A Practical Guide to Behavioral Research

A Practical Guide to Behavioral Research

Tools and Techniques

FOURTH EDITION

Barbara Sommer
Robert Sommer

New York   Oxford
OXFORD UNIVERSITY PRESS
1997

Oxford University Press

Oxford   New York
Athens   Auckland   Bangkok   Bogota   Bombay   Buenos Aires
Calcutta   Cape Town   Dar es Salaam   Delhi   Florence   Hong Kong
Istanbul   Karachi   Kuala Lumpur   Madras   Madrid   Melbourne
Mexico City   Nairobi   Paris   Singapore   Taipei   Tokyo   Toronto

and associated companies in
Berlin   Ibadan

Copyright © 1980, 1986, 1991, 1997 by Oxford University Press, Inc.

Published by Oxford University Press, Inc.
198 Madison Avenue, New York, New York 10016

Oxford is a registered trademark of Oxford University Press

Library of Congress Cataloging-in-Publication Data
Sommer, Barbara Baker, 1938–
A practical guide to behavioral research: tools and techniques /
Barbara Sommer, Robert Sommer. — 4th ed.
p. cm.
Includes indexes.
ISBN 0-19-510419-6 (paper). — ISBN 0-19-510418-8
1. Social sciences—Research.   2. Social sciences— Methodology.
3. Psychology—Research.   4. Social sciences—Research—Data
processing.   I. Sommer, Robert.   II. Title.
H62.S724734   1997
150'.72—dc20   96-35531
                                                    CIP

3 5 7 9 8 6 4 2

Printed in the United States of America
on acid-free paper

Contents

Preface

As in previous editions, we continue to offer a multimethod approach, describing a wide range of techniques. But through our continued experience in using this book with undergraduate students, we have improved the overall clarity and comprehensiveness of the text throughout.

Since the 1991 edition, major changes have occurred in the behavioral sciences. Particularly in regard to the use of the Internet in research, we are running just to keep up. The computer is now a major presence in the behavioral sciences. Earlier it had seemed to be a tool, like its predecessor, the calculator, which had over time become increasingly more sophisticated. While uses of the calculator were limited largely to data analysis, the computer has pervaded all aspects of research. Statistical software packages have revolutionized data analysis. We have added a new chapter describing the research opportunities provided by the Internet. The chapter on equipment (formerly, apparatus) now includes a description of computers in running research studies (Chapter 15), plus a section on use of the camera in behavioral research. A guide to using computers in data analysis is provided in an appendix. The library chapter provides detailed information on how to access and use electronic databases. Other computer applications are integrated into the appropriate individual chapters.

Writing this book has led us to confront the difference between the ideal and the actual practice of behavioral research. Ideally, experimentation is the paramount method of finding cause-and-effect relationships. It is a powerful method for testing theory and permits ruling out alternative explanations. Within memory, the terms "research methods" and "experimental design" were synonymous. However, the questions asked behavioral scientists by policy makers, practitioners, and the public rarely involve tests of theory, as such, but rather reflect a search for accurate information on issues of social importance. Experiments often do not yield this type of information. We do not neglect experimentation but consider it one method among many for obtaining behavioral information.

We advocate a hands-on approach to research and provide many easily-understood examples. There is information about making conference presentations and writing technical reports, as well as the more typical guidelines for writing journal-style papers.

We have also tried to make this edition more international. A sabbatical leave spent teaching in Estonia and a continuing collaboration with researchers in Brazil have expanded our awareness of research methods appropriate for other nations. This edition includes more references to work outside North America. Additionally, we are impressed by international networks of researchers studying similar problems in different nations, such as aspects of parent-child interaction or the response of people to natural disasters. Electronic communication has made it easy for researchers to contact those working on related issues in other locations and to undertake collaborative studies.

The book is suitable for students in research methods courses and for nonstudents who wish for a clear guide to conducting behavioral studies. Behavioral research methods are too important to be left in the hands of a small group of specialists. The long-run interests of a democratic society are served by the widest possible understanding and acceptance of these methods. The hands-on approach advocated in the book is ideally suited for small-scale program evaluation as well a more general research. For example, an innovative project at a university, such as providing residence halls for specific majors, could be tried out in one or two residence halls with students from a small number of majors, and the results evaluated using interviews, questionnaires, an examination of student grades, and other criteria of program success. A similar approach could be used in a city-sponsored program of giving food vouchers to the homeless. The program could be tried out in one or two neighborhoods, carefully evaluated, and the problems reduced before the program is extended to the rest of the city.

We are indebted to those colleagues and students who have read and evaluated this and earlier editions. In particular, the comments of Ron Goldthwaite, Michael Winter, Harmut Guenther, and John Bower helped remove ambiguity, jargon, and the occasional error.

Davis, California
March 1996

B.S.
R.S.

A Practical Guide to Behavioral Research

1 Multimethod Approach

What Is Behavioral Research?

Behavioral research is everybody's business. It is difficult to imagine an occupation in which systematic information about human behavior is not relevant. Forest rangers are increasingly concerned about vandalism, arson, and litter in wilderness areas. NASA wants to know how groups of astronauts will react during space flights to distant planets. Manufacturers are concerned about the public response to new products. Politicians want to know how the public feels about key issues. The lives of all of us have been touched, directly or indirectly, by the procedures and results of behavioral research.

There is an important difference between thinking about human behavior and doing research. Research is careful, patient, and methodical inquiry done according to certain rules. It is not simply an exchange of views among friends, colleagues, or experts. Anyone whose job depends on information about what people do or want should know how to obtain that information in a valid and systematic manner. Specifically, they should know how to interview, construct a questionnaire, observe natural behavior, and conduct an experiment.

Even professions whose primary concerns are with machines must take account of human behavior. What is the most efficient way to place letters on a PC keyboard? What is the best way to arrange instrument dials in a jet aircraft to minimize risks of confusion and error? The answers to such questions will be based, to some degree, on the results of behavioral studies. Of course, not all questions are behavioral. A comparison of the gas consumption of two types of engines is an engineering problem. Yet at some point that question will have behavioral aspects, perhaps in terms of the noise level of the two engines. Behavioral research cannot answer nonbehavioral questions. Whether adultery is good or evil is a moral and not a behavioral question. The interpretation of a court decision is a legal question. Such questions have behavioral implications, but the researcher must realize what parts of them are behavioral and what parts are not.

There are limits to how far behavioral science can go in terms of description. Personal tragedy can be studied by psychologists but the experience is probably more sensitively portrayed by poets and novelists. Nor does the slow patient inquiry characteristic of the behavioral sciences suit fast-breaking events. Journalists are trained to go out in the morning and come back in the afternoon with a story. A behavioral scientist is not likely to be comfortable with such tight time constraints. There are also limits to the behavioral sciences in regard to advocacy. There is no evidence that behavioral scientists are better suited than others for suggesting and implementing solutions to critical social problems such as crime or drug addiction. Research can provide systematic and reliable information on such problems (for example, the amount of crime in a community, how people feel about it, what it means to be a victim, and so on) without pointing directly to practical solutions. This has raised awareness about the need for better dissemination of research findings, in terms of getting the information into the hands of those who can use it.

This book emphasizes systematic methods for gathering information. Visual inspection of a shopping mall is better than nothing, but a systematic observational study over a period of time will yield information that is more accurate and believable, and probably more useful. The game warden who believes that fluorescent blue would be more suitable than orange for hunting jackets under conditions of poor visibility could question several hunters on the issue. A better approach would be to do an experiment to determine the appearance of each color under different degrees of illumination. The range of questions that can be examined using the methods of behavioral research is enormous. It is the task of the researcher to set priorities for the questions to be asked, as well as to identify the best methods to be used.

Theory and Research

There are two components of a scientific body of knowledge: empirical research and theory. *Empirical research* involves the measurement of observable events— for example, the effect of a particular drug on reaction time, people's responses to questionnaires, or individual characteristics measured by a personality inventory. Empirical refers to information that is sense-based—what we directly see, hear, touch, smell, or taste. It is demonstrable; that is, it can be shown to other people. Subjective qualities such as feelings and beliefs become empirical when expressed by means of attitude scales, interviews, ratings, or some other measurement procedure.

Theories are logical constructions that explain natural phenomena. They are not in themselves directly observable but can be supported or refuted by empirical findings. The criteria of a good theory are accuracy, scope, simplicity, and fruitfulness (Kuhn, 1970).

There is a reciprocal relationship between theory and research. Research shapes a theory by bringing it into accord with the observable world and thereby increasing the theory's explanatory and predictive power. Theories go beyond a single observation and link a number of sometimes-diverse observations into coherent wholes. Theories suggest additional questions to be examined and answered, which leads to further research and subsequent refinement of the underlying theory.

Theory and empirical research are connected by means of *hypotheses*—testable propositions that are logically derived from theories. The "testable" aspect is very important in that scientific hypotheses must be capable of being accepted (confirmed) or rejected (disconfirmed). For example, many religious statements are not directly testable in that they can be neither supported nor refuted on the grounds of direct observation. Thus they fall outside the realm of science. As an example, the proposition that "People were placed on earth to rule over other creatures" is not directly testable in an empirical sense.

Validity and Reliability

Behavioral research is conducted in accord with the scientific method. The subject matter is directly observable, or can be made so through some type of representation (e.g., questionnaire responses). Generally, a scientist uses an *operational definition*; that is, defining something by the means used to measure it. For example, hunger might be defined as hours since last eating, or racial attitudes by a score on an attitude scale. Sometimes operational definitions may not be agreed upon—for example, defining masculinity as being able to grow a beard—but they have the advantage of being clear, and thus open to scrutiny.

In order to be scientific, the obtained information (data) must be valid and reliable. *Validity* is the degree to which a procedure produces genuine and credible information. Two aspects of validity are internal validity and external validity. *Internal validity* is the degree to which a procedure measures what it is supposed to measure. Is the operational definition consistent with other ways of identifying and measuring the behavior or characteristic? Number of hours since eating is probably a valid measure of hunger as research has shown the two are associated. Defining sociability in terms of the number of interactions that a person has each day would be of questionable validity because some people may have jobs that require interactions, whereas other people are in more isolated situations. A more valid measure would take into account whether an interaction was more or less voluntary.

External validity refers to the generalizability of the findings. Do the results extend beyond the immediate setting or situation? Research in natural settings often provides higher external validity than does research from the laboratory. In contrast, laboratory research may be higher on internal validity. By having more control over the situation, the researcher can be more confident about what is being measured.

In addition to being valid, research should also be *reliable*. Reliability refers to the repeatability or replicability of findings. Instruments and procedures should produce the same results when applied to similar people in similar situations, or to the same people on a second occasion. Reliability is an important contributor to validity. However, a study can be reliable but not be valid. For example, we might propose strength of hand grip as a measure of intelligence. We can measure hand grip with a high degree of reliability, but that does not mean we have a valid measure of intelligence. The measure lacks validity.

Why Do Behavioral Research?

The very general reasons for doing behavioral studies are (1) to obtain answers to pressing questions and (2) to contribute to theories of human behavior. Providing answers to pressing questions is called *applied research*. It is motivated primarily by the need to solve an immediate problem. One type of applied research that is receiving increasing attention is *program evaluation*. This involves determining the effectiveness of a program. Some government agencies now require evalua- tion to accompany all new projects. This has created the need for researchers who can adapt themselves to the politically charged and hurried world of legislation, government budgets, and bureaucratic jargon. Program evaluation must be done quickly or else it is useless. There is a growing recognition that evaluation, when done properly, can help to guide government-supported programs.

Investigations designed to answer general long-range questions about human behavior are considered *basic research* and are motivated largely by the re- searcher's curiosity. Most behavioral research arises from a combination of at- tempts to answer specific questions and the researcher's curiosity. A third cate- gory of behavioral studies, which may include your own interests, is *instrumental research*. This includes studies done as training exercises or as part of a job as- signment. Many people doing behavioral research for industry, the military, or government agencies work on problems chosen by others. Some students become intrigued with research done as part of a class project and continue work on it af- terward, or the instructor may continue and extend a class project to the point where it becomes a publishable paper.

Although it is useful to make a conceptual distinction between basic and ap- plied research, the line between the two is often blurred and indistinct. A researcher may have mixed motives in conducting a study, seeking to test part of a theory while answering a practical question at the same time. Social psychologist Kurt Lewin (1946) pioneered *action research* as a means by which behavioral scien- tists could contribute simultaneously to theory and practice. Lewin and his asso- ciates used this approach in communities attempting to reduce racial prejudice. The programs to change attitudes became experiments to be evaluated and revised before they were implemented elsewhere. Action research involves the potential users of the information in doing the research. Lewin believed it reduces the gulf between research and application. Other reasons for doing action research are to increase people's involvement in an issue or problem, to develop a constituency for change, to reduce the distance between researchers and the public, to base program changes on sound information (the fruits of research) rather than guesses, to test theories of human behavior in natural settings, and to provide feedback to researchers on the utility of their work. Action research is an important approach in community psychology and action anthropology, both of which seek to increase people's control and self-determination over their affairs. As an example, action anthropologists work collaboratively with native peoples in defining and facilitating the latter's goals.

Specific Methods

There are dozens of methods available to the behavioral researcher. Not all of these will be equally useful. Four techniques—observation, experiment, questionnaire, and interview—account for more than nine-tenths of the articles in social science journals. Some rules of thumb for selecting among methods are presented in Box 1–1. Observation is well suited for discovering what people do in public. For private behavior, the personal diary is more appropriate. The experiment is an immensely powerful tool for deciding between alternative explanations of a phenomenon. It is less useful, however, for studying natural behavior or opinions.

BOX 1–1. Choosing among Research Techniques

Problem	Approach	Research technique	Chapter
To obtain reliable information under controlled conditions	Test people in a laboratory	Laboratory experiment, simulation	6, 7
To find out how people behave in public	Watch them	Systematic observation	4
To find out how people behave in private	Ask them to keep diaries	Personal documents	12
To learn what people think	Ask them	Interview, questionnaire, attitude scale	8, 9, 10
To identify personality traits or assess mental abilities	Administer a standardized test	Pyschological testing	16
To find patterns in written or visual material	Systematic tabulation	Content analysis	11
To understand an unusual event	Detailed and lengthy investigation	Case study	13

With opinions and attitudes, the questionnaire and interview are very efficient. Standardized tests are used to assess mental abilities.

Multimethod Approach

Each technique for gathering information has its shortcomings. Experimentation is limited by artificiality, observation by unreliability, interviews by interviewer bias, and so on. There is no ideal research technique in the behavioral sciences. The advantages may lie along one dimension, such as economy; the disadvantages along another, such as objectivity. The goal of the researcher is not to find the single best method.

For most problems, several procedures will be better than one. Even though each has its limitations, these tend not to be the same limitations. The artificiality of the laboratory can be supplemented by observation, which is high on naturalness but low on reliability; the questionnaire, which can be given to many people quickly, can be supplemented by detailed interviews with a few people to probe more deeply into significant issues. This has been described as the method of *converging operations* (Webb, Campbell, Schwartz, Sechrest, & Grove, 1981). A number of different research techniques are applied, each with somewhat different limitations and yielding somewhat different data. Conflicts between the information from different sources will sometimes occur. In one case, the letters received by a director of a veterinary hospital consisted mostly of complaints. On the other hand, interviews with pet owners bringing their animals to this same hospital showed a high level of satisfaction. There was no basic contradiction between the two sources of information. People dissatisfied with the hospital wrote letters of complaint and went elsewhere, while satisfied customers continued to visit the hospital. Both the complaints and the interviews contributed to an understanding of how the hospital worked.

The multimethod approach provides flexibility in dealing with obstacles encountered in carrying out a project. Sometimes the most appropriate procedure cannot be used so the researcher must fall back on a combination of other techniques. When experimentation is not possible, the researcher may use a combination of observations and interviews, and if neither of these is possible, the researcher will try simulation (creating an artificial reality in the laboratory), or read autobiographical accounts. Having a variety of methods available, even when they are not all used, provides a flexibility beyond what is possible with a single procedure.

Although flexibility is desirable, the choice of methods should be guided by the questions to be answered, and the time and resources that are available. There is no point in planning an elaborate survey if there is no one to carry it out, or in preparing an observational study of a prison whose superintendent will not permit observers inside the walls. You may have to settle for interviews with ex-prisoners and a reading of prison diaries.

A multimethod approach is also useful in dealing with the unforeseen circumstances that arise in field research. Beginning researchers are likely to be discouraged when they go out to a shopping center and there is no one around to interview because it is too cold, windy, or simply an inactive period. One solution is to use such occasions to practice other data-gathering techniques. If there are no customers in the shopping center, then this may be a good opportunity to interview store employees or examine wear on carpets or linoleum, oil stains in the parking lot, graffiti, or other residues that will provide clues to usage. The experienced researcher always has several methods in reserve for occasions when the primary method cannot be employed. Making good use of unforeseen circumstances will increase the likelihood of the accidental discovery of new relationships.

Knowledge Is Connected

An introduction to research techniques would be easier if the methods and disciplines could be kept separate. This is not realistic; procedures overlap. Constructing a questionnaire might involve interviews. An interview study will be preceded by observations to find out the questions to be asked. Interviews often are scored using a method known as *content analysis*. Academic disciplines cannot be kept separate either. A sociologist undertaking participant observation among teenage youth will have more in common with anthropologists than with other sociologists who analyze census records. The psychologist observing children in a nursery may feel more kinship with zoologists than with laboratory-based experimental psychologists. It is important for students interested in human behavior to learn a wide range of techniques. This will not only help them choose the best methods for a project but will also be indispensable for understanding relevant studies from other fields. To understand why people act as they do, one cannot view their actions solely in psychological terms, economic terms, or historical terms. Knowledge will be more thorough and accurate when it includes ideas and findings from many different sources.

An interdisciplinary approach is essential for research on complex problems. A small study of only one aspect of a problem, such as the relationship between airplane engine types and the amount of noise, might involve only a mechanical engineer and an acoustical consultant, but a larger study on airport noise might include an engineer, architect, physician or public health worker, and a behavioral scientist. Team members must avoid the jargon of individual specialties and develop a shared language. Each single investigation must be integrated into the larger effort and timetable.

Studying complex social issues virtually requires multiple methods, not only for breadth of coverage, but also to allow for a check on the validity of individual methods. To understand how people in Germany were affected by the nuclear accident at Chernobyl in the Soviet Union, Kaminski (1988) combined interviews with content analyses of media. Members of his research team interviewed government officials and experts who had manned special telephone hotlines installed shortly after the accident. They also interviewed people most likely to be affected by the accident, such as pregnant women, mothers with small children, farmers, and produce store managers. They tabulated letters and calls to television and radio stations, and collected a year's issues of the city newspaper to analyze all references to the accident.

Dealing with Reactivity

To be of most value, the data obtained from the different methods should be independent. When more than a single procedure is used in the same location or with the same respondents, there is the risk that the first procedure may affect the results of subsequent ones. The effect of the research upon the participants and the data collected is termed *reactivity*.

One method for reducing reactivity is to subdivide the sample and use different procedures in each subsample. In a survey using both a mail questionnaire and interviews, the researcher could divide the potential subjects randomly into two different groups, using interviews with one group and mail questionnaires with the second. Another way to minimize reactivity among different procedures is to carefully plan the sequence in which they are used, starting with the least and going to the most reactive procedures. As an example, in combining observations and interviews, the rule would be to observe first and ask questions later. Mailed questionnaires are generally less reactive than personal interviews, so if you were combining these two approaches, the mail survey should precede the personal interviews.

Pilot Study

No matter how carefully you reviewed the background literature and designed the study, there is no substitute for a pilot study before the actual data are collected. A *pilot study* is a preliminary use of a procedure designed to identify problems and omissions before the actual study is conducted. Remember Murphy's Law—if something can go wrong, it will. Even the best designed experiments will have flaws, and the most carefully developed interview sheet will have ambiguous questions or words that the respondent will misinterpret. There is no way to predict all potential problems in advance. Not even the most experienced survey researcher can compose a perfect questionnaire on the first try. Survey research firms test out their questions in a pilot study before beginning formal data collection. You should plan to do the same in your own research. Set aside a designated time for this after the procedures have been developed. Don't skip the pilot study in a rush to collect data. A little effort put into it will pay big dividends in improving the precision, reliability, and validity of the data collected in the actual study.

Longitudinal and Cross-sectional Research

Sometimes a researcher is fortunate enough to be able to study a situation or group of people over time. For example, a research team might study children of divorced parents as they grow to adulthood and have children of their own. Research over a long period of time is termed *longitudinal*. Although researchers recognize the value of longitudinal studies, in practice few are able to do them because of the expense and time commitment. As an alternative, they undertake *cross-sectional* studies in which different groups of people are compared on a single occasion. Instead of studying the same group of children over many years, researchers might compare groups of 5-, 10-, and 15-year-olds.

General Laws and Local Conditions

Much of the research in the behavioral sciences aims at producing *general laws*. These are principles that help explain behavior in a variety of situations. However, general laws will not be adequate for understanding local conditions. Homelessness in Rio de Janeiro is not the same as it is in Cleveland, and two research methods classes at the same university taught by different instructors are likely to vary in content.

Many of the questions asked behavioral scientists by outside groups and agencies deal with local conditions. If the police in Melbourne, Australia, want to know whether the residents are satisfied with the existing level of police response and how it can be improved, the answer cannot come from reading previous studies of crime, but only from *local research* focused upon a particular neighborhood or city. Local research is site-specific in that the investigator seeks to understand conditions in a particular location. If one were attempting to deal with crime in Melbourne, it would be *helpful* to know previous research on crime issues, but *essential* to know the characteristics of the city. Each place has its own character or spirit. The methods of the behavioral sciences can be used to identify and understand the special nature and character of communities, and how general principles are expressed at the local level. There is no contradiction between studying local conditions and thinking about general principles. This is similar to the maxim of the environmental movement to "act locally and think globally." The behavioral researcher can study local conditions with possibilities of applying the findings there, while at the same time seeing them as an expression of general principles.

Research in other nations should be undertaken with a full recognition of social, economic, and political realities. The choice of topic, method, and even the wording of the questions must be suited to local conditions. A printed questionnaire is inappropriate in a developing nation with a high rate of illiteracy. A telephone survey is a poor choice in a nation where few households have phones. Under those conditions, the researcher would do a door-to-door survey. Observational techniques are threatening in an authoritarian nation whose citizens worry about being spied upon. The untimely death of Ignacio Martin-Baro, director of the University of Central America's Institute of Public Opinion and editor of the respected journal *Revista de Psicologia* illustrates the hazards of undertaking public opinion research under conditions of state terrorism. After he rejected the Salvadoran military's demand to censor his survey findings, there were seven attempts on his life, the last of which was fatal (Aron, 1990).

There are philosopical differences among nations in their approaches to behavioral research. Europe has a long tradition of qualitative research in the social sciences. Researchers in Germany perceive an overemphasis on quantification and hypothesis-testing among American researchers. Researchers in France are likely to pay more attention to small groups and larger social units than to individuals (Jodelet, 1987). National priorities affect the choice of research topics. Israeli social scientists focus attention on relations between Arabs and Jews. Researchers in Brazil examine the consequences of development, such as deforestation and migration of people to the cities. Japan's geographical location has been responsible for a particularly high number of natural disasters, including floods, fires, and earthquakes. This has stimulated a considerable amount of disaster research.

Practical Experience

Specific techniques can be learned from a book. You can read the definition of a questionnaire, how it differs from an interview, and its advantages and disadvantages. To acquire skill in using the questionnaire as a research tool requires something more—experience. The difficulty in writing clear questions may not be evident yet. Thus, when you construct your first questionnaire, you are likely to make all the mistakes you have read about. Nor is it obvious how boring it can be to spend a day observing children in a playground. Another thing that may not be apparent yet is the intellectual thrill of finding patterns and meaning in the mass of data you have collected. The emotional side of research, the joy and excitement, as well as the frustration and boredom, are best learned by *doing* research. Like other skills, specific research techniques are learned most readily by following accepted procedures. After some proficiency is acquired, you can decide when to modify the rules.

With experience, you will find yourself more attracted to some procedures than to others. Don't worry if one or more techniques turn you off. It happens to professional researchers. Some like nothing more than spending their days in a laboratory using sophisticated equipment. They may feel uncomfortable conducting observations in the field where nothing is controlled. Other researchers enjoy sending out questionnaires in mail surveys and letting the postal service do the work. Some researchers do not collect original data but rely on secondary sources, such as health statistics and census records, or undertake content analyses of the mass media. Depending upon the problem studied, each of these approaches has the potential to yield theoretically significant or useful information.

Even if you dislike a particular method, it is still important to learn about it so that you can evaluate the work done by others. You may someday find yourself part of an interdisciplinary team whose members employ different methods. If you consider a technique to be dull or difficult, it is useful to reflect upon the reasons, as this will help you define your personal research style. Presumably you will do a better job using methods with which you feel comfortable. Knowledge of your own preferences will help you set priorities for future involvement in research projects.

Summary

Theory and research are two components of scientific knowledge. Empirical research involves systematic measurement of observable events. A theory is a logical construction that explains natural phenomena. Hypotheses, which are testable propositions, connect theory and research.

An operational definition defines something by how it is measured. Internal validity is the degree to which a procedure measures what it is supposed to measure. External validity refers to the generalizability of the findings. Reliability refers to their repeatability or replicability.

Basic research aims at answering long-range questions. Applied research tries to provide solutions for immediate problems. Instrumental research is undertaken as either a training exercise or a job assignment. Action research combines the testing of theory with application.

For most problems, several procedures will be better than one. Even though each method has its limitations, these tend not to be the same limitations. In designing a research project, reactivity (the effect of the research procedure on behavior) needs to be minimized. Pilot tests uncover problems at an early stage. Longitudinal studies extend across time while cross-sectional research investigates different groups or events on a single occasion.

Local conditions as well as national differences must be taken into account. Practical experience will be of value in honing research skills, as well as discovering one's own particular research strengths and capabilities.

References

Aron, A. (1990). A tribute to Ignacio Martin-Baro. *SPSSI Newsletter, 181*, 4.

Jodelet, D. (1987). The study of people-environment relations in France. In D. Stokols & I. Altman (Eds.), *Handbook of environmental psychology* (pp. 1171–1193). New York: Wiley.

Kaminski, G. (1988). *Is the development of a psychological ecology useful and possible?* (Report No. 28). Tuebingen, West Germany: Psychological Institute, University of Tuebingen.

Kuhn, T. S. (1970). *The structure of scientific revolutions* (2nd ed.). Chicago: University of Chicago Press.

Lewin, K. (1946). Action research and minority problems. *Journal of Social Issues, 2*, 34–36.

Webb, E. J., Campbell, D. T., Schwartz, R. D., Sechrest, L., & Grove, J. B. (1981). *Nonreactive measures in the social sciences* (2nd ed.). Boston: Houghton Mifflin.

2 Ethics in Behavioral Research

Leroy, an undergraduate education major, wants to do a study of the stress that students experience during finals week. One of his professors agrees to sponsor the project. Leroy asks the Student Health Center for permission to review admission records for the past five years, in order to compare student visits during finals week with the other weeks in the semester. A number of ethical questions arise with regard to the project:

1. Whose permission and approval should Leroy obtain in order to conduct the study?

2. If the study is approved, what information should the Health Center release to Leroy?

3. If the study is approved, what safeguards should be established to protect the privacy of students who have visited the Health Center?

4. Are there conditions that should be established regarding publication of the findings?

Institutions such as universities and governmental agencies have established Institutional Review Boards (IRBs) to deal with ethical and procedural questions regarding human and animal research. The procedures for ethical review on our campus typify that of most universities. Investigators fill out and submit one of several forms depending upon the type of research undertaken. The following categories of studies are usually exempt from reviews (i.e., do *not* require a formal review):

1. Studies conducted in established educational settings involving formal educational practices; for example, evaluation of different teaching methods and curricula.

2. Research using educational tests when the information is recorded in such a manner that respondents cannot be identified.

3. Surveys or interviews in which the respondents cannot be identified, and when the responses do not place the respondents at risk. Research which deals with sensitive aspects of the subject's own behavior, such as illegal conduct, cannot be exempt from review.

4. Observation of people in public locations, except when the observations include identifying information, might place the individual at risk, or deal with problematic behaviors.

5. Research using existing records or public documents, o if the information is recorded by the investigator in such a manner that people cannot be identified.

6. Research or demonstration projects evaluating certain agency or public service programs. These studies should be approved by the department or agency heads responsible for the program.

7. Taste and food quality evaluations and consumer acceptance studies that involve eating wholesome foods without additives, or with food ingredients at or below the levels found to be safe by the appropriate government agency.

Researchers who believe that their studies meet the preceding conditions submit a "Statement of Exemption" to the IRB, which is responsible for determining that the conditions for exemption have been met.

Many student research projects fit into the exempt category. This is particularly true in observational and questionnaire studies where the respondents' names are not obtained. Statements of exemption are typically reviewed by a department head or department committee to ensure that the conditions for exemption have been met. For nonexempt studies whose methods are scrutinized by the IRB, a more detailed research approval form is used. When students are the principal investigators, their faculty advisors assume responsibility for seeing that all the proper forms are filled out. When instructors assign or supervise a student project, the instructor is responsible for seeing that the student will safeguard the health and well-being of the subjects and that proper human subjects forms are completed and submitted for review. Box 2–1 shows a completed Human Subjects Approval Form for a student project. All of the instruments to be used, such as questionnaires and rating scales, should accompany the approval form when it is submitted.

Box 2–2 shows the consent form that subjects were asked to sign for the study described in Box 2–1. The procedures are presented in a straightforward and clear manner, avoiding the use of jargon. At the conclusion of the session, the subject was given a full account of the goals and hypotheses of the study.

Researchers who study vulnerable populations such as children, the elderly, hospital patients, or jail inmates have special responsibilities in terms of protecting human subjects. Questions can be raised about the legitimacy of informed con-

BOX 2–1. Example of a Completed Human Subjects Approval Form

1. *Investigator:* Raphael Moore; Faculty Sponsor: J. Poirot.

2 *Title of Research:* Learning Strategies in University Students.

3. *Sponsor Name and Address:* None.

4. *Duration of Study:* Start January 1997; conclude July 1997.

5. *Location:* Social Psychology Laboratory, Young Hall.

6. *Subjects:* 70 undergraduate students.

7. *Contact Method:* Notice on Department bulletin board, in-class announcement.

8. *Procedures:* Instructions to subjects attached

9. *Purpose of Study:* To determine whether a constant rhythm during learning or recall improves retention of nonsense syllables.

10. *Procedure:* Subjects will be randomly divided into four groups: A. sound during memorization; B. sound during recall; C. sound during both memorization and recall; and D. no sound. Students will be tested in groups. Each student will have a headset connected to a master control tape unit. The session will begin with recorded instructions. After this a slide with a list of words will be shown. Those in groups A and C will hear music as the words are being shown. During recall groups B and C will hear music.

11. *Risks and Benefits:* The procedure poses no potential risk to the subjects. After the session is finished, students will receive a description of the objectives and procedures, and can request a copy of the data analysis. The experience should be of educational value to the students.

12. *Costs to Subjects:* None

13. *Personal or Financial Interest in the Research Study:* None

14. *Informed Consent:* This will be obtained by the investigator before starting the experiment. See attached form. (Example is shown in Box 2–2.)

sent for people in dire or difficult circumstances. These ethical problems are sometimes discussed at professional meetings and in the technical literature. The "Further Readings" section at the end of this chapter lists several good sources.

The research community relies heavily upon self-regulation in the form of standards developed by professional organizations and institutional review boards that screen research proposals. The conduct of scientific research involves two general categories of ethical principles and rules: those developed to protect research participants against undue risks, and those concerned with scientific misconduct in other areas, such as falsification of data, plagiarism, and undeserved credit. The codes of ethics of social science professional organizations deal with both of these.

Protecting the Welfare of Research Participants

The need for these procedures first became apparent in medical research, where people might be exposed to dangerous drugs or radioactive materials. For legal as well as ethical reasons, procedures were needed to ensure (1) that the research plan was reviewed by a committee of competent scientists, (2) the rights and welfare of the subjects were protected, and (3) the subjects were adequately informed of the risks and benefits involved. It was not long before federal granting agencies extended these requirements to behavioral research. Several studies had gained notoriety because of the unorthodox procedures and/or the risks to unknowing participants.

BOX 2–2. Example of a Completed Consent Form

Consent to Participate in Research Study

Title of Study: Learning Strategies in University Students

Investigator: Raphael S. Moore, Dept. of Psychology, University of California, Davis. Phone 555-8228

You are being asked to participate in a research study investigating strategies of learning.

Procedures: If you decide to participate, you will be given a short ability test, measuring your knowledge of words. You will then be asked to follow the instructions heard through your headset, which will include the task of learning words seen on the screen in front of you.

Risks and Benefits: The method of research creates no potential risk to you as a subject. It is a minimal risk study, where the risk-benefit ratio leans heavily toward your benefit. Other than the extra credit you might receive from your psychology class, you may also request printed matter explaining your role in the study. This will include a description of the hypotheses, and final analysis of the data. If you choose not to participate, your instructor has other options for you to obtain extra credit.

Confidentiality: Ability test data will be computer coded and used for analysis only. Original information will be destroyed.

Costs/Compensation: There is no cost to you beyond the time and effort required to complete the procedures described above.

Right to Refuse or Withdraw: You may refuse to participate. You may change your mind about being in the study and quit after the study has started.

Questions: If you have any questions, please feel free to ask. If at a later time you have any additional questions, the principal investigator can be reached at 555-8228.

Consent: Your signature below will indicate that you have agreed to volunteer as a research subject and that you have read and understood the information provided above.

Date	Signature of participant
Date	Signature of investigator

Outside Review

Asking an IRB, or some other group not directly involved in the research, to make a formal assessment of the risks of the procedure is an important part of behavioral research. A researcher can become so involved in a project that some ethical problems are overlooked. The researcher may not be aware of all the risks involved. Even experts can disagree about the likelihood or amount of risk to participants. Some research carries hazards for the participants or for society. The issues are whether the potential benefits are worth the risk, and the people subjected to the risk are informed of its nature and magnitude. Full disclosure can pose special problems for the behavioral researcher. To tell people the full nature of a study *in advance* can alter their actions. A common solution is to withhold information during the session and debrief the participants afterward. Some researchers will tell people that they are taking part in a psychological experiment that will not involve pain or any physical danger, and ask them for permission not to tell them about the experiment until afterward in order to obtain unbiased responses. Immediately following the session, each participant is given a printed sheet describing the purposes and methods of the study, and the experimenter is present to answer any questions.

Confidentiality and Anonymity

Two methods used by researchers to protect participants in behavioral studies are confidentiality and anonymity. *Confidentiality* means that the respondent's identity is known to the investigator but protected from public exposure. The researcher keeps any identifying information out of published reports. Confidentiality is particularly important when people's statements or actions would cause them some embarrassment if they became known. It is best for the researcher to maintain as much confidentiality as possible because it is difficult to predict how people's answers might be interpreted or used by others. Instead of identifying organizations or cities by name, a general description, such as "a middle-sized industrial city in the Northeast" or a fictitious name such as Yankee City or Worktown, is used instead.

The best way to ensure that the people you have interviewed or observed will not be embarrassed by your research is to remove identifying information, such as names and addresses, as soon as the data are tabulated. Some researchers use a special code at the time of the interview so that no names or other identifying information exist even in the researcher's files. The exact methods used to protect your respondents will vary according to the situation, but it is important to realize that behavioral researchers do not have the special right to confidential communication that the courts grant to physicians, lawyers, and the clergy.

Anonymity means that the researcher does not know the identity of the participants in the study. The best protection for people in an observational study is anonymity. It makes more sense to observe people in a public park or courtyard without knowing their names than to ask each person to sign a written consent form. Anonymity is also a useful safeguard in questionnaire and public opinion research. Most questionnaire studies do not ask people to sign their names. Often this is emphasized by telling respondents *not* to sign their names.

Deception

Among the most difficult ethical decisions facing the behavioral researcher is whether or not to use deception. Deception can range from relatively minor omissions, such as not telling people the full story of what you are doing, to outright falsehood about your identity and the nature of the study. To deceive is to deliberately mislead others. The issue is most relevant in experimentation where personal knowledge of the purposes might change people's behavior.

Following publication of Stanley Milgram's (1974) classic studies of obedience in which unwitting volunteers were asked to apply supposedly painful electric shocks to another person (in reality, no shock was administered and the supposed victim was a confederate of the researcher), the use of deception in social psychological research increased in popularity along with criticism from those opposed to it. A survey of the social psychological literature revealed that 47% of the published studies had employed some type of deception (Fisher & Fyrberg, 1994). Experimenters who employ deception are responsible for debriefing the participants. This involves describing the nature of the deception, why it was done, why the approach was chosen over other procedures not involving deception; and allowing the participants to express their feelings about what happened.

There are a number of problems with using deception. Even when debriefed afterward, some participants may become angry and wonder whether the researcher is simply practicing a further deception. Rosenthal (1976) found that many participants in experiments were aware of the purposes even when the experimenter attempted to keep the purposes hidden. Deception may have a negative effect on the participants' attitudes toward behavioral research. People dislike being lied to and research subjects are no exception. Finally, there is the negative effect on the researcher when forced to lie to other people. It can produce cynicism and distance from the people being studied.

With full consideration of the ethical and practical problems in using deception, many researchers find instances where they feel it is warranted. *Impersonation*, or acting as someone other than oneself, has been found to be useful in understanding life in mental and penal institutions. Researchers had themselves admitted as patients or inmates to see the institution from the inside. To the degree that others are aware of the impersonation, the validity of the observer's experience may be reduced. Consumer researchers may impersonate customers in order to investigate misleading marketing practices. In this case one deception is used to study another. Social psychologists employ impersonation to investigate discrimination. Researchers of different races pose as prospective apartment renters or house buyers and visit real estate agencies to inquire about the types of housing available. This is probably a more valid method than asking realtors if they discriminate among prospective tenants or homeowners on the basis of race.

Our personal views about deception have been shaped by our experiences. We feel that researchers should try to avoid deception as much as possible. The majority of complaints received by IRBs concern deception (Keith-Spiegel & Koocher, 1985). Even when it appears that it might be advantageous to mislead others, there are alternative ways to obtain the information without telling lies. Ask yourself whether it is absolutely necessary to deceive other people or whether the same information could be obtained with full disclosure or through some sort of simulation that people know has been staged. Regarding conditions in jail and mental hospitals, where some researchers have used impersonation, others have created artificial prisons and jails in which volunteer subjects spent various periods of time in "captivity." As described in Chapter 7, important aspects of confinement have been studied in these simulation environments without the use of deception.

Comment on Participant Risk

The risks to participants in behavioral research should not be exaggerated or over-dramatized. Most surveys, observational studies, and laboratory experiments pose little or no risk to the participants. Students asked to learn lists of words can be told the exact nature of the procedure, what is going to be done with the results, and so on. People whose movements are charted throughout the day would be told of the potential inconvenience of having an observer following them around. The researcher may decide to reserve information about how the results are to be used (e.g., comparing the time younger and older people spend sleeping) until the observations are concluded, but this withholding does not increase the risks to the participants, who know exactly what the researcher will be doing.

Issues of Scientific Misconduct

It is important to note that instances of outright misconduct on the part of researchers, regarding either deliberate falsification of data or fraudulent credentials, are very infrequent. It is this infrequency of occurrence that makes them newsworthy. More common are the gray areas where something is claimed that is not technically true. When John Bailar was a statistical consultant for the *New England Journal of Medicine*, he reviewed a large number of manuscripts. He noticed that some of them seemed deceptive—not that authors deliberately provided false data, but rather, they exaggerated the strength of the evidence or inappropriately implied a statistically significant result. This experience inspired Bailar, now chair of the epidemiology department at Montreal's McGill University, to teach a course on research ethics for both students and faculty. Those enrolled in the course reviewed both real and hypothetical instances where scientific misconduct has been alleged (Science home page, 1995).

Sign-up board outside Psychology Department office. Announcements describe each study and advise students of their rights and responsibilities before they volunteer.

Other universities have similar courses for students and faculty. Because research has increasingly become an international operation, such courses are particularly valuable for researchers visiting from other nations who use the course to become familiar with the ethical rules of the host nation, which may be different from the ethical rules in their own countries.

The case study method is frequently used for teaching scientific ethics and what to do when possible misconduct occurs. The case study or scenario provides information about a real or hypothetical ethical violation and asks readers to judge whether or not there has been misconduct, and if so, what should be done about it. The studies are designed to stimulate discussion among the participants. As in real life, some important information may not be known, or there may be disagreement among the various parties. Box 2–3 shows an ethical scenario regarding possible misconduct in a behavioral research study. Again, we emphasize that instances of such misconduct are rare. Even so, it is important that the scientific community has procedures and principles to deal with allegations of fraud or misconduct.

Science magazine used its home page on the World Wide Web for an electronic project called "Science Conduct Online." The project involved ethical scenarios developed by a panel of five experts who taught courses on scientific ethics. The five scenarios cover a range of issues connected with scientific conduct, including accusations of fraud, plagiarism, and undeserved credit. Viewers were invited

---

BOX 2–3. Teaching Research Ethics

Scenario: Who gets the publication credit?

Lisa came up with an interesting idea for her senior thesis. She discussed it with her instructor who agreed to sponsor the project. Lisa completed the study during her senior year, turned in her report, graduated, and went on to graduate school where she became interested in other topics, and did no further work on the subject of her senior thesis.

A few years later Lisa discovered an article published by her former sponsor that included the data Lisa had collected along with some new data collected by the former instructor working with other students. The instructor was the sole author of the published paper, with the contributions of Lisa and the other students mentioned in a footnote. Lisa immediately wrote a letter to the instructor complaining that her data were used without her permission and that she should have been listed as a co-author of the paper, as the original idea was hers. The instructor wrote back to say that acknowledgement in a footnote was sufficient, and that because Lisa's study was submitted as her senior thesis, the data were available for use by others, especially as Lisa had not continued to pursue this line of research.

    1. Do you think that Lisa's claim to co-authorship is legitimate?

    2. Was the instructor required to contact Lisa to obtain her permission to use the data from the senior thesis?

---

to respond to each scenario, and the experts replied to the comments online. Although the interactive format has ended, the cases and the discussions are available on the home page (Science home page, 1995). The variety of responses to the scenarios shows the difficulty in making decisions based on incomplete and conflicting information. This is a common situation when accusations of misconduct are made. Person A claims one thing and Person B claims the opposite. Discussion of the claims may not always identify who is at fault, but is useful in deciding what should be done, not only in the specific instance, but as a matter of future policy, to minimize the likelihood of future occurrences.

Simulation exercises (see Chapter 7) have been developed to teach ethical principles in research. In the game *Integrity or Misconduct*, players become familiar with the facts of a practice case from newspaper articles about a scientist who is accused of falsifying data in the clinical tests of a new drug (Halleck, 1995). Participants in the exercise play the roles of government officials at the National Institutes of Health who supplied the money for the research, other government officials concerned with scientific fraud, colleagues of the researcher who want him to have a fair hearing, politicians, and members of the public who suspect a cover-up of scientific fraud. The exercise and a follow-up discussion with a trained facilitator allow the exploration of the complex issues involved in determining if an ethical violation has occurred, who is to blame, and what, if anything, should be done about it. The game helps participants develop a tolerance for ambiguity when having to make decisions where some of the information is contradictory and not everything can be known with certainty.

Psychologists' Code of Ethics

Professional organizations in the social sciences have developed guidelines for the ethical conduct of research with human participants. The first version of the ethical code for members of the American Psychological Association (APA) was published in 1953 and has been revised several times on the basis of the experiences of researchers (American Psychological Association, 1992). The code can also be accessed through the home page of the APA (http://www.APA.org). Most sections of the current ethical code for psychologists concern professional practice, such as clinical testing and psychotherapy, which are outside the scope of this book. The relevant sections on research are summarized in Box 2–4.

The code places joint responsibility on the individual investigator to conduct research in an ethical manner and on institutional review boards to screen proposals in order to minimize risks to participants and ensure informed consent. The language of the code is legalistic, but the issues are important both from an ethical standpoint and in educating investigators and participants about the nature of research.

The key element for most studies, apart from those involving unobtrusive observation in public locations or the review of available documents, is *informed consent*. As described in Box 2–3 those who participate in research studies should understand what is involved (i.e., specifically what they will be asked to do and if there is any risk or discomfort involved), and be informed of their rights to decline to participate in the experiment (with alternative activities available if course extra credit is given for participation in research), and to withdraw from the study at any point.

After the research, participants should be provided with information about the study. This can be done with individuals or groups. When a class of students has participated in a study, the researcher or the instructor describes the goals of the research immediately following the procedure, and after the data have been analyzed, will report to the class on the results.

The ethical code also discusses the use of animals in behavioral research, especially the need to adhere to professional and governmental standards in the care of laboratory animals.

Additional sections discuss the need to avoid *plagiarism* in research and to give proper credit when research findings are published. Plagiarism is a type of theft, in which one person "steals" another person's data by representing it as his or her own. This is avoided by giving proper credit where it is due. There is nothing unusual or unethical in analyzing data collected by others. Researchers do this all the time. You might, for example, analyze survey data collected by a government agency or re-analyze the published data collected by another investigator. What is important is that the identity of the source be identified by referring specifically to the government agency of the other investigator, rather than implying that you collected the information yourself.

When data are collected jointly by several different investigators, as occurs on research teams, there are legitimate questions about who "owns" the data and to

BOX 2–4. Excerpts from the APA *Ethical Principles of Psychologists and Code of Conduct* (1992), sections 6.06 through 6.26

6.06 Planning Research

(a) Psychologists design, conduct, and report research in accordance with recognized standards of scientific competence and ethical research.

(b) Psychologists plan their research so as to minimize the possibility that results will be misleading.

(c) In planning research, psychologists consider its ethical acceptability under the Ethics Code. If an ethical issue is unclear, psychologists seek to resolve the issue through consultation with institutional review boards, animal care and use committees, peer consultations, or other proper mechanisms.

(d) Psychologists take reasonable steps to implement appropriate protections for the rights and welfare of human participants, other persons affected by the research, and the welfare of animal subjects.

6.07 Responsibility

(a) Psychologists conduct research competently and with due concern for the dignity and welfare of the participants.

(b) Psychologists are responsible for the ethical conduct of research conducted by them or by others under their supervision or control.

(c) Researchers and assistants are permitted to perform only those tasks for which they are appropriately trained and prepared.

(d) As part of the process of development and implementation of research projects, psychologists consult those with expertise concerning any special population under investigation or most likely to be affected.

6.08 Compliance With Law and Standards

Psychologists plan and conduct research in a manner consistent with federal and state law and regulations, as well as professional standards governing the conduct of research, and particularly those standards governing research with human participants and animal subjects.

6.09 Institutional Approval

Psychologists obtain from host institutions or organizations appropriate approval prior to conducting research and they provide accurate information about their research proposals. They conduct the research in accordance with the approved research protocol.

6.10 Research Responsibilities

Prior to conducting research (except research involving only anonymous surveys, naturalistic observations, or similar research), psychologists enter into an agreement with participants that clarifies the nature of the research and the responsibilities of each party.

6.11 Informed Consent to Research

(a) Psychologists use language that is reasonably understandable to research participants in obtaining their appropriate informed consent (except as provided in Standard 6.12, Dispensing With Informed Consent). Such informed consent is appropriately documented.

(b) Using language that is reasonably understandable to participants, psychologists inform participants of the nature of the research; they inform participants that they are free to participate or to decline to participate or to withdraw from the research; they explain the foreseeable consequences of declining or withdrawing, they inform participants of significant factors that may be expected to influence their willingness to participate (such as risks, discomfort, adverse effects, or limitations on confidentiality, except as provided in Standard 6.15, Deception in Research); and they explain other aspects about which the prospective participants inquire.

(c) When psychologists conduct research with individuals such as students or subordinates, psychologists take special care to protect the prospective participants from adverse consequences of declining or withdrawing from participation.

(d) When research participation is a course requirement or opportunity for extra credit, the prospective participant is given the choice of equitable alternative activities.

(e) For persons who are legally incapable of giving informed consent, psychologists nevertheless (1) provide an appropriate explanation, (2) obtain the participant's assent, and (3) obtain appropriate permission from a legally authorized person, if such substitute consent is permitted by law.

6.12 Dispensing With Informed Consent

Before determining that planned research (such as research involving only anonymous questionnaires, naturalistic observations, or certain kinds of archival research) does not require the informed consent of research participants, psychologists consider applicable regulations and institutional review board requirements, and they consult with colleagues as appropriate.

6.13 Informed Consent in Research Filming or Recording

Psychologists obtain informed consent from research participants prior to filming or recording them in any form, unless the research involves simply naturalistic observation in public places and it is not anticipated that the recording will be used in a manner that could cause personal identification or harm.

6.14 Offering Inducements for Research Participants

(a) In offering professional services as an inducement to obtain research participants, psychologists make clear the nature of the services, as well as the risks, obligations, and limitations.

(b) Psychologists do not offer excessive or inappropriate financial or other inducements to obtain research participants, particularly when it might tend to coerce participation.

6.15 Deception in Research

(a) Psychologists do not conduct a study involving deception unless they have determined that the use of deceptive techniques is justified by the study's prospective scientific, educational, or applied value and that equally effective alternative procedures that do not use deception are not feasible.

(b) Psychologists never deceive research participants about significant aspects that would affect their willingness to participate, such as physical risks, discomfort, or unpleasant emotional experiences.

(c) Any other deception that is an integral feature of the design and conduct of an experiment must be explained to participants as early as is feasible, preferably at the conclusion of their participation, but no later than at the conclusion of the research. (See also Standard 6.18, Providing Participants With Information About the Study.)

6.16 Sharing and Utilizing Data

Psychologists inform research participants of their anticipated sharing or further use of personally identifiable research data and of the possibility of unanticipated future uses.

6.17 Minimizing Invasiveness

In conducting research, psychologists interfere with the participants or milieu from which data are collected only in a manner that is warranted by an appropriate research design and that is consistent with psychologists' roles as scientific investigators.

6.18 Providing Participants With Information About the Study

(a) Psychologists provide a prompt opportunity for participants to obtain appropriate information about the nature, results, and conclusions of the research, and psychologists attempt to correct any misconceptions that participants may have.

(b) If scientific or humane values justify delaying or withholding this information, psychologists take reasonable measures to reduce the risk of harm.

6.19 Honoring Commitments

Psychologists take reasonable measures to honor all commitments they have made to research participants.

6.20 Care and Use of Animals in Research

(a) Psychologists who conduct research involving animals treat them humanely.

(b) Psychologists acquire, care for, use, and dispose of animals in compliance with current federal, state, and local laws and regulations, and with professional standards.

(c) Psychologists trained in research methods and experienced in the care of laboratory animals supervise all procedures involving animals and are responsible for ensuring appropriate consideration of their comfort, health, and humane treatment.

(d) Psychologists ensure that all individuals using animals under their supervision have received instruction in research methods and in the care, maintenance, and handling of the species being used, to the extent appropriate to their role.

(e) Responsibilities and activities of individuals assisting in a research project are consistent with their respective competencies.

(f) Psychologists make reasonable efforts to minimize the discomfort, infection, illness, and pain of animal subjects.

(g) A procedure subjecting animals to pain, stress, or privation is used only when an alternative procedure is unavailable and the goal is justified by its prospective scientific, education, or applied value.

(h) Surgical procedures are performed under appropriate anesthesia; techniques to avoid infection and minimize pain are followed during and after surgery.

(i) When it is appropriate that the animal's life be terminated, it is done rapidly, with an effort to minimize pain, and in accordance with accepted procedures.

6.21 Report of Results

(a) Psychologists do not fabricate data or falsify results in their publications.

(b) If psychologists discover significant errors in their published data, they take reasonable steps to correct such errors in a correction, retraction, erratum, or other appropriate publication means.

6.22 Plagiarism

Psychologists do not present substantial portions or elements of another's work or data as their own, even if the other work or data source is cited occasionally.

6.23 Publication Credit

(a) Psychologists take responsibility and credit, including authorship credit, only for work they have actually performed or to which they have contributed.

(b) Principal authorship and other publication credits accurately reflect the relative scientific or professional contributions of the individuals involved, regardless of their relative status. Mere possession of an institutional position, such as Department Chair, does not justify authorship credit. Minor contributions to the research or to the writing for publications are appropriately acknowledged, such as in footnotes or in an introductory statement.

(c) A student is usually listed as principal author on any multiple-authored article that is substantially based on the student's dissertation or thesis.

6.24 Duplicate Publication of Data

Psychologists do not publish, as original data, data that have been previously published. This does not preclude republishing data when they are accompanied by proper acknowledgment.

6.25 Sharing Data

After research results are published, psychologists do not withhold the data on which their conclusions are based from other competent professionals who seek to verify the substantive claims through reanalysis and who intend to use such data only for that purpose, provided that the confidentiality of the participants can be protected and unless legal rights concerning proprietary data precludes their release.

6.26 Professional Reviewers

Psychologists who review material submitted for publication, grant, or other research proposal review respect the confidentiality of and the proprietary rights in such information of those who submitted it.

---

what degree team members are allowed to use portions of the joint data for their own purposes. Such issues are typically discussed at the beginning of the research, but when disputes arise, they should be discussed among the participants, and if no resolution is possible, brought to the attention of an IRB or other agency familiar with ethical issues in research.

Publication credit is another area in which disputes occasionally arise. There may be questions about who counts as an author and who simply merits acknowledgment in a footnote, and the order of authorship may be an issue (whose name appears first, second, and third). There are several ways to resolve order of authorship when members of a research team have made equal contributions. One method is to flip a coin in deciding the order in the published article with a footnote indicating that the authors have made equal contributions. When several papers result from a research program, the order of authorship can be varied among them. With class projects, the name of the class can be listed as author, with the individual students listed alphabetically in a footnote, along with the instructor's name. It is important not to leave issues of publication credit to the end of the study when team members are likely to have different conceptions of the importance of their own contributions.

Researchers are required to retain their data for a prescribed period and make it available to others who want to examine or reanalyze the data providing that confidentiality rules regarding the original participants can be protected.

Anthropologists' and Sociologists' Code of Ethics

Anthropologists who conduct their research in other nations and cultures face special problems. They must be concerned about their relationship with host governments and local people. Their actions reflect on their own government. The statement of ethics adopted by the American Anthropological Association (1990) describes anthropologists' responsibilities in six major areas:

1. Anthropologists' first responsibility is to those whose lives and cultures they study. Should conflicts of interest arise, the interests of these people take precedence over other considerations.

2. Anthropologists have responsibility to be truthful to the publics that read, hear, or view the products of their work.

3. Anthropologists bear responsibility for the good reputation of the discipline and its practitioners.

4. Anthropologists should be candid, fair, and nonexploitative in their dealings with trainees and students, and committed to their welfare and progress.

5. In all dealings with employers, clients, and sponsors, anthropologists should be honest about their qualifications, capabilities, and aims. Prior to entering any professional commitment, anthropologists must review the purposes of sponsors, employers, or clients, taking into consideration their past activities and future goals.

6. Anthropologists should be honest and candid in all dealings with their own governments and with host governments. They should ascertain that they will not be required to compromise either their responsibilities or anthropological ethics as a condition of permission to engage in professional activities.

The American Sociological Association (1989) has a code of ethics that is similar to those of the psychologists and anthropologists but places more emphasis on the proper use of research findings. It also recognizes the wide range of contexts within which sociologists find employment.

Local Procedures

In carrying out your own studies, be sure to find out the procedures within your own organization, agency, or school for protecting research subjects. If you are at a university or research institution, you will probably fill out a form, such as that described at the beginning of this chapter, that will be reviewed by an official committee. *This may involve a delay of several weeks before you can begin your research.* You should plan for this delay beforehand. Don't wait until the last minute to submit your approval form. Filling out these forms is a valuable learning experience. You will have to answer questions that you may not have considered: How much should the participants be told beforehand? How can the confidentiality of the completed questionnaires be maintained? Will the researcher specify the name of the institution being observed? What happens if the observer sees illegal behavior? Answering these questions is a good opportunity to foresee potential problems and develop ways of handling them before they arise.

The type of inducement allowed in recruiting research participants can also be an ethical issue. Students participating for extra credit in college classes must be allowed to withdraw from the study at any time, and be provided with alternative activities if they do not want to participate in the study but still want to earn extra credit. Participants should be given opportunities to learn about the study. This is done both during informed consent so that people know what they are getting into and after the testing during debriefing, when they are given further details about the methods and goals of the research.

Research done as part of class projects may be exempt from some of the more cumbersome procedures, providing the instructor takes responsibility and there is no risk to the participants. Even if your specific project does not require you to fill out the human subjects questionnaire, the responsibility for maintaining ethical standards remains. You will have to develop your own procedures for protecting participants from inconvenience or risk.

Summary

Most colleges and universities have IRBs to review the ethical aspects of behavioral studies. A major concern is protecting the rights and welfare of participants and seeing that they are adequately informed about the risks and benefits of their participation.

Two methods used to protect participants in behavioral studies are confidentiality and anonymity. *Confidentiality* means that the respondent's identity is protected from public exposure. *Anonymity* means that the researcher does not know the identity of the participants in the study. Use of deception in research should be avoided whenever possible.

A second area of concern is scientific misconduct. Blatant misconduct is very rare. There are areas of ambiguity where misunderstandings can occur, leading to accusations of fraud, plagiarism, and taking undeserved credit. Following ethical guidelines reduces the likelihood of claims of misconduct.

Some colleges and universities have developed courses in research ethics which use case studies or scenarios to examine allegations of scientific misconduct. As in real life, the information in the scenarios is often incomplete and contradictory. Professional organizations have developed guidelines for the ethical conduct of behavioral research. When embarking on a research plan, familiarize yourself with the procedures of your institution regarding research review, informed consent, and inducements for participation.

Ethical guidelines phrased in general terms are often difficult to apply in specific instances. It is also difficult to specify in advance all the ethical problems that might arise in the course of the study. Committees charged with protecting the rights and welfare of research subjects may be inflexible in interpreting rules and policies and thus delay valuable research. On the other hand, committees may be unfamiliar with the risks in frontier areas of research and approve studies that expose people to unknown risks.

References

American Anthropological Association. (1990). *Professional Ethics: Statements and Procedures of the American Anthropological Association*. [brochure]. Washington, DC: Author.

American Psychological Association. (1992). Ethical principles of Psychologists and Code of Conduct. *American Psychologist, 47*, 1597–1611. http://www.APA.org/ethics

American Sociological Association. (1989). *Code of Ethics*. [brochure]. Washington, DC: Author.

Fisher, C. B., & Fyrberg, D. (1994). Participant partners: College students weigh the costs and benefits of deceptive research. *American Psychologist, 49*(5), 417–427.

Halleck, G. B. (1995). Academic integrity. In D. Crookall & K. Arai (Eds.), *Simulation and gaming across disciplines and cultures: ISAGA at a watershed*, (pp. 37–44). Thousand Oaks, CA: Sage Publications.

Keith-Spiegel, P., & Koocher, G. P. (1985). *Ethics in psychology: Professional standards and cases.* New York: Random House.

Milgram, S. (1974). *Obedience to authority; an experimental view.* New York: Harper & Row.

Rosenthal, R. (1976). *Experimenter effects in behavioral research.* New York: Irvington.

Science home page. (1995). *Beyond the printed page.* http://www.aaas.org/science/science.html

Further Reading

Bersoff, D. N. (Ed.). (1995). *Ethical conflicts in psychology.* Washington, DC: American Psychological Association.

Canter, M. B., Bennett, B. E., Jones, S. E., & Nagy, T. F. (1995). *Ethics for Psychologists: A commentary on the APA ethics code.* Washington DC: American Psychological Association.

Erwin, E., Gendin, S., & Kleiman, L. (Eds.). (1994). *Ethical issues in scientific research: An anthology.* New York & London: Garland Publishing.

Lee, R. M. (1993). *Doing research on sensitive topics.* London & Newbury Park, CA: Sage Publications.

Penslar, R. L. (1995). *Research ethics: Cases and materials.* Bloomington, IN: Indiana University Press.

Sieber, J. E. (1992). *Planning ethically responsible research: A guide for students and internal review boards.* Newbury Park, CA: Sage Publications.

U.S. Public Health Service, Office of Research Integrity (ORI) home page. http://phs.os.dhhs.gov/phs/ori/ori_home.html

3 Library Search

An important part of a researcher's task is to learn what has been done before. Finding out about previous research is called *reviewing the literature*. Not only will you learn additional information and facts about your area of interest, but you will probably come across new ideas and methods that will improve your project. It is also exciting to encounter others who share an interest in your topic. There is not one source of information on a topic, but many. Most can be found in a college library.

Source Credibility

There are various places where behavioral research is mentioned. A study may be described on television, in the newspapers, on the internet, or in a secondary source such as a textbook or review article (a review of the scientific literature on a topic), or it can be seen in its original form in a scientific journal. Although no source type is 100 percent credible, some sources are more credible than others. The following descriptions will help you in judging the quality of information.

Primary and Secondary Sources

A *primary source* is the original research report, such as a journal article or book chapter. Sometimes the information is only available in a conference report or unpublished manuscript. *Secondary sources* are textbooks, review papers, or general articles that mention the study. Typically, the description is brief and provides only a general idea of the topic without much information about methods or findings. If you wish to know the details, you need to find the original paper. Most secondary sources contain reference information, such as a journal reference, that allows you to locate the original paper, which is the *primary* source of the information. Each of the following information sources may contain either primary or secondary levels of information, and sometimes hearsay (information with little credibility).

Scientific Journal Articles

When an article is published in a scientific journal, you can generally assume it has passed through a *peer review process* (i.e., it has been read and evaluated favorably by researchers familiar with the topic). Journals that follow a peer review procedure are called *refereed* journals. Some have higher standards than others and are more credible sources. Consult an experienced researcher to find out the most reliable and credible sources in your area of interest.

Books of Readings

Collected articles can be a mixed bag in terms of credibility. There can be classic papers that have been through the peer review process, have stood the test of time, and are printed in their entirety. Sometimes an original journal article is abridged or adapted for inclusion in a book of readings. There may also be new chapters that have not passed through peer review.

Behavioral Science Books

A college or university library contains an assortment of books on behavioral science issues. Some are textbooks written primarily for specific courses. There are technical books and monographs directed to advanced specialists. There may also be popular books written for a general audience. Some of these will be authored by well-known scholars who want to reach a general audience, or they may be written by professional writers specializing in behavioral science issues.

The important thing to remember about virtually all books is that they have not been peer reviewed. A publisher typically sends a book manuscript to several people for their comments, but the major concern is likely to be the potential market (will it sell?), which is very different from the type of evaluation given to a journal article.

Each of the preceding outlets is intended to reach a specific audience. A researcher who studies animal behavior will publish articles in refereed technical journals to be read by colleagues. To reach a general audience, it is entirely proper and sensible for her to write an article for *Natural History, Audubon,* or the *Smithsonian,* all of which are nonrefereed but still have high editorial standards. If the findings were particularly interesting, a commercial publisher might ask the author to prepare a popular book for a general audience.

Mass Media

The popular media, such as newspapers, television, and magazines, tend to focus on topics or portions of studies that are controversial or sensational. News reports do not present the context of research in terms of previous studies, and they frequently omit important aspects of the methods and findings. This makes it risky to rely on their descriptions of a research study. You should check the original source, which can probably be located in a library.

Internet

The quality and completeness of information available on the Internet and through the World Wide Web is variable. It depends mainly on who is responsible for compiling the information and how conscientious they are in presenting it. Some lists and groups are better than others, and it is difficult to determine viability without already being an expert in the particular subject.

Defining Technical Terms

As you conduct your literature review, you are likely to encounter unfamiliar technical terms and abbreviations. These are used by authors to save time and space. It is much simpler to use MMPI than the full name of the test, the Minnesota Multiphasic Personality Inventory. When you encounter an unfamiliar word or abbreviation, you can look it up in the index of a textbook in the same field or consult one of the many dictionaries in the behavioral and social sciences. Some are listed at the end of the chapter in the "Further Reading" section. There are dictionaries of statistical terms and symbols, and of terms used in psychology, sociology, and other fields. Some terms are defined in the glossary of this book.

Using the Library

Set aside a specific time for your library work, and do it in advance of the deadline for your paper. You might not be able to find everything you need on a single trip, and it will take a while to become familiar with the various information sources.

The most important and useful information resource in the library is not found on the shelves, but is sitting at a desk waiting to assist you. The reference librarian is a trained professional whose job is to help people gain access to information. Don't just ask and run; explain your needs in detail. There are many ways in which a librarian can help.

Consider the depth to which you want to explore the topic. For a broad overview, and to get a feel for previous research on the topic, the index of a general textbook in the field is a good place to start. There are general encyclopedias of social and behavioral science and more specialized encyclopedias in the areas of Education, Social Work, Women's Studies, and many other fields. The material in an encyclopedia has been carefully selected to stand the test of time. Finding your topic in a textbook or encyclopedia will ensure that it is, in fact, what you think it is. Every field has its own jargon (specialized language), which often differs from common usage.

Your report is likely to require more information than is available in general sources such as encyclopedias and textbooks (secondary sources). You probably will need to review both periodicals (journals) and books. It is wise to begin with the most *recent* publications, working back to earlier sources, as needed.

The computer age has led to tremendous increases in the ease of literature searches. In the past, one dealt with card catalogs and bound index volumes in order to locate books and articles. Now, in most libraries, the search for titles and authors can be done by computer using *electronic databases*. A *database* is a listing of information—of books, articles, and related descriptive information, generally categorized by author and subject. A library card catalog is a database in print form. The *Readers' Guide to Periodical Literature* is a print database. Over the past years, a number of these print databases have been transformed into computer-based systems, and new ones have been added. Governmental and business libraries are likely to have electronic databases covering subjects of interest to them. Some databases are available to the public via the internet. For example, YAHOO on the World Wide Web provides access to a number of library catalogues (databases) around the world. You won't be able to get the actual publication over the net (unless you are willing to pay for it), but you will be able to obtain the reference and find out whether the publication is available in a particular library.

Finding Books on Your Topic

At most libraries, the familiar card catalog of the past is now available online. A computerized catalog allows you to search by subject headings, authors' names, and titles. If you want to locate a specific journal article or a chapter in an edited book, you will need to use other databases described in subsequent sections.

Most library online catalogs use the Library of Congress subject headings. These may be accessible using a BROWSE command on the computer, or you may need to consult the *Library of Congress Subject Heading Index*, a very large red 4-volume set of books, probably placed nearby. For example, assume you are interested in *alcohol-related accidents*. That heading is *not* one of the Library of Congress subject headings, and entering it into the computer will not provide any references. However, under the Library of Congress listing for *alcohol*, you will see NT (for Narrower Terms) and the following listings:

Drinking and airplane accidents
Drinking and automobile accidents
Drug-alcohol interactions

These subject headings will produce a list of relevant books. Copy the *reference* information (author, date, title, publisher, and city of publication) and the *call number* (in order to locate the volume).

Finding Journal Articles and Book Chapters

Librarians refer to journals, magazines, and newspapers as *periodicals* because they are issued periodically (daily, weekly, etc.). In addition to the online catalog, there are many databases in both electronic (computer-based) and print form (bound volumes) that use subject headings, author names, or other keywords for locating relevant books, chapters, and articles in periodicals. When a book or article is originally entered into a database, a list of keywords is included. This list provides the basis for a subject matter search. You can also locate items by using the author's name or possible title words.

Some databases reflect subject matter areas, such as education or anthropology. Others access specific media, such as magazines or newspapers. Because of differences among the various databases, we cannot provide a detailed how-to-do-it sequence, but we will lay out the basic steps in the hope of making it easier for you to learn about the databases available to you.

Navigating a Database by Computer

Usually you can accomplish a computer search with a few commands. At the beginning, all you need are the commands for finding references and for saving and printing. These will help you find the actual book or article. It is also easy to download the references that you have saved to a disk or send them to your own e-mail address.

Terms that tell the program what to do are called COMMANDS, for example

F (Find)
D (Display)
EXPLAIN
SAVE
HELP

The F (Find) command is usually used with an INDEX term. INDEXES refer to the categories used as the basis for the search. For example,

SU (Subject)—to search by thesaurus terms or descriptors assigned to items.
AU (Author)—to search by author's last name, preferably followed by initials or first name.
TW (Title Word)—to search by words in titles.
KW (KeyWord)—to search by words in the titles or abstracts.

Pay attention to blank spaces in a command. For example,

F AU MIDOROVICH (author's name).

There are other index terms that you will find listed in your library.

The Logic of the Search

Most of the time you will want to search for a particular topic. A good way to start is to write a phrase or two describing the subject of interest. For example, perhaps you are interested in sport psychology. That is a very broad subject and would yield hundreds of references. Thinking further, you decide that your particular interest is in the effect of imagery training (mentally visualizing the particular activity) on improving performance. Now you can derive the key terms (subjects or keywords) to guide your search—"sport psychology" and "imagery." These are the words to use in your subject search. It is best to have two or more terms in order to narrow your search to a manageable number of references.

The computer simply goes through all the available citations (references) seeking keywords. You guide the search by using commands and index terms (described above) followed by your specific search terms (e.g., Find SUbject sport psychology). The command and index terms can be abbreviated, and you can use more than one word as the search term (e.g., f su sport psychology). If you were searching the PsycINFO database, here is what you might see on the computer screen. The first line is your entry. The second and third lines are the computer's response.

f su sport psychology
Search request: F SU SPORT PSYCHOLOGY
Search result: 414 citations in the PsycINFO database

You can reduce the number of references by including your second index term.

> f su sport psychology and su imagery
> Search request: F SU SPORT PSYCHOLOGY AND SU IMAGERY
> Search result: 10 citations in the PsycINFO database

If you think this step might have reduced your search too much, use KeyWord in place of SUbject.

> f su sport psychology and kw imagery
> Search request: F SU SPORT PSYCHOLOGY AND KW IMAGERY
> Search result: 24 citations in the PsycINFO database

Alternatively, you can reduce the number of references by telling the computer to eliminate certain subjects. This is done by adding "AND NOT" to the command, as follows:

> f su sport psychology and kw imagery and not kw dance
> Search request: F SU SPORT PSYCHOLOGY AND KW IMAGERY AND NOT KW DANCE
> Search result: 23 citations in the PsycINFO database

Each database will have its own list of subject and keyword headings. For example, both psychology and sociology have a *thesaurus* of subject headings (Booth & Colby, 1986; Walker, 1994). Other databases may use what are called "descriptor" terms.

Your subject or keyword may have alternate forms, such as adoles*cence*, adoles*cent*, adoles*cents*. Most information systems allow you to search for alternate forms by using a symbol such as # or * (for truncation or as a wild card) with no preceding space (for example, adoles#), and all forms will be covered.

Finding the Right Database(s)

Learn about the different databases available to you. Some of them may still be in printed form (i.e., bound volumes). Decide which ones are most likely to contain the literature that you wish to search.

Box 3–1 describes several databases that are particularly useful in searching behavioral and social science literature (including education). There are many more databases. Although they may differ with regard to particular terms, once you have learned how to use one database, it is easy to figure out how to navigate new ones.

Online and CD-ROM Databases

Some databases are accessible through a connection with another online public access catalog (called OPACs) such as EUREKA, FIRSTSEARCH, and MELVYL. Others are available on CD-ROM. PsychLIT is similar to the online PsycINFO database and the print *Psychological Abstracts*. The Educational Resources Information Center database (ERIC) is available on CD-ROM. Sociology references

BOX 3–1. Selected Databases for the Behavioral and Social Sciences

ONLINE/CD-ROM

PsycINFO: (PsychLIT on CD-ROM) scholarly psychology journals, conference proceedings, dissertations, reports, books, and book chapters in psychology and related disciplines; from 1967.

Anthropological Literature: journals and book chapters in anthropology and archaeology; art history; ethnohistory; biological, cultural, physical, or social anthropology; geography; genetics; folklore; geology; history; linguistics; music; religion; from 1984.

ERIC: Educational Resources Information Center of the U.S. Department of Education; scholarly journals and unpublished reports in microfiche format in all areas of education; from 1966.

Current Contents: citation subsets for the Social/Behavioral Sciences and Arts/Humanities, from 1989.

Magazine & Journal: general interest and scholarly journal articles, especially in the humanities and social sciences, from 1988. Some references include abstracts, and some include the full text of the article.

ABI/Inform: articles on companies, products, industries, public policy, trends, research results, technology, health care, and social issues; from 1971. Some references include abstracts, and some include the full text of the article.

GPO: Government Printing Office; subjects of interest on the U.S. Government, including Congressional hearings, reports, debates, and records, judiciary material, documents issued by the executive branch; from 1976.

ArticleFirst: citations to journal tables of contents in science, technology, medicine, social science, business, the humanities, and popular culture; broad coverage; from 1990.

Sociofile: scholarly sociology journal articles; available on CD-ROM, probably online in near future; from 1974.

PRINT

Psychological Abstracts
Abstracts in Anthropology
Sociological Abstracts
ERIC (Education)
Current Contents
Reader's Guide to Periodical Literature
Social Sciences Index
Business Periodical Index (also on CD-ROM)
GPO Monthly Catalog (Government Printing Office)

and abstracts are available on *Sociofile*; the print equivalent is the *Sociological Abstracts*. Dissertation Abstracts (summaries of doctoral dissertations) are available on CD-ROM and in print form.

Print Databases

A number of more specialized databases are available only in print form, but in the future may be online or on CD-ROM. Examples are

Sage Race Relations Abstracts
Women's Studies Abstracts
Social Work Research and Abstracts
Child Development Abstracts and Bibliography
Criminology and Penology Abstracts
Exceptional Child Education Abstracts

Your library may have others not mentioned here.

Less Technical Sources

Sometimes the information you want will be in the mass media—newspapers and magazines. In addition to the Magazine and Journal database listed in Box 3–1, there is an online Newspaper Articles Database listing articles from five major U.S. newspapers. In either print or electronic form, the *Reader's Guide to Periodical Literature* is one of the best guides to general literature.

Accessing the Database

After selecting the database most likely to meet your needs, find out how to access it, that is, how to log on to the program on the computer or how to use the print volumes. There will be several aids available: written instructions, instructions appearing on a computer screen, help menus, and, not the least, the reference librarian.

In using printed indexes, check the front matter for instructions. Online sources usually have both general and context-specific screens retrievable with a standard command such as "help" or "explain."

What to Save from the Search

The most important elements are the references and the locations of the articles and books that you wish to review. You will cite the reference when you refer to the book or article in your paper. See examples of references at the end of each chapter in this textbook and in the manuscript shown in Appendix D. The *location* includes the call number, which enables you to find the actual book or article of interest.

In addition, many of the databases provide an *abstract* which is a very brief summary of the article. This is extremely helpful because it gives you a better idea of what is in the article and whether or not it is really what you want. Viewing the abstract allows you to narrow your search even further, avoiding dead ends and finding the pertinent articles. The abstract may also contain some details on method and sample characteristics. In addition to saving or printing the reference, consider keeping the abstract if it appears useful.

Saving the References

There are a number of ways to save references. You can copy the relevant ones down by hand. With an electronic database, usually you can save the references that you want by simply typing in SAVE and the number of the reference. That puts the reference on a list. When you have finished your search and *before* you leave the database, you can either print your list or download it to a file for future use. As noted above, the key elements you want to transfer, either to typed copy or a file, are the full *reference* and the *location* of the article or book. You might want to save and transfer the abstract, if available, along with the reference. Obtaining the call number may require your consulting the library's electronic card catalog using the book or periodical title. The database you are using may not have the location information.

There are a number of ways to print a list of references. For details, consult the reference librarian or posted information regarding literature searches. Here are a few possibilities:

1. In the library, print out the results of your search (the listing that you have saved) at the computer where you are working.

2. Mail the results to yourself at another computer via e-mail.

3. If working from a modem at home or in your office, download the file containing the search results to your computer and print it out, or transfer the references to a bibliographic program.

There are computer software packages that manage references and format them in various styles. Examples are EndNote Plus, Pro-Cite, and Reference Manager. Reviews of these programs with purchase information can be found by accessing the *Computer Articles Database*. Use the search terms "bibliographic software" or "reference management software." The software allows you to directly download the results of your literature search by computer, so that you do not need to re-type the references.

Citation Search

A citation search is a technique for finding recent work that references an earlier article. You can use a citation search to locate all the subsequently-published articles that have referenced a person's work or a particular study.

In the behavioral and social sciences, the most useful citation database is the *Social Sciences Citation Index (SCCI)*. The actual search involves a series of steps, which we will not describe here. The print volumes of SCCI are available at many college or university libraries. You can also inquire about access to online citation searches, where you pay a citation service to locate all the papers that have included the study or author in the reference list.

How Far to Search?

Begin with the most recent work. If the topic is limited to a specific discipline such as psychology, then using the electronic card catalog for books and an electronic database (PsycINFO OR PsycLIT) or print database (*Psychological Abstracts*) for journals will probably be sufficient. If you are researching an interdisciplinary subject—for example, recreation and leisure—you may need to use more than one database.

How far back in time you should go will depend on the amount of recent material you find. If there are many recent articles, these will probably contain reviews or summaries of earlier work and save you the trouble of having to read through all the earlier papers. If the earlier work is especially close to your interest, you should read the original paper rather than rely on someone else's interpretation. If there is very little current research, then you will have to go further back in time to find out what is known about the topic. The key is to find the most relevant articles. How many will depend on the amount and quality of published research.

Sometimes you will be fortunate enough to be doing research on a topic for which a literature review is available. Some journals in the behavioral sciences, such as *Psychological Bulletin,* specialize in literature reviews. For many databases there is a specific index term for searching by *document type.* In PsycINFO, our library uses PT (Publication Type). The following phrase will produce a list of published reviews of anorexia:

f su anorexia and pt review

You may be able to locate a published *bibliography*, a compilation of titles of earlier work. A useful library reference tool is the *Bibliographic Index*, a semi-annual topical index (Cooley, Donohoe, & Borodkin, 1994). Some bibliographies are published separately, and others may be buried within books or articles. The *Bibliographic Index* provides the exact location, even to the page numbers, of the bibliography. Some government agencies periodically publish bibliographies of research studies in particular fields. "Bibliography" is also used as a document type index term in many databases such as PsycINFO and Current Contents.

If you are fortunate enough to be working in an area where a previous review exists, you will still need to update the material. Because of the publication lag, a review article published in 1995 is probably current only through 1993. There may be additional sources or references not included in the review.

When there are no published literature reviews or bibliographies, you can still get review information by reading the introductory sections of published papers on the topic. The introduction to a research study always includes a brief review, and references to relevant articles will be listed in the reference section at the end of the article. Each source can supply bits of information that point you toward other sources. When the names and titles that you encounter begin to look familiar, then you have come close to a good overview of the area. Your information on a topic will never be complete, and new bits of information are likely to come in while your project is underway. Box 3–2 provides a checklist of the the steps in doing a literature search.

Library Access through the Internet

Things are changing rapidly on the Internet with new features, home pages, lists, and new laws regulating access and permissible uses of material. The Internet has such potential as a research tool that we wanted to say something about it, even in its present form, recognizing that by the time this edition appears in print, things will have changed. Here we will mention its relevance to literature searches. Other uses of the Internet are described in Chapter 14.

On the Internet, you can access OPACs (Online Public Access Catalogs) and the catalogs of libraries around the world. Depending upon the database, you may be able to obtain tables of contents and library call numbers and be able to store these in a list.

A word of caution is needed. Access to the Internet does not eliminate the need for firsthand reading of material. One can use the Internet to locate titles and perhaps abstracts of articles, but it is hazardous to rely completely on a brief abstract for understanding the findings of a study. The abstract simply reveals whether or not a study is relevant, thus increasing the efficiency of the search and the actual visit to the library (or using interlibrary loan services).

Electronic access can be used to check references for accuracy (after you have left the library and when you are writing your paper). In writing a report, it frequently happens that key reference information is missing, such as the volume number, year of an article, or the proper spelling of someone's name. It is not uncommon to possess contradictory information, as when a name is spelled in two different ways or the first and second initials are reversed. These inconsistencies may be resolved by electronic communication without the need for an additional visit to the library.

Getting Your Hands on the Materials

There are differences among libraries in the degree of access users are given to the main book collection. Libraries with open stacks (bookshelves) allow readers to browse the collection and select what they need themselves. Such libraries often have tables in the stack area for people to sit down and read books and articles on the spot. Libraries with closed stacks prohibit readers from entering the collection area. The books and journals must be requested at a central desk and then retrieved by the librarians.

If your library has an open stack policy, check the library shelves around the call numbers that you turned up in your search. Librarians tend to place books on a topic close together. You may discover titles that were missed in the online search.

BOX 3–2. Steps in a Literature Search

1. Write out a couple of phrases describing the topic of interest.
2. For further clarification, look up the topic in textbooks and encyclopedias.
3. Check the library's electronic card catalog under subject heading for relevant books, obtaining the reference and call number for each.
4. Find the appropriate database(s) for journals that cover the topic.
5. Check with reference librarian.
6. Search the databases by subject or keyword and by authors (if known) who do research on the topic.
7. Obtain the complete references and the call numbers (location) for articles of interest.
   References should include the following information:
   A. For **books**
      1) Last name and initials for all authors
      2) Year of publication
      3) Title, including edition or volume number, if appropriate
      4) Place published, city and state/province
      5) Publisher
   B. For **book chapters**
      1) Last name and initials for all authors
      2) Chapter title
      3) Page numbers
      4) All book information as in A1-5 above.
   C. For **journal articles**
      1) Last name and initials for all authors
      2) Year published
      3) Title of article
      4) Periodical name
      5) Volume number
      6) Page numbers
   D. For **other sources**, such as newspapers or electronic media, consult style manual (see Ch. 20)
8. Consider other possible information sources (e.g., interlibrary loans, direct contact, information on the Internet).

There are online vendors who, for a fee, will provide you with copies of articles. Check with your librarian or examine Internet resources to get more specific information. These document delivery services are profit oriented and can be expensive.

Interlibrary Loan

Some books or key articles turned up in your literature search may not be available at your library. The book may be missing, the journal may have been sent out for binding, or the library does not subscribe to the particular periodical. When an unavailable article or book seems particularly important, consider using *interlibrary loan*. The librarian who handles these requests has computerized lists of materials at other libraries, or you might have located the source via the Internet. Typically, you fill out a request card for each book or periodical needed. When it arrives, the interlibrary desk sends a postcard or e-mail message telling you to pick it up and how long you can have it. For brief articles, the situation is somewhat easier, since the library that subscribes to the periodical can make a photocopy and send it for you to keep. The chief problem with interlibrary loan is the time delay. Several weeks can elapse between the initial request and the arrival of the book or journal. Eventually this may be done online.

What to Look for in a Research Article

Your first screening is the title of the article and keywords. If you are studying the effects of television violence upon aggression in children, you would look for "television," "aggression," "violence," and "children's aggression." At least one of these terms should be present if the article addresses that topic. Read the abstract. If it looks promising, then locate the article.

Some studies are of better quality than others and should be given more weight in your review. You need to know how to distinguish between good and less-good studies. You also need to know what information is more important and what is of lesser importance in order to take notes. To some extent, this will come with experience. To get a general idea of what to look for, skip ahead to Chapter 20 and look at Box 20-3 (Checklist for Reviewing a Research Report). Key points of information that should be included in a journal article are listed. These are also the points that you may wish to cover in the introduction section of your paper (i.e, what the researchers were looking for, what they did, and what they found).

If your topic is a broad one, such as gender differences, you will need to make it more narrow and be selective in your review. More manageable topics would be gender stereotypes in the media, gender differences in aggressive behavior, or children's perceptions of gender roles.

In reading an article do not overlook the Method and Results sections. These are often the distinguishing features between good and mediocre studies. The method determines the reliability and validity of the findings. The results section presents the findings without subjective interpretation. Some journal formats combine the Results and Discussion, requiring a more critical reading to separate findings from interpretations.

As the prose is more tightly packed with information, reading a technical article is slower than reading a newspaper or novel. You may need to consult other sources for definitions, as noted in the section on Defining Technical Terms, earlier in this chapter.

Direct Consultation

Find out the names of local individuals and agencies knowledgeable about the topic. They can supply information specifically about the situation in the community that may be included in a report. They can also be asked for the names of knowledgeable individuals.

It is gratifying to find how helpful outside people can be if they are approached in the right way. A further advantage of local consultation is the possibility of making valuable contacts. During conversations with local officials, students may learn about new programs and job opportunities.

Distant officials and authorities are more difficult to use as information sources. If you write to the author of a book on a topic, make your requests specific. Some famous people are extraordinarily helpful with student inquiries. If you have a specific question that you think some distant authority can answer, don't hesitate to write a personal letter. Enclosing a stamped self-addressed envelope will increase the likelihood of a reply. Many people at academic and governmental institutions can be contacted by e-mail. A search by institutional name, using the Internet, may get you the address you need. See Chapter 14 for information on locating e-mail addresses.

Summary

Reviewing the literature means finding out what previous research has been done on a topic. Primary sources such as journal articles and books by scholars provide the most credible information on a research topic. These can be located in reference libraries using the online catalog and other databases. Electronic databases, such as *PsycINFO* or *Sociofile*, contain references and sometimes abstracts for journal articles and books. Do not hesitate to enlist the help of the research librarian. Select the database(s) most suited for your topic. Explore others, as needed. Begin the search with the most recent publications, and either narrow or broaden your focus, depending on the information available. Save the relevant references and obtain the call numbers in order to locate the book or article. Be selective (i.e., choose articles that are directly relevant to your specific topic) and use only credible sources and reports.

There will also be situations in which direct consultation with known authorities will be helpful. Allow sufficient time for finding the necessary materials.

References

Booth, B., & Colby, A. Y. (1986). *Thesaurus of sociological indexing terms* (1st ed.). San Diego, CA: Sociological Abstracts.

Cooley, L., Donohoe, L. E., & Borodkin, J. (Eds.). (1994). *Bibliographic index*. New York: H.W. Wilson.

Walker, A., Jr. (Ed.). (1994). *Thesaurus of psychological index terms* (7th ed.). Washington, DC: American Psychological Association.

Further Reading

American Psychological Association. (1993). *Journals in psychology: a resource listing for authors* (4th ed.). Washington, DC: Author.

Braun, E. E. (1994). *The Internet directory*. New York: Fawcett Columbine.

Colman, A. M. (1994). *Companion encyclopedia of psychology*. London, New York: Routledge.

Gilster, P. (1994). *Finding it on the Internet: The essential guide to archie, Veronica, Gopher, WAIS, WWW (including Mosaic), and other search and browsing tools*. New York: Wiley.

Gregory, R. L., & Zangwill, O. L. (1987). *The Oxford companion to the mind*. New York: Oxford University Press.

Hahn, H., & Stout, R. (1994). *The Internet complete reference*. Berkeley, CA: Osborne McGraw-Hill.

Harre, R., & Lamb, R. (1986). *The Dictionary of developmental and educational psychology*. Cambridge, MA: MIT Press.

Harre, R., & Lamb, R. (1986). *The Dictionary of ethology and animal learning*. Cambridge, MA: MIT Press.

Kuper, J. (1988). *A Lexicon of psychology, psychiatry, and psychoanalysis*. London, New York: Routledge.

Ramachandran, V. S. (1994). *Encyclopedia of human behavior*. San Diego, CA: Academic Press.

Reber, A. S. (1985). *The Penguin dictionary of psychology*. New York: Penguin Books.

Statt, D. A. (1990). *The concise dictionary of psychology*. London, New York: Routledge.

Westerman, R. C. (1994). *Fieldwork in the library: A guide to research in anthropology and related area studies*. Chicago: American Library Association.

Wolman, B. B. (1989). *Dictionary of behavioral science* (2nd ed.). San Diego, CA: Academic Press.

4 Observation

There is a popular belief that people in groups drink and eat faster than people alone, as the slow members of the group try to keep up with the fast ones. This belief has been proven false in a succession of observational studies in bars, restaurants, and coffeehouses in Canada, New Zealand, and the United States. People in groups do drink and eat more, but not because they drink or eat faster, but rather, because they tend to stay longer than do lone individuals, and length of stay is strongly related to food and beverage consumption (Graves, Graves, Semu, & Sam, 1982; Sommer & Sommer, 1989).

For those who enjoy people-watching, observation is the ideal research method. Observation is useful not only as a method in its own right but as an accompaniment to other procedures. Before beginning an interview study, it will be necessary to observe the situation first. You will want to know where to find people, how long they are going to be available, and possible distractions. Before beginning an experiment, you will want to know about the behavior in its natural state. Otherwise you run the risk of creating conditions in the laboratory that do not exist in the real world.

An advantage of observation is that it does not require conversation. You can observe pedestrians crossing a busy street or people who do not speak your language. Observation is the ideal method for studying commonplace nonverbal behaviors, such as gestures, postures, or seating arrangements, in which people may not be consciously aware of how they are acting.

Unobtrusive observation is commonly used in transportation research as the procedure does not interfere with the behavior being studied. In the case of bicyclists, the recording can be done by a researcher without the use of fancy equipment, i.e., just recording how bicyclists ride in traffic or whether they stop at lights or stop signs. In observing automobiles, traffic researchers are likely to use radar for measuring vehicle speed. This method was used by Icelandic researchers to study the effects of posting safety signs along the road. The observations which were undertaken on twenty consecutive weekdays, revealed that the signs significantly reduced speed on the roadways (Ragnarsson & Bjorgvinsson, 1991). Researchers in the Netherlands used systematic observation to measure the success of a campaign to increase seat belt usage at military bases. Observations were made before and after an extensive publicity and incentive campaign. At a dozen military bases in the Netherlands, a trained observer stood next to the gate entrance and recorded shoulder belt usage of all drivers. Observations before and after the safety campaign revealed that the publicity had been effective, increasing seat belt usage both immediately after the campaign and three months later (Hagenzieker, 1991).

Observation is economical in terms of money and equipment but expensive in terms of time. One invests long hours of waiting. This is well known to animal researchers, who spend weeks scouting the terrain and establishing observation posts before catching a glimpse of a rare bird or mammal. More than any other method, observation requires patience and luck. There is no certainty about who will appear and what will happen. It may rain or snow while you are there, be too hot or too cold, the setting too crowded or too empty. The time, discomfort, and required patience may severely test the observer's skills. On the other hand, it is intensely satisfying to notice things that other people overlook.

Behavior is more variable in natural surroundings than it is in a laboratory where everything is arranged by the experimenter or in response to questionnaire items posed by the researcher. The results of natural observation can be unexpected and surprising, and include behaviors not previously reported in the setting. Generalization to the real world is easier when you have studied natural behavior. There are three types of observational procedures—casual observation, systematic observation, and participant observation.

Casual Observation

Casual observation is done without prearranged categories or a scoring system. It refers to eyeball inspection of what is happening. It is most useful at an early stage of research or as an accompaniment to some other procedure. For example, before one approaches hospital patients for interviews, it is desirable to spend some time watching behavior in the setting. This will yield information that is indispensable for developing good questions. Casual observation is not a substitute for more systematic and detailed study, but occasionally it is the only method possible. For example, a city planner from France visiting a housing project in India may have only a limited time to look around. This may mean a single tour in the company of a guide without the opportunity to talk to local residents. Keen powers of observation are required under these circumstances.

The vivid impressions of a first visit are worth recording. After several sessions, it is easy to become accustomed and desensitized to what is happening. First impressions are most useful when they are written down immediately. There can be no substitute for field notes kept on a day-by-day basis. These notes need not be typed or written in perfect grammar. A final report is best written after a long period of reflection, data gathering, and several drafts, but first impressions are most valuable when written while they are still fresh.

The notes in Box 4–1 were written by a student observer following an observation session in a self-serve restaurant. The visit was intended to be preliminary to detailed systematic observations of health and sanitation problems in different types of self-serve food outlets. Based on the initial observation, this particular

Casual observation is an ideal technique for people watchers. Observing the people in a zoo can be as interesting and rewarding as watching the animals.

BOX 4–1. A Visit to the Rialto Restaurant

This was one of the most unappetizing meals I've every been offered. You pay as you walk in—no real chance to check out the counter first—as you usually do in a salad bar. The buffet was one-sided, surrounded by a high wall—making it impossible for me to observe other customers.

The food included meats and fish, as well as salads and rolls. Everything was unappetizing and the mess was unreal. All foodhandles were dirty and the place you slid your tray along the counter collected the spills from everyone before you. The food shield worked well, except for children, and there were lots of kids, mostly unsupervised. The roast beef and ham were carved by an employee (Bruce said the meat wasn't bad, but I didn't eat any).

Drinks, except for beer and wine, were self-serve. Bruce was offended that you had to dig your hands in the ice to retrieve the serving scoop, raising questions about the sanitation of the ice. Desserts were self-serve, a food shield over the custard and cake. Self-serve ice cream is available from a machine. There was no food shield over the toppings, which had many spills. I observed one employee taking out empty food tubs and putting full ones into the buffet. The way the counter is designed required the employee to place his hands inside the tubs to avoid pinching his fingers or dropping the tub.

The clientele is mostly working-class families, older people, and many street folks. This place is constantly busy, but Bruce and I were getting the "willies" so we only lasted an hour. The barriers made customer observations more difficult. This may not be a place suitable for those weak of stomach.

restaurant was deemed unsuitable for further study because the high partitions made it too difficult to observe unobtrusively.

Systematic Observation

Systematic observation employs a scoring system and prearranged categories that are applied consistently. This usually requires an observation checklist, on which information is recorded under the proper headings. Categories on the checklist should include those items of behavior that occur naturally in the situation and can be observed and recorded. Not everything that takes place is open to view. Casual observation is helpful for developing the categories to be used in systematic observation. In a study of alcohol consumption in fifteen bars in a New England city, two researchers found that they could record the following items on napkins without appearing conspicuous.

Number of drinks	Alone or in a group
Type of drink	Type of clothing
Number of sips per drink	Height estimate
Time to consume	Weight estimate
Total time in bar	Age estimate

The items were limited to what could be seen directly. What the patrons said to one another, their marital status, and their political attitudes lay beyond the range of an observational study. In establishing the reliability of the observational categories, two researchers went to a selected bar, sat either at a table or at the bar with instructions to independently observe the next patron entering the premises who sat in clear view of both observers. The patron was then observed throughout his or her stay in the bar. Agreement was high between the two observers using this procedure (almost 100 percent) except in the case of the age estimates (Kessler & Gomberg, 1974).

The observer must choose a location from which behavior can be seen and recorded. This will be easier in some settings than in others. In bars, observers can sit at tables to record activities. A city planning student studying behavior in a city park found a good view from a tall building overlooking the park. The choice of an observational post depends completely on local circumstances. The Rialto restaurant described in Box 4-1 had partitions surrounding the buffet table that made it difficult for the observer to watch people serve themselves. As a result, no further observations were conducted. There is no way to know in advance where the best vantage point will be. A videocamera can be useful in observational research. Interactions can be recorded at one time and transcribed later (see Chapter 15). Box 4–2 lists the steps for doing observational research.

How to Be a Good Observer

The first principle of good observation is to heed the Greek maxim "Know thyself." Careful attention to your own responses provides valuable insights into what

---

BOX 4-2. Basic Steps, Systematic Observation

1. Choose topic.
2. Conduct casual observation.
3. Specify questions to be answered.
4. Design the measurement instruments (i.e., checklists, categories, coding systems, etc.).
5. Train observers.
6. Do a pilot test.
   a. Test the procedure.
   b. Check reliability using at least two independent observers.
7. Revise procedure and instruments as needed. If substantial changes are made, run another pilot test.
8. Develop a sampling plan for data collection (timing and locations).
9. Collect data.
10. Compile, analyze, and interpret results.
11. Write report.

---

is happening in the situation and in you. Make it a practice to acknowledge and *name* your feelings: "I am beginning to become tense . . . I feel uncomfortable . . . something seems odd here." Try practice observations with a friend and share your feelings aloud. See if you can identify the internal cues for these feelings. Notice whether you hold your breath or stand differently when you are tense. Practice plus feedback will increase your sensitivity to such feelings.

Pay attention to nonverbal cues in the environment. These include people's postures, gestures, and privacy-seeking behaviors, such as turning away and gaze avoidance. When an anthropologist was observing a mental hospital ward, he found that patients acted disturbed when he sat out in the dayroom, and the nurses were bothered when he was inside the nurses' station. He gradually found himself forced back into a small area outside the nurses' station. Monitoring other people's reactions to his presence taught him which places were open and which were closed to him.

During your observation, occasionally ask yourself about what you are *not* seeing. Did you expect something to happen that is not actually taking place? The non-event may be as important as what does occur. For example, an interesting finding in the self-serve restaurants was that customers hardly ever returned for second portions.

Systematic observation in natural settings requires the researcher to take notes in an unobtrusive manner. The closer the recording procedure resembles normal activity in the setting, the better. One observer in a restaurant recorded observations on napkins; another in a classroom recorded participation in a notebook. Certain locations are more suitable than others for recording what is happening. Watching bicyclists at an intersection proved difficult when the observers stood on the street corner; cyclists became curious and altered their behavior. It was more effective to watch from inside a parked car. The researcher studying a playground might bring along a young child as a cover, to make the observer's presence more comprehensible. "Fitting in" is an art that develops through practice. The objective of the naturalist is to study nature while disturbing it as little as possible. Most of the time, it pays to have an observer who can blend into the setting. In laboratory research, it is often assumed that the physical appearance of the experimenter does not matter. Whether this assumption is true is an interesting question, but no one ever assumes it in a natural setting. Researchers who get their first introduction to observational procedures in a setting in which they do not fit will probably soon become discouraged. A white researcher who spent a year among street-corner men in a black neighborhood in Washington, D.C. realizes that he would always be an outsider:

> This brute fact of color, as they understood it in their experience, and I understood it in mine, irrevocably and absolutely relegated me to the status of outsider. . . . I used to play with the idea that maybe I wasn't as much of an outsider as I thought. Other events, and later readings of the field materials, have disabused me of this particular touch of vanity. (Liebow, 1966, p. 248)

A researcher, studying gorillas in their natural habitat, describes the gradual process of becoming a good observer in the jungle:

In civilization, one loses the aptitude for stillness, the habit of moving gently. It takes time to cease to be an outsider, an intruder, and be accepted once again by the creatures of the forest. The return to the wilderness is a gradual process, unconscious for the most part. Once the senses have been relieved of the incessant noise and other irrelevant stimuli that are a part of our civilization . . . the sights, sounds, and smells of the environment become meaningful again. Slowly the courage and confidence of man, previously nurtured by his belief in the safety of his civilized surroundings, slips away. Finally he stands there, a rather weak and humble creature who has come not to disturb and subdue but to nod to the forest in fellowship and to claim kinship to the gorilla and the Sunbird. (Schaller, 1964, p. 107)

Box 4–3 provides additional information on observing animal behavior. Those who observe behavior in natural settings can expect to endure physical discomfort and occasionally danger. It is not uncommon for zoologists studying animal behavior to stake out an area and spend weeks in fruitless waiting in a stuffy, hot, insect-ridden blind. Watching children play in the streets of Philadelphia during July and August may be no less uncomfortable and occasionally more dangerous.

Reliability in Systematic Observation

In systematic observation it is desirable to employ at least two independent observers at an early stage of study. Independent observers are two or more indi-

---

BOX 4–3. Observing Non-human Species

Observation is well suited for research on the behavior of animal species. For over forty years, Charles Darwin did occasional studies of earthworms, conducting both systematic observations and worm-related experiments. The famous population biologist Paul Ehrlich has spent every summer for the past thirty years watching butterflies in the meadows of western Colorado (McVay, 1993).

An instructor teaching a comparative psychology course in our department asked his students to conduct observational studies of animal behavior. The studies covered the feeding behavior of thoroughbred horses, territories of domestic cats, food searching behavior of blue jays, social grooming by mallard ducks, and how chimpanzees spent their day.

When observing animals it is important to avoid *anthropomorphism*, the tendency to ascribe human characteristics to other species. For example, a lowered head may not have the same significance for another species as it does for humans, where it sometimes means sadness. In New York's Central Park, some animal lovers felt that the horses were being mistreated because their heads appeared droopy. In contrast, a stable owner declared "That means she's a calm horse. A high head means high strung. We look for what we call a cold-blooded horse, with the head down" (Talk of the Town, 1993, p. 36).

Observation is also suited for studying human-animal interaction. Instead of looking exclusively at animal behavior, the focus becomes the two-way relationship between people and animals. This approach is being used in the new field of companion animal therapy for elderly, shut-ins, and autistic children. Observation is used to document the benefits of interacting with animals for people with reduced opportunities for human contact.

---

viduals who take notes separately and compare them afterward. Such comparisons may reveal ambiguities and overlaps in scoring categories. These comparisons should be made before the main body of observations is collected (e.g., during the pilot study). After you have finished making all your observations, if you learn then that some of the categories are not reliable, the value of the data will be diminished. When such problems can be identified beforehand, the scoring system may be improved to eliminate them, and then reliability checked a second time so that the observations can begin with confidence that the scoring system is reliable. Box 4–4 lists some of the potential problems in systematic observation.

Qualitative Approaches

The two observational methods described so far, casual and systematic observation, involve an outside observer coming in for short periods to watch and record what is happening, while remaining apart from the participants. Qualitative approaches put more emphasis on the observer spending long periods of time in a setting, becoming acquainted with the participants, and keeping detailed confidential records. Two types of qualitative observation are *participant observation* and *ethnography*.

BOX 4–4. Pitfalls to be Avoided in Systematic Observation

1. Reactive effects from being observed; a guinea pig effect in which awareness of being watched changes behavior.
   a. People becoming self-conscious and not behaving as they normally would.
   b. People attempting to accommodate the observer, doing what they believe the observer wants them to do.
   c. Influence of the observer's specific appearance or manner on people's actions.
   d. Changes in accommodation to the observer during the course of the study.
2. Investigator error
   a. Unclear and unreliable observational categories.
   b. Bias on the part of the observer.
   c. Changes in the observational procedures in the middle of the study.
   d. Not checking reliability before the study begins. Learning too late that the categories for observers are not reliable.
3. Selection bias
   a. People being observed are not representative of the groups to which the results will be generalized.
   b. Inadequate time periods selected for observation.
   c. Sources of bias due to weather, day, location, etc.

Participant Observation

In *participant observation* the observer becomes part of the events being studied. The emotional learning on the part of the researcher can be as important as the documentation of external events. One participant observer described what he had learned over a 6-month period, "It wasn't a question of discovering new facts, since most of what I had found was already known, but of discovering what it meant to *feel* the facts."

Frank Farley, a former president of the American Psychological Association, is a risk taker. He rides rapids and crosses the ocean in balloons. While participating in these activities, he observes the other participants in formal and informal settings, interviews them, and records his own experiences. His research led him to develop the concept of the Type T (thrill-seeking) personality. Type T people are independent-minded and less concerned than others with rules and regulations, but they are not crazy or suicidal. They spend considerable time preparing for their adventures, and they do not take undue personal risks if the risks can be avoided. They do not practice their skills to the degree required by Olympic athletes. "They are not perfectionists" and "they achieve a level of skill they are comfortable with, they have their own internal rules" (Farley, 1993, p. 5).

In this case, participant observation has several advantages. There is the personal enjoyment that he achieves from his experiences, and he has converted his hobby into a research study. His involvement in these activities gives him direct access to other risk-takers that it would be difficult for a non-participant to achieve. He can observe his fellow balloonists at close range, while a non-participant would be limited to interviews following the ride. He understands the specialized vocabularies, the slang expressions whose meaning is clear only to the participants. He can also use his own experiences as a yardstick in gauging the responses of others.

Another social scientist used participant observation to study housing projects. Participant observation allowed time to break down barriers of suspicion and mistrust. There were things that she learned living in a project that would go unnoticed by outsiders. When she found herself picking up litter in "her" courtyard while ignoring it on the other side of the building, she became aware of the importance of territorial divisions in stimulating caring attitudes toward one's surroundings. From her third floor balcony she became aware of extensive outdoor activities. Her experiences living in the building provided so many insights that she vowed never again to do a study of a housing project unless she could experience it first-hand (Marcus, 1990).

A participant-observer has a defined and active role in what is happening, as distinct from being a spectator, bystander, or customer. This is not to imply that customers cannot make observations. The restaurant studies described at the start of this chapter were done by observers posing as customers. This seems more properly classified as systematic observation rather than participant observation. Had the observer been a waiter or bartender who took the job specifically to record eating patterns, then it would have been participant observation.

Researchers sometimes find themselves in a participant observation role through circumstance—for example, after an automobile accident or physical disability. Research through participant observation is a means of understanding the experience and also a way for them to use their professional training while in an unusual situation.

Ethnography

The in-depth description and study of specific peoples and places is known as *ethnography*. Through intensive field work, the ethnographer attempts to dig out multiple layers of meaning. At one time, ethnographers were concerned primarily with pre-industrial societies. More recently they have turned their attention to the study of contemporary peoples in special settings, such as courtrooms, banks, and shopping malls. The observer looks, listens, asks questions, and records what is seen and heard. From all this emerges a picture of what is happening. This is not the picture of the artist who sketches a scene from a single perspective. It is more the approach of the detective who examines and puts together all sorts of evidence, including smudged fingerprints, bloodstains, torn clothing, and eyewitness accounts (Sanders, 1974).

Although the terms *ethnography* and *participant observation* are often used interchangeably, ethnography, like other related terms used in the social sciences, such as qualitative sociology and field work, is more of an approach than a research method, because it combines several research techniques, including interviews, observations, and physical trace measures. The best ethnography remains true to the place and people studied; it does not distort or reduce them to arbitrary abstract categories. This is nicely stated by an ethnographer in Northern Ireland:

> (Research) is distorted and reality is mangled when disciplines harden into ideology, categories freeze into facts, and the sweet, terrible wholeness of life is dismembered for burial . . . [In good ethnography] the categories will slip and shift, and then melt away as we find the place where social science joins the humanities, where art and culture and history, time and space connect, where theoretical and empirical studies fuse. (Glassie, 1982, p. xiv)

Studying the effect of tourism on the island of Ionia off the west coast of Scotland, a graduate student used observation and in-depth interviews to gather qualitative information. In addition, quantitative data were collected from the ferry service to the island. Hotel registers yielded information on tourists' home addresses. Housing records showed the number of houses on the island owned by outsiders, and historical documents were found in the archives of a local newspaper (Butts, 1995).

Unlike the participant observer who has a defined role in the setting and is part of the action, the ethnographer typically is identified only as a researcher. An example is the use of ethnography to study spatial separation in a large corporate office building. The researcher identified himself from the outset as a social scientist whose goal was to learn how people felt about the building. He found that the building was a social pyramid, with the executives at the top, the technical and administrative employees in the center, and the clerical employees and data processors on the lower floors and in the basement. There was infrequent travel between the different levels of the building, and when people visited another floor, they felt they were on unfamiliar terrain. The separation reduced communication and contact; lower level employees felt ignored and disrespected, and the top executives felt isolated and ignorant of what was happening in the rest of the building (Mazumdar, 1994). Ethnography was a good choice for this type of project. The researcher did not have a specific role in the organization (he was not an employee), and he only needed to spend enough time on each floor to get to know the people, so that they would express their opinions to him.

Ethnography is particularly useful in the early stages of research where little is known about a phenomenon, in situations where other methods are not feasible, and as part of an overall multimethod strategy. An anthropologist employed ethnography in studying the drug trade in New York City neighborhoods. In this type of situation formal survey techniques are not practicable. He commented on his anomalous position,

> Looking around me on the street corner I sensed that I was the only one not there to buy or sell drugs or needles, or to assist or "steer" a buyer for a "taste" of the bag, or to "tout a bag" or "look out for" or "rip off" a dealer, or to "set up" or arrest a buyer or seller. (Goldsmith, 1994, p. 3)

In both participant observation and ethnography, impressions are written down in rough form and may be typed later. The final notes should be legible, indicating places, dates, and names (often these are written in a code known only to the researcher), and a clear distinction between events witnessed and the observer's impressions or feelings should be made. It is quite useful in field notes to describe one's own interpretations in brackets or otherwise distinguish them from actual events. These records are later summarized and discussed with colleagues or a research supervisor. Collecting field notes is often done by a single researcher, but the subsequent validation of observations and interpretations is a shared enterprise.

Doing Qualitative Observation

Flexibility is a required attribute for a participant observer or ethnographer. Methods will evolve during the course of the research, and procedures will be added, modified, or dropped. Unlike a laboratory study, new sources of information will appear during the course of the investigation, requiring new approaches or contacts. During field work, it will be impossible to keep track of everything happening at one time. Some selection among different variables or processes will be necessary, along with constant monitoring of how they interact and measure in importance.

Kirk and Miller (1986) describe the four phases of field work as invention, discovery, interpretation, and explanation. *Invention* refers to preparation for the study and the development of the research plan. This includes reviewing previous work in the field and training in appropriate methods. *Discovery* refers to data collection, the production of information through a variety of methods. *Interpretation* is ongoing as the researcher reflects on what is happening and discusses it with colleagues, but it is also a separate phase following data collection in which there is formal analysis of what has been learned. *Explanation* refers to the packaging of findings for an outside audience. Typically this involves writing a report or article based on the study.

Stresses on the Observer

Of the techniques described in this book, participant observation and ethnography are among the most stressful for the investigator. A researcher studying psychiatric patients living in the community felt alone and isolated because there was no one with whom she could share the intimate facts of the daily observations and her own personal reactions. She couldn't express her occasional feelings of frustration, depression, or even elation about clients, staff, their interaction, or her own reactions to a roller coaster set of experiences (Estroff, 1981). The ethnographer studying the drug trade in New York City (mentioned earlier) saw himself being pulled into relationships, especially when faced with emergencies. "You have to decide how to respond," he wrote, "whether to take someone to an emergency room, drive people to visit a gunshot victim in a hospital . . give out bleach bottles to persons about to inject. . . ." (Goldsmith, 1994, p. 6).

Culture shock was experienced by a researcher doing field work among business people in a city and becoming aware of possibly illegal activities. There were also dirty tricks played on her by the people she was studying. In one instance a handgun was placed in her briefcase, as one of many jokes to see if she was "a good sport." Fortunately her research skills helped her to maintain both distance and objectivity in an ethical mine field (Stumpf-Carome, 1995).

As a participant observer, one is privy to backstage behaviors. It is virtually *inevitable* that one will see illicit, unethical, and illegal acts. A participant observer working in a restaurant, for example, is likely to notice unsanitary conditions. One could put this more strongly and say that the observer *will see*, over a period of time, unsanitary conditions. There is probably no restaurant in the world where this would not occur at least occasionally. How the observer deals with the situation is likely to be a source of severe personal stress. Should he or she "rat" on the other employees or keep quiet and risk exposing the public to a health risk? Ethical dilemmas are inevitable in participant observation.

There is also legal ambiguity about the status of field notes written by researchers. The courts have not determined that such field notes are protected against subpoena. They might become part of the public record in court proceedings.

Reliability and Validity in Qualitative Research

The field notes of a single participant observer or ethnographer necessarily lack reliability. An observer may have blind spots for certain things that occur and exaggerate the importance of other events. Sometimes a participant observer gets so deeply into a role that perspective is lost, a process known as "going native." The observer's presence may affect the behavior of the people in the setting. These effects are difficult to specify in advance and interpret. There are also problems in generalizability with this method—how much can be learned from the study of a single health clinic or police department?

Although it is difficult to eliminate these problems completely, it is possible to minimize their occurrence and effect on the research and to specify when they have occurred. Most of the remedies involve *triangulation* or the use of more than one method, observer, and site to provide additional checks on a single observer's account (Hunt, 1985). Triangulation allows the researcher to pinpoint aspects of a phenomenon more accurately by approaching it from different vantage points using different methods (Brewer & Hunter, 1989). Successful triangulation requires careful analysis of the type of information provided by each method, including the strengths and weaknesses.

The likelihood of a researcher going native can be reduced by having a team of researchers in the field who interact with one another and thereby prevent total immersion in the local culture. Frequent contact between the researcher and the supervisor can also provide opportunities for reflection on what is taking place. Observer effects can be dealt with through a multimethod approach that uses independent sources of information, such as public or private records, previous research studies, and so on. When an observer's account contrasts markedly with what is known about the setting and the occupants, as when a participant observer finds no illegal gambling at a social club that has been raided by police on previous occasions and numerous convictions obtained on gambling charges, the researcher will have to seriously reflect on his or her impact upon the setting. Reliability can be improved by the use of more than one observer. This does not have to be done routinely. Only a few visits by a second observer may be sufficient to determine whether the first observer is picking up the important things that are happening and reporting them correctly. Generalizability can be improved by increasing the number of settings observed. Instead of focusing all of the attention on a single setting, several representative locations can be observed. If the same behaviors are seen in all the settings, then the observer can have more confidence in the findings. Again this does not require a detailed observational study in all locations. The additional sites can be observed briefly if the observer is not interested in everything that occurs, but only in specific items.

Limitations

Observation, whether casual, systematic, or qualitative, deals with behavior, not with attitudes or beliefs. Attitudes can be deduced from behavior only with caution. If you want to find out what people do, you should observe them. If you want to find out what they think, you should ask them directly. There are exceptions to both of these rules, but observation is generally a good method for studying natural behavior, while interviews and questionnaires are more appropriate for opinions and beliefs.

Reliability is always a problem in observation. In casual and systematic observation, the use of two independent observers is recommended during the early stages of the study. No matter how simple and straightforward the behavior being studied, it is still wise to check on reliability. If two independent observers cannot agree on what they see, then the conclusions of the study are in doubt.

In qualitative observation, solutions to reliability problems involve triangulation, or the use of more than one method, observer, and site to provide additional checks on a single observer's account. The immersion of the observer into the situation for extended periods can be stressful. There are also potential ethical problems when the researcher becomes part of ongoing events.

Summary

Observation is useful in behavioral research as a method in its own right and as an accompaniment to other procedures. It can produce unexpected and surprising findings. It is economical in terms of money and equipment but expensive in terms of time.

Casual observation does not use prearranged categories or a scoring system. It is most useful at the beginning stages of research. Systematic observation employs detailed categories and a scoring system. Possible sources of error in systematic observation are reactive effects from being observed (the guinea pig effect), investigator error, and biased sampling.

Two qualitative approaches are participant observation and ethnography. In participant observation the observer becomes part of the events being studied. Ethnography is the in-depth study of specific peoples and places. Both techniques place considerable demands upon the observer. There may be problems of reliability and generalizability.

Limitations: Since observation deals with behavior, it is difficult to deduce beliefs, attitudes, or opinions. In many settings, reliability is difficult to establish.

References

Brewer, J., & Hunter, A. (1989). *Multimethod research.* Newbury Park, CA: Sage Publications.
Butts, S. L. (1995). Tourism for whom? *Practicing Anthropology, 17,* 13–16.
Estroff, S. E. (1981). *Making it crazy: An ethnography of psychiatric clients in an American community.* Berkeley, CA: University of California Press.
Farley, F. (1993). Psychology thrills President Farley. *APA Monitor, 24,* 4–5.
Glassie, H. H. (1982). *Passing the time in Ballymenone: Culture and history of an Ulster community.* Philadelphia: University of Pennsylvania Press.
Goldsmith, D. S. (1994, April). *Confidentiality in ethnography: Drugs, sex, and AIDS in the lives of informants in New York City.* Paper presented at the 53rd annual meeting of the Society for Applied Anthropology, Cancun, Mexico.

Graves, T. D., Graves, N. B., Semu, V. N., & Sam, I. A. (1982). Patterns of public drinking in a multi-ethnic society: A systematic observational study. *Journal of Studies on Alcohol, 43*, 990–1009.

Hagenzieker, M. P. (1991). Enforcement or incentives? Promoting safety belt use among military personnel in the Netherlands. *Journal of Applied Behavior Analysis, 24*, 23–30.

Hunt, M. M. (1985). *Profiles of social research: The scientific study of human interactions.* New York: Russell Sage Foundation.

Kessler, M., & Gomberg, C. (1974). Observations of barroom drinking: Methodology and preliminary results. *Quarterly Journal of Studies on Alcohol, 35*, 1392–1396.

Kirk, J., & Miller, M. L. (1986). *Reliability and validity in qualitative research.* Beverly Hills, CA: Sage Publications.

Liebow, E. (1967). *Tally's corner.* Boston: Little, Brown.

Marcus, C. C. (1990). From the pragmatic to the spiritual. In I. Altman & K. Christensen (Eds.), *Environment and behavior studies: Emergence of intellectual traditions* (pp. 111–140). New York: Plenum Press.

Mazumdar, S. (1995). How birds of a feather flock together in organizations: The phenomena of socio-physical congregation and distancing. *Journal of Architectural & Planning Research, 12*, 1–18.

McVay, S. (1993). Prelude: "A Siamese connexion with a plurality of other mortals." In S. R. Kellert & E. O. Wilson (Eds.), *The Biophilia Hypothesis* (pp. 3–19). Washington, DC: Island Press.

Ragnarsson, R. S., & Bjorgvinsson, T. (1991). Effects of public posting on driving speed in Icelandic traffic. *Journal of Applied Behavior Analysis, 24*, 53–58.

Sanders, W. B. (1974). *The sociologist as detective: An introduction to research methods.* New York: Praeger.

Schaller, G. B. (1964). *The year of the gorilla.* Chicago: University of Chicago Press.

Sommer, R., & Sommer, B. (1989). Social facilitation effects in coffeehouses. *Environment and Behavior, 21*, 651–666.

Stumpf-Carome, J. M. (1995). On becoming one of the boys. *Practicing Anthropology, 17*, 17–20.

Talk of the Town. (1993, April 5). Horse play. *The New Yorker*, 36–37.

Further Reading

Banister, P. (1994). *Qualitative methods in psychology: A research guide.* Philadelphia: Open University Press.

Lofland, J., & Lofland, L. H. (1995). *Analyzing social settings: A guide to qualitative observation and analysis* (3rd ed.). Belmont, CA: Wadsworth.

Marshall, C., & Rossman, G. B. (1995). *Designing qualitative research* (2nd ed.). Thousand Oaks, CA: Sage Publications.

Miles, M. B., & Huberman, A. M. (1994). *Qualitative data analysis: An expanded sourcebook.* Thousand Oaks, CA: Sage Publications.

Shaffir, W., & Stebbins, R. A. (Eds.). (1991). *Experiencing fieldwork: An inside view of qualitative research.* Newbury Park, CA: Sage Publications.

Strauss, A. L., & Corbin, J. M. (1990). *Basics of qualitative research: Grounded theory procedures and techniques.* Newbury Park, CA: Sage Publications.

Suen, H. K., & Ary, D. (1989). *Analyzing quantitative behavioral observation data.* Hillsdale, NJ: Lawrence Erlbaum Associates.

Webb, E. J., Campbell, D. T., Schwartz, R. D., Sechrest, L., & Grove, J. B. (1981). *Nonreactive measures in the social sciences* (2nd ed.). Boston: Houghton Mifflin.

5 Mapping and Trace Measures

Mapping

Mapping is used in the behavioral sciences to study people's relationship to the environment, including how they imagine it to be and how they use it. Two types of mapping procedures are used in behavioral research. *Behavioral mapping* deals with people's locations and movements, how people actually distribute themselves in a particular area or location. *Cognitive mapping* refers to mental images of places. People have images of places based on a combination of personal experience, what they have heard or read or seen on TV. Procedures for measuring the two types of maps are very different, so we will begin with a discussion of behavioral mapping (the actual distribution of people and where they spend their time) before discussing procedures for examining people's mental images of places.

Behavioral Maps

A special application of observational procedures, behavioral mapping is a technique for systematically recording people's locations and actions. A behavioral map is an actual chart of individuals' locations in space. It is an empirical document that illustrates where and what behaviors actually occur, which may contrast with what was planned for the space. For example, a neighborhood street is more than a transit corridor; it also may be a place where people congregate, children play, and commerce occurs. Behavioral maps are used in fields such as environmental psychology and urban planning where knowledge of people's use of space (where they spend their time and what they do there) is important. An environmental psychologist who specializes in retail stores uses a combination of video cameras and time-lapse photography to record customer behavior, traffic flow patterns, areas of congestion, bottlenecks, and other information.

In constructing a behavioral map, a researcher can record only those items that are readily observable, such as approximate age, sex, whether the person is alone or in a group, and what he or she is doing. There are various ways to record an individual's locations in space, including time-lapse photography, videotape, and prepared diagrams on which an observer records people's locations. Whatever method is used to record behavior, the researcher must determine its effects upon the behavior of the respondents. It may also be possible to compare people's behavior when they know they are being watched to their behavior when they are unaware.

Whether collecting information directly or interpreting data from photographs or videotape, the technique requires observers who are trained to record behavior in a systematic and reliable manner. They must be familiar with the terms and symbols used to record behavior. This will require practice, feedback, more practice, and more feedback. Testing for the reliability of the categories is essential. Some researchers use 90 percent agreement among observers in each category as a criterion. Where the observers cannot agree at this level on a specific behavior (not overall, but on a specific behavior), that behavior may be dropped from the data analysis.

Behavioral mapping is often used with children for whom interviews or questionnaires are less appropriate. Teams of psychologists in Finland and the Netherlands charted the movement of school children with particular reference to street crossings (Nummenmaa & Syvänen, 1974; Van der Molen, Kerkhof, & Jong, 1983). In both nations, the observations were used to develop traffic education programs for children.

Behavioral maps can be *place-centered* or *individual-centered*. In *place-centered mapping* observers station themselves to watch the action at a particular site. On prepared diagrams they record people's locations and activities. An *individual-centered map* requires following a particular individual or individuals across time and location. Because of the movement and amount of descriptive detail, an individual-centered map usually involves only a few cases. The choice of mapping procedure will depend on the researcher's goals. If the objective is to assess a particular location, such as usage of a store or play area, place-centered methods are preferable. If the goal is to learn about a group or individuals, such as the social life of older people living by themselves, the observer will probably choose an individual-centered approach.

Place-centered Maps

The first task is to draw a diagram showing all those architectural/environmental features that affect behavior. This should be based on your own measurements rather than the architect's blueprints, which are probably out of date and do not contain the portable features of the environment, such as chairs, tables, bulletin boards, wall clocks, and information signs. You can use existing floor plans or charts as a guide, but be sure to check the measurements yourself.

The next step is to list the behaviors to be recorded. Special scoring symbols are then used for each behavior, (i.e., Si = sitting, St = standing, Wa = walking, etc.). The list is compiled through casual observation of the setting. Categories should cover 80 to 90 percent of the behaviors found in the setting. Special symbols such as 01 and 02 can be used for "other behaviors," which are described in detail at the bottom of the map. The setting is then sampled at predetermined times and the behaviors are recorded. Selecting the right times for doing the mapping is important.

A research team in a mental hospital ward found that the categories listed in Table 5–1 included most of the behaviors they observed in the dayroom. When an unusual event occurred on the ward, such as a group sing led by the recreation therapist that took place about twice a month, this was scored in the "other" category and described at the bottom of the record sheet. Such events occurred so infrequently on the ward that the "other" category was not often used. The clearest finding from the observations was the minimal level of activity in the dayroom. Most of the occupants were sitting and doing nothing most of the time.

Behavioral maps. Place-centered maps were used to study space utilization in a university library. Students preferred to sit at the ends of table, as this minimized eye contact with others.

TABLE 5–1. Activity List for a Mental Hospital Dayroom

Activity	Scoring symbol
Reading	R
Playing cards	C
Watching TV	TV
Listening to radio	Rad
Talking to other patient	T-P
Talking to nurse	T-N
Jigsaw puzzle, games	G
Sitting, doing nothing	S
Standing, doing nothing	St
Sleeping	Sp
In transit (walking)	W
Other (describe)	O_1, O_2

The reliability of the notation system should be checked. Some behaviors are difficult to categorize. On the hospital ward mentioned earlier, the researchers had a hard time distinguishing between patients sitting and watching television. Observers disagreed among themselves so often in making this determination that sitting (S) and watching television (TV) were combined into a single category. There is no point in including categories of behavior that cannot be reliably scored. Some of the more common methods for estimating scoring reliability are a percentage agreement score or a correlation coefficient (see Chapter 19). When observers disagree frequently as to the category in which a behavior belongs, further refinement of the scoring system and/or training of the observers is needed.

The map should cover all of the possible times when the area is being used. Some of the most interesting information from behavioral maps is recorded when nothing is supposed to be happening. For example, a researcher was mapping the use of outdoor play areas in a San Francisco apartment complex. Initially she decided to end the behavior mapping at 8 p.m. because it was assumed that children would be inside the buildings by that time. Subsequent observations revealed a heavier use of the play area at 10 P.M. by teenagers than in mid-afternoon by children (Marcus, 1990).

A design team studying a school yard was struck by the number of times during the week when the yard was unoccupied. This led the designers to search for ways to increase community use of the school yard outside of school hours by including a picnic area, amphitheater, and other facilities in the renovation plan (Hester, 1975). The observation sheet used by the research team is shown in Figure 5–1. The actual usage patterns of the school yard are shown in Figure 5–2.

The Project for Public Spaces, an interdisciplinary team of social scientists and urban planners, uses time-lapse photography to measure the use of parks, plazas,

FRED OLDS SCHOOL OBSERVATION SHEET _____

| Date | Hour | Weather | Observer |

	Pre-School		1-8 Grade		9-12 Grade		College		Adult	Elderly		Social Activity *	Setting for Interaction **
	F	M	F	M	F	M	F	M		F	M		
a. Walking													
b. Sitting													
c. Working													
d. Stop to talk													
e. Neighborhood meeting													
f. Active recreation													
g.													
h.													
i.													
j.													
k.													
l.													
m.													
n.													
o.													
p.													
q.													
r. Commercial													
s. Waiting for transportation													
t. Art													
u. Fantasy play													
v. Construction													
w. Role play													
x.													
y.													

*Record the Interaction Process associated with each activity and the number of people interacting in that manner. Use the key: P = Private, I = Impersonal, C1 = Cooperation, C2 = Competition, C3 = Conflict, A = Accommodation.
**Indicate the setting in which each activity takes place and the numbers of people, particularly in that setting.

FIG. 5–1. Observational sheet used in the behavioral mapping of a school yard.

and other public spaces. The pictures provide an objective record of how the spaces are actually being used, regardless of how they were planned. Where possible, the researchers place a camera in a tall building overlooking a park or public place. The camera automatically takes pictures at designated intervals. A composite of the photos illustrates usage across the area. The research team has studied parks and other public spaces in over 700 communities in the United States, Europe, Asia, Australia, and New Zealand (PPS, 1995; Whyte, 1980).

FRED OLDS SCHOOL
INTENSITY OF ACTIVITY
TYPICAL WEEKDAY

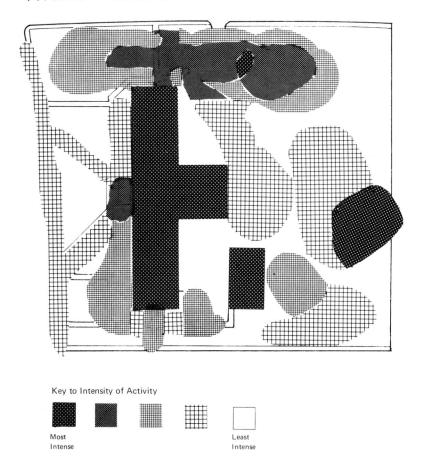

FIG. 5–2. Composite map of interaction throughout the week, made by combining observational records over time.

In scheduling the observations, do not space the sessions too closely together on the same day. Otherwise, you are likely to see the same people doing the same things. To cover all the morning hours, 8 A.M. observations could be made on Monday, 9 A.M. sessions on Wednesday, 10 A.M. observations on Tuesday, and so on.

You will be pleasantly surprised how quickly place-centered observations can be done even for a comparatively large area. A place-centered map deals with instantaneous cross sections of behavior. Generally you will want to record what people are doing when you first see them. What they do afterward is *not* recorded. This will yield a series of behavioral maps at representative intervals throughout the day. Individual maps can later be combined into a single *composite map* showing location, density, and usage for all time periods (see Figure 5–2).

Individual-centered Maps

Individual-centered maps are especially useful in understanding how and where people spend their time. In constructing an individual-centered map, the first task is to identify the sample and obtain subjects' cooperation. At the outset, the subjects should realize the implications of being followed. They must be assured that anything seen or heard will be kept confidential. For recording activities, it is helpful to use a coded notation system that does not involve actual names or details of conversations.

No matter how skillful you are in gaining cooperation, a period of adjustment will be necessary to accustom the person to your presence. Observations may be omitted during this time. Not writing things down during the early sessions will shorten the adjustment period. You might try observing the person in stages—1 hour the first day, 2 hours after that, a morning observation next, and finally an 8-hour session.

As there are only a few people to be observed, you can expect to be bored much of the time. While you cannot avoid being drawn into conversation occasionally, becoming the person's best friend will detract from the validity of the procedure. Thus, the notation "talking to the observer" should appear infrequently on your scoring sheet.

Individual-centered maps can also be done unobtrusively in public locations. Consumer researchers have followed people through their shopping trips. Tracking at a distance is relatively non-reactive in that shoppers seldom notice the observer in a crowded store or shopping mall. Box 5–1 illustrates behavioral mapping of animals.

Observations can be continuous or periodic. Continuous observations involve following an individual over a period of time (e.g., an 8-hour work shift or an entire school day). Periodic observations involve observing the same individual at intervals throughout the day. This requires a *time sampling procedure* in which the observer prepares a list of specific times when the person's activities will be charted, such as 9:18 A.M., 10:04 A.M., and 2:35 P.M. At the designated time, the observer notes the person's location and activity. Time sampling does not require the observer to watch a single subject all the time. The researcher can schedule

High traffic density makes individual-centered mapping a good option in a shopping mall.

BOX 5–1. Behavioral Mapping of Penguins in an Oceanarium

Zoos and animal parks are wonderful places for observing animal behavior, human behavior, and human-animal interactions. Sue Joseph obtained permission from Sea World, a large oceanarium in San Diego, California, to conduct observations in the penguin exhibit. She wanted to learn how use of the various parts of the exhibit changed over the breeding cycle. Her first step was to develop categories of penguin behavior that could be reliably scored by an observer stationed 8 to 10 feet away. She and her assistants used the categories over a 6-month period to observe the penguin exhibit.

The categories on the observation sheet (Figure 5–3) were abbreviated and not always meaningful to an outsider. Longer descriptions of each category were given to her assistants during the training sessions in which the reliability of the observers was determined. For example, "ecstatic" refers to a display in which the penguin slowly stretches its head and bill straight upwards while slowly flapping its wings and emitting a staccato vocalization. "Bill-to-axilla" refers to the bird leaning forward at an angle of approximately 45° with slowly flapping wings while rocking its head from side to side with the tip of the bill directed to the base of one wing (after Sladen, 1958).

A map of the observation area was drawn and divided into rectangular grids that could be identified through a coordinate system (e.g., Bird 102 was in section B–6 at the time of the observation). Maps of the observation area were placed at the top of the behavioral categories on each score sheet. This score sheet was used for ten 30-second observations of a single penguin throughout a 5-minute period.

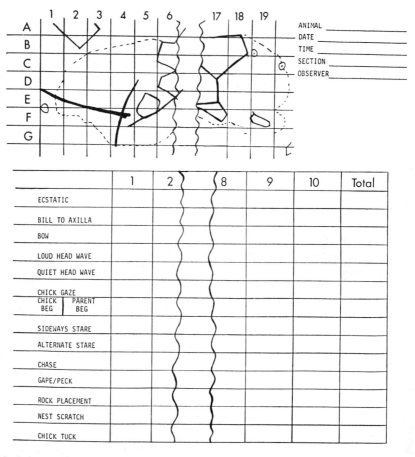

FIG. 5–3. Observational sheet used for behavioral mapping and recording behavior of penguins.

other activities, including observational sessions with other subjects, during the intervals.

With people whose schedules and activities are regular and predictable, little is gained by extending the observations indefinitely. At some point, it should be more profitable to move to the next person in your sample. Eventually you may want to return to the first person for a second series of observations, but this is optional. The decision as to how many people to include depends more on economics and interpersonal relations than on theory. How long will subjects permit your observation? How valuable are the additional data? If there is an impressive consistency in people's movements and activities, a small representative sample is probably sufficient.

After you have collected a series of individual-centered maps, they can be converted to spatial form. For adults this may be accomplished by using an ordinary

Behavioral mapping. Several times a day, the location of each penguin in the Sea World Exhibit was indicated by the researcher on prepared maps (Sea World photo).

Posed picture of behavioral mapping of the penguin exhibit showing the observer with grid diagram on the clipboard and penguins marked with flipper bands. Normally the observations were made from a longer distance away from the birds. (Sea World photo).

city map. The person's travels each day are recorded as single lines, which become thicker with more frequent travel. The maps can also be summarized in tables showing the percentage of time spent in various locations and activities (e.g., for children on a playground, the amount of time or number of occasions of swing use, sandbox play, climbing, or games).

One technique for quantifying the findings of individual-centered maps is to calculate the *behavioral range*, the number of different settings that an individual enters during a given time period. Consider the situation of two employees of a company, one of whom remains in a single location, while the other spends time in five different locations. It is likely that the second employee will be more knowledgeable about the organization and of informal channels of communication. The behavioral range may also predict job satisfaction (Schoggen, 1989). In animal behavior studies, the behavioral range may be indicative of dominance patterns, vary across age, or show seasonal fluctuations.

Individual-centered mapping can also be done retrospectively (after the fact) using interviews. This approach was used to study traffic patterns in a mall (Cherulnik, 1990). A random sample of shoppers leaving the mall was approached by the interviewer and asked to participate in a study of shopping patterns. Those who agreed had the opportunity to win a gift certificate for use in the mall. They were shown a simplified map of the mall and asked to draw the routes they had followed. The individual maps were combined to find the percentage of shoppers entering each section of the mall and into various stores. This procedure was far less time-consuming than first-hand observation of peoples' behavior as they shopped. Another labor-saving approach to individual mapping is to use a beeper. When the beeper goes off, the person records where they are and what they are doing.

Place-centered mapping can be combined with individual-centered mapping as was done in a large public market in Montreal, Canada. Place-centered mapping was done at 28 key locations in the market. At specified times, the researchers noted how many people were present in each location and what they were doing. In addition, 122 customers were followed throughout their entire visit to the market (Zacharias, 1995). Although each method alone yielded valuable data, the combination provided added insights.

Safeguarding the privacy of your respondents is important. Check your data carefully to ensure that individuals cannot be identified by name. When it is impossible to prevent identification, as in mapping the activities of a lone school nurse, consider omitting detailed information on his or her activities in any published report.

Limitations

Individual-centered mapping can be both tiring and intrusive. Except for crowded public locations, an observer following someone around will have difficulty remaining in the background not only for the person observed but for others encountered. Combining maps from several individuals observed at various times can make interpretation difficult.

Place-centered mapping can also be intrusive. A combined behavioral map for 10 observational sessions in a school yard may show 10 dots at a specific location. The reader does not know whether this refers to one child observed at that location ten times or ten children on one occasion. This confusion of within- and between-individual variation makes it difficult to deal with behavioral maps statistically.

Because of the time and effort involved in their construction, individual-centered maps tend to involve only a few individuals. This also makes it difficult to test the data statistically.

Finally, individual-centered mapping reveals environmental choices with no information as to why these choices are made. For any practical purpose, the maps must be supplemented with interviews or other procedures to find out why certain locations are chosen and others avoided.

Cognitive Maps

Cognitive maps are mental representations of places. The term was first introduced by psychologist E. C. Tolman (1948) to explain how rats learned the locations of rewards in a maze. A cognitive map provided the rat with a useful model of the environment. Some information was omitted from the map because it was not useful or important. For this reason, cognitive maps can be very different from the actual place. The distortions found in cognitive maps reveal much about what organisms believe to be important in the environment, where they go, and the routes they use to get there.

The most common method of studying people's cognitive maps is to give them blank sheets of paper and ask them to create "sketch maps" of a given area, indicating the main features, buildings, landmarks, and anything else that they think is important. Sometimes the procedure is standardized by providing an outline map showing major features and asking people to fill in the details. This method has been used to study global awareness by giving people outline maps of the world showing all land masses, which they are asked to identify. A similar approach is used in the study of cities or neighborhoods, in giving respondents an outline map containing one or two key features, such as a river or a highway, as reference points and asking people to fill in the landmarks, parks, major buildings, and neighborhoods. Other researchers use outline maps with all the geographic features identified and ask people where certain activities take place or which are the most desirable locations. To locate gang territories, researchers would probably give people maps of the city with the neighborhoods and streets named and ask the respondents to draw the boundary lines of gang turf.

A cognitive map is a useful tool for exploring people's images of small and large environments, indoors or outdoors. It can be used in spaces as small as a house or as large as the planet. Cognitive maps have been used to study how children's conception of space expands and becomes differentiated as they mature.

Cognitive maps can provide insight into the worlds of those with sensory deficits and physical handicaps. The maps of blind people make more use of sound and tactile cues than do those of sighted people. People in wheelchairs emphasize physical barriers in their maps, obstacles that are missing from the maps of those able to move more freely. Geographers use cognitive maps to supplement their knowledge about the physical characteristics of places. Knowing how people view a location, what stands out in their minds, provides additional information about physical characteristics. Cognitive mapping is of practical use in many fields including community design, architecture, and recreational planning.

Limitations

Although the selectivity and distortion of cognitive maps are informative, it is also possible that they may reflect stereotyped images rather than people's actual experiences.

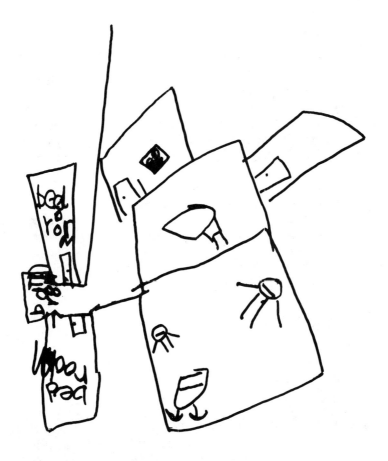

Cognitive mapping. A five-year-old produced this drawing of her family's apartment.

Trace Measures

Trace measures are the physical remains of interaction. When investigating a crime, police operate under the assumption that "every contact leaves a trace" (Canter, 1994, p. 68). Hence the police, at the crime scene and elsewhere, look for traces of the criminal, in fingerprints, footprints, fiber from clothing, blood type, and so on. Behavior scientists use traces in the study of interaction.

There are two general types of physical traces useful in behavioral research—accretion and erosion (Webb, Campbell, Schwartz, Sechrest, & Grove, 1981). *Accretion* refers to the buildup of a residue or product of the interaction—something added to the situation. *Erosion* refers to deterioration or wear and provides an index of usage patterns. With erosion, something is worn down or removed.

Painted or sprayed graffiti are a form of accretion. "Vals must die!" Is this gang graffiti in the inner city? No, it is surfer talk. Locals patrol the parking areas and the beaches to keep away outsiders, sometimes slashing tires or physically assaulting non-locals, as outside surfers are called. Such practices have been seen in beach communities in Australia, Hawaii, and California. Some view the behavior as territorial defense; others view it as greed with local surfers wanting to keep the waves for themselves. Police in oceanfront cities watch the walls for signs as to where the next conflicts are likely to erupt.

Specialized knowledge of group symbols is required to read the handwriting on the wall. Surfer graffiti, with its emphasis on defending beaches against outsiders,

Trace measures: Graffiti can provide a record of gang activity in an area.

emphasizes location. In the opening example "vals" referred to valley youth coming to the beaches looking for surfing spots. Hip hop is a particular graffiti style found in major urban areas in industrialized nations, linking graffiti to rap music and break dancing (Brewer & Miller, 1990). Gang graffiti is different from hip hop in form and content, with frequent use of symbols and numbers. When a police detective gave a presentation to parents warning about gang activity, he noted the significance of numbers "13" and "14," representing M and N, the 13th and 14th letters of the alphabet, which were "tags" of local gangs. Crossing out the "tag" of another gang is an invitation to violence, particularly when it occurs at the border zone between gang territories. Police in California pay special attention to numbers 187 and 245, which refer to state statutes for homicide and assault with a deadly weapon.

The eruption of Mount Vesuvius in 79 A.D. covered the city of Pompeii with a heavy layer of volcanic ash that cooled as it fell to earth. The dense layer of ashes protected the buildings, the walls, and many common household objects for over a thousand years. When the city was excavated, the writing scratched on walls was found to be intact and provided many clues to the day-to-day life of ordinary people.

A special type of illegal wall writing is *latrinalia*, the technical name given to graffiti on public toilet walls. This writing has been studied by anthropologists and others in an effort to learn about cultural values. Latrinalia tend to express attitudes and sentiments that are socially disapproved. Most American toilet walls reveal a preoccupation with sexual experience, excretion, ethnic hostility, and divergent political views.

The systematic study of graffiti typically involves an application of content analysis, a technique described more fully in Chapter 11. The researcher selects an area for a single or periodic sampling of graffiti. This can be a single wall or several walls in a neighborhood or the restrooms on campus. Then a classification system is developed for the style and content of the messages. As an example, Box 5–2 contains scoring categories for a study of graffiti in college restrooms (Williams, 1995). The score sheet is accompanied by more detailed definitions of the categories, including examples to assist those doing the scoring.

In some societies tattoos and other body markings are trace measures of social status. For over twenty years a Russian criminologist collected photographs of tattoos found on prison inmates. Initially he used them as a means of identification of criminals, but soon became interested in the meaning of the symbols. Among career criminals, tattoos were a mark of seniority and status. The more serious the offense and longer the sentence, the more likely there were to be tattoos. Men were more likely than women to be tattooed, but even among women there were more tattoos in the maximum security prison than in the minimum security prison (Bronnikov, 1993).

Tattoos are also a part of American prison life. Unlike graffiti, which is relatively easy to paint over, a tattoo can last a lifetime. A gang symbol may place an inmate in danger of retribution by rival gang members. A tattoo can also be a se-

---

BOX 5–2. Coding Categories for Studying Graffiti in College Restrooms

Location
Building (1, 2, 3 ... 8)

Gender		Form	
1	Men's room	1	Words or letters
2	Women's room	2	Drawing
Primary content		3	Drawing plus words
1	Sex and relationships (heterosexual)	4	Poetry
2	Sex and relationships (homosexual)	5	Other
3	Politics	Affective (emotional) tone	
4	Religion	1	Positive
5	School	2	Neutral
6	Sororities and fraternities	3	Negative
7	Names	4	Mixed
8	Places	5	Other
9	Drugs	Responses to other graffiti?	
10	Nonsense	1	Yes
11	Miscellaneous	2	No or cannot say

---

rious impediment on discharge. When they see the tattoo, many employers refuse to hire former inmates.

A cultural anthropologist who studied illegal drug use in New York City used discarded paraphernalia as a trace measure. In neighborhoods where there was heavy drug trade, he found sidewalks strewn with variously-colored crack vial tops, intact or discarded syringes, and spent butane lighters. In the same way that archaeologists use bone fragments and pottery shards as signs of early settlement, this anthropologist uses the crack vial tops and other materials to indicate a work site or use location for illegal drugs. He spends time in these neighborhoods developing relationships with the participants in the drug trade in an attempt to understand their world. The trace measures give him added confidence that he is studying the right people in the right locations (Goldsmith, 1994).

The study of trace measures requires knowledge of both people and of their environments. If you want to study tattoos, you probably won't want to use a sample of accountants or physicians. If you want to analyze gang graffiti or discarded drug paraphernalia, you need to go to the places where the key players hang out. Archaeologists follow this principle in selecting sites for excavations. They learn to "read the landscape" to find promising places. A California forester described how he used trace measures to locate an Indian settlement. Looking across the Eel River, he noticed a large flat area at the confluence of a stream. The river location promised salmon and steelhead trout, staples of the North Coast Indian diet. A canopy of old oak trees fueled his hunch as it offered shelter and acorns. All the indicators encouraged the forester to search the area for artifacts. As he scrambled over big boulders, he found dozens of inscriptions carved hundreds of years earlier. Near the boulders were fire pits, foundations of huts, and an abundance of arrowheads and tools (Bowman, 1993).

Trace measures are also used in the study of animal behavior. Researchers count the number of bird nests to obtain information on density and breeding behavior. There are studies of animal droppings and the gut contents of dead animals (often road kills) to learn what animals eat. A team of researchers in England used trace measures to investigate feeding habits of domestic cats. Through personal contact, all but one of the households in a small village agreed to bag the remains of any animals that the cat caught. These were collected by the researcher on a weekly basis and tabulated. The study showed that small mammals represented almost three-quarters of the prey of these domestic cats. Contrary to what many people believed, birds were always in the minority as prey except during the coldest part of the winter, when mammals stayed below ground. Cats in houses near the middle of the village caught fewer prey than cats living near the edge of the village (Churcher & Lawton, 1989).

Certain types of usage create erosion or wear. Deterioration of campus lawns and the extent of footprints in the snow reveal informal pathways. Astute university administrators delay installing walkways until after these informal pathways have been located. Such pathways can be used to assess the social relationship between people in different buildings. Footprints do not provide an infallible measure of contact, but this clue may be worth following up if there is a significant number of footprints in the snow going from one dormitory to another and none between that dormitory and another equally close. According to Webb et al. (1981), the floor tiles around the hatching chick exhibit at Chicago's Museum of Science and Industry must be replaced every 6 weeks, while tiles in other parts of the museum last for years. Tile wear, they suggest, is a good index of the relative popularity of exhibits. In the hallways on our campus, the floor tiles showing the greatest amount of wear are those directly outside classrooms where students congregate between lectures. Although it is easy to record waiting patterns through systematic observations, worn floor tiles increase confidence in the findings.

Limitations

Apart from archeology, trace measures have not found wide acceptance in behavioral research. Most social scientists prefer to study live interaction rather than carpets and lawns.

The information provided by trace measures can be misleading. Deterioration of certain library books, for example, may reflect the activities of a single destructive individual rather than a large general circulation. The absence of graffiti in a restroom may reveal more about the cleaning policies of the janitors than about the social attitudes of the people using the restroom. The wear on the floor tiles around drinking fountains may result from the combination of usage and dripping water.

Trace measures: Informal paths shed light on the interaction networks among apartment dwellers.

Summary

A behavioral map records individuals' locations in physical settings. These maps can be place-centered or individual-centered. A place-centered map shows how individuals arrange themselves in a particular setting. A individual-centered map is based on recording an individual's behavior over time. Behavioral mapping can be both tiring and intrusive. Further research will be needed to explain the behaviors observed.

Cognitive mapping is used to investigate people's images of places. People are asked to sketch a map of an area showing the location of landmarks, buildings, parks, and other significant features. Cognitive maps are selective and may be based on stereotypes rather than direct experience.

Trace measures are the physical remains of interaction. Accretion refers to the buildup of a residue or product of the interaction. It is something added to the situation. Erosion refers to deterioration or wear and provides an index of usage patterns. With erosion, something is worn down or removed. The interpretation of trace measures is limited by the possibility of their resulting from factors that are not immediately obvious.

References

Bowman, C. (1993, December 10). State forester's hunch reveals ancient Eel River Indian site. *Sacramento Bee*, p. B3.

Brewer, D. D., & Miller, M. L. (1990). Bombing and burning: The social organization and values of hip hop graffiti writers and implications for policy. *Deviant Behavior, 11*, 345–369.

Bronnikov, A. G. (1993, Nov). Telltale tattoos in Russian prisons. *Natural History, 102,* 50–59.

Canter, D. V. (1994). *Criminal shadows: Inside the mind of the serial killer.* London: HarperCollins.

Cherulnik, P. D. (1990, April). *A study of traffic flow patterns in West Park Mall.* Paper presented at the annual meeting of the Environmental Design Research Association, Urbana, IL.

Churcher, P. B., & Lawton, J. H. (1989, July). Beware of well-fed felines. *Natural History,* 40–47.

Goldsmith, D. S. (1994, April). *Confidentiality in ethnography: Drugs, sex, and AIDS in the lives of informants in New York City.* Paper presented at the 53rd annual meeting of the Society for Applied Anthropology, Cancun, Mexico.

Hester, R. T. (1975). *Neighborhood space.* Stroudsburg, PA: Dowden, Hutchinson, & Ross.

Marcus, C. C. (1990). From the pragmatic to the spiritual. In I. Altman & K. Christensen (Eds.), *Environment and behavior studies: Emergence of intellectual traditions* (pp. 111–140). New York: Plenum Press.

Nummenmaa, T., & Syvänen, B. (1974). Teaching road safety for children in the age range of 5–7 years. *Pedagogica Europaea, 9*(1).

PPS. (1995). *The Center for Rebuilding Communities.* New York: Project for Public Spaces.

Schoggen, P., Barker, R. G., & Fox, K. A. (1989). *Behavior settings: A revision and extension of Roger G. Barker's Ecological psychology.* Stanford, CA: Stanford University Press.

Sladen, J. J. L. (1958). The pygoscelid penguins, parts 1 and 2. *Scientific Reports of the Falkland Islands Dependency Survey, 17.* London.

Tolman, E. C. (1968). Cognitive maps in rats and men. *Psychological Review, 55,* 189–208.

Van der Molen, H. H., Kerkhof, J. H., & Jong, A. M. (1983). Training observers to follow children and score their road-crossing behavior. *Ergonomics, 26,* 535–553.

Webb, E. J., Campbell, D. T., Schwarz, R. D., Sechrest, L., & Grove, J. B. (1981). *Nonreactive measures in the social sciences* (2nd ed.). Boston: Houghton Mifflin.

Whyte, W. H. (1980). *The social life of small urban spaces.* Washington, DC: Conservation Foundation.

Williams, R. (1995). *Ladies' latrinalia.* Unpublished manuscript, University of California, Davis.

Zacharias, J. (1995, March). *Attractions and distractions, wandering and stopping in a public market.* Paper presented at the 26th conference of the Environmental Design Research Association, Boston, MA.

Further Reading

Shettel-Neuber, J. (1988). Second- and third-generation zoo exhibits: A comparison of visitor, staff, and animal responses. Special Issue: Zoological parks and environment-behavior research. *Environment & Behavior, 20,* 452–473.

Webb, E. J., Campbell, D. T., Schwartz, R. D., Sechrest, L., & Grove, J. B. (1981). *Nonreactive measures in the social sciences* (2nd ed.). Boston: Houghton Mifflin.

Wicker, A. W. (1987). Behavior settings reconsidered. In D. Stokols, & I. Altman (Eds.), *Handbook of environmental psychology* (pp. 613–649). New York: Wiley.

6 Experimentation

TV VIEWING AFFECTS KID'S CHOLESTEROL announced the headline in the newspaper. "Habitual watchers have higher levels." The article went on to describe a study reporting that children who watched television four hours a day were four times as likely to have high cholesterol as children who watched TV less that two hours a day. Does this mean that watching television raises cholesterol levels? That is certainly what the headlines imply. If that were an accurate conclusion, TV viewing in and of itself would increase cholesterol levels. That doesn't seem logical.

The light rays emanating from the TV set haven't much to do with the level of lipids in the blood (cholesterol level). What is being reported is an association between cholesterol level and time spent watching television. But alone, this association really can't tell us what the underlying cause of that relationship is. It provides hints and clues but no certainty. We can't assume that if children stop watching television, their cholesterol levels will decline. We would have to test it in a systematic way, keeping track of all the other factors that might be influencing cholesterol level. The finding of the association between time spent watching television and cholesterol level generates a number of hypotheses. *Hypotheses* are testable statements, educated guesses that can be either confirmed (accepted) or disconfirmed (rejected). One hypothesis (note the singular form) is that lower cholesterol levels result from TV viewers getting less exercise. Another hypothesis is that children who watch TV are exposed to more advertising for fatty foods and as a result have a diet higher in cholesterol. A third hypothesis is that children watching a lot of TV have parents who are unable to or unwilling to supervise either their exercise patterns or their eating habits. A fourth is that social class may be influencing both diet and TV watching. One can even venture to hypothesize about genetic contributions to sedentary behavior. Having generated so many hypotheses, it becomes apparent that it would be very foolish to take the headline at its word. What we are after in this example is an understanding of cause-and-effect, which brings us to the special nature of the experiment.

The Special Nature of the Experiment

One of the purposes of research is to understand *causal relationships*, that is, to find out what causes what—how events or behaviors affect other events or behaviors. In the previous example, it is finding out what television watching has to do with cholesterol level. There are three criteria that must be met in order to scientifically show that Event A (presumed cause) in fact causes Event B (presumed effect). The first is *co-occurrence*. Both elements A and B must be observable and measurable. The television example meets this criterion. Time spent watching television and cholesterol level in the blood can be observed and measured.

The second criterion pertains to *sequence* or direction. The presumed cause must precede (come before) the presumed effect. Cause and effect cannot work backward in time, nor can simultaneous events cause each other. If Event A is the cause of Event B, A must occur first in time. Our example didn't meet this criterion. No information was provided as to the timing of cholesterol increases and how long the current television viewing pattern had been in effect.

The third criterion and often the most problematic requirement is that all other possible causes (in the situation under study) must be eliminated. Co-occurrence and sequence in time are not sufficient in and of themselves to confirm that Event A causes Event B. The problem is that both Event A and Event B may be the result of Event C, a third factor. This is where the alternative hypotheses came into play. They illustrated the multiplicity of possible explanations for the association between time spent watching television and cholesterol level.

Experiments are especially important with regard to the third criterion—ruling out alternative explanations or causes. Properly-designed experiments provide an opportunity to confirm that Event A is the cause of Event B by keeping other causal factors out of the test. This is accomplished through the systematic manipulation and control of variables. An experiment allows us to systematically examine relationships that we have observed in natural settings.

It is possible to design an experiment to test the relationship between cholesterol levels and TV watching in children. Measures of children's existing TV watching (amount per day) and cholesterol levels would be obtained. These initial measures could be used to form groups with similar average levels of cholesterol and TV watching. Then, by agreement with the parents and with occasional checking by the researchers to see that the plan was being followed, one group of children would watch TV for 1 hour a day, another group for 3 hours a day, and the last group for 5 hours a day. The experiment might run for 3 months, with cholesterol levels measured at the end of each month. In order to confirm the hypothesis, children who watch TV for 5 hours a day should have higher cholesterol levels than those who watched 3 hours a day, and those who watched 3 hours a day should have higher levels than those who watched only 1 hour a day.

This true experiment would be difficult to implement in practice. There would be the tasks of getting permission from all the parents for their children to participate in the study, arranging for cholesterol tests, and making sure that the experimental plan was being followed (i.e., children watching for the required number of hours). These difficulties are not insurmountable, but they do encourage some researchers to take shortcuts and avoid doing true experiments.

John B. Watson, the pioneer figure of behaviorism, was a strict experimentalist, but at the same time recognized the value of field observation. He saw the methods of observation and experimentation as complementary, and wrote the following comments in 1914:

> Unquestionably it is a mistake to neglect field work . . . no one who has ever used monkeys as subjects can help feeling how handicapped we are at the present time in our laboratory studies . . . through lack of systematic knowledge of their life in the open. What is true in the case of the primates is true with respect to nearly every other animal form . . . on the other hand, it can hardly be claimed that mere observation of field activity, even when made by competent students, can ever hope to answer in any scientific way the basic questions which must be asked about the mechanics of stimulus and response. Even the most superficial observation of field activity by the trained student raises at once a host of questions, the answers to which must be sought in the laboratory. (Watson, 1914, p. 30)

In his book *Zen and the Art of Motorcycle Maintenance*, Robert Pirsig (1974) describes the purpose of the experimental method as making sure that Nature has not misled you into believing you know something you actually don't know. As Pirsig describes it, the power of the scientific method, and experimentation in particular, outweighs the elaborate preparation and formalities required. This does not mean that an experiment always provides predicted results. Nature can jealously guard her secrets and you can end up learning a fraction of what you expected. Alternatively, you may discover more than you ever imagined. An experiment fails only when it does not adequately test the hypothesis. If an experiment is properly conducted, even results that do not support the hypothesis are important. Disconfirmation can be as valuable as confirmation because it allows us to eliminate possible explanations.

Variables

In experiments, the elements that are manipulated, compared, and controlled are *variables*. A *variable* is any characteristic or quality that differs in degree or kind and can be measured. Examples of variables are height, hair color, sex, running speed, income, IQ, education, social class, and political party. Simply put, variables vary. Qualities that do not vary are called *constants*. One rarely finds reference to constants in behavioral research. The concept of a *variable* is fundamental. Just about anything we measure can be called a variable.

Variables possess *values* or *levels*. These are the dimensions on which they vary. Gender is a variable whose values or levels are female and male. The values or levels of the variable, hair color, can be described as brunette, blond, redhead, or grey. Time spent watching TV is a variable that can range from zero to most of the waking day.

Independent and Dependent Variables

Whether a variable is independent or dependent depends upon how it is used by the researcher in an experiment. The variable that is manipulated or systematically altered by the experimenter is called the *independent variable*. In the study just described, TV watching is an independent variable. Synonyms for the independent variable are *experimental variable* or *predictor variable*. The levels of the independent variable are sometimes referred to as *treatments*. They reflect the manipulation of the independent variable. In the TV watching experiment, time spent watching TV is the independent variable whose three treatment levels are 1, 3, and 5 hours per day.

The variable that is affected, the consequence or outcome of the manipulation, is called the *dependent variable*. The term "dependent" is used because the changes in it depend upon the manipulation of the independent variable. Synonyms for the dependent variable are *outcome*, *response*, or *criterion variable*. If we decide to test the hypothesis that increasing levels of TV watching produces increased levels of cholesterol in the viewer, then cholesterol level is the dependent variable.

Variables in Experiments

Now we can phrase the experimental question as "What is the effect of the independent variable on some outcome (dependent variable)?" The effect or absence of an effect is discovered by manipulating the *levels* of the independent variable and seeing their effect on the dependent variable. There must be at least two levels used (to provide a comparison). The levels may be defined simply as presence or absence or may represent different degrees of the independent variable.

Generating Hypotheses

It is general research practice to restate questions as statements that can be tested. These are called *hypotheses* (singular form is *hypothesis*).

Example

ORIGINAL QUESTION: Do students who complete a driver education course get fewer citations than those who do not take the course?

HYPOTHESIS: Students who completed the driver education course will receive fewer citations in the following year than students who did not take the course.

The variables of the hypotheses must be clearly specified and defined. In this example, completing the driver education course is the independent variable; its two levels are YES and NO. Number of traffic citations the following year is the dependent variable. Its levels or values can range from zero to maximum possible in a year.

Operational Definitions

Variables are usually specified by their operational definitions. An *operational definition* defines something by how it is measured. Intelligence may be operationally defined as a score on an IQ test. Success in driver's training is defined above as the absence of traffic citations the following year. Operational definitions can vary from experiment to experiment. Worker satisfaction may be defined by a number of operations—turnover rate, productivity, expressed satisfaction on a questionnaire, and rate of absenteeism. Although operational definitions may differ, they are not arbitrary. They must show a logical relationship to the concept under study. Contradictory research findings sometimes can be traced to researchers' having used different operational definitions.

The primary reason for giving an operational definition is to specify clearly and precisely what is being measured so that the study can be repeated by someone else using exactly the same procedures and measurements. The operational definitions reduce the likelihood of misunderstanding.

Example: Dressing for Success

A question of interest might be "What is the effect of a job candidate's clothing on the outcome of a job interview?" Does one need to "dress for success"? The question needs to be transformed into a statement (hypothesis) that either can be accepted or rejected on the basis of the results of the experiment. We also need to operationally define the terms and concepts being used, which means specifying the variables, whose levels will be manipulated and compared, with regard to their effect on some outcome. We must generate an operational description of clothing/attire, defining its *levels* or *values*. One possibility is to use categories of casual (jeans and tee shirt), sporty (slacks and sportshirt for men, dress or slacks and blouse for women), and business-like (suit and tie for men, suit and high-heeled shoes for women). These categories (casual, sporty, and business-like) represent three levels of the independent variable (clothing/attire). The outcome or *dependent variable* can be operationally defined in several ways: being hired or not (two levels, yes/no), or ranking among job candidates (first choice, second choice, to last choice).

Now that the concepts are operationally defined, we can transform the question "Does clothing affect the outcome of a job interview?" into a series of testable propositions (hypotheses):

A job candidate dressed in business-like attire is more likely to be hired than a candidate wearing casual clothes.

The sportily-dressed candidate will be ranked somewhere between the casually-dressed and the business-attired candidate.

To make the experiment more realistic, we can add job type as a second independent variable. Job type can have two levels, clerical and managerial. With the additional factor, we would probably revise our hypotheses to take into account the particulars of the job. For example, we might hypothesize that type of attire would have less of an effect on selection of the clerk than it would on selection of the manager.

Outline of the Variables
Independent Variable A:　　Clothing/attire
　　　　Levels/Values:　　1. Casual
　　　　　　　　　　　　　2. Sport
　　　　　　　　　　　　　3. Business
Independent Variable B:　　Job type
　　　　Levels/Values:　　1. Clerk
　　　　　　　　　　　　　2. Manager
Dependent Variable:　　Interview outcome
　　　　Levels/Values:　　1. Hired
　　　　　　　　　　　　　2. Not hired

In this example, we now have 6 treatment conditions: all combinations of the 3 levels of Treatment A, clothing/attire, and the 2 levels of Treatment B, job type—casually-dressed clerk applicant, casually-dressed manager applicant, sport-dressed clerk applicant, . . . business-dressed manager applicant. The treatments are the various combinations of the levels of the independent variables. The experiment involves manipulating the levels of clothing/attire and job type and comparing the effects of that manipulation (the various combinations) on the outcome of the interview.

Experimental Control

Remember the third factor problem discussed at the beginning of the chapter? To be sure that our experimental manipulation is truly having an effect, we must rule out all other variables that might have an influence. These are called *extraneous variables*. In the clothing/attire study described above, perhaps people were hired because of their facial appearance, irrespective of what they were wearing; or maybe their gender played a role. These other factors are examples of extraneous variables. They are not what the experimenter is attempting to either manipulate or measure, but they might affect the interview outcome (dependent variable).

The experimenter must avoid *confounding*, that is, confusing the effect of the independent variable with that of other variables. Extraneous variables are potential sources of error as they mask or cloud the observable effects of the independent variable. There are three general ways of controlling the effects of extraneous variables: (1) eliminate or hold them constant across the different treatment conditions, (2) measure them in order to take their effect into account, and (3) use a control group or control condition.

Eliminating or Holding Extraneous Variables Constant

Extraneous variables arise from five general sources: subjects, experimenters, setting, apparatus, and procedure. The following sections describe these sources of error and ways of controlling them.

Subjects

The participants in an experiment are called *subjects*. Their individual characteristics are likely to influence the outcome of the experiment. Examples of such characteristics are age, education, socioeconomic background, ability, personality, and temporary conditions such as fatigue, nervousness, or preoccupation with other matters. The subjects' expectations and beliefs about the experiment may also influence the results.

    1. Eliminate or reduce extraneous variables when possible. For example, reduce fatigue by making the procedure brief.

    2. Holding subject variables constant by creating the same conditions in all groups used in the experiment. There are two ways to do this.

        a. *Random assignment*—Random assignment means that a person is as likely to be put in one group as in another; that the decision depends on chance alone. Such assignment can be made by a table of random numbers.

        Using a table of random numbers: Turn to the table of random numbers, Appendix A-5. Assume an experiment with 20 subjects and 2 treatment conditions. Pick a point anywhere on the table and assign each subject a number from the table moving consistently in any direction, up or down, or to left or right. The subjects can initially be listed in any order—alphabetical, order of signing up, or by age. It doesn't matter because the numbers they are getting were randomly generated. The ten people with the lowest numbers are assigned to one level of treatment, and the remainder are assigned to the other.

   b. *Matched groups*—Assign subjects so that all the groups are equal with regard to the extraneous factors. In the TV example, one could assign participants so that each group has the same average level of cholesterol and the same ratio of boys to girls. In a different study, one might want to structure groups with equal percentages of Catholics, a similar mix of socioeconomic level and age range, and any other relevant extraneous factor. If the variable has nothing to do with the outcome, there is no need to match for it. For example, in a study of reaction time to lights flashed at different intensities, one wouldn't be concerned about a participant's religious preference. On the other hand if the stimuli to which one reacts were religious symbols, then religion would be an important factor to take into account.

Experimenter

Experimenters, like subjects, possess a variety of characteristics and expectations that might influence the outcome of an experiment. These must be eliminated or kept the same for all subjects under all of the experimental conditions.

1. Use the same experimenter for all conditions.
2. If more than one experimenter is used,
   a. train them so that they are all doing exactly the same thing in the same way.
   b. have each experimenter run an equal number of subjects in each treatment condition, *or* randomly assign experimenters to run subjects under the various treatment combinations.

Setting

Situational aspects of the experiment—the room, the equipment, time of day, weather, temperature, other variables associated with the setting—are potential confounds or sources of error. The only thing that should differ across subjects is level of the independent variable.

1. Run all subjects the same time of day.
2. Keep the laboratory conditions (lighting, temperature, noise, etc.) as similar as possible for all subjects.

Apparatus

The apparatus refers to the equipment used in the experiment—for presenting stimuli, monitoring reactions, or recording responses. *Stimuli* (singular form is *stimulus*) is a general term used to refer to the material to which participants are expected to respond.

    1. Check equipment frequently to make sure that it is functioning properly.

    2. Make sure that all materials, handouts, pencils, and anything else used in the study are of the same quality across conditions.

Procedure

The procedure refers to actual manipulation of the levels of the independent variable(s). Some experiments involve presenting stimuli to subjects; for example, lists of words to be memorized, different types of arguments to find out which are more persuasive, or combinations of objects and colors for judgments of attractiveness. In these procedures, order of presentation may operate as an extraneous variable. The fact that an item is encountered early on may influence the subject's judgment of it. Subjects may become tired or bored as the experiment progresses, and these factors, rather than some quality of the stimulus, may influence their reaction. Factors associated with presentation order (boredom, novelty, practice, fatigue) can be controlled by counterbalancing or randomizing the order in which stimuli are presented.

    1. *Counterbalancing*—the order of the presentation of stimuli is systematically balanced within the treatment group: for example half of the subjects are presented the materials in reverse order.

    Example: In the study where subjects are asked to make a hiring decision based on three types of clothing in two job situations, there are six combinations to be judged.

Independent Variable A:	Clothing/attire
Levels/Values:	Casual, Sport, Business
Independent Variable B:	Job type
Levels/Values:	Clerk, Manager
Dependent Variable:	Interview outcome
Levels/Values:	Hired, Not hired.

    The initial order can be reversed for some subjects. Further counterbalancing can be done by reversing each half of the presentation order, yielding four sequences for the six items:

Stimuli order #1:	1,2,3,4,5,6
Stimuli order #2:	6,5,4,3,2,1
Stimuli order #3:	4,5,6,1,2,3
Stimuli order #4:	3,2,1,6,5,4

How much counterbalancing is needed depends on the degree to which order effects are expected. It is always a good idea to provide at least one counterbalanced order of presentation.

2. *Random order of presentation*—the order of presentation is randomized for each subject or for groups of subjects, so that extraneous effects such as fatigue will be randomly distributed across the various presentations. Use a table of random numbers (see earlier discussion) to assign numbers to conditions and re-order accordingly. Note that random is *not* simply haphazard. Being in random order means that a particular order is due to chance only and is unaffected by any source of bias. A haphazard arrangement may be biased in some way.

Measurement of Extraneous Variables

Extraneous variables in one experiment can become independent variables in another. In the clothing example, we could include gender as a third independent variable, manipulating and thereby assessing its effect across all the other levels of the independent variables.

Another possibility is to measure an extraneous variable and statistically take it into account when analyzing the results of the experiment. This involves statistical techniques that are beyond the scope of this textbook. A crude technique would involve a sort of handicapping—for example, in an experiment testing the effectiveness of driver training, taking a fixed number of points off the scores of subjects who started out with greater ability.

If we had an experiment run by two different experimenters, we could compare the results of subjects tested by each. This would tell us whether or not the experimenter made a difference, and this factor could then be taken into account in assessing the overall findings, either by considering experimenter as an independent variable or by making a statistical adjustment.

Using a Control Group

The group of subjects exposed to the levels of the independent variable is called the *treatment group* or the *experimental group*. In order to control for extraneous variables, many experiments use a *control group*. The control group should be similar to the experimental group in every way *except* for exposure to the independent variable. All of the extraneous variables should be affecting the control group just as they are affecting the experimental group. The effect of the independent variable can be measured by comparing changes in the control group with changes in the experimental group. Here is an allergy treatment example:

Hypothesis: Drug X relieves hay fever symptoms.

Independent Variable:	Drug X
Levels:	1. Control condition = drug absent.
	2. Treatment condition = drug present
Dependent Variable:	Symptom relief
Values:	Scale of 0 to 5 (0 = no relief, 5 = total relief)

In this example, if the medication were in pill or capsule form, people in the control group would receive a non-active substance (sugar or corn filler) packaged in the same manner. This is called a *placebo*. Originally, placebos were sugar pills given to soothe medical patients. Now the term is used more generally to refer to pills, liquids, or injections that look like the treatment but don't contain any active chemical elements.

Using Subjects as Their Own Controls

In the above example, subjects could be put on several cycles of treatment, sometimes receiving the drug and other times receiving the placebo. This is called a *repeated measures* or *within-subjects* design. The effects of the drug would be evaluated by subtracting symptom reports in the control (placebo) condition from symptom reports in the treatment condition for each subject and then seeing if any effect remains.

Another example of using subjects as their own controls is to employ before-and-after measurement. This technique is often used to evaluate various interventions such as training in some task or finding out whether exposure to persuasive arguments changes attitudes.

Limitations of Repeated Measure Designs

The drawback with using people as their own controls is that the change might occur from the testing itself—that the pre-test may affect the post-test outcome (the dependent variable). A second limitation is that some outside event taking place at the same time as the experiment may make the comparison invalid (e.g., a change in the pollen count while testing the effects of Drug X). In such instances, it is better to compare a treated and untreated group at the same point in time. The trade–offs between comparing two groups (treated and untreated) versus the same group (before and after treatment) must be considered in the light of the particular study.

Doing an Experiment

Experiments are particularly powerful in untangling cause-and-effect relationships. However, they tend to be artificial and require time and planning in order to meet

the requirements of systematic manipulation, comparison, and control. Many interesting research questions do not lend themselves to experimental design and are
better explored through other techniques such as observation, surveys, case studies, or other research techniques.

Getting Ideas

Ideas for experiments can be found in many places—a theory, an observation, a
case study, or from reading the research literature. Theories are broad and over-
arching statements connecting concepts and generally cannot be tested directly.
Their credibility or truth value depends on the results of testing the hypotheses
that they generate.

There is no special order of development among theory, hypotheses, and observations. Any one of them may serve as a starting place for an experiment. Observation can lead to the development of theory but so can a case study or reading other research articles.

Designing and Running an Experiment

The experimental design lays out the procedures for manipulation, comparison,
and control. Box 6–1 provides a checklist of the necessary steps.

Types of Experiments

All experiments involve the manipulation of the levels of one or more independent variables and examining the effects on the dependent variable, but experiments differ with regard to researchers' ability to directly manipulate the independent variable. Generally the issue is one of assigning subjects to the various
conditions. When the experimenter is able to assign subjects to treatment and control conditions either randomly or by some other unbiased method, the experiment
is described as a *true experiment*. If the subjects are already in groups due to external circumstances, the experiment is a *quasi-experiment* rather than a true one.
In the third category, only one subject is used, serving under all treatment conditions. These are labeled *single-subject* experiments. Any of these three types of
experiments can be conducted in the laboratory or in the field under more natural
real-world conditions.

True Experiments

In a true experiment, subjects are randomly assigned to treatment groups. Such assignment generally requires that the experimenter has direct control over the independent variable.

BOX 6–1. Basic Steps: Designing and Running an Experiment

1. Clearly describe the problem, issue, or question being addressed.
2. State the hypothesis or hypotheses to be tested.
3. Provide operational definitions of the independent and dependent variables and describe their levels or values.
4. Design the study, including the controls for extraneous variables associated with
   a. subjects
   b. experimenter(s)
   c. setting
   d. apparatus
   d. procedure
5. If you are using a control group, see that its composition and treatment are like that of the experimental group in every way except for the levels of the independent variable.
6. Meet local requirements concerning the use of human or animal subjects.
7. Pilot test (trial experiment).
   a. Are directions clearly understood?
   b. Does the apparatus work correctly?
   c. Is the experimenter performing as required?
8. Correct any problems. If they are extensive, run a second pilot experiment and upon satisfactory completion, proceed with the experiment.
9. Carefully record any problems or insights that occur during the experiment.
10. On completion, debrief participants.
    a. Thank them for their cooperation.
    b. Explain the study.
    c. Answer any questions.
    d. Explain where and when the results will be available.

True experiments are more easily done in the laboratory where it is possible to control the relevant variables. Temperature, lighting, and other aspects of the environment are easily held constant, and distractions such as noise and other activity can be eliminated or reduced. Treatment conditions can be created and changed according to schedule. For convenience to the researcher, it is hard to beat the laboratory.

It is difficult to conduct true experiments in the field because there are so many uncontrolled factors that can affect behavior: distractions, interruptions, weather, and other environmental conditions. The major advantage of field experiments is their naturalness compared to the presumed artificiality of the laboratory. For example, Kim Garrity worked as a server at Charley Brown's Restaurant in Huntington Beach at the same time she was enrolled in an experimental psychology class at a local college. She decided to combine the two parts of her life in a field experiment to test the effects of a personal introduction on tipping behavior. Twenty-one two-person tables at the Sunday buffet were randomly assigned to one of two conditions. In one condition, Kim introduced herself by name (treatment condition); in the other, she did not (control condition). She found that the name identification resulted in a statistically-significant increase in tip size. The results were interpreted in terms of social impact theory (Garrity & Degelman, 1990). This is an example of a true experiment done in the field.

Quasi-experiments

The distinguishing characteristic of a *quasi-experiment*, also known as a *natural experiment*, is that the experimenter cannot fully control assignment of subjects to conditions. Sometimes the treatment may be a natural event, a new law or program, or something else beyond the researcher's control.

Examples: Quasi-experiments/natural experiments
Pre-event vs. post-event comparisons

> The rate of highway fatalities before and after raising the speed limit.
> Rate of drunk driving arrests before and after implementing a community awareness campaign.
> The number of migratory geese in Chesapeake Bay after farmers switch from growing tobacco to planting corn.
> Number of tranquilizers sold in a community before and after a natural disaster.

Treatment vs. control comparisons

> School achievement in two districts, one with a lower-than-average student-teacher ratio.
> Sales of tranquilizers in two similar communities, one of which has been struck by a tornado.
> Achievement motivation in first-born children compared with later-born children.

These studies gain much in external validity because they take place in the real world. Unfortunately they lose internal validity. The experimenter cannot know all the factors associated with the subjects' being in the various treatment groups. Because subjects were not randomly assigned to conditions, there may have been self-selection or some other form of bias. Clear interpretation of the findings is not possible because varying levels of extraneous variables are confounded with the levels of the independent variable. For example, people living in the school district with a lower student-teacher ratio may be better off economically, so that differences in children's school achievement may in fact be due to factors other than the teacher-student ratio. Even if you matched the districts by socioeconomic level, there might be other historical, cultural, or situational factors that contribute to differences in student achievement. Quasi-experiments can be extremely valuable and informative, but they don't establish cause-and-effect relationships to the degree that is possible in true experiments.

Well-designed laboratory experiments that superficially appear to be true experiments in fact may be quasi-experiments. An obvious example is using gender as an experimental variable. Gender can serve as an independent variable and male-

Quasi-experiment. To learn how much distance motorists kept between themselves and a bicyclist riding at different speeds, a bicyclist rode on a straight path along a road with separate 25-mile, 35-mile, and 45-mile an hour speed limits. Another researcher photographed the "shy distance" kept by cars in each speed zone.

female comparisons are easily made, but gender is not directly manipulated by the experimenter. The experimenter cannot assign an individual to be a man or women (outside of role-playing). A comparison of the performance of women and men on mental rotation tasks conducted in the laboratory under highly controlled conditions would be a quasi-experiment rather than true experiment because subjects were not randomly assigned to the treatment conditions—being male or female. Well-designed laboratory studies can produce reliable information about gender differences under specified conditions, but don't reveal what it is about maleness or femaleness that is causing the difference. Factors of biology, upbringing, training, experience, modeling, situational influences, and a host of other interacting influences are confounded with being female or male.

Single-subject Experiments

Up to now, we have discussed experimentation from the standpoint of groups of people in different treatment conditions. Within experimental psychology, particularly in the branch known as applied behavior analysis, an alternative model is single-subject research. Instead of testing many people at one time, a researcher tests one individual over an extended period.

This research design is known as ABA or ABAB, in which A is a baseline (non-treatment or control) phase prior to the introduction of the treatment condition. B is the period covering the application of the treatment that produces some effect. Then the experiment returns to A (removing the treatment condition) to see if the effect disappears. Sometimes the researcher follows the second non-treatment phase with a repeat of treatment (ABAB design).

The confirmation obtained by adding a second cycle of the control condition (ABA) or a second cycle of both control and treatment (ABAB) increases the reliability and internal validity of the findings. Consider a case where treatment with a drug to reduce hyperactivity is prescribed for a disruptive child. The A phase involves systematic observation before treatment. During the B phase, behavior is observed while the child is taking the drug. It is important to be certain that it is the drug rather than some other effect (e.g., placebo effects, attention paid by the researchers, or other uncontrolled changes in the environment) that is producing the change in behavior. Return to the non-treated (A) condition provides an important confirmation or disconfirmation regarding the effectiveness of the drug treatment.

The fact that the design is powerful doesn't mean that it is always appropriate or necessary. Consider the following: A child sees a frightening mask on a wall, screams in terror, and starts to cry. We turn the mask to the wall, and the child stops crying. Was it mask removal that caused the change in behavior, or was it our soothing words and assurances that "It can't hurt you"? The test is to return the mask to its original position. If our words had little effect, the child will start screaming and crying again. Do we really need to know the precise cause of a change in behavior in this case? Is the benefit of pinning down the cause sufficient to justify the potential increase in discomfort for the child? When considering an experiment, the value of systematic manipulation needs to be placed within the larger contexts of concern for participants and potential benefit to society.

There are a number of advantages in studying a single individual over time: (1) the effects of the treatment are not hidden or masked in a group average; (2) only one subject is needed; (3) observations can be made in naturalistic, real-world settings; (4) clinical practice is concerned with changes in individual behavior and this is what single-subject research measures; and (5) the procedure and interpretation of findings do not involve complex manipulation and statistical information and are more readily understood by the general public (Geller, 1987).

Limitations

The primary limitation of true experiments is that they are often highly artificial in separating variables that naturally occur together. They sacrifice external validity (generalizability) for internal validity (control of extraneous variables). Experiments often require a considerable amount of time and effort in their design and implementation.

Quasi- or natural experiments possess more external validity, but fail to meet the third criterion of cause-and-effect. If we demonstrate that a campaign to reduce drunk driving in a community was followed by a decline in such arrests, we have increased our confidence that the program works. Perhaps success was due to some third unknown factor or simply chance, but our confidence in the positive outcome is strengthened by the evidence we have. Single-subject experiments are limited in their generalizability as the person selected for study may be unusual or atypical, or unknown circumstances may be affecting the particular outcome. It is possible to repeat single-subject studies with additional individuals.

Another point about experiments of any type is that demonstrating one likely cause of a behavior doesn't eliminate other possible causes. For example, a clear and strong demonstration that a particular training program improves one's ability to play the clarinet doesn't rule out the possibility that clarinet-playing skill has a genetic component that is distributed differentially through the population, leading some people to be better at it than others. We may have pinned down one contributing factor, but others might exist.

Summary

The major value of experiments is in determining cause-and-effect relationships. The three criteria for cause-and-effect are co-occurrence, sequence, and elimination of alternative causes (third factors). These criteria can be met in a true experiment by the systematic manipulation, comparison, and control of variables. An *independent* or *experimental* variable is a variable that is systematically manipulated in order to measure its effect on some outcome. The outcome is the *dependent* variable. Additional variables, besides the independent variable, that might be affecting the outcome (dependent variable) are termed *extraneous*.

Hypotheses are testable propositions or statements. They often describe relationships among variables. *Operational definitions* define variables by the way in which they are measured. *Confounding* refers to an inability to separate the effects of the independent variable from those of extraneous variables. Extraneous variables may arise from subjects, experimenters, setting, apparatus, or procedures. If extraneous variables cannot be eliminated, they can be controlled by holding them constant across all conditions or by counterbalancing or randomization. Extraneous variables can also be measured and taken into account. Another alternative is to use a control group that is treated exactly like the experimental group, except for exposure to the independent variable.

Ideas for experiments come from observations, theories, case studies, or reviewing previous research, and generally involve testing hypotheses. Running a successful experiment takes care and planning.

There are three general types of experiments. In *true experiments* subjects are randomly assigned to the levels of the independent variable. In *quasi-experiments* there is nonrandom assignment to conditions; the experimenter lacks direct control over the independent variable. In *single-subject experiments* the independent variable is manipulated for a single subject.

As a method, experimentation tends to be high on internal validity but may be low on external validity (generalizability). The main strength of true experiments is in determining cause-and-effect relationships. Quasi-experiments gain in external validity but do not permit ruling out third-factor explanation because of limited control over extraneous variables. Single-subject experiments also posses limited generalizability.

References

Garrity, K., & Degelman, D. (1990). Effect of server introduction on restaurant tipping. *Journal of Applied Social Psychology, 20*(2, Pt. 1), 168–172.

Geller, E. S. (1987). Applied behavior analysis and environmental psychology: From strange bedfellows to a productive marriage. In D. Stokols & I. Altman (Eds.), *Handbook of environmental psychology* (Vol. I, pp. 361–388). New York: Wiley.

Pirsig, R. (1974). *Zen and the art of motorcycle maintenance.* New York: Morrow.

Watson, J. B. (1914). *Behavior: An introduction to comparative psychology.* New York: Holt.

Further Reading

Christensen, L. B. (1994). *Experimental methodology* (6th ed.). Boston: Allyn & Bacon.

Levin, I. P., & Hinrichs, J. V. (1995). *Experimental psychology: Contemporary methods & applications.* Madison, WI: Brown & Benchmark.

Levine, G., & Parkinson, S. (1994). *Experimental methods in psychology.* Hillsdale, NJ: Lawrence Erlbaum Associates.

McGuigan, F. J. (1993). *Experimental psychology: Methods of research* (6th ed.). Englewood Cliffs, NJ: Prentice-Hall.

7 Simulation

What does close confinement in a space capsule under conditions of zero gravity do to one's personal space? How close is "too close" when a fellow astronaut floats by in a horizontal position? Studying interpersonal distance during actual space flights would be expensive and difficult to control. A solution used by a team of researchers under contract to the American space agency was to employ a cardboard model of a space station with astronaut dolls. Earlier research had established that the conversational distance people used for dolls in simulated conversation was similar to the distances real people used in actual encounters.

> In front of you are two male figures and a space station scene. I'm going to ask you to put the men in the space station in a comfortable conversational arrangement with one another. Keep in mind that they are in zero gravity. Every time you put them in position, keep their feet off the floor. When you have put them in a comfortable conversational distance, tell me and I will measure them.

These were the instructions used by psychology student Susan Westfall to study interpersonal distance under conditions of weightlessness. The blond-haired "Ken" doll and the dark-haired "Derek" doll were dressed in specially designed one-piece blue jumpsuits with an American flag on the left sleeve and a black name patch on the left side of the chest (see photo). To simulate zero gravity (weightlessness), the figures were mounted on the ends of desk lamp arms that could be rotated 360 degrees. The space station scene was a cardboard panel containing silver pipes, control dials, and other mechanical items found in earlier space vehicles. In a control condition, the doll figures were placed in a living room scene. Westfall found that conversational distance was greater in the simulated space station than in the control condition of the living room. The longest conversational distances occurred when one of the "astronauts" was vertical while the other floated either horizontally or upside down.

What Is a Simulation?

Behavioral simulations are imitations of actual conditions. They are intended to resemble the true situation in many of its functional characteristics without being mistaken for it. None of the participants mistook the cardboard model for a true space station, but seeing the scale model and the dolls in various positions helped them to imagine what weightlessness would be like. Although they vary in complexity, simulations generally depict complex situations involving many variables. Unlike a true experiment, little effort is made to untangle them.

There are many ways to imitate natural conditions. Re-creating an environment using scale models or other media is possible. Other options are games and role-playing.

Environmental Simulations

Showing photographs, videos, or models of setttings is often less costly than taking viewers to the site. Presentation modes for environmental simulations can include slides, video, photographic prints, maps, floor plans, drawings, scale models, computer graphics, and various combinations of the above.

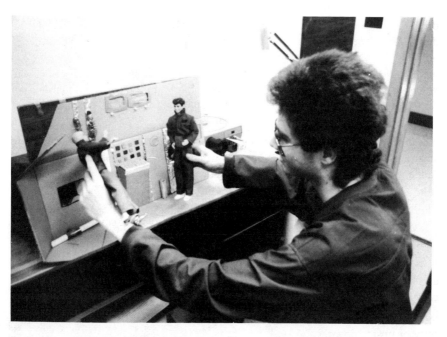

To simulate conversational distance at zero gravity, students adjusted the distance between dolls in various spatial arrangements.

Landscape researchers use slides to obtain ratings of environmental quality. People are shown slides of different parts of a coastline and asked to rate scenic attractiveness, naturalness, excitement, and other characteristics. Ratings by people viewing slides and photographs tend to be similar to those given by people rating the actual scene (Stamps, 1990). Slides and other pictures can be digitized and manipulated by the researcher. Individual items in a picture can be blown up or shrunk or changed in specific ways, or distracting elements can be removed. The newly-created stimuli can be transferred to videotape for easy presentation to subjects.

The economy of simulation is illustrated in the following situation: a zoo administrator wants to improve the information signs. She is interested both in different types of lettering and placement (i.e., at eye level, bottom, top, or either side). She first considered making the signs and trying them out in various locations throughout the zoo. Four different signs with five placements yields 20 combinations. Each of the 20 would have to be posted somewhere in the zoo, and then visitor responses obtained. As a simulation would be less awkward and time consuming than a field experiment, she decided to create the four signs and photograph them in five locations within an enclosure. At a testing booth at a convenient location, zoo visitors could be shown a display of the 20 photographs and asked for their preferences. Extraneous factors that might influence the viewer, such as type of animal or individual exhibit layout, could be held constant by photographing the 20 combinations at the same enclosure.

Simulation is widely used in the human factors field, in such applications as driving simulators that include video images of the roadway and potential accident sources for greater realism. Virtual reality is the most current form of technological simulation. By means of a helmet containing earphones and a color TV monitor, a computer can control what a person sees and hears, coordinating this with actual body movements. With proper adjustment in the computer-controlled displays, stereoscopic vision is created with the visual experience of depth, just as in ordinary visual perception (Tart, 1990). The technology is becoming more available and has research applications in studying how people will respond in different situations and environments without the need to actually place them in these situations. There are several mailing lists on the Internet specifically devoted to virtual reality technology in the behavioral sciences.

Games

In simulation games people take on the roles of participants and make decisions appropriate to their assigned roles. Simulation helps participants understand the complexities of institutional arrangements, brings together and allows each person to view multiple perspectives (how others see things in the gaming situation), and enables players to experiment with policy options in a safe environment.

One of the most popular computer games is *SimCity*, in which players create their own cities. They must build and maintain roads, provide services, and at the same time hold taxes at reasonable levels and keep the citizens happy. The game teaches lessons of complexity and connectedness. If the budgets of schools, libraries, and museums are reduced, SimCity will be less able to attract high-tech industries. But high taxation will put them off as well. The game is the basis of a national competition among schools to design the ideal city, and it has many research applications in urban planning.

Environmental conflicts, because of their complex mix of political, economic, geographic, and ecological issues, lend themselves to simulation. The MIT Harvard Public Disputes Program has developed over a dozen simulations on environmental and energy issues. *Harborco* is a simulation based on a dispute between those who want to build a deep-water port and environmental, labor, and other interest groups. *Development Dispute at Menehune Bay* is a six-person multi-issue game involving a conflict between environmental groups, advocates for native peoples, and commercial development interests in Hawaii. *DirtyStuff* is a series of games involving toxics in the workplace and the role of outside neutral parties who try to resolve disputes. The *National Energy Policy Game* begins with a 15-minute video of a news broadcast which sets the mood for the game. At least 27 players are needed, including 16 commissioners, 9 lobbyists, and 2 media commentators. The game can be played in a single day or over a few weeks. It requires a table large enough to seat everyone with additional space for lobbyists to observe and to hold separate meetings.

The Internet permits cross-national participation in simulation games. Project IDEALS was one of the largest attempts at cross-cultural simulation on the Internet. It involved participants from 14 different nations. They ranged in age from junior high school through university students and practicing professionals. Project IDEALS provided a democratic forum for communication in that there were no direct cues to age, background, and status of the participants. As a result, college students found themselves dealing with junior high school students as equals. Sometimes the older participants had difficulty believing that the responses they saw were from 13-year-olds. The game had a positive impact on all sides, challenging the stereotypes of the older students and raising the self-esteem of the younger players. People had to communicate not only across national borders but also across different fields of specialization. Important lessons about interdisciplinary cooperation were learned as the students represented different academic and vocational majors (e.g., a Russian class in technical electronic education, a political science class in Kentucky, a high school class from Ontario, Canada). Because there were no direct consequences of the decisions, the simulation allowed a wide-ranging exploration of problems and solutions in a low-risk context. The subsequent learning produced insights that were applicable to real-world problems (Sutherland, 1995). The e-mail addresses of some of the major international simulation games can be found in Crookall (1995).

Social psychologists use simulated conflict-of-interest games in order to study the conditions likely to promote cooperation and conflict. In games based on Prisoners' Dilemma and The Tragedy of the Commons, players attempt to reach an accommodation when individual short-term gain comes into conflict with mutual long-term benefit. Each game has numerous variations depending upon the researcher's specific goals. The games can involve multiple participants in face-to-face interactions or one or more individuals interacting with a computer. A Swiss psychologist used the computer simulation of fishing in a large lake. For there to be a sustained yield of fish, players had to restrict their catch to an allowed quota (Mosler, 1993).

Role-playing Exercises

In addition to models and games, there are more open-ended forms of role-playing for simulation purposes. For example, physical handicaps and sensory deficits can be simulated by the non-disabled wearing blindfolds or moving about in wheelchairs. One would not want to draw conclusions about the experiential world of the impaired solely on the basis of college students using blindfolds or wheelchairs, but it might provide useful leads in the absence of better information and serve to sensitize the participants to overlooked aspects of the setting.

Simulations are particularly useful in situations where observation and experimentation are not feasible or ethical. For example, a furor was caused when it was found that jury deliberations in Chicago were being taped as part of a research project. Researchers now avoid controversy by recruiting volunteers to play the part of jurors in mock trials.

Role-playing exercises are used in intergroup research, where some people become minority group members for the duration of the experiment, or a class of students is randomly divided into two groups, the reds and the blues, and efforts made to see how they get along in situations likely to produce conflict.

Because of the freedom allowed the participants in their role-playing, the situation requires close monitoring to keep it from getting out of hand. A simulation develops its own pace and momentum. Unlike an experiment, it can very quickly move beyond the control of the researcher.

An artificial jail was created in the basement of Stanford University's psychology building with paid volunteers as prisoners and guards. The experience had tremendous emotional impact upon the participants. Students playing the guards became cold, aloof, and hostile. Those who became inmates were at first angry and rebellious but in the end became sullen, bitter, and emotionally burned out (Zimbardo & Musan, 1992).

Debriefing is an important part of role-playing exercises. After the simulation exercises are completed, the participants and the facilitator should discuss and reflect on what occurred and how they felt about the experience. The debriefing elaborates the lessons learned from the simulation for real-world application and is also important for dealing with the emotional after-effects of the experience. Simulations have many uses in teaching and clinical practice that will not be covered here.

General Comments

A good simulation should be realistic. When people are able to see out the corners of their blindfolds, the experience isn't like being blind. If the images on a videotape simulation are fuzzy and indistinct when people in ordinary life see things clearly, then viewer responses may not be valid. It is necessary to capture the significant elements of the setting or experience being studied. The realism of a game will depend on the validity of the issues raised and questions being asked. A successful simulation also requires cooperation from the participants. If they are not willing to "pretend," then their responses are not going to be useful in predicting actual behavior. To gauge realism, the results from the simulation can be compared with the behavior of people in the actual situation. For example, to what degree do people in a simulated jail act in the same way as genuine prisoners and guards? The latter information can be obtained from interviews with people in jail or from reading autobiographies of prisoners and guards. A second method is to question the respondents afterwards about their experiences. Did they feel like jail inmates and did the "guards" treat them as if they were?

Simulations vary in cost and complexity. They may be as modest as asking students in a class to imagine themselves participants in a United Nations conference or as complex as constructing a stationary space capsule in the basement of a NASA laboratory. While the mock-up of a spaceship and the detailed monitoring of people's responses cost thousands of dollars, an actual flight trial of a space ship would cost tens of millions. Because it depends heavily on the ability of participants to "fill in" omitted items through imagination, a simulation is less expensive than constructing the actual object.

Simulation procedures may come close to being full-fledged experiments. An experiment involves an artificial situation in which events that generally go together are separated. A simulation involves an artificial situation, such as a space capsule or wheelchair ride, whose components are left together. To the extent that the researcher attempts to separate items that occur naturally together, the simulation may become indistinguishable from the experiment. If non-handicapped students in wheelchairs are asked to perform specific tasks and then timed, the procedure would qualify as an experiment. However, if a person is asked to spend the entire day in a wheelchair and keep notes of everything that occurs, it seems more logical to call this a simulation.

Limitations

Two criticisms of simulations are that they are too realistic in some instances and not realistic enough in others. The imitation jail constructed in the basement of Stanford University's psychology building was extremely stressful for the participants. Even milder forms of role-playing can be upsetting. People become so identified with their roles that they say and do things they regret later. It is difficult to predict in advance how people will respond in a role-playing exercise and thus protect them from personal revelations or actions that may be harmful to them or upsetting to others. For example, when people take part in role-playing exercises, they reveal themselves in the presence of co-workers, friends, fellow students, supervisors, and others. When the mayor and the county air pollution officer play a city planning game, each has the opportunity to observe the other's performance, and if the mayor is in charge later on, this may have serious implications for the air pollution officer's job. Ethical problems of simulation exercises outweigh their usefulness as a research tool in many situations.

The second major criticism of simulations is that they are artificial and unrealistic. Playing games is not the same as real life. Board games such as chess and Monopoly are less a copy of actual conflict situations than another level of reality (i.e., game playing). The brief duration of play, the fixed rules, and the illusory quality of the rewards and penalties make the situation different from ordinary life.

Summary

Simulations are imitations of actual conditions, intended to resemble an actual situation without being mistaken for it. Compared to testing people's responses to actual situations, simulation is more economical and provides more control. Unlike an experiment, little attempt is made to untangle all the variables operating in a situation. Three types of simulations are environmental simulations, games, and role-playing exercises. Debriefing participants is important after the session. Simulations have been criticized as being too realistic and thereby stressful for the participants and of being too artificial and lacking relevance to the actual situation.

References

Crookall, D. (1995). A guide to the literature on simulation gaming. In D. Crookall & K. Arai (Eds.), *Simulation and gaming across disciplines and cultures: ISAGA at a watershed* (pp. 151–177). Thousand Oaks: Sage Publications.

Mosler, H.-J. (1993). Self-dissemination of environmentally-responsible behavior: The influence of trust in a commons dilemma game. *Journal of Environmental Psychology, 13*, 111–123.

Stamps, A. E. (1990). Use of photographs to simulate environments: A meta-analysis. *Perceptual & Motor Skills, 71*(3, Pt. 1), 907–913.

Sutherland, D. (1995). Cross-cultural communication, the internet, and simulation/gaming. In D. Crookall & K. Arai (Eds.), *Simulation and gaming across disciplines and cultures: ISAGA at a watershed* (pp. 89–100). Thousand Oaks. CA: Sage Publications.

Tart, C. T. (1990). Multiple personality, altered states and virtual reality: The world simulation process approach. *Dissociation: Progress in the Dissociative Disorders, 3*, 222–233.

Zimbardo, P. G., & Musan, K. (1992). *Quiet rage: The Stanford Prison Experiment* [videotape]. Stanford, CA: Stanford University.

Further Reading

Bell, R. C. (1990). *Board and table games from many civilizations*. Mineola, NY: Dover Publications.

Kalawsky, R. S. (1993). *The science of virtual reality and virtual environments: A technical, scientific and engineering reference on virtual environments*. Reading, MA: Addison-Wesley.

Savetz, K. M. (1994). Internet games. *Internet World, 5*, 29–33.

Simulation and Gaming: An International Journal. Thousand Oaks, CA: Sage Publications.

Van Ments, M. (1994). *The effective use of role-play: A handbook for teachers and trainers* (Rev. ed.). London: Kogan Page.

8 Interview

Face-to-face interviews provide an excellent way of exploring complex feelings and attitudes. The following interview was designed to explore the attitudes of truants and a matched sample of nontruants.

Question. What sorts of things do you like to do in your spare time?

Answer. I like to play football and go out with my friends. Whatever my friends like to do.

Q. Do you spend most of your time alone or with friends?

A. I hang out with a whole bunch of friends, mostly after school.

Q. Where do you and your friends usually like to go?

A. Sometimes we go to the Graduate to play video games. I don't know. . . . just find some place (seems shy and embarrassed at lack of words).

Q. What do you think about school?

A. I like it. It's better than doin' nuthin'. If it weren't for the homework, I'd like it better. I don't like my geography teacher. He's kind of senile.

For this project, there were several reasons why the interview was a better method than other techniques. If the researcher had tried to hand out questionnaires in class, many of the truants would not have been present. Second, an interview allows the researcher to pursue half-answered questions and to encourage more thorough and detailed responses. Finally, the face-to-face contact allows for observation of general appearance, overall health, personality, nonverbal behavior, and other individual characteristics.

There are times when interviews will produce more accurate information than other types of procedures that seem on the surface to be more rigorous and objective. Researchers found that interviews were more accurate in detecting alcoholism than were laboratory tests. The best of the laboratory tests used in the study detected only a third of those with serious alcohol problems while interview procedures detected 95 percent of them (Bernadt, Mumford, Taylor, Smith, & Murray, 1982).

Some biographers have come to a similar conclusion regarding the value of interviews relative to other forms of gathering information. Relying strictly on the written record can be hazardous. Documents may be incomplete or edited to remove sensitive material. The biographer of a famous American Secretary of State noted that "Almost every document regarding foreign policy in the . . . archives was written to mislead someone and, as a result, interviewing was essential" (Biographers' lunch, 1993, p. 41). The ideal situation is not to rely strictly on interviews or on any single source of information, but to combine information from different sources.

Interviews can provide a rich and fascinating source of research data. Their intrinsic interest stems from the personal interaction that is the core of the procedure. Modern technology has led to a broadening of the face-to-face concept to include interviews by telephone, video, and other extended means of communication. However, the key element of the interview is the verbal give-and-take between two people with the questions and answers providing its form. Another way of describing an interview is that it is a "conversation with a purpose" (Bingham & Moore, 1959).

It is surprising to discover all that people are willing to talk about. With encouragement and the recognition of genuine interest on the part of the interviewer, people will reveal a great deal about themselves and about their beliefs and feelings. In collecting case histories on sexual behavior, Alfred Kinsey and his associates appealed to the willingness of people to contribute information that would be of scientific value and of help to others (Pomeroy, 1963). The basic pitch was to altruism, but its mode varied for each group interviewed. Professional people responded when they recognized the social significance of the study. Less educated people responded positively when told simply that doctors needed their help in knowing more about these things. The researchers were also quick to show their appreciation and esteem for those who helped. The success of the studies of sexual behavior was due not only to the scholarly competence of the investigators but also to their recognition of the fundamental importance of the human interaction which occurs between the interviewer and the respondent.

Uses and Types of Interviews

The interview is particularly useful for the exploration of topics like truancy and sexual behavior, which are complex and emotionally loaded. Interviews are also useful in areas where opportunities for observation are limited. They can be used to assess beliefs and opinions as well as personality characteristics. A person's answers may reveal both manifest and latent content. *Manifest* content is that which is obvious and conveyed in the spoken information of the interview. It refers to what the person says. *Latent* content is the less obvious or more hidden information conveyed by hesitations and nonverbal responses, such as avoidance of eye contact, nervous gestures, or restlessness. Latent content indicates what the person means. The interviewer pays special attention when the latent content contradicts the manifest content. When interviews are recorded on videotape, the analysis of particular movements, gestures, and facial expressions, as well as changes in voice quality, hesitations ("um . . . you know . . ."), and pauses, provide a wealth of data for assessing the latent aspects of the communication. Such material may then be tabulated in a content analysis (see Chapter 11).

Interviews may focus on personality characteristics rather than on the content. One example is the *clinical interview*, an in-depth exploration of personality. These purposes may be combined. Social work interviews often serve the dual function of obtaining necessary factual information as well as gaining insight into a client's personality. Job interviews also combine these goals, where character as well as competence is evaluated. Newspaper and television interviews provide factual information but also give glimpses into the respondent's personality. In watching an interview with a famous writer or artist, most of us are as interested in what she is like as in what she says. Research interviews also provide this dual function. As we explore facts and opinions, we learn about the respondent as a person.

An interview gives people the opportunity to tell their stories in their own words. It can provide a release for pent-up feelings and can be empowering as it recognizes people as experts on their own experiences.

A further advantage of the interview is that people who may be unwilling or unable to write out a long, coherent answer are often willing to say it to an interviewer. Of course this may also become a disadvantage when the interviewer encounters a long-winded respondent who wanders off the subject and won't stop talking. In such cases, the interviewer needs to be firm but polite in guiding the respondent back to the point.

Unstructured Interviews

In an *unstructured* interview the main goals are to explore all the alternatives in order to pick up information, to define areas of importance that might not have been thought of ahead of time, and to allow the respondent to take the lead to a greater extent. The interviewer has a general topic in mind and may want to ask specific questions. However, there is no predetermined order or specified wording to the questions.

An unstructured interview leaves room for improvisation on the part of the researcher. Studying the use of the coca plant (the basis of cocaine) in Peru, a sensitive topic in discussions between locals and foreigners, Kirk and Miller (1985) were dissatisfied with the stereotyped replies they received. People were saying what they thought the interviewers wanted to hear. The interviewers became suspicious of the sameness of people's statements. As they put it, their measurement was too reliable! The discrepancy between what they were hearing and what they knew from other sources to be local practices compelled the interviewers to change their approach. To minimize the likelihood of stereotyped, consistent answers, the researchers decided to ask novel questions, such as "When do you give coca leaves to animals?" Or "How did you find out you didn't like coca?" These seemingly "silly" questions produced new and useful information. An unstructured interview is desirable as a preliminary step in developing a structured form for an interview or a written questionnaire, or may stand as part of a qualitative study.

The *depth* or *intensive* interview is a special form of unstructured interview. The interviewer follows the respondent's answers with a request for more information at an increasing level of depth. It is this process of using the respondent's answers to delve more deeply into the topic that gives the depth interview its name.

Example

Does your school operate on a semester or a quarter system?
How do you feel about that? (rather than "Do you like it") Why?
Could you be more specific?

As one line of questioning runs out, the direction is shifted.

Have you ever attended a school with a different calendar system?
How did that work?

or

Do you have friends at colleges with the (semester/quarter) system? What did they think about it?
What would you do if the current system at your school were changed?

In pursuing the topic, the tone of questions remains neutral, giving the respondent as much freedom as possible to express feelings on the topic.

It requires practice and sensitivity to know when to change direction. When a new topic emerges in the discussion, it is difficult to know whether to follow it and risk losing continuity or to stay on the major theme and risk the omission of additional information. The decision should rest on your assessment of the respondent and how much shifting of questions can be tolerated. Some people are easily confused and distracted by sudden shifts. Others become bored with a direct and obvious sequence. If the respondent begins answering questions before you ask them, consider picking up the pace and expanding the scope of your interview.

Structured Interviews

If information from a number of respondents is to be combined, as in an attitude survey or opinion poll, then a *structured* or *standardized* interview is desirable. The questions are formulated beforehand and asked in a set order and in a specified manner. The structure is provided to obtain consistency from one situation to the next. In survey research where hundreds of people are contacted by several different interviewers, structured formats are essential in getting information which can be combined. The Gallup and Harris polls utilize mostly structured interviews to make their projections of public opinion.

The questions may be open-ended, for example "What do you think about X?" and "Why do you feel that way?" Or respondents may be asked to select from a set of choices. Chapter 9 describes the technique for constructing clearly-worded items. The important point is that the same questions must be asked in the same manner for all respondents.

Semistructured Interviews

Sometimes it is necessary to design a *semi*structured interview where all respondents are asked the same questions, but the order in which they are asked differs from one person to the next. In some cases, even the manner in which they are asked varies, for example, changing the wording or sentence structure to better fit the respondent or the situation. This arrangement may be more suitable for obtaining in-depth information where the interviewer does not want to be restricted by a prescribed question order but would like the advantage of having asked the same questions of all respondents. Interviews with a cross-section of the population may require adaptation of wording and sentence structure to better fit the respondent's age or social background.

Using a semistructured interview, one loses the consistency provided by following the same procedure for all respondents. The further one moves from a structured procedure, the greater the risk of interviewer bias.

Telephone Interviews

Telephone interviewing has become more feasible due to various technological advances. There is random digit dialing which overcomes some sampling problems. There are statistics on telephone ownership and usage that can be used as a check on your sample of respondents (Frey, 1989). For researchers on a limited budget, there are special rates that have decreased the cost of long distance calls. A telephone survey of 100 households in a community is far more economical in time than door-to-door interviews. There are, however, problems unique to telephone interviewing, including households with no telephones or unlisted numbers, answering machines, bias in terms of who is likely to be home at certain times of the day, and the possibility of intrusion during mealtimes or other personal activities.

Despite these disadvantages, there are many situations in which telephone interviewing is the most feasible and economical approach. As an example, the student organization on our campus uses the telephone to survey student opinions on current issues, based on a random sample of telephone numbers from updated student directories. With the assistance of the Registrar's Office, special lists can be obtained for different categories of students, such as those living in the residence halls or off campus, undergraduate or graduate students, and so on. Telephone contact allows excellent sampling of students plus rapid turnover time. Using five or six interviewers, the student organization can obtain interviews from a random sample of 200 students in a few days. A mail survey would take longer and be more expensive. Possibilities of contact through e-mail are being explored.

How to Interview

Interview techniques are learned through a combination of practice and feedback. Practice with other people before doing the actual interviews. Such role playing will give you a chance to familiarize yourself with the procedures and provide an opportunity for feedback. Videotaping and watching a playback of yourself conducting an interview will be helpful in improving your skills. Also, watching skilled interviewers and evaluating their performance is instructive. If a group of you are planning to work on a project, practice on each other and evaluate each other's performance.

Deciding What to Ask

In many cases, the topic will not be a matter of choice but is determined instead by the demands of the situation. The interview process will be considerably simplified if you pick a topic with which most people are familiar. If your questions refer to rare experience or knowledge, you will spend a lot of time searching for people who know something about the topic. Another consideration is to select an

Interviewing children poses special problems. This interviewer felt that getting down to the child's own level increased rapport.

issue that is nonthreatening. Ethical considerations require care in interviewing about illegal or taboo subjects. The respondent should be protected from any possible harmful effects of the interview, for example, against court subpoena of interview records or publication of embarrassing information. Sensitive topics must be pursued sensitively. If they are not, the likelihood of a successful completion of the interview is markedly reduced.

A final consideration is to pick a topic you find interesting. Your interest or lack of interest is likely to be conveyed to the respondent. A ho-hum reaction on the part of an interviewer quickly extinguishes any enthusiasm a respondent might have about answering the questions.

Begin with the more general and more interesting questions. By starting in a general manner, you are less likely to inadvertently influence the answers. A specific question may establish a *set* (a tendency to respond in a particular way), that then influences subsequent answers. Remember, respondents tend to make judgments about what a questioner wants to hear. Starting with more general questions reduces the likelihood of this happening. The reason for beginning with interesting questions is fairly obvious—to engage the interest and attention of the respondent. Also, questions that might be more challenging or complicated are better asked early. The routine ones that require little thought can be placed at the end when fatigue is more likely—information covering name, birth date, place of birth, and so on. This procedure reduces some uncertainty because the respondent knows exactly what content will be associated with his or her identification.

Questions should follow one another in a logical order without abrupt changes in subject. If a change is necessary, a bridge statement from the interviewer eases the transition.

Examples

Now, to change the subject, are you in favor or opposed to _____ ?
Changing the subject, what do you think about _____ ?
The next few questions will deal with _____ .

Each subsection of the interview should contain questions that move from the general to the specific.

The first questions asked should determine whether or not the respondent has knowledge of the topic you wish to cover. *Don't assume anything.* A graduate student was once interviewing a young man hospitalized for a suicide attempt. The patient explained that he had quarreled with his lover and had then become despondent. After having already asked several questions which the respondent had willingly answered, the student asked, "How long had she been living with you?" The respondent said heatedly, "It's not a she, my lover is a man." There was an awkward pause as the graduate student readjusted his frame of reference. The interview continued, but there was a loss of rapport between interviewer and respondent.

Obtaining Permission

Before considering a household survey, you should find out if it is legal. In an effort to regulate the activities of door-to-door salespeople, many communities require a license for any sort of solicitation. Because this was designed for salespeople, it probably won't affect a legitimate research study. However, some unscrupulous salespeople use the "I'm doing a survey" approach to get a foot in the door. This has given survey research a bad name. To be on the safe side, you should check with the local police department before embarking on a community survey. The police like to know what is going on around the precinct in case they receive telephone inquiries. There are certain neighborhoods where researchers may require police protection. Under those circumstances, it would be wise to switch to another data-gathering technique or another neighborhood. Some projects send out interviewers in pairs, one of whom always waits outside while the interview is in progress.

The interviewer's task becomes easier when people expect them or at least know that the survey is being undertaken. Knocking on doors will provoke many refusals from people who are disinterested, suspicious, or afraid of strangers. An advance letter or phone call announcing that the interviewer is coming will be useful. Another helpful device is a leaflet placed in the mailbox or under doors the day before, announcing that the survey is being undertaken and explaining its goals. Having the sponsorship of a recognized community agency will make your work easier. Sometimes even government sponsorship may not be sufficient, as in this case of responses of Minnesota farmers toward interviewers from the United States Department of Agriculture:

> The farmer scowls. "I won't give you anything, I'm disgusted." The interviewer walks away empty handed. Later the farmer explains his reaction to a reporter. "When she says 'Department of Agriculture,' I see red."
>
> The interviewer is accustomed to such treatment, especially nowadays, with agriculture in a near depression and many farmers blaming Washington for much of what is wrong. Although the majority continue to discuss their business and plans with federal pollsters when asked, thousands refused, and not always politely. (Birnbaum, 1982, p. 1)

First impressions are important. Appropriate dress and grooming will reduce reluctance or suspicion. Make a clear and honest introduction, giving your name and institutional affiliation and an explanation of the purpose of the interview. Your manner and voice should be friendly, courteous, and nonthreatening. Overfamiliarity should be avoided. In explaining the purpose of the interview, be sure to give the person time to understand what you are saying. It may be the fortieth time you have rattled it off, but it will be the first time your potential respondent has heard it.

Example

Good afternoon. My name is Robin Jones and I represent the International Research Corporation. We are doing a household survey on transportation needs in the community. May I please ask you a few questions on this topic? The interview should take no more than 15 minutes of your time.

It may be difficult to obtain an unbiased sample in a household survey. Who is at home will vary by time of day. In the afternoon there will be a disproportionate number of homemakers, older people, and children. It is also difficult to interview people in a crowded household. Securing privacy is a problem, and there are the distractions of chores, children, telephones, and television.

Street Corner Interviews

To avoid the problems of a house-to-house survey, some researchers prefer to collect their interviews on street corners, in parks, shopping malls, and other public locations. Again, it is important to gain the permission of the agency or corporation that controls the space. Local authorities should be consulted about a street corner survey, and the management of a shopping mall regarding a survey conducted on its premises. Most of the time people are willing to oblige a worthwhile and legitimate project. However, some of them may have been burned by individuals or groups promoting political causes, religious concerns, or commercial projects in the guise of doing a survey. It may be helpful in gaining an interview if you can state factually that the management of the shopping center or the park department has agreed to let you do the survey. Such permission adds legitimacy to your study.

Stopping people walking on the sidewalk may not be as easy as it sounds. Many people are in a hurry and others have developed a tunnel vision for strangers. They simply won't see you as you approach. It is best to dress neatly and carry an obvious clipboard that conveys your purposes at a glance. If you are mistaken for a panhandler, then you are doing something wrong.

Choose a location where people can see you from a distance. That way you won't surprise them with your request. This will enable them to convey through their actions their own curiosity, willingness to help, or clear disinterest. The best sort of location is where people are seated or moving slowly. Interviewing office workers eating lunch in a courtyard outside their building will be easier than stopping them on the street as they leave the building after work. Your success rate will be higher if you pick people who are strolling or window shopping than those who are walking hurriedly toward an obvious destination. Don't try to stop people who are rushing to catch the 5:02 train or trying to get on a bus. If you can get permission from the manager, an airport where people spend hours with nothing to do is a fine place to conduct a survey. Parks, beaches, museums, and shopping areas are also good locations for interviews.

Ingenuity and a knowledge of the characteristics of the population to be studied contribute to the success of an interview. A team studying housing preferences in the Navajo nation was having difficulty obtaining information through conventional means. The Navajo had been surveyed so often with so few results that they were uninterested in answering questions. Knowing the Navajo interest in traveling about their territory, the research team gained much of its information from hitchhikers. They picked up and interviewed riders as they drove them to their destinations. Under these circumstances, people were very cooperative (Snyder, Stea, & Sadalla, 1976). Sometimes you have to be creative in approaching the people you want to interview (see Box 8–1).

Setting the Stage

A major consideration in putting another person at ease is to be at ease yourself. Role playing and practice interviews will increase your confidence. Respondents generally are more likely to be candid when they are convinced that their responses will be kept confidential and when they perceive that no moral evaluation of them is being made by the interviewer. This observation was borne out by the researchers in the Kinsey studies of human sexual behavior. Despite the extremely intimate

BOX 8-1. Creative Technique for Interviewing Bicyclists

The easiest way to find bicyclists, the research team decided, was to seek them out on the streets. A door-to-door survey would be unlikely to turn up more than a handful of dedicated riders. The first problem was to get the cyclists to stop long enough to be interviewed. The research team stationed themselves on a clear stretch of road frequently traveled by bicyclists. They placed a sign 100 feet ahead of them, "Bicycle survey ahead." This aroused the curiosity of most cyclists. The researchers carried obvious clipboards and had big signs across their chests that read "Bicycle survey". Most cyclists, alerted by the earlier notice and spotting the two sign-bedecked interviewers frantically waving their arms, pulled over, and answered the questions. The novelty of the approach proved successful in that situation. Undoubtedly, if the procedure were repeated many times, the novelty would wear off. How would you go about conducting a survey about the attitudes of motorcyclists? Would you use the same procedure as in the bicycle survey or would you have to do something different?

and sensitive nature of their questions, they obtained remarkable cooperation. The need for a nonjudgmental attitude and for assurances of confidentially cannot be overemphasized. Human beings are very good at detecting deceit. If the interviewer is making strong moral judgments, it will come across during the interview. Such feelings must be reduced prior to the interview. This may be accomplished by recognizing the legitimacy of other people's views. Another means of reducing the emotional intensity of feelings is through discussion, which may make a topic less sensitive. If your own feelings remain strong, perhaps another person should be found to do the interviews.

Find a place for the interview that is free from distraction and serves to maintain confidentiality. Your respondent is not likely to be candid within earshot of others. Also, telephone calls and other interruptions interfere with the respondent's train of thought. Be sure your own needs for a writing surface and a comfortable location for recording are taken care of before you start. Otherwise, you may have to interrupt the session and miss important information.

Nonverbal Aspects

A degree of eye contact is important in establishing rapport between interviewer and respondent. However, don't stare. An unbroken or penetrating gaze will make the respondent uncomfortable. On the other hand, the absence of eye contact makes you appear untrustworthy or uncomfortable. Again, the best preparation for interviews is practice and getting honest feedback from classmates, colleagues, or friends.

The rest of your face, as well as your eyes, communicates your feelings, particularly those of approval and disapproval. Respondents are very likely to pick up even flickers of feeling. Thus, it is very important for an interviewer to show an attentive but nonjudgmental interest. As most of us are not trained actors, we will probably perform best when asking questions that interest us but that do not arouse intense emotions. For emotionally-arousing questions, a considerable amount of practice is essential in desensitizing feelings.

While conducting practice interviews, notice the set of your mouth, your body posture, and your position in relation to the respondent. When do you lean forward? When do you lean back? What might these behaviors communicate? Also, pay attention to your hands. Do you tend to cover you mouth when asking a question? The latent message of that movement is that you don't really want to ask it. Just as videotapes are widely used in training psychotherapists, so are they of value in providing feedback for research interviews. Observe the professional interviewers on television. Notice the effects of their behavior upon the respondents, and vice versa.

The quality of the interview data rests on the interaction between interviewer and respondent. Good questions can be ruined by improper techniques. Poor questions may be salvaged by a good interviewer. Remember, the purpose of an interview is to obtain information about another person's beliefs, opinions, feelings, or attitudes. Responding to the person's answers in a positive way is essential. One need not be vigorous in approval, but rather, through an occasional nod or eye contact, indicate attention and respect for the views expressed.

Interviewing people of different ethnic background, nationality, or social class brings special problems of nonverbal communication. In some cultures, for example, avoidance of eye contact is a sign of respect rather than an indication of untrustworthiness. Physical distance between interviewer and respondent has different meanings for persons of different backgrounds. Northern Europeans and Anglo-Americans often become uncomfortable within the close range quite acceptable for those of Latin background (Hall, 1959). Familiarity with the slang expressions of another social stratum may be necessary. A respondent will soon lose interest if the interviewer can't understand what is being said; for example, probing the drug culture requires knowledge of the various terms used for the drugs and persons associated with them.

Characteristics of race and sex as well as social class can affect the interview. However, the heart of the issue is the degree to which these characteristics will detract from obtaining candid responses. Persons of the same social or ethnic background also introduce a bias of conformity to expected attitudes. The quality of the interview depends more on the interviewer's capacity to convince the respondent of a nonjudgmental attitude and a sincere interest in and respect for the respondent's point of view than upon the specific characteristics of race, sex, or class. However, in some situations, these characteristics may be particularly influential and require a matching or deliberate contrasting of interviewer and respondent characteristics.

Pacing and Timing

A major mistake of beginning interviewers is the failure to allow enough time for the respondent to answer. The interviewer, especially after having formulated the questions, becomes very familiar with the outline and may forget that it is totally new to the respondent. A person needs time to think about each question and to prepare an answer. The interviewer must learn to be comfortable with long silences, yet recognize the point at which the silence is no longer productive and is making the respondent uncomfortable. If an answer is not forthcoming, a reformulation of the question may be appropriate. Sometimes the discomfort caused by silence may be used to the interviewer's advantage. It may lead the respondent to be more self-revealing than he or she originally intended.

To practice how to tolerate delay, look at a watch or clock with a second hand and observe the passage of 30 seconds. As silence, it may seem a conspicuously long period of time. Yet, while attempting to formulate an answer to a complicated or controversial question, 30 seconds is hardly time at all. The main point is for you to become less self-conscious about silence.

The interview should not be allowed to drag. When the respondent has finished answering a question, move on to the next. Otherwise, boredom, irritability at the interviewer's unpreparedness, or rambling into irrelevant comments may ensue. The interview should move at a pace that is rapid enough to retain interest but slow enough to allow adequate coverage of the topic.

Probes

When a respondent gives an unclear or incomplete answer, it is necessary to probe for additional information. A *probe* is a question or comment designed to keep the person talking or to obtain clarification. If the respondent does not seem to understand the question or strays from the topic, it may be sufficient to repeat the question. If that does not work, or if only a partial response is given, other probes are necessary. An expectant pause accompanied by the usual facial expressions of waiting, or repeating the respondent's reply followed by a pause, should draw added comment. Failing that, use neutral questions or comments or simply ask for further clarification.

Examples of probes

Anything else?
Could you tell me more of your ideas on that?
What do you mean?

It is very important that probing questions or comments not bias the response. They should not direct a person to a particular answer.

Recording the Information

The extent to which notes should reflect exactly what was said depends on how the interview will be used. When the information is the final source of data, a precise transcript is essential. This is accomplished by recording the respondent's replies exactly as spoken. These *verbatim* transcripts would include ungrammatical statements, requests for more information, and so on. Verbatim recording from speech requires a rapid notation system in order to avoid the respondent's losing interest. On the positive side, it is flattering to have someone write down one's statement in detail, even though some delays and interruptions occur.

Tape or video recording increases the accuracy of the information and also permits analysis of hesitation phenomena, the various "ahems" and "ahs" and "ers" made by the respondent. However, transcription is a long process, taking four or five times the amount of time spent in the interview itself. Many respondents are made uncomfortable by the presence of a recorder, and confidentiality may be compromised.

Depending on the purpose of the interview, it may not be necessary to produce a verbatim transcript of the interview. Instead the interviewer can *paraphrase*—a paraphrase is the interviewer's impression of what the respondent meant. Phrases that are irrelevant, unnecessary, or ungrammatical are omitted. For example, in response to the question, "What is your opinion of the President's handling of the budget?"

> *Verbatim* statement: "I think . . . umm . . . that he is . . . well . . . doing the best he can. They are good . . . they are trying hard. It is not easy to be in the White House for any one."
>
> Interviewer's *paraphrase*: The President is doing a good job.

Slips of the tongue, pauses, and defensive gestures that would be very important in a clinical interview probably won't be worth recording if the responses are going to be put into categories of agree/disagree or satisfied/dissatisfied. The task of classifying answers into fixed categories is called *coding*. This task becomes more time consuming when the coder must wade through a lot of irrelevant detail.

Extensive paraphrasing by an inexperienced interviewer is risky. It is better to write down more, rather than less, detail. What is irrelevant can be ignored at the time of coding. When dealing with groups of people who have a special way of expressing things, such as adolescents or professional engineers, there is value in recording some statements exactly as they are said. Instead of talking about adolescents' attitudes toward adults, the researcher can express their attitudes in the teens' own words. For example, "bad man" may be a term of respect. Direct quotations can be used to make a report more readable.

Various shorthand codes can be used when replies are lengthy. A self-developed notation may be adequate if notes are reviewed immediately following the interview, with scribbles and shorthand terms correctly spelled out while the conversation is fresh in mind. A common convention is the use of a hash mark (/) to indicate where a probe has been made.

Example

> Question: What do you think about forced retirement at age 65?
>
> Answer: Well, it is probably a good idea in general, but then for some people not so good. / Well because some people are still pretty sharp and have a lot of experience to offer. / Like judges and politicians, things like that.

Other conventional marks may be adopted in an interview project. The University of Michigan Survey Research Center (1976) uses a standardized set of abbreviations for probes (see Table 8–1).

In their ground-breaking research on human sexuality, Kinsey and his associates developed a very elaborate code system that required 3 months to learn and 6 months to practice with ease. No written words were used, only mathematical signs and numbers. These coded data have never been transcribed into a longhand or typewritten account. The coding during the actual interview served several functions. It enabled the interviewer to record all pertinent data without slowing up the interviewing and risking loss of rapport. It preserved the confidence of the record since the code has never been publicly explained. It facilitated the transfer of the data from the original interview notes to statistical analysis. If a written record had been used, then the data would have required coding anyway. Thus an intervening step was omitted by coding the information as it came from the respondent.

Minimizing Sources of Error

In interviews, as in social conversation, people try to avoid saying things that will offend others. These are called *socially-desirable responses*—statements that fit social norms or are modified according to what the respondent thinks the interviewer wants to hear. It is very important in conducting interviews to convey to the respondent that you want them to state their opinions openly and that their statements will be treated confidentially.

Respondents may over-estimate their abilities and under-estimate their limitations. A survey of a million high school seniors found that 70% reported themselves to be above average in leadership ability and only 2% reported that they were below average (Gilovich, 1991). Tendencies toward socially-desirable responses or exaggeration can be reduced by making the questions specific and de-

TABLE 8–1. Codes Used by the University of Michigan Survey Research Center

Interviewer's probe	Code
Repeat question	RQ
Anything else?	AE or Else?
Any other reason?	AO?
How do you mean?	How mean?
Could you tell me more about your thinking on that?	Tell more
Would you tell me what you have in mind?	What in mind?
What do you mean?	What mean?
Why do you feel that way?	Why?
Which would be closer to the way you feel?	Which closer?

tailed. Instead of asking whether students' leadership skills are above or below average, they can be asked how often they have served as officers in an organization, organized a club or group, become captain of a team, or been elected to some
position.

In some cases, there is value in having two interviewers present. This has the
advantage of a built-in reliability check in that there are two people to record and
remember what took place. It also permits more detailed note-taking as one person can write down answers while the other asks questions.

Tact and Diplomacy

You must learn when to probe and when to end a sequence of questions. This is
particularly important in the less structured situations. Depending on format or
procedural constraints, an interviewer may choose to vary the order or phrasing of
the questions, adapting them to the situation and mood of the respondent. Another
aspect requiring tact is to recognize when a respondent is being untruthful or wandering off the subject. A direct indication of mistrust on the interviewer's part may
terminate the interview. On the other hand, false information is of little value unless its assessment is a purpose of the interview. There are no simple guidelines
for dealing with these problems. If you are working in an area where misinfor-
mation or irrelevancies are likely to crop up, then you should plan beforehand how
you will deal with them.

Some topics may be too "hot" for an interview study. When passions are in-
flamed, it is difficult to get people to answer questions in a rational manner. There
can be expressions of anger and hostility. People are likely to break off the interview, to change questions or ignore them. During an interview, if the respondent
becomes tense or hostile, it may be desirable to terminate the session, either per-
manently or until another time. People occasionally take out their resentment about
an issue on the interviewer. Because of the number of violent confrontations that
occur during questioning, police in several cities have switched to bulletproof clipboards. You will probably not need to consider such extreme measures, but you
should be alert to the possibility and, over time, the inevitability of someone becoming upset and angry. When this happens, soothe the respondent's feelings and
end the interview politely and quickly.

Ending the Interview

At the outset, tell the respondent how long the interview will last and stick as close
to that limit as possible. If it is a paid interview, the means and time of payment
should be explained. On completion, express appreciation for the person's time
and effort. The respondent should be encouraged to ask any questions about the
research, and should be told how the results will be used, and where and when
they will be available.

Example of a closing sequence of comments

Thank you very much for your time and effort. Is there anything you would like to add to the interview? (pause) The results of our survey will be sent to the State Department of Transportation. You will receive a check for $5.00 in the mail in about 2 weeks. If there is any problem, please telephone. You have my card. Do you have any further questions about the survey? (pause) Thank you again. Goodbye.

The ethics of research require as much feedback as possible to the respondents about the nature, purposes, and intent of the project. Common courtesy requires acknowledgment of the value of a person's time and effort.

Analyzing the Results

Keep your survey data in a safe place. The unspoken fear of researchers is graphically depicted in a newspaper report of an apartment house fire:

Alan Rosin, who had lived in one of the buildings for 14 years, had just completed a political poll. Now, the damp and partially burned surveys containing 1,352 interviews lay in a mound of debris on the sidewalk. "All the (data) were in my apartment. Now they are all over the street," he lamented. (Lambert, 1984)

When the interview is the primary source of research data, it becomes necessary to devise systematic ways of summarizing information. The first step is generally to provide for transcription and quantification. Transcription refers to putting the responses into clear form for data analysis, such as transcribing answers from a tape recorder to typed copy or a computer record, and recopying handwritten notes that contain symbols and abbreviations. Quantification means tabulating the results in numerical form.

Coding

Coding is the process by which lengthy answers are reduced and sorted into specific response categories. The easiest items to code are categorical characteristics, such as sex, age group, and religion. These are categorical in that a person clearly belongs in one or another category (e.g., male, below age 25, and Catholic).

Example

Question: When in your life did you decide upon your present career?
Coding categories:
1 = Childhood (10 yrs. or under)
2 = Adolescence (11 through 17 yrs.)
3 = Young adulthood (18 through 24 yrs.)
4 = Later years (25 yrs. or older)
5 = Still undecided about career

Note that the numbers used for the categories (e.g., 4 = Later years) reflect a *nominal* level of measurement in that they are labels only, and do not provide quantitative information (see Chapter 10).

It is very important to keep a record (in duplicate) of the coding numbers used. Your data summary won't make sense if you have 354 cases of code 6 under religion and cannot remember whether these are Catholics or Protestants.

The coding process becomes more complicated for complex answers. Box 8–2 illustrates the coding process for an item taken from college students' recollections of their experiences of puberty. Another example of coding can be found in Chapter 11.

Reporting Interview Results

The most clear and significant results should be described first. Areas of less agreement and importance come next. Trivial or irrelevant findings should be ignored, or placed in an appendix. You are not bound to the interview format when presenting the results. It is not necessary to give the answers to question 1 first, then question 2, and so on. The order in which information is presented to a reader or an audience usually is different than that of the original interviews. At this point, importance or consistency of the findings determines order.

Indicate the number of people contacted, the number of refusals, replies that had to be discarded for one reason or another, and the final number of respondents. Discuss the means by which people were contacted, the dates, time of day, and something about the training and background of the interviewers.

Remember to safeguard the identity of your respondents. This can be done through the use of code names rather than real names and the removal of statements that contain identifying information not essential to the reader's understanding of the study.

Limitations

What people say is not always what they do. The information obtained in interviews is limited to the spoken content and to inferences made by the interviewer. The data are highly subject to bias introduced by the human interaction of the interview process. Interviewers may unintentionally encourage or discourage the expression of particular facts and opinions. Although no research method is absolutely free of interpretation, the interview is more open to bias than most other research methods. However, this is not to say that bias is inevitable; rather, to warn that great care in constructing the question format and in training interviewers is essential if valid information is to be gained. The necessary care may be costly. The need for training, coupled with the time-consuming aspects of the interview itself, creates an economic disadvantage. A written questionnaire distributed to a hundred people takes a small fraction of the time required for individual interviews. The coding of the open-ended questions used in interviews is time-consuming and

BOX 8–2. Coding Open-ended Responses

A. Skim the responses and generate a set of categories into which they can be classified. The following categories were constructed from the answers to the question: "What social changes or events did you, at the time, associate with puberty?"

1. Interest in other sex; social activity with other sex—dances, dating, parties, going steady.
2. Increased independence and/or responsibility.
3. Self-consciousness; attention to appearance.
4. Need for social acceptance, seeking friendship, joining clubs and organizations.
5. Withdrawal from family, problems in communication with family.
6. Increased social sensitivity (i.e., awareness of cliques, feeling social pressure, conformity concerns).
7. Other (if too many of the responses fall into "other," you need to make up additional categories).
8. No changes, or can't recall.

B. Check reliability. Give another person the description of the coding categories. Independently score a sufficient number of interviews to test the reliability of the categories. If the rate of agreement is less than 90%, revise your coding categories and check reliability on a new set.

C. In this example some responses fall in more than one category. In other cases the researcher may be able to assign responses to one category only. The choice between multiple categories or mutually-exclusive ones will depend on the type of questions and answers.

Code #	*Male respondents*
6,4	More aggressive, needed to prove self and to be accepted.
1,5	Increased social activity, less interaction with parents and family.
3,1	Shy, withdrawn. Girl friends—or at least I tried!!!

	Female respondents
5,4	Trouble communicating with family, turned more to friends.
8	Not much.
1,6	Dances, relationships with guys more than girls, pressure to conform, and I began a relationship with a guy when I was not really ready.

D. The coded responses can now be quantified and shown on a table in descending order of mention.

Number of females and males mentioning each category

Code #	Coding category	Female (n = 14)*	Male (n = 14)*
1.	Interest in other sex	4	5
4.	Social acceptance	2	3
3.	Self-consciousness	3	1
6.	Social sensitivity	3	1
2.	Independence/responsibility	1	1
5.	Withdrawal from family	1	1
7.	Other	0	1
8.	No changes, can't recall	2	1

*n refers to the number of respondents in each sample.

also expensive. Results from more than one interviewer may not be combined unless each has proceeded in the same manner.

Focus Groups

A *focus group* is a type of group interview designed to explore what a specific set of people (such as teenagers, senior citizens, or police) think and feel about a topic. Focus groups are useful for clarifying the meaning of images, words, or products, and locating points of concern, disagreement, or ambiguity. A trained moderator asks questions and facilitates discussion. A second observer may serve as a recorder. Group size ranges from eight to twelve people—small enough to permit genuine discussion, but large enough so that a single person is unlikely to dominate, and not so large as to inhibit participation. The use of focus groups was pioneered in the 1940s by sociologists at Columbia University. The focus group has been an important research tool in marketing, advertising, politics, and communications.

Commercial firms routinely use focus groups in developing and designing new products. What do consumers like and dislike about existing items? Do they feel they have sufficient choice? What product needs are currently not being addressed? What would consumers like to see if they could design products themselves? These and many other questions can be discussed in an *exploratory* focus group. At a later stage in product development focus groups can be *confirmatory* in observing people's responses to items that have not yet been marketed. People can be shown and asked to try out and discuss their responses to models in various sizes or styles. They can describe how they might use the product, when and where it would be appropriate, and select the best name. A company that produced a genetically-engineered tomato tested brand names in focus groups and settled on the name of the farmer from a well-loved children's story in the belief that it would produce a positive response from consumers.

In political campaigns, focus groups can be used in an exploratory manner to learn what issues are important to voters. They can also be confirmatory in finding out the responses of people to slogans and advertisements. Public efforts to change behavior, such as health promotion or reducing litter, utilize focus groups to test messages and images. Do they address the targeted group? Does the message make the point? Will the slogans catch on? The Center for Substance Abuse Prevention has published a brief bulletin on managing focus groups (CSAP Communications Team, 1994). They recommend using them at various stages in a prevention program—for learning about the audience, testing campaign themes and images, and for measuring the appropriateness and effectiveness of materials.

Focus group sessions generally last from 1.5 to 2.5 hours to allow full exploration of the topic. In order to establish a good relationship with the participants, the moderator must be a skilled interviewer with knowledge of group processes. The moderator should maintain a neutral attitude concerning opinions expressed and should respond positively to comments. It is necessary to keep the discussion on track and prevent any person from dominating. All this must be done with tact and diplomacy. Organizers often provide light refreshments.

It may be useful to record the session for subsequent analysis, requiring a room with audio or video potential. Research ethics require that participants give their consent to any observation or recording. It is common practice to offer light refreshments and payment as an incentive to participation.

Strengths and Limitations

Focus groups can produce stimulating discussions that reveal perceptions and concerns that might go undetected in a survey. They are more efficient than individual interviews (more people are contacted at a single time), although there can be a problem of social pressure influencing responses. A good moderator actively encourages all the participants to express their opinions, but people may be reluctant to make statements that go against the majority view.

The depth and variety of responses in a focus group session has its disadvantages in that the proceedings may be difficult to summarize. Complex issues cannot be explored with individuals to the same degree that it is possible in an interview.

The use of focus groups can supplement other methods. For example, a survey on a topic can obtain the opinions of a random sample of the community. Adding focus groups would provide depth to the answers, helping to explain why people answered the survey questions as they did. The focus group is an excellent method for exploring opinions in depth, but for generalizable information, they cannot substitute for a survey using a representative sample of the target population.

Summary

The key element of an interview is the verbal give-and-take between interviewer and respondents. Interviews are particularly useful for exploring complex and emotionally-arousing topics. Interviews can be used to explore beliefs, opinions, and personality characteristics. In a *structured* interview, questions are formulated beforehand and asked in a set order in a specified manner. In an *unstructured* interview, the interviewer has in mind a general topic but not set questions or a predetermined order to the questions. In a *depth* or *intensive* interview, the interviewer follows the respondent's answers with a request for more information at an increasing level of depth. Interview techniques are learned best through practice combined with feedback. Responses can either be recorded verbatim or paraphrased. The classification of the respondent's answers into categories is called *coding*. The results of an interview study are presented in order of importance rather than in order of the questions asked.

Focus groups are a type of group interview in which people's feelings or opinions about a specific topic are explored in depth. It is important to have a skilled moderator. The discussion may be exploratory (generating ideas) or confirmatory (testing out concepts and images).

Compared to questionnaires, the interview is time consuming and expensive. The responses are subject to bias introduced by the human interaction during the interview process. Respondents may give socially-desirable responses that do not truly reflect their opinions.

References

Bernadt, M. W., Mumford, J., Taylor, C., Smith, B., & Murray, R. M. (1982, February 6). Comparison of questionnaire and laboratory tests in the detection of excessive drinking and alcoholism. *The Lancet, 8267,* 325–326.

Bingham, W. V. D., & Moore, B. V. (1959). *How to interview* (4th ed.). New York: Harper.

Biographers' Lunch. (1993, March 29). *The New Yorker, 69,* 40–41.

Birnbaum, J. H. (1982, December 22). Farmers need savvy, as do agents who ask them for data: For U.S. to forecast a crop, 'enumerators' must get farmers to talk about it. *Wall Street Journal,* p. 1.

CSAP Communications Team. (1994). *You can manage focus groups effectively for maximum impact.* (Technical Assistance Bulletin). National Clearinghouse for Alcohol and Drug Information, P.O Box 2345, Rockville, MD 20852.

Frey, J. H. (1989). *Survey research by telephone* (2nd ed.). Beverly Hills, CA: Sage Publications.

Gilovich, T. (1991). *How we know what isn't so: The fallibility of human reason in everyday life.* New York: Free Press.

Hall, E. T. (1959). *The silent language.* Garden City, NY: Doubleday.

Kirk, J., & Miller, M. L. (1986). *Reliability and validity in qualitative research.* Beverly Hills, CA: Sage Publications.

Lambert, M. (1984, October, 8). Apartment fire leaves only sorrow. *Sacramento Bee,* p. B1.

Pomeroy, W. B. (1963). Human sexual behavior. In N. L. Farberow (Ed.), *Taboo topics* (pp. 22–32). New York: Atherton Press.

Snyder, P. Z., Stea, D., & Sadalla, E. K. (1976). Socio-cultural modifications and user needs in Navajo housing. *Journal of Architectural Research, 5,* 4–9.

University of Michigan. Survey Research Center. (1976). *Interviewer's manual* (Rev. ed.). Ann Arbor: Institute for Social Research, University of Michigan.

Further Reading

Fink, A. (1995). *How to analyze survey data.* Thousand Oaks, CA: Sage Publications.

Fink, A. (1995). *How to ask survey questions.* Thousand Oaks, CA: Sage Publications.

Fink, A. (1995). *How to report on surveys.* Thousand Oaks, CA: Sage Publications.

Fowler, F. J. (1995). *Improving survey questions: Design and evaluation.* Thousand Oaks, CA: Sage Publications.

Frey, J. H., & Oishi, S. M. (1995). *How to conduct interviews by telephone and in person.* Thousand Oaks, CA: Sage Publications.

Gordon, R. L. (1992). *Basic interviewing skills.* Itasca, IL: Peacock.

Ives, E. D. (1995). *The tape-recorded interview: A manual for field workers in folklore and oral history* (2nd ed.). Knoxville: University of Tennessee Press.

Krueger, R. A. (1994). *Focus groups: A practical guide for applied research* (2nd ed.). Thousand Oaks, CA: Sage Publications.

Lavrakas, P. J. (1993). *Telephone survey methods: Sampling, selection, and supervision* (2nd ed.). Newbury Park, CA: Sage Publications.

Vaughn, S., Schumm, J. S., & Sinagub, J. M. (1996). *Focus group interviews in education and psychology.* Thousand Oaks, CA: Sage Publications.

9 The Questionnaire

Sir Francis Galton, a nineteenth-century versatile English genius, was fond of measuring things. Among his other interests, he explored visual imagery. Galton presented people with a list of written questions about their ability to picture breakfast that morning. Was the image dim or clear? Was it in color or black and white? Were the colors distinct and natural? This was one of the first uses of the questionnaire in psychological research. Respondents were asked to rate the vividness of their images along a scale from 0 (no image at all) to 100 (clear and distinct as the original).

Galton found that artists reported better imagery than scientists. Some scientists, in fact, doubted that imagery existed. They felt that the expression "seeing in the mind's eye" was only a figure of speech and that the very notion of mental pictures was fanciful. Galton discovered not only important differences in the way people think but also the value of the questionnaire as an instrument for studying behavior that could not be observed or experimented on directly (Galton, 1907).

A *questionnaire* is a series of written questions on a topic about which the respondent's opinions are sought. It is a frequently-used tool in *survey research*—the systematic gathering of information about people's beliefs, attitudes, values, and behavior. A self-administered questionnaire is very efficient in time and effort. For example, copies of a questionnaire can be distributed to 100 employees, filled out by them, and collected within an hour's time. Conducting 100 individual interviews would be much more arduous and time consuming. However, a self-administered questionnaire requires clear instructions and a very careful wording of items. The most difficult aspects of a questionnaire are its construction and the interpretation of the results. Distributing and scoring a well-constructed questionnaire are usually easy (although the amount of data to be processed can be extensive). Overall, it is difficult to surpass a questionnaire for economy. That is why it is such a popular and widely used research tool.

Questionnaire Construction

There are two general aspects to every questionnaire: content and format. The *content* of a questionnaire refers to the subject matter. The *format* pertains to its structure and appearance—how the items are worded, their appearance on the page, and the form used for answering the questions.

Content

In general, it is best to restrict a questionnaire to a single issue. If you want to find out what college students think about the cafeteria, stay with that topic. Don't ask about teaching methods or the adequacy of the library. If others are interested in these topics, let them do another survey. It will be easy for students sitting in the cafeteria to see the relevance of questions about the food and service.

Is yours the first survey on this issue? Sometimes a beginning researcher is halfway through a survey before discovering that someone else studied the same topic a year earlier. The cafeteria manager or a long-term employee may be a good source of information on this. It is surprising how many surveys are finished, filed, and forgotten. You can save considerable time and effort if the previous survey developed suitable questions. You can always add new questions, but try to include some of the old ones. Wherever possible, retain the same wording. If the previous questionnaire asked whether the employees were "helpful," don't change the word to "courteous" even though you believe this means the same thing. Even a slight change in wording can invalidate the comparison between answers from two surveys.

Assuming you are going to construct your own questionnaire, you will start by using two other methods: casual observation and interview. The purpose of casual observation is to learn the *range of activities* about which questions must be asked. You need to know what goes on in order to ask questions about it. This requires brief inspection rather than systematic observation with detailed categories. Interviews should accompany the observations to learn the range of opinions students hold regarding the food. At this stage, a loose, open-ended interview is preferable. This will avoid suggesting answers to people. Replies will be used primarily to find out which topics should be included in the questionnaire. The following brief list of questions would probably be appropriate for a casual interview on this topic:

Hello, my name is _____ . The Campus Planning Committee is doing a survey of student attitudes about the cafeteria. I would like to ask you a few questions. This will only take a few minutes. Your answers will help us improve food service on campus.

1. What do you think of the food here?
2. What do you like most about it?
3. What do you like least about it?
4. What do you think about the service and facilities?
5. Is there anything else you would like to say about the food or the service?

These general questions would not be sufficient for a formal interview. However, the purpose is not to use the answers as primary data but only to learn what questions should be asked on the questionnaire.

Format

Open-ended and Closed Questions

There are two major categories of questions: open-ended and closed. With *open-ended questions*, the respondents write in their own answers:

Example

What do you like most about this cafeteria?
What do you like least about this cafeteria?

Closed questions, also known as *multiple-choice questions,* ask the respondent to choose among alternatives provided by the researcher.

Example

What do you think of the salads here?
(like) (dislike) (indifferent) (cannot rate)

What do you think of the cost of the meals here?
(expensive) (inexpensive) (about right) (cannot rate)

An open-ended format is desirable (1) when the researcher does not know all the possible answers to a question; (2) when the range of possible answers is so large that the question would become unwieldy in multiple-choice format; (3) when the researcher wants to avoid suggesting answers to the respondent; and (4) when the researcher wants answers in the respondent's own words. Multiple-choice (closed) answers are desirable (1) when there is a large number of respondents and questions; (2) when the answers are to be scored by machine; and (3) when responses from several groups are to be compared.

The beginning researcher often prefers open-ended questions because they allow respondents more freedom to answer as they please. This infatuation with open-ended questions tends to be short-lived. Once the researcher attempts to compare one person's answers with another's, and the replies from one group with those from another group, the disadvantages of open-ended questions quickly become apparent. People tend to ramble in their answers to open-ended questions. It is therefore necessary for the researcher to read lengthy statements in order to pick out the respondent's intent or meaning. Often it shows more respect for people's opinions to let them classify their answers themselves as positive, negative, or neutral than for the researcher to do this for them.

Salience refers to the importance of an issue in people's minds. Open-ended questions are very useful for determining the salience of opinions. It is generally assumed that in answering an open-ended question, those items that stand out in a person's mind will be mentioned first. Another method for determining salience is to ask respondents to *rank* a list of items in terms of importance. This can be done using either an open-ended or a closed format.

Example (open ended)

List those qualifications you would look for in hiring a secretary. Place a 1 next to the most important qualification, a 2 next to the second most important, and so on, until all qualifications on your list are ranked.

Example (closed)

Rank each of the following qualifications in terms of its importance for a secretary in your office (1 = most important).
____ General clerical skills
____ Computer skills
____ Word processing speed
____ Telephone answering skills
____ Meeting the public
____ Other (please specify)

Ranking versus Rating

Rank-order questions tend to confuse many respondents. They are also more difficult to analyze. Some people will list only their top choices or use check marks instead of numbers. Others interpret the scales in the wrong direction, using 5 for the most important skill and 1 for the least important skill, even though the instructions say the opposite. Other people will list two number 3s and omit number 4 entirely. The larger the number of items to be ranked and the more complicated the format, the more mistakes will be made. With more than 10 items, rating is more efficient than ranking. Sometimes a combination of rating and ranking can be used.

Example

Rate each of the following qualifications in terms of its importance for a secretary in your office. Please use the following scale:
1. Very important
2. Moderately important
3. Slightly important
4. Not at all important
_____ General clerical skills
_____ Computer skills
_____ Meeting the public
(etc.)
Now place a check next to the single most important qualification and two checks next to the second most important qualification.

Matrix Questions

Arranging the items and answers in a matrix is very efficient. Answer headings are placed across the top, and items to be rated down the side, as illustrated in this example:

For each statement below, please indicate whether you Strongly Agree (SA), Agree (A), are Undecided (U), Disagree (D), or Strongly Disagree (SD).

	SA	A	U	D	SD
The food in the cafeteria is well prepared.	( )	( )	( )	( )	( )
Lines are too long.	( )	( )	( )	( )	( )
Table arrangements encourage conversation.	( )	( )	( )	( )	( )

The degree of detail desired by the researcher determines the number of response categories. If earlier interviews revealed that the students either strongly liked or strongly disliked the cafeteria food, there would not be much point in using 10 categories. Because the students do not expect the cafeteria to be the equal of a fine restaurant, there is little reason to include an "excellent" category. Three terms would probably be sufficient: "good," "ok," and "poor." Those terms will take up little space, will be easily understood by the respondents, and will serve to distinguish between positive, neutral, and negative opinions. In other situations where a finer differentiation of opinion is required, 5 or 7 categories can be used.

Examples

Excellent, good, satisfactory, poor, terrible
Strongly agree, moderately agree, slightly agree, undecided, slightly disagree, moderately disagree, strongly disagree

Measuring the Middle Position

The middle position in a rating scale uses terms like "neutral" or "undecided." It isn't always clear what is meant when a respondent checks the middle category. Sometimes it means a balance between positive and negative feelings on the issue; other times it means a lack of interest or knowledge on the topic. Some investigators eliminate the middle position, creating a forced-choice item where the respondent must agree or disagree, or take some kind of a stand. Having a middle category will decrease the number expressing a clear opinion at one end or the other. Not surprisingly, middle category responses occur more often when people don't have strong feelings on the issues (Schuman & Presser, 1981). Although it is possible that people who actually have an opinion might use the middle ground, others may, in fact, feel neutral about an issue. We favor providing the middle alternative in order to avoid forcing a false appearance of opinion one way or the other, and out of respect for the respondent's right to neutral feelings. Several students interviewed in the cafeteria expressed these types of opinions.

> The food's okay, I guess.
> What do you expect of cafeteria food?
> It's better than what you get at Jack-in-the-Box.

A neutral category seems appropriate for vague opinions like these. Some terms useful for the middle category are: "neutral," "undecided," "neither good nor bad," "satisfactory," "OK." Often it is helpful to include the additional response category "not applicable (NA)" for questions that are not relevant. Students who never eat a particular food item may feel more comfortable checking NA than saying that it is neither good nor bad.

Example

> What do you think of the desserts served here?
> Good OK Poor NA

Combining Question Types

Following the chapter on multimethod approach, it will come as no surprise that the authors recommend a combination of closed and open-ended items, ratings, and ranks, rather then relying on a single type of item. The customary procedure is to use open-ended, general questions at the beginning of a questionnaire, followed by more specific, multiple-choice rated and ranked items. Coupling several types of items provides checks on each. In a survey designed to learn student attitudes toward library reading areas, students were first asked an open-ended question, "What do you like most about the library reading areas?" The most common response was the quiet in the library compared to the student's dormitory room or apartment. Later, students were asked to rate specific aspects of the library environment as "excellent," "satisfactory," or "needs improvement." Paradoxically, the item of library environment that provoked the largest number of complaints was the noise.

This illustrates the value of including both open-ended and closed questions in the same survey. If only the general question about why the student came to the library had been asked, the researchers probably would have concluded (incorrectly) that the noise situation was good. Yet the ratings indicated just the opposite. Students came to the library in search of quiet, but noise problems still existed.

Number of Questions

Beginning researchers often include too many items in a questionnaire. In their desire to omit nothing, they forget that the respondents will become fatigued and lose interest as they plod through an unending barrage of questions. For most purposes, the shorter the instrument, the better. Avoid complex formats, such as, "If yes, skip to question 9, part B. If no, answer question 7, part A."

Wording Your Questions

Your questions should be clear and meaningful to the respondents. Terms should not be too difficult. Don't overestimate the vocabulary level of your respondents. Define all difficult or jargon terms. It is helpful to include synonyms. Instead of asking a question about *nuclear energy*, you can ask about *nuclear or atomic energy*. The synonym may reach some people who miss the primary term.

Avoid loaded terms, scare words, and phrases that immediately raise a red flag. Don't ask questions about *dangerous* drugs, *noisy* trucks, or *excessive* government spending. Such adjectives produce a reflex-like negative response. If you want to know what people think about cocaine, ask them directly; don't ask about dangerous drugs. *Noise* is a technical term for the unpleasant aspects of sound. Asking employees to evaluate the *sound level* in the office is preferable to asking them about noise, which by definition is unpleasant.

Avoid double-barreled questions. Ask about one thing at a time. Don't ask about the cost *and* efficiency of municipal services. It is preferable to divide this into separate questions, one concerned with efficiency and the other with cost.

Whenever possible, avoid phrasing questions in the negative. It is surprising how often people confuse "do" and "don't," "will" and "won't," "can" and "cannot." If you must use a negative, be sure to underline it or have it printed in italics so that it will *not* be missed.

Example

Of all the classes that you took in high school, which was the single class that you liked *least?*

Question wording must be culturally sensitive. When a questionnaire for American high school students was adapted for use in Australia, several questions had to be reworded. In Australia, the term *college* refers to what would be the last 2 years of high school in North America. Questions about "going to college" were changed to "attending a tertiary institution." As background information, Australian students were asked if they were of Aboriginal descent, a question that would have little meaning in the United States. Also, the Australian students were asked if they had ever lived on a "farm or station," the latter term referring to what would probably be a ranch in the United States. Changing the wording makes it difficult to compare the results of different surveys, but may be necessary in order to make the questions understandable to a different group of respondents.

A common mistake in writing questions is to use jargon terms. Many American workers do not know the meaning of "FICA" or "SSI" even though social security payments are deducted from their paychecks every week. Some words have more than one meaning. When a survey team asked residents of a fundamentalist community about the need for government to regulate profits, they were surprised to find exceptionally strong resistance to the idea. Subsequent interviews disclosed that some people thought the question referred to regulation of prophets!

Balance

Balance refers to the neutrality of questions, or providing sufficient items so that the number leaning toward one view are balanced by an equal number leaning toward the other view. The goal of balance is to counteract implicit influence from the questions themselves. The following shows imbalance in questions about cafeteria food.

Is the meat too salty?
Are the vegetables overcooked?
Is the coffee watery?

This set of questions is unbalanced at two levels. Individually, the items imply a direction to the answer. Balance can be provided by asking respondents to circle an alternative from a balanced set: "Is the coffee (too weak) (too strong) (about right)?" The second level of bias is that the implied responses for all the items are in the same direction—that the food isn't very good. An alternative to balancing each individual item is to balance them overall. For example, leave the implicit bias in the question "Are the vegetables overcooked?" but balance it with another item of the reverse implied bias, such as "Is the meat properly prepared?" Providing balance not only reduces the effects of a possible response bias, it also makes the survey itself seem more fair, and thus more difficult for partisans of one view or another to ignore or dismiss.

Don't be discouraged if your questionnaire isn't perfect on the first try. It is extraordinarily difficult to anticipate all sources of ambiguity and confusion. Experienced survey researchers always construct a preliminary version, pretest it, and then revise it before distributing the actual survey. The secret of learning to write clear questions is practice, feedback, more practice, more feedback, and still more practice. No one writes a perfect questionnaire the first time. Box 9–1 provides a checklist for evaluating questionnaire items.

BOX 9–1. Checklist for Evaluating Questionnaire Items

1. Is the question necessary? How useful will the answers be?
2. Is the item clear and unambiguous?
3. Is the respondent competent to answer the question as asked?
4. Will the respondent be willing to answer the question as asked?
5. Have double-barreled questions been eliminated?
6. Is the item as short as possible, while remaining clear and precise?
7. Do the multiple-choice questions provide a comprehensive set of choices? Do they include a "don't know" or "not applicable" category? Is there an "other" category, if appropriate?
8. Is the answer likely to be affected by social desirability (saying the "right thing")? If so, can the question be altered to reduce this bias?
9. Have negatives such as "no" and "not" been underlined?
10. Are the questions balanced so that the number of favorable items equals the number of unfavorable items?

Layout

A self-administered questionnaire must begin with an introductory statement, present the questions in an easily read and easily answered format, and end with a note of thanks or appreciation.

Introductory Statement

At the top of the questionnaire, briefly describe the purpose, identify the person or group conducting the survey, request assistance, and provide general instructions. For example,

> The purpose of this questionnaire is to learn about attitudes toward the cafeteria. The survey is being conducted by Ms. Nguyen and Mr. Smith, students in a research methods class at _____ College. We would very much appreciate your assistance in answering the questions below. Please do not write your name on this form in order that the replies remain anonymous.

Additional instructions might be included. For some rating scales, the respondent is asked not to dwell on the choice, to just check the first response that comes to mind. In other cases a well-considered response is requested.

Question Order

Begin with factual, noncontroversial questions. These help to establish a good relationship that can smooth the way for more difficult or controversial questions later. General questions on a topic should precede specific questions, as in this example.

1. What do you think of this playground?
2. Is there enough play equipment?
3. Do you feel that any of the play equipment is dangerous?

This sequence avoids suggesting danger to the respondent on the first two questions. If danger is mentioned in the first question, it is likely to influence answers to the other questions.

Maintain a logical order understandable to the respondent. Routine items such as age and gender can be included at the end. The questionnaire should *not* begin with overly personal or sensitive questions regarding illicit activities, sex, or controversial religious or political opinions. If such items are to be included, begin with the less controversial ones.

Answer Format

There are various answer formats in which a respondent inserts a checkmark, number, or letter. The response blanks that are placed either to the right or left of the question usually take one of five forms: ____ , /____ / , ( ), [−], or O.

With regard to neatness and appearance, the [−] has been rated best, and the /__ / was the worst (Major, Jacoby, & Sheluga, 1976). Another acceptable practice is to have the respondents circle their choice. Arrange the response blanks to permit easy tabulation and computer entry (if needed).

Example

What is your class in school?	Fr Soph Jr Sr 1 2 3 4
Are you a full-time or part-time student?	Full-time Part-time 1 2
What is your gender?	Male Female 1 2
What is your age?	_____ years

Closing Statement

At the end of a the questionnaire, ask for any other comments or suggestions and then thank the respondents for their time and effort—a simple THANK YOU VERY MUCH may be sufficient.

Pretesting

The first draft of your questionnaire will need revision. Nobody writes a perfect questionnaire on the first try. The need for changes should be accepted gracefully. No matter how carefully you phrase the original questions, there will still be some words that are difficult or unclear, some topics left out. The impressive economy of the questionnaire is partially offset by the researcher's inability to clarify the

BOX 9–2. Basic Steps: Constructing a Questionnaire

Content

1. Exploratory interviews of an in-depth type and/or casual observation, if appropriate.
2. Decide on aspects of problem to be covered. Be specific.
3. Generate items.

Format

4. Decide item format, for example, open-ended vs. closed.
5. Re-examine items (see Checklist for Evaluating Questionnaire Items, Box 9–1).
6. Have a knowledgeable colleague or instructor look at the questions.
7. *Pretest*—pilot test the questionnaire *before* putting it into final form.
   a. Check for confusing or ambiguous items.
   b. Estimate the time needed for administration.
8. Revise questionnaire in accord with pilot results. If new items are added, be sure to pretest them.
9. Final editing—include clear instructions to the person distributing the questionnaires and to the respondents.

meaning of terms. Elaboration is easy in an interview, almost impossible on a questionnaire. Because there may be no person physically present to help explain the meaning of difficult terms or confusing questions, you must anticipate all possible sources of error. An adaptation of Murphy's Law* applies here:—The slightest opportunity for respondents to go wrong means that some of them will.

The best way to reduce ambiguity is to pretest the questions. Try them out on a group of people who are asked the items *and,* in addition, asked to comment on their wording and clarity. The first draft of the cafeteria questionnaire might be given to eight customers and two cafeteria employees. The respondents would be told that this is a trial version of the survey instrument and that we would like their opinions on the food *and* the questions. Pretesting can be done in a short period of time. There is no need for detailed sampling or statistics. A small sample should be sufficient unless serious problems are found, in which case a major revision and further pretesting will be necessary. Pretesting can be done orally. Try it out on a few people who will not be in the final sample but are similar to that sample.

A basic rule in questionnaire construction is that the first draft should never be put in finished form. Write it down in longhand or type it, make 10 copies, but no more. Once you have a large stack of printed questionnaires in front of you, it is easy to overlook minor errors and inconsistencies and to continue to use the copies because they are available. If you do this, you will regret it afterward. It is easier to change a first draft than to interpret people's answers to ambiguous questions. Box 9–2 provides a summary of the basic steps in constructing a questionnaire.

*Murphy's Law: If something can go wrong, it will.

Reproducing the Questionnaire

Eye appeal is important. Make sure all questions are legible. Don't squeeze things together. Use a second sheet of paper if necessary for a clear presentation. A nicely designed and printed questionnaire will increase reader interest. With the advent of low-cost photocopies, this is your most likely means of questionnaire reproduction, although mimeograph or ditto, if available, are cheaper. Before you distribute your questionnaires, go through them to see that pages are in the correct order and there are no blank pages. Numbering the pages will make it easier for you (and the respondent) to notice when pages are out of order or one is missing.

The readability of two-sided copies depends on the thickness of the paper, so try it and see whether the print shows through before committing yourself to multiple copies. If you use the back, be sure to write PLEASE COMPLETE THE REVERSE SIDE at the bottom of the first page. Even with that warning, you can assume that in a self-administered questionnaire, some respondents will fail to complete the back page. The same expectation applies to multiple pages. If the questionnaires are being picked up individually, it is wise to make a general scan to see that all pages have been filled out.

There is no reason for a questionnaire to look dull and uninteresting. Copy technology and computer clip art make it easy to include borders or illustrations. For most purposes, paste-and-copy will be sufficient. We have made frequent use of pictures from the inexpensive Dover Books series of copyright-free illustrations. There are specialty volumes on transportation, food, money, children, and so on. Care should be taken to use appropriate illustrations that do not put off the respondent or bias the results. If pictures are a problem, one can still use attractive borders and backgrounds to enliven the format.

In deciding on the number of copies needed, consider your sample size and request additional copies. You will need these not only for follow-up or spoilage, but also for data tabulation, discussion copies, as appendices for reports, and as samples for other researchers.

Distributing the Forms

If the questionnaire is properly constructed and brief, you will be pleasantly surprised at how quickly it can be distributed, filled out, and collected. This is the stage at which the economy of this instrument is most evident. It may take more than a month to get permission to conduct a survey among office workers, another few weeks to write and pretest the questions, get them approved by management and an institutional review board, and have the forms printed, but only a few hours to distribute them, have them filled out, and collected. Once you have the instrument already available, a second survey can be carried out in a wondrously short time.

As a questionnaire is to be answered in writing, it is more easily given to people sitting down than to those standing or on the move. One would probably choose an interview rather than a written questionnaire for customers in a shopping center or teenagers at the Dairy Queen. The questionnaire is ideally suited for office workers, students, library readers, and others who are seated at desks or tables. An alternative for people in public settings or who have problems reading or writing is for the researcher to read the questions and check the answers as they are given by the respondent.

There are various methods of distributing questionnaires to potential respondents. Questionnaires can be circulated at a group meeting, handed to people individually, or mailed. Each approach is likely to work better in some situations than in others. *Sampling* is an important consideration in distributing a survey. This topic is discussed in Chapter 16.

Group Meetings

When an organization, club, or class meets regularly, you have a good opportunity to distribute a questionnaire. If the survey is brief and relevant to the group's purpose, it may be possible to have the questionnaires filled out during the meeting and returned directly to you. There is likely to be a problem of a biased sample if only a small number of members attend because they may not be representative of the total membership.

Individual Distribution

Individual distribution is efficient when the behavior studied involves solitary people rather than groups or organizations. Researchers studying wilderness use have employed this approach in combination with mailing. The questionnaire is given to people as they enter or leave the area, perhaps in a parking lot or at the trailhead, with the request that the questionnaire be filled out and placed in a designated collection box or returned through the mail in an attached postage-paid return envelope. When this approach was used among people engaged in river recreation in Vermont, the return rate for completed surveys was 61 percent, which is very high for a survey (Manning & Ciali, 1980). The people contacted had a direct connection with the topic of the survey, and that contributed to the good return rate. We would not recommend handing questionnaires to people walking by on the street or placing them on automobile windshields with a request that they be filled out and returned by mail. Most of these questionnaires are likely to end up in the street or in a trash can. A positive personal relationship with the researcher or sponsoring agency is crucial for a good return rate.

Mail Surveys

A mail survey is efficient for covering a large geographic area quickly. It is expensive for researchers to travel to distant locations to conduct surveys. The advantages of a mail survey are its low labor and travel costs and complete standardization. There is no need to train interviewers, and all respondents receive the same questions posed in the same manner. A mail survey also provides more anonymity to the respondents than is possible in a personal interview. A follow-up study of former employees may secure more valid information when conducted by mail without requiring names to be associated with the responses. If contacted directly, individuals might fear that their opinions would be used against them. However, there will be many other situations where controversial opinions can be explored more fully through a personal interview than in a mailed questionnaire.

Disadvantages of a mail survey are its impersonality, low return rate, slowness, and financial cost. Many commercial firms and political organizations send out fake surveys as promotional tools. Respondents are asked to answer questions deliberately intended to create favorable attitudes toward a product or organization. This misuse of survey methodology has led many householders to classify all mail surveys as junk mail. Fortunately, most fake surveys do not have college return addresses, employ hand-written envelopes, or use first class postage. Taking advantage of this fact, genuine survey researchers personalize the envelope, the cover letter, and the questionnaire to the greatest degree possible.

A mail survey of households randomly selected from a city telephone directory will probably result in a 10–40 percent return rate, thus requiring the researcher to send out from three to five times as many questionnaires as are needed for the final sample. Three mail surveys of districts in Brasilia yielded return rates of 30%, 36%, and 38%, respectively (Guenther & Flores, 1994).

There is a problem of potential response bias when a small percentage of questionnaires is returned. The return rate is likely to be much higher if the recipients have a prior interest in the topic of the survey. For example, a mail survey of former high school alumni accompanied by a cover letter from the school principal is likely to yield a return rate in excess of 60 percent of delivered questionnaires.

A mail survey is slower than a telephone survey, which can be done in a few days. Questionnaires take several days to be delivered by mail and weeks before the bulk of replies return. A mail survey is not appropriate when timely information is needed. The costs of printing, mailing, and return postage may seriously deplete the budget of a small organization or agency.

Cover Letter

A cover letter should accompany a questionnaire sent through the mail. The letter introduces the person conducting the survey, describes why it is being done, how the results will be used, and approximately how long it will take to fill out the questionnaire. Personalization is very important in the cover letter. For example, provide a genuine signature in ink, and perhaps a hand-written note at the bottom "We are especially interested in comments from people in _____ neighborhood" or "Your comment will be very helpful in the planning process."

A survey of people's attitudes toward the trees on their street contained the species name of the tree (red oak or Norway maple) hand-written at the bottom of the page. It would have been possible to type this in the letter, but the handwriting made the letter more personal. Box 9–3 shows the cover letter used in the tree survey. Questionnaires were sent to neighborhoods where different species of trees had been planted. The goal of the survey was to find out how people felt about their street trees and whether the presence of the trees improved neighborhood life.

Increasing Return Rates

Notifying people about the survey beforehand will increase cooperation. Placing a notice in a neighborhood newsletter or at a community center telling people that a survey is underway and explaining its purposes might arouse interest and encourage cooperation. Office workers could be sent a note describing the goals of the survey and why it is important for them to participate. No matter how fine

---

BOX 9–3. Street Tree Cover Letter and Questionnaire

Cover Letter
Dear Householder:
   Your local tree organization (name) in collaboration with researchers at the University of (name) is examining the health of trees in (city name) and in the contributions that trees make to the quality of neighborhood life. This research is supported by the (name of agency).
   We hope you will take a few minutes to fill out the enclosed questionnaire. The questions refer to the trees in *your* front yard. Please return the completed questionnaire in the enclose stamped envelope.

                                             Sincerely,
                                             (Researcher's name and affiliation)
Questionnaire
   The four-page questionnaire was photocopied on both sides of a single 11 × 17 page and then folded in half. A picture of a tree-lined street was placed at the top to increase interest. Only a few of the actual questions are shown here.
   The following questions refer to the tree planted in your front yard.

   1. How do you rate the way in which the tree was staked or supported when it was planted? (circle one)
         (excellent)   (good)   (OK)   (poor)   (very poor)
   2. How satisfied are you with the location selected for the tree?
         (excellent)   (good)   (OK)   (poor)   (very poor)
   3. Did you or another family member assist in the planting of your front yard tree?
         (yes)   (no)   (don't know)
   4. Did you get to know any of the neighbors better in the process of receiving or planting your tree?   (yes)   (no)   (don't know)
   5. What is your overall opinion of this tree?
         (excellent)   (good)   (OK)   (poor)   (very poor)

your motives, people are doing you a favor when they invest time and effort answering your questions. Therefore, try to convince them of the usefulness of their answers. This can be done *both* in the advance letter and in the introductory paragraph of the questionnaire. Enclosing money or a chance to win a prize increases return rates, and a brief questionnaire is more likely to be completed and returned than a long one.

Postcards can be sent before and after mailing to increase return rate. Several days beforehand, you can send a postcard describing the purposes of the survey. A week after sending the questionnaire, a follow-up reminder can be mailed asking people to please return the surveys and providing an address to which people can write if they mislaid the original survey and would like another copy.

Example

Dear Resident,

About a week ago you were sent a questionnaire about your attitude toward your front yard tree. If you have not yet sent in your questionnaire, please do so as soon as you can so that our data will be truly representative of your area. If you have already mailed in your questionnaire, please accept this as a thank you for your cooperation.

Sincerely,

(signature)

(title and affiliation or sponsor)

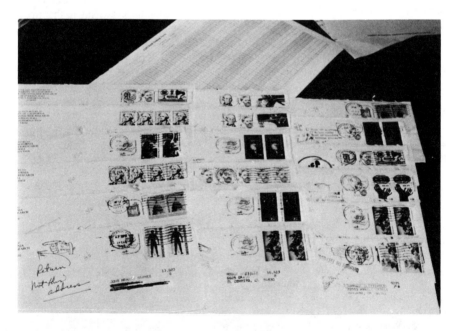

Undeliverable surveys will be returned if mailed first class. Note the use of attractive stamps to increase respondent interest.

Addressing envelopes by hand increases the likelihood of a response in mail surveys.

Obtain current addresses. Use the most recent version of the telephone directory or other information source.

Send questionnaires first-class mail so that the post office will return the undelivered questionnaires. First-class letters are more likely to be noticed than bulk mail.

Hand address the letters and use attractive stamps. Some market researchers believe that a stamp placed at a slight angle on the envelope increases the return rate.

Scoring

Scoring a properly constructed questionnaire is quite simple. Open-ended questions must be coded by hand. See Chapter 8 for a detailed account of coding. A brief questionnaire with a small number of respondents can be scored by hand and allow you to stay closer to the data and get a better sense of the responses to the questions. With a lengthy questionnaire and/or many respondents, you will probably want to use a computer. Nothing surpasses computer analysis for speed and accuracy in comparing the responses of different groups of people. Plan for ease of computer entry and analysis when designing and formatting your questionnaire.

This survey from a national magazine was accompanied by a crisp new dollar bill as an inducement, along with a stamped return envelope.

Interpretation

Up to now, everything has gone well. You've written your questionnaire, pretested it, revised it, distributed, and collected the final version. You are now the proud owner of 96 completed questionnaires. Two people didn't finish the questionnaire and one didn't follow the instructions. Another person didn't take the questions seriously and wrote funny answers. This last is the moron factor, and the response should be disregarded. As long as it is not done to bias the results, it makes sense to discard bizarre answers. A person who puts an exclamation point after "sex" or writes "I am for it" is kidding. If some of the person's other replies look humorous, it is probably best to discard the entire questionnaire. On the other hand, someone putting a question mark after "age" may be shy about revealing how old he or she is. You can be sure that some of your respondents will omit one or two items. Either the question is not clear or the item was missed in going through the questionnaire. Don't be concerned if you lack replies to all the questions. When you convert to percentages, there will be no problem.

When you deal with people who are rushed or busy, you can expect that some of them won't finish the questionnaire. Generally the replies from the completed portions can be added to the total sample without significant bias. This is not true of people who object to your questions. Even a mild question can upset some people. For example, an employee may use the questionnaire to vent hostility toward an employer. Before discarding these replies, it is best to check with a colleague or co-worker to see that you are not biasing your results. Occasionally an apparently humorous response is meaningful and a refusal is appropriate. Even though you have promised your respondents anonymity, some of them won't believe you. This is not totally unrealistic if they don't know you. Abnormal conditions can provoke abnormal responses. Do not expect to get honest answers from people who believe that the survey results will be used against them.

Removing the two incomplete questionnaires, the person who didn't follow the instructions, and the joker, our sample in the cafeteria survey now consists of 96 respondents. If we had wanted to finish with a perfect 100, we could have aimed for 115 completed questionnaires and put 15 aside as replacements for any rejections. For our purposes, however, there is no significant difference between 96 and 100 completed replies. We will probably be presenting our results in overall percentages, as in Table 9–1.

This is a straightforward presentation of the data. For many purposes, it is all that is needed. However, if you want to know how the attitudes of male freshmen living off campus compare with female freshmen living on campus, the computer is a very efficient way of making these detailed comparisons, but unless you are careful, the computer can overload you with data. It will take very little extra ef-

TABLE 9–1. Number of Students Rating Each Aspect as Good, OK, or Poor, ($N = 96$)

Aspect of the Cafeteria	Percentage rating		
	Good	OK	Poor
Meats	10	55	35
Vegetables	7	44	49
Salads	53	38	9
Desserts	43	35	22
.			
.			
.			
Seating arrangement	22	61	17
Sound level	0	32	68

fort to ask the computer how the replies of 17-year-old Protestant men compare with those of 19-year-old Catholic women. We advise against asking trivial questions. The computer does not indicate which results are important and which are trivial.

Describing Survey Results

People's likes can be as significant as their dislikes. The point of a survey is not to reveal only failure and frustration. Success and satisfaction should also be identified. A beginning researcher often identifies important results with surprises. Can a survey be worth anything if the results are not shocking? The answer is clearly yes. A survey that finds there is no problem may be just as important as one that identifies a source of tension. For example, if your survey tells you that students are satisfied with the cafeteria food, this is a perfectly valid and useful finding. You have found that your cafeteria is better than most. There still may be some room for improvement in other areas, such as noise and crowding.

There is no need to present the results in the sequence that the questions were asked. Rather, present the results in terms of topical areas beginning with the most important. In a cafeteria survey, food will be the most important issue, so present that first. Then you can go into hygienic considerations and environmental issues such as sound level, crowding, and decor. There is nothing more frustrating to the reader of a report than to have every percentage described. Don't bury your reader under a mountain of statistics. Some findings may be unimportant or too ambiguous to have meaning. Don't exaggerate the importance of small differences. Often the similarities among various percentages are more impressive than small differences. The body of the report should be devoted to the major findings. It is realistic to assume that most readers will look only at the summary. It is still necessary to make the actual data available for those readers who want them. The best place to include detailed percentages is in the appendix, where they will not interrupt the flow of the report. Here is the summary from the cafeteria survey:

Report on Students' Attitudes Toward the Cafeteria: Summary
To learn students' attitudes toward the food and service, a 25-item questionnaire was constructed, pretested, revised, and distributed to 100 students in the cafeteria during lunch on Thursday and Friday, June 6–7, 1996. Three-quarters of the respondents had purchased cafeteria food and one-quarter brought their meals with them. The main reason students brown-bagged their lunches was the cost of the food. Areas of most satisfaction with the cafeteria were size of portions (very ample), the green salads (tasty and nutritious), cleanliness, fast service, and the possibility of going back into the line for seconds. The problems indicated by at least one-third of the sample included quality of the meats (poor), tastiness of the vegetables (overcooked), noise in the table area, and the drab decor of the cafeteria. On most of the other items, people were satisfied but not particularly enthusiastic.

This summary presents the highlights of the report. It includes what people liked as well as what they disliked. Specific complaints are placed in the context of the overall general level of satisfaction. This is accurate as well as diplomatic. It would have been biased and shortsighted to list only the complaints and omit the compliments. A good summary, like a good report, describes the full range of attitudes, including weak and noncommittal responses. The summary should be brief and to the point. The discussion comes in the body of the report, and the detailed percentage totals appear in the appendix. Store the raw data on computer diskettes and always make a back-up copy. The original questionnaires should be kept a few months after the final report has been distributed in order to allow you to answer any questions that arise; later, the paper can be recycled.

Comparison of Interviews and Self-administered Questionnaires

In deciding whether to do interviewing or to distribute self-administered questionnaires, carefully consider your project needs and resources in time and money. Self-administered questionnaires are generally more economical in that they require less time and assistance in scoring, provided that they have been designed with a closed-ended response format. A questionnaire ensures standardization of measurement in that all respondents are asked precisely the same questions in the same manner, thereby eliminating the potential for interviewer bias. People at distant locations can be reached by mailed questionnaires. When administered to an organized group, such as a class or club, collecting completed questionnaires can be quick and efficient. Questionnaires also have the advantage of offering anonymity, so they may be more desirable for investigating sensitive attitudes or behaviors.

Interviews have the advantage of allowing for observation in addition to answers to questions. Interviewers can assess nonverbal behaviors as well as elements of the setting. Even telephone interviews allow for recording intonation and comments. The interview is less likely to be incomplete and yields a higher response rate. It is better for dealing with complex issues. An interviewer can reword questions, define terms that the respondents do not understand, and probe for additional information.

Internet Surveys

Questionnaires can be administered on the Internet. They can be sent to a discussion group or mailing list of people concerned with a specific topic. As discussion groups are open to people throughout the world, this approach can yield a heterogeneous international sample. At present the demographic and other characteristics of newsgroup members are unknown. Data may be available in the future as groups collect more information about their membership, perhaps as a condition for joining.

Another possibility for conducting surveys is e-mail. This is a particularly good method when an entire organization, residence hall, or community is connected with a central registry of e-mail addresses, which in turn would permit use of so-phisticated sampling procedures currently used in mail and telephone surveys.

Internet surveys are likely to become much more popular due to their speed and low cost. A survey can also be made more interactive than is possible on a printed page, with follow-up questions tailored to specific replies. Selecting alter-native A can lead directly to a follow-up question, with the selection of alterna-tive B providing a different item, and still another linked with alternative C.

At this writing, use of the Internet for surveys is in its infancy. An Internet sur-vey might suggest questions or hypotheses, rather than testing or confirming them. For example, a researcher could ask members of a discussion group on obesity whether or not they notice weight fluctuations associated with different seasons. Due to sampling limitations, the answers by themselves will not be confirmatory, but they may be useful in proving leads that can be tested more systematically.

Limitations

A questionnaire is of little use with respondents who are very young, very old, in-firm, or uninterested in the topic. As a written document, it is not appropriate for people on the move or who are busy with other activities. The typical question-naire with multiple-choice answers evokes "bare bones" responses. You can learn the general structure of the situation but not the details. Follow-up interviews will help to make sense out of the trends.

A poorly worded question can create the appearance of attitudes where none exist. People may believe they are helping the researcher by providing answers that he or she wants to hear. Questionnaire replies are more useful for identifying attitudes than for predicting behavior. Do not confuse people's opinions as ex-pressed on a questionnaire with their behavior.

Questionnaires strike many respondents as impersonal, mechanical, and de-meaning and the response categories as limited, artificial, and constraining. Un-less the researcher asks precisely the right questions, the information will not be very useful. Questionnaires are not suitable for examining deeper levels of moti-vation or opinions on complex issues. Individual interviews will probably be more appropriate for these purposes. Although this chapter has emphasized the econ-omy of the questionnaire, the work involved in writing questions, pretesting the instrument, and tabulating the responses should not be underestimated. If opinions from only a small number of respondents are needed, the open-ended interview, in which a few general questions are followed by specific questions tailored to the respondents' replies, will be more economical.

Summary

A questionnaire is typically a series of written questions on a topic about which the respondents' written opinions are sought. Because it is so economical to administer and score, the questionnaire is widely used in behavioral research.

Open-ended questions provide space for the respondents to write in their own answers. With closed or multiple-choice questions, respondents choose from among alternatives provided by the researcher. Open-ended questions are desirable when the researcher does not know all the possible answers to a question, when the range of possible answers is so large that the question would become unwieldy in a multiple-choice format, when the researcher wants to avoid suggesting answers to the respondent, and when the researcher wants answers in the respondent's own words. Multiple-choice answers are desirable when there is a large number of respondents and questions, when answers are to be scored by computer, and when answers from different groups of individuals are to be compared.

Salience refers to the importance of an issue in people's minds. Open-ended questions are well suited to determining the salience of an issue. In a multiple-choice format, salience can be determined by asking the respondent to rank or rate a list of answers in terms of importance.

In many cases you will need a middle-response category such as "neutral" or "undecided," and need to include a "not applicable" or "don't know" response.

Check all items for clarity. Avoid double-barreled and negative questions. Provide balance. Always pretest the questionnaire before putting it into final form.

The questionnaire is of little use with respondents who are very young, very old, infirm, or uninterested in the topic. The typical questionnaire with multiple-choice answers evokes "bare bones" responses. Questionnaires are more successful in identifying attitudes than in predicting behavior.

References

Galton, F. (1907). *Inquiries into human faculty and its development* (2nd ed.). London: J.M. Dent.

Guenther, H., & Flores, E. P. (1995). Sense of neighbourhood and model quadras. *Trialog, 46*(3), 40–45.

Major, B. N., Jacoby, J., & Sheluga, D. A. (1976). Questionnaire research on questionnaire construction. *Purdue Papers in Consumer Psychology,* No. 166.

Manning, R. E., & Ciali, C. P. (1980). Recreation density and user satisfaction: A further exploration of the satisfaction model. *Journal of Leisure Research, 12,* 329–345.

Schuman, H., & Presser, S. (1981). *Questions and answers in attitude surveys: Experiments on question form, wording, and context.* New York: Academic Press.

Further Reading

Bourque, L. B., & Fielder, E. P. (1995). *How to conduct self-administered and mail surveys.* Thousand Oaks, CA: Sage Publications.

Fowler, F. J. (1995). *Improving survey questions: Design and evaluation.* Thousand Oaks, CA: Sage Publications.

Frey, J. H. (1989). *Survey research by telephone* (2nd ed.). Newbury Park, CA: Sage Publications.

Mangione, T. W. (1995). *Mail surveys: Improving the quality.* Thousand Oaks, CA: Sage Publications.

Oppenheim, A. N. (1992). *Questionnaire design, interviewing, and attitude measurement.* London: Pinter Publishers.

Rossi, P. H., Wright, J. D., & Anderson, A. B. (1983). *Handbook of survey research*. New York: Academic Press.

Schuman, H., & Presser, S. (1981). *Questions and answers in attitude surveys: Experiments on question form, wording, and context*. New York: Academic Press.

Sudman, S., & Bradburn, N. M. (1982). *Asking questions*. San Francisco: Jossey-Bass.

10　Attitude and Rating Scales

What Is a Scale?

Originally from the Latin word *scala,* meaning a ladder or flight of steps, a scale represents a series of ordered steps at fixed intervals used as a standard of measurement. Scales are used to rank people's judgments of objects, events, or other people from low to high or from poor to good. Commonly used scales in behavioral research include attitude scales designed to measure people's opinions on social issues, employee rating scales to measure job-related performance, scales for determining socioeconomic status used in sociological research, product rating scales used in consumer research, and sensory evaluation scales to judge the quality of food, air, and other phenomena. These scales provide numerical scores that can be used to compare individuals and groups.

Rating Scales

There are various methods for making ratings. With *graphic rating scales,* the respondent places a mark along a continuous line. The ends and perhaps the midpoint of the line are named, but not the intervening points. The person can make a mark at any point along the line. The score is computed by measuring the distance of the check mark from the left end of the scale.

Example

Place a checkmark somewhere along the scale to indicate the quality of this loudspeaker system.

Terrible   (score = 5.2 cm)   Excellent

A *step scale* requires the rater to select one of a graded series of levels. Intermediate points cannot be used. The intervals can be letters, numbers, or adjectives. For scoring purposes, these may be numbered from 1 to 5.

Example

How would you rate the quality of this sound system? (circle one)

excellent   very good   good   poor   terrible

Comparative rating scales are commonly used on recommendation forms. The person is asked to compare the applicant with others in the same category.

Example

Compared to other students in the class, how does this student rate in terms of motivation for graduate work?

Top 1%___   Top 5%___   Top 10%___   Top 25%___   Top 50%___   Bottom 50%___

Limitations

Rating scales are easy to construct and easy to answer, but they may not be reliable. If the respondent were asked to answer the same question tomorrow, how similar would the ratings be? Also, a single rating may catch only one aspect of a more complex concept. Even something as simple as rating a sound system may involve several aspects such as frequency range, distortion with volume change, etc. The problem can be solved by using a multi-item measure, an instrument that includes more than one question. Such scales are frequently used in the measurement of attitudes.

Levels of Measurement

Before describing more complex scales, it is necessary to look more closely at what scale numbers actually represent. When interpreting the meaning of a score on a scale, it is necessary to have a clear idea of the level of measurement that the scale represents. The process of assigning numbers to events, ratings, or behavior occurs at a particular *level* of measurement. These levels can be nominal, ordinal, interval, or ratio.

Nominal measures are qualitative or categorical, providing no information about quantity. Presence or absence is perhaps the most simple form, often indicated by 1 versus 0, a dichotomous or binary classification (examples are yes/no, present/not present, student/non-student, citizen/non-citizen). Male/female is a nominal measure. There may be more than two categories, for example, homeowner, renter, and other. Numbers may be used, but only to represent categories (e.g., 1 = male, 2 = female).

An *ordinal* scale provides additional information about size or direction. Street addresses are ordinal measures. They indicate direction but provide no certain information about the distance between individual buildings. A ranking of contest winners into first, second, and third place is ordinal if there is no description of the size of the differences between them.

An *interval* scale possesses the qualities of an ordinal scale, plus the additional characteristic of equal intervals between scale points. Such scales contain units similar to a temperature scale, on which the difference between 85° and 87° F is comparable in degrees to the difference between 47° and 49°. Time of day (e.g., 10 A.M., 2 P.M.) is measured in equal intervals.

Ratio scales not only have equal intervals, but have the additional property of an absolute zero point. This permits comparisons such as "twice as much" or "three times as many." Grade point average (GPA) is a ratio measure (a student who received all Fs would have a GPA of 0). A student with a 4.0 has twice as many grade points as a student with a 2.0. Time, distance, and physical qualities such as weight, age, and size, are easily expressed in ratio measures.

Most subjective rating scales, like those described in this chapter, are ordinal rather than interval or ratio. In an opinion survey, we can say that someone who strongly disagrees is more opposed than someone who slightly disagrees, but we don't know how much difference there is between the two attitudes. The level of measurement in a study influences comparisons and generalizations that are justified, as well as the selection of statistical tests. Here is a summary of the characteristics of the four levels of measurement:

Scale type	Distinguishing features	Example
Nominal	Characteristics assigned to categories. No underlying continuous dimension.	Yes, No; Mountain bike, Ten-speed, Three-speed, Other
Ordinal	Characteristics can be ordered along an underlying dimension, but no information is provided about the distance between points.	Rank ordering preferences— 1st, 2nd, and 3rd choice
Interval	Equivalent distance between points (steps) along the underlying dimension.	Temperature, Time of day
Ratio	Has characteristics of an interval scale, plus an absolute zero point.	Measures of income, GPA

Attitude Scales

An attitude scale is a special type of questionnaire designed to produce scores indicating the intensity and direction (for or against) of a person's feelings about an object or event. There are several types of scales that can be constructed, but the most common is the Likert-type. The scale is constructed so that all its questions concern a single issue.

Attitude scales are often used in attitude change experiments. One group of people is asked to fill out the scale twice, once before some event, such as reading a persuasive argument, and again afterward. A control group fills out the scale twice without reading the argument. The control group is used to measure exposure or practice effects. The change in the scores of the experimental group relative to the control group, whether their attitudes have become more or less favorable, indicates the effects of the argument.

Likert-type Scale

A Likert-type scale, named for Rensis Likert (1932) who developed this type of attitude measurement, presents a list of statements on an issue to which the respondent indicates degree of agreement using categories such as Strongly Agree, Agree, Undecided, Disagree, and Strongly Disagree.

Construction

The first step is to collect statements on a topic from people holding a wide range of attitudes, from extremely favorable to extremely unfavorable. Duplications and irrelevant statements are discarded. For example, college students provided the following examples of positive and negative statements about marijuana:

> I don't approve of something that puts you out of normal state of mind.
> It has its place.
> It corrupts the individual.
> Marijuana does some people a lot of good.
> If marijuana is taken safely, its effects can be quite enjoyable.
> I think it is horrible and corrupting.
> It is usually the drug people start on before addiction.
> It is perfectly healthy and should be legalized.
> Its use by an individual could be the beginning of a sad situation.

A Likert scale includes *only* statements that are clearly favorable or clearly unfavorable. Statements that are neutral, ambiguous, or borderline are eliminated. This can be accomplished by asking a few people, who are called "judges" in the procedure, to rate each statement as to whether it expresses a favorable or unfavorable opinion about the topic. Where there is little agreement among these judges or difficulty in deciding whether the item is favorable or unfavorable, the statement is eliminated. For example, the statement "Marijuana use should be taxed heavily" was rejected because it was ambiguous. Some judges thought it was pro-marijuana because it implied legalization, while others felt it was anti-marijuana because it advocated a heavy tax. The statement "Having never tried marijuana, I can't say what effects it would have" would be eliminated because it is neither positive nor negative.

Initial Administration and Scoring

The statements are arranged in random order on a questionnaire with a choice of degrees of agreement. Each statement is followed by five degrees of agreement (strongly agree, agree slightly, undecided, disagree slightly, strongly disagree). Favorable statements are scored 5, 4, 3, 2, and 1, respectively. Unfavorable statements are scored in the reverse direction (1, 2, 3, 4, and 5, respectively).

Example

Indicate your degree of agreement or disagreement with each of the following statements about marijuana by circling one of the following letters

SA = Strongly Agree
 A = Agree
 U = Undecided
 D = Disagree
SD = Strongly Disagree

SA A U D SD 1. Marijuana use corrupts the individual.
SA A U D SD 2. Its use by the individual could be the beginning
                    of a sad situation.
SA A U D SD 3. Marijuana does some people a lot of good.

People who are very favorable toward marijuana use would be expected to strongly agree with the favorable statements and strongly disagree with the unfavorable statements. They would earn a high score on the scale when the item scores are added together. Conversely, people with very unfavorable attitudes would be expected to strongly disagree with the favorable statements and strongly agree with the unfavorable statements, and would score low on the scale. Note the importance of reverse scoring the negative items. A person who strongly disagrees with the statement "Marijuana use corrupts the individual" is expressing a *positive* attitude toward marijuana use, and hence the item is scored as a 5 rather than 1.

Selecting the Final Items

The point of constructing the scale is to measure a person's attitude toward something. Thus, a scale should consist of items that distinguish people with a positive attitude on a topic from people with a negative attitude. Here is a method for getting rid of items that do not distinguish between people with different attitudes.

1. Sort the questionnaires from lowest to highest on the basis of the total score (with negative items scored in the reverse direction).

2. Take the top and bottom quarters (which will be the people with the most and least favorable attitudes).

3. For each group, calculate the average (mean) score for each individual item.

4. Keep only those items that distinguish the two groups. In other words if both the high (very favorable) and low (very unfavorable) scorers rated an item in the same way, that item is not discriminating and should be dropped.

Another way of cleaning up an attitude scale is to use items that cluster or hang together. If people who strongly agree with item #3 also strongly agree with item #5, then it is likely that #3 and #5 are measuring similar or closely-related attitudes. Precise assessment requires the use of correlation, either among items or between an individual item and the total score. This can be done using correlation coefficients (described in Chapter 19). The final version of the scale is administered and scored as described in the preceding section.

Validity and Reliability

The *validity* of an attitude scale is the degree to which it measures a specified attitude or belief system. A common method for assessing validity is to administer the attitude scale to individuals known to hold strong opinions on both sides of an issue. For example, a scale measuring attitude toward smoking could be administered to smokers and to members of an anti-smoking organization. If the scale is valid, there will be a large difference between the responses of the two groups.

An attitude scale should yield consistent results. Consistency in measurement is known as *reliability*. There are three common methods for testing the reliability of an attitude scale: test-retest, split-half, and equivalent forms. With the *test-retest* method, the scale is given to the same person on two occasions and the results are compared. Unless something significant happened during the interval, the two scores should be similar.

The *split-half* method involves dividing an attitude scale into two halves, which are then compared. This is generally done by combining all the even-numbered items into one scale and all the odd-numbered items into another. Scores on the two halves are compared and should be similar if the scale is reliable. A more technical split-half technique uses a computer program to calculate Cronbach's Alpha coefficient, which is an average of various logical splits.

The third method of measuring reliability involves the use of *equivalent forms*. Two different scales on the topic are constructed, Form A and Form B. If the scale are reliable, scores on the two forms should be similar.

These three methods for determining reliability rest on a comparison between two sets of scores. This comparison is made through a statistical test known as the correlation coefficient, described in Chapter 19.

For readers who do not want to construct their own attitude scales, a selection of scales whose reliability has already been established is available in Robinson, Shaver, and Wrightsman, *Measures of Personality and Psychosocial Attitudes* (1991). Chapter 16 (Standardized Tests and Inventories) also lists a number of sources for locating attitude scales. Journal articles and reviews are a good sources for references to scales currently in use on specialized topics. There are computerized databases available at many campus and agency libraries. For example, the *Health and Psychosocial Instruments (HAPI)* database contains information about questionnaires, rating scales, and other instruments used in published studies. For each instrument, there is a brief description of its form and uses, plus information about the authors, year of publication, length, reliability and validity, and published references.

Limitations

There are questions about the validity of attitude scales. Often they predict behavior poorly or not at all. The words on the printed page bear little resemblance to the actual situation. Another problem with attitude scales is the assumption that attitudes lie along a single dimension of favorability. People's opinions on a topic like marijuana are complex and multidimensional. A person may be in favor of reducing the penalties on marijuana possession but not on cultivation or sale, and may want strict penalties for anyone driving under the drug's influence. A single favorability score cannot reflect the specificity of these concerns. Questionnaires allow for a more in-depth and detailed assessment of such complexity.

Semantic Differential

The semantic differential is a procedure developed by psychologist Charles Osgood and his associates to measure the meaning of concepts (Osgood, May, & Miron, 1975). The respondent is asked to rate an object or a concept along a series of scales with opposed adjectives at either end.

Example

Rate the park nearest your residence along each of the following scales.

Quiet ___:___:___:___:___:___:___ Noisy

Dangerous ___:___:___:___:___:___:___ Safe

Sad ___:___:___:___:___:___:___ Happy

The semantic differential is a good instrument for exploring the *connotative meaning* of things. Connotation refers to the personal meaning of something, as distinct from its physical characteristics. For example, a panther, in addition to being a large cat, connotes stealth and power. Crêpes Suzette suggest elegance and expensive dining.

Selection of Terms

In the research that developed the semantic differential, three major categories of connotative meaning were found: value (e.g., good–bad, ugly–beautiful), activity (e.g., fast–slow, active–passive), and strength (e.g., weak–strong, large–small). Table 10–1 presents four adjective pairs high in value, activity, or strength. Not surprisingly, the value dimension (good-bad, valuable-worthless) is of greatest importance in evaluative research. When you want to know whether or not people like something, you will probably want to include good–bad, ugly–beautiful, and friendly–unfriendly. Activity and strength are important dimensions in certain circumstances. A comparison of people's images of cities and small towns found major differences on the activity and strength dimensions. Cities were full of bustle, hurry, and activity, while in small towns the pace was more slow, relaxed, and leisurely. Cities were also rated as larger, stronger, and more powerful than small towns. Other adjectives may be more relevant to a particular topic. An investigation of religious concepts used adjectives closely related to religious belief, such as sacred–profane, mysterious–obvious, and public–private. The nature of the project will determine the selection of adjectives.

The most common error made by inexperienced researchers using this technique is to overestimate the respondents' vocabulary level. Although most college students know the meaning of "profane" and "despotic," a substantial number of students may not, which reduces the validity of the results when these terms are included on a rating scale. Pretesting the adjective pairs is essential for eliminating difficult or ambiguous terms. Even if adjectives have been used by other researchers, it will still be necessary to test them on your particular respondents. Adjectives that have one meaning for one group of people may mean something else to another group.

Length and Layout

Don't burden your respondents with too many scales. After a while, the lines become a blur. We do not recommend using more than 20 adjective pairs to measure a concept; 10 to 12 adjective pairs seem preferable. Remember that the value of your results depends on the voluntary cooperation of your respondents.

TABLE 10–1. Polar Adjective Pairs*

High on value dimension	High on activity dimension	High on strength dimension
good-bad	active-passive	strong-weak
beautiful-ugly	energetic-inert	large-small
friendly-unfriendly	fast-slow	hard-soft
wise-foolish	excitable-calm	heavy-light

*Adapted from Osgood, Miron, and May (1975).

Counterbalance the order of positive and negative adjectives. Begin some scales with the positive term (happy–sad) and others with the negative term (noisy–quiet). This will prevent the respondent from falling into a fixed pattern of always checking to the right or left.

Make sure that people put their marks in the right place. Researchers often use solid lines for the responses and colons as spacers.

Example

Light ___:___:___:___:___:___:___ Dark

It is important that answers be marked on the lines and *not* on the dots. Tabulating the responses becomes more complicated when people have checked on the dots. When this occurs, you can assign the response a mid-point value such as 2.5. Another possibility is to assign the score to the right or left line in random or alternating order. That is, if a person has checked midway between the second and third line, the response will be scored as a 2 the first time and a 3 the next time this occurs.

Most researchers follow Osgood in using seven-point scales. This includes a midpoint, which is useful when the item is neither happy nor sad or neither light nor dark, but somewhere in the middle. However, if machine scoring limited to a five-point scale can be done cheaply and quickly, this option should be seriously considered. Five-point scales are more easily tabulated by hand, too. Many researchers find that differences among the three scale points to the right or left of the midpoint have little meaning. The direction of response (e.g., whether the cafeteria is seen as a happy place) is more important than whether it is seen as extremely happy, moderately happy, or somewhat happy. If you plan to combine all three categories to the right of the neutral point later, you might as well begin with a smaller number of scale points—five or even three.

Example

Rate the cafeteria along each of the following scales:

friendly ___:___:___ unfriendly

light ___:___:___ dark

quiet ___:___:___ noisy

dirty ___:___:___ clean

Scoring

On a seven-point scale each level is given a numerical value from 0 to 6 or 1 to 7, going from left to right. The average is computed separately for each pair. Thus, 3 is the midpoint value of the happy–sad scale, whose endpoints are 0 and 6. Anything below 3 means that the item is generally happy, and anything above 3 means that the item is generally sad. In summarizing the results in a report, it is helpful to the reader to reorganize all the scales so that the favorable end is on the left and the unfavorable end on the right. Note that this differs from the order of the scales given to the respondents. Placing all the favorable adjectives on the left in the report allows the reader to see at a glance how the ratings came out.

The results can be presented graphically as well as in averages. Figure 10–2 shows student ratings of a reading room in a university library. The room is seen as valuable and strong but relatively low in activity.

Limitations

The semantic differential is usable only with intelligent and cooperative adults. People with little education often focus on the ends of the scale and do not use the middle points. We would not recommend using the semantic differential with children, with people whose command of the language is limited, with older people who would have difficulty seeing the various scale points, or with any group of respondents who are not accustomed to making fine distinctions.

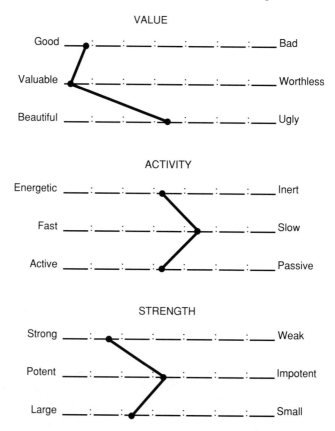

FIG. 10–2. Library reference room, ratings from the semantic differential.

Performance Rating Scales

Many companies require the work of all employees to be formally rated periodically. The procedure is intended to give the supervisor firsthand contact with the employee's work and to ensure a minimum level of competence. Performance scales contain a built-in evaluative component. Behavior is rated along dimensions such as skilled–unskilled, organized–disorganized, competent–incompetent, etc. It is desirable to make the behaviors assessed very specific; instead of asking a general question about work habits, the rater is asked about the employee's response to supervision, ability to work under pressure, relationships with fellow employees, and so on. The items can be tailored to specific tasks by asking workers and supervisors to suggest qualities that are important on the job. Previous research on worker productivity may also be a source of items. It is important to pretest both the job-related characteristics and the rating scales to eliminate ambiguous or unclear terms.

Experience with performance ratings in industry, the civil service, and the armed forces has been disappointing for several reasons. One is the problem of halo effects. A *halo effect* refers to the tendency to make ratings of specific abilities on the basis of an overall impression. If you like someone, it is easy to see everything he or she does as good. If you don't like the person, it is easy to give poor marks to all his or her work. Another problem is that raters are not willing to make honest judgments. There are severe pressures against saying unkind things about another person. If a supervisor wants to be known as a "good guy," all employees routinely receive good evaluations. Also, low ratings for employees reflect badly on the supervisor.

Because those doing the rating know that extremely positive evaluations are the rule, anything less than the top score is seen as likely to jeopardize the person's career. With a shrug of the shoulders because "everybody does it," the rater routinely checks "outstanding" for all categories. This happened in the U.S. Army Officer Efficiency Ratings. In this scale, "Excellent" was a typical score and "Very Good" became a mark of disapproval. This tendency to inflate a person's abilities is readily apparent on recommendation forms that use performance scales. A high proportion of recommendation letters describe the applicant as being in the top 5 or 1 percent.

One method used to minimize the tendency to give top ratings to everyone is to make the questions specific and personal. Instead of asking whether an employee is a good worker, supervisors are asked how likely they would be to recommend the employee for advancement in their department. A professor writing a letter of recommendation would be asked not only whether the applicant was a good student but whether the professor would admit the student to his or her own graduate program. Personalizing the questions helps reduce the ho-hum attitude on the part of the rater.

Limitations

Performance rating scales have not been very useful in research because of the reluctance of raters to say unkind things about people, halo effects, and a lack of standards for judging employee effectiveness. If other criteria of effectiveness are available, such as production records or customer ratings, the supervisor's rating may provide useful supplementary information.

Consumer Rating Scales

After checking into a motel room, it is common to find a short questionnaire on the dresser asking for an evaluation of the service, facilities, and food. The purchaser of a new car is likely to receive a questionnaire in the mail from the national distributor asking about the quality of dealer service and maintenance. Consumer organizations collect evaluations of products from members and volunteers. Rating scales are ideal for evaluating items or services with which the person is familiar. They are less useful for defining needs and wants. Interview and focus groups are the preferred methods for market research aimed at discovering the levels of demand.

Product and service rating scales offer an efficient method for collecting responses from large groups. It would be awkward and time-consuming to interview 100 motel customers in their rooms, but it is easy to collect a similar number of responses to a rating scale from room occupants over a period of time. Instead of using a representative sample of the community, it is common to use a convenience sample of those who have had direct experience with the product or service. Ratings of an airline would be obtained from passengers during a flight. A camera manufacturer might include a brief questionnaire along with the warranty card. Commercial firms employ methods that vary in complexity and sophistication to obtain customer feedback. Some cast their nets widely in the hope of finding something useful; others prefer detailed ratings from a carefully selected sample.

The first step in developing a consumer rating scale is to identify those characteristics of the product or service that are relevant and important. This is done by examining ratings of similar products and by consulting with suppliers and customers.

The next step is to establish scale points. For a brief questionnaire that accompanies the product or is filled out by customers, a three-point scale plus "cannot say" or "no opinion" is probably sufficient.

Example

We would appreciate your opinions regarding your stay in this motel. Please rate the quality of the following:

desk clerk	above average	average	below average	no opinion
cleanliness of room	above average	average	below average	no opinion
coffee shop service	above average	average	below average	no opinion
elevator	above average	average	below average	no opinion

For children and others not accustomed to making verbal ratings, a series of facial expressions can be used to indicate liking.

Example

Which face shows the way you feel about this product?

There is no reason why a rating scale should be dull and lifeless. A restaurant used movie titles to increase customer interest in filling out the rating scale:

1. Rate our food
   A. Some Kind of Wonderful
   B. Bound for Glory
   C. Touch and Go
   D. Crimes and Misdemeanors
   E. Mississippi Burning
   F. Unable to rate
2. Rate our service
   A. All the Right Moves
   B. Dream Team
   C. We're No Angels
   D. Missing
   E. Ruthless People
   F. Unable to rate

No matter how carefully the rating scale is constructed or how interesting the categories, there will always be some items that some people will be unable to rate. The easiest way to deal with this, as illustrated in the examples, is to include a separate category "unable to rate" or "no opinion." Another possibility is to instruct people to leave blank any item they are unable to rate. However, if space is available, it is better to add a specific category for those unable to express an opinion.

Limitations

Rating scales attached to the product or left on motel dressers are subject to response bias. Persons most likely to fill out and send in questionnaires will be those with strong opinions pro and con—and generally the latter. Response rates will vary with the consumer's interest in helping the manufacturer or service agent.

Sensory Evaluation

Sensory evaluation began in the laboratories of early experimental psychologists who were interested in the basic properties of odors, tastes, sound, and other sensations. The connection between the physical qualities of objects and their sensory attributes is called *psychophysics*. A key assumption in psychophysics is that people can make meaningful ratings of the degree of their sensory experiences (e.g., rating items as more or less bright, loud, sweet, and so on).

The food and beverage industries rely heavily on sensory evaluation. Before a new product is marketed, its consumer acceptance will be tested. Products are often first rated by expert judges who have exceptionally well-developed palates, noses, or visual sensitivity before being tried out on a panel of nonexperts. Researchers in Norway examined consumer response to black currant juice, which varied in strength, color, acidity, portion size, and time of testing (before or after lunch). Preference was found to be mainly influenced by color, acidity, and portion size (Martens, Risvik, & Schutz, 1983).

The qualities to be rated depend as much on the interests of the investigator as on the objective characteristic of the item. A firm might be interested in the vi-

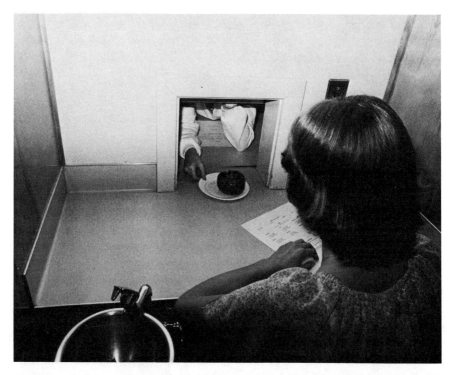

Sensory evaluation. The student was asked to rate the flavor and appearance of tomatoes.

sual appearance of a bar of soap, the texture of canned fruit, or the sound level of fluorescent lights. Deciding what characteristics are relevant should be done in consultation with the client or consumer organization, or it can be based on previous research.

Various methods have been used to present material to the judges. One approach is to present the judges, at the beginning of the session, with *standards*. For an investigation of taste qualities, the judge will first taste four different compounds, one very sweet, one very sour, one very salty, and another very bitter to use as standards in making subsequent judgments.

Example

Rate the item you have tasted along each of the following scales. Place a check anywhere along the line.

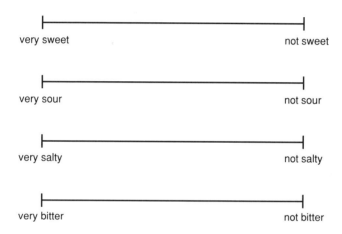

Note that the four taste qualities are rated separately. Sweet is not considered the opposite of sour. Grapefruit and pineapple can be both sweet and sour.

In the method of *paired comparisons*, two items are presented and the person asked to compare them. This method is useful in deciding whether or not a change represents an improvement relative to a standard.

Example

Compared to B (the standard), item A is:

spicier	less spicy	equal
sweeter	less sweet	equal
more dense	less dense	equal
more fragrant	less fragrant	equal

Since the subject compares only two items at a time, each comparison can be done quickly and easily. There is very little dependence on memory. Comparison procedures are useful with inexperienced raters who can express a preference for one item over another without being specific as to their reasons.

Example

Which of these two wines is sweeter, A or B?

Which of these two wines would you choose to accompany a steak dinner, A or B?

Such sessions are conducted as *blind taste trials*. The term *blind* indicates that the subject is not aware of the origin or identity of the item being rated. The subject is told its general category (wine) but not the specific variety, cost, or place of origin. Blind tasting minimizes the effects of labels and stereotypes. Subjects may be more likely to give high ratings to wines with expensive labels or fancy names. A further refinement of this procedure requires two experimenters, one who replaces all identifying information with code numbers before the sessions. The second experimenter, who has no information on the coding system, conducts the actual taste trials. This is called a *double blind procedure*, as both the subject and experimenter conducting the tests are in the dark about what is being tasted.

Limitations

Like performance rating, sensory evaluation is subject to a halo effect. When people like a product, they tend to see most things about it as good; if they dislike it, they see everything about it as bad. Without careful explanation, the terms used in sensory evaluation may not be clear to those doing the rating; for example, people may have difficulty distinguishing among fragrant, fruity, and spicy. Expert judges, such as food critics and wine tasters, use different criteria than those used by ordinary consumers. Sensory evaluation requires people to make artificial distinctions. When they taste ketchup on a hot dog, most people do not divide the taste into separate degrees of sweetness, sourness, and saltiness.

Summary

Rating scales are used to rank people's judgments of objects, events, or other people from low to high or from good to poor. They provide numerical scores that can be used to compare individuals and groups.

On a graphic rating scale, the respondent places a mark along a continuous line. On a step scale, the rater checks one of a graded series of steps without intermediate points. On a comparative rating scale, the person is asked to compare the object or person with others in the same category.

The numbers on a scale will reflect one of four levels of measurement: *nominal*—contains information only on qualities, or the presence or absence of something; *ordinal*—contains information on direction, such as increasing or decreasing size or order; *interval*—contains information on direction, and the intervals between each step are the same size; and *ratio*—contains information on direction, possesses equal intervals, and an absolute zero.

An attitude scale is a special type of questionnaire designed to produce scores indicating the overall degree of favorability of a person's feelings about a topic. A Likert-type scale contains only statements that are clearly favorable or clearly unfavorable. No neutral or borderline statements are included. The respondents rate each statement along a five-point scale of agreement, from strongly agree to strongly disagree. Validity is increased by eliminating items that fail to discriminate between persons holding very positive and very negative views on the topic.

Reliability refers to consistency of measurement. There are three common methods for estimating the reliability of an attitude scale. In the test-retest method, the scale is given to the person on two occasions and the results are compared. The split-half method involves splitting an attitude scale into two halves which are then compared. The third method of measuring reliability involves constructing two equivalent forms of the scale. If the scale is reliable, the person's score on the two forms should be similar. The chief limitation of attitude scales is that they may not predict behavior.

The semantic differential is a procedure developed to measure the connotative meaning of concepts. Connotation refers to the personal meaning of something as distinct from its physical characteristics. Three major categories of connotative meaning are value, strength, and activity.

Performance rating scales are used to judge the competence and efficiency of employees. Experience with performance scales in most settings has been disappointing. Many supervisors are not willing to make honest judgments. The halo effect refers to the tendency to rate specific abilities on the basis of an overall impression.

Consumer ratings are used to find out people's opinions about products and services with which they are familiar.

Sensory evaluation is used to test the psychophysical properties of products, particularly food and beverages. Sometimes people are asked to rate items along graphic rating scales (e.g., sweet–not sweet, salty–not salty). In the method of paired comparisons, items are presented two at a time and the person is asked to compare them. In a blind taste trial, the respondent does not know the origin or specific identity of the item being rated. In a double-blind procedure, neither the subject nor the investigator knows the origin or specific identity of the item being rated.

Without careful explanation, the terms used in sensory evaluation may not be clear to those doing the rating. Expert judges such as food critics use different criteria than those used by ordinary consumers.

References

Likert, R. (1932). A technique for the measurement of attitudes. *Archives of Psychology, 140,* 1–55.

Martens, M., Risvik, E., & Schutz, H. G. (1983). Factors influencing preference: A study on black currant juice. *Proceedings of the Sixth International Congress of Food Science and Technology, 2,* 193–194.

Osgood, C. E., May, W. H., & Miron, M. S. (1975). *Cross-cultural universals of affective meaning.* Urbana, IL: University of Illinois Press.

Robinson, J. P., Shaver, P. R., & Wrightsman, L. S. (Eds.) (1991). *Measures of personality and psychosocial attitudes*. San Diego, CA: Academic Press.

Further Reading

Anderson, A. B., Basilevsky, A., & Hum, D. P. J. (1983). Measurement: Theory and techniques. In P. H. Rossi, J. D. Wright, & A. B. Anderson (Eds.), *Handbook of survey research* (pp. 231–287). New York: Academic Press.

Beere, C. A. (1990). *Gender roles: A handbook of tests and measures*. New York: Greenwood Press.

Beere, C. A. (1990). *Sex and gender issues: A handbook of tests and measures*. New York: Greenwood Press.

Dunn-Rankin, P. (1983). *Scaling methods*. Hillsdale, NJ: Lawrence Erlbaum Associates.

ETS. (1991). *The ETS Test Collection catalog Vol. 5: Attitude tests*. Phoenix, AZ: Oryx Press.

Henerson, M. E., Morris, L. L., & Fitz-Gibbon, C. T. (1987). *How to measure attitudes*. Beverly Hills, CA: Sage Publications.

Mueller, D. J. (1986). *Measuring social attitudes: A handbook for researchers and practitioners*. New York: Teachers' College Press.

Oskamp, S. (1991). *Attitudes and opinions* (2nd ed.). Englewood Cliffs, NJ: Prentice Hall.

Robinson, J. P., Shaver, P. R., & Wrightsman, L. S. (Eds.) (1991). *Measures of personality and psychosocial attitudes*. San Diego, CA: Academic Press.

11 Content Analysis

A 1989 Gallup Poll reported that 63 percent of Americans had "lost confidence" in airline safety. This did not, of course, mean that they stopped flying but only that the respondents felt less secure when they flew on airlines. However, statistics on airline safety did *not* show that things had gotten worse. During the decade preceding the survey, air travel was far safer than it had been earlier. Even the most frequent fliers faced a very tiny cumulative risk. It was estimated that a person could go on one flight a day for 18,000 years before having a fatal crash. To understand the paradox of increased fear at the same time of greater safety, a researcher looked at the way that air crashes were treated in the media relative to other risks. He undertook a content analysis of front page stories in the *New York Times* for a one-year period in 1988–89 (the same time period as the Gallup Poll mentioned earlier). He counted the number of stories dealing with six prominent sources of mortal danger: AIDS, automobiles, cancer, commercial jets, homicide, and suicide. The comparison among the six mortality risks was striking. The *Times* carried far more front page stories about the dangers of flying than any of the other risks. Despite the media interest in AIDS, the *New York Times* gave 60 times as much front page coverage per death to commercial jet crashes as to AIDS. The situation was even more extreme in the case of cancer. The same newspaper gave 8,100 times more front page attention to commercial air crashes than to cancer. The author of the study suggested that media attention might explain the contrast between the increased nervousness of air travelers and the actual air safety statistics (Barnett, 1990).

Quantification in Content Analysis

Content analysis is a technique for systematically describing the form and content of written or spoken material. It has been used most often in the study of mass

169

media. However, the technique also is suitable for any kind of material, including publications, recorded interviews, letters, songs, cartoons, advertising circulars, and so on.

The basis of a content analysis is *quantification* (i.e., expressing data in numbers). Instead of impressions about trends and biases, the investigator comes up with precise figures. For example, a content analysis of televised food ads aimed at children found that 64% were characterized by some combination of violence, conflict, and trickery (Rajecki et al., 1994). Private organizations and government agencies use content analysis to document the amount of violence shown on prime time television. Bleary-eyed researchers sit in front of multiple TV screens and make check marks on record sheets every time someone is shot, stabbed, or otherwise assaulted. Records of television violence over time can be compared with actual crime statistics.

A content analysis covers both the content of the material and its structure. *Content* refers to the specific topics or themes in the material. Whether or not an article discusses events in Asia is a content question. Also, whether or not the article is favorable to the subject is a content question. *Structure* refers to form. Whether an article is prominently featured on the front page of a newspaper or buried in the middle section is a structural question. Another example of structure is use of illustrations and their location on the page.

Uses

The content analysis method has been applied to the following materials, and other possibilities exist:

Visual media—television, film, videos
Verbal print media—newspaper, magazines, books
Visual print media—drawings, cartoons, other illustrations
Artistic productions—painting, sculpture, music
Personal documents—autobiographies, letters, diaries
Open-ended questionnaire or interview responses

Content analysis allows a person to do social research without coming into contact with people. There is no need to check with a human subjects committee. No laboratory equipment or expensive facilities are required. The materials for a content analysis are probably available in a library or newspaper file. In some cases, it will be necessary to dig for scarce materials in back issues of a periodical that is difficult to locate. A reference librarian can be helpful in finding materials.

An additional advantage is that the investigator can use material that is already available, thus eliminating the possible bias that occurs when the researcher generates the data in an interview or observational study. Content analysis is unobtrusive. The observer has no effect upon the material collected. The material is the same after the study as before. This is not true in an experiment or interview study.

Content analysis permits the comparison of trends over time and across cultures. How have the subjects of newspaper photographs changed over the decades? What sorts of models are used for sculpture in different cultures? These are the sorts of questions that can be answered. A systematic analysis of Australian horoscopes in the *Brisbane Sun* revealed themes similar to those found fifteen years earlier in the *Los Angeles Times*. Both sets of horoscopes were described as encouraging dependency, helplessness, and blind obedience to authority (Svensen & White, 1995).

An Israeli researcher reviewed a large body of Hebrew children's literature published after the Six Days War of 1967. The early picture of Arabs as seen in most stories was not attractive. The situation began to change in the 1980s with articles appearing that presented Arabs as individuals, rather than as stereotyped figures or national representatives. They were depicted as human beings among whom there were some good and some bad ones (Cohen, 1990). Moore and Kramer (1993) have continued this line of research, bringing the systematic study of stereotypes of Arabs in Hebrew literature up to the present.

In another example, a researcher compared the obituaries of male and female managers in major newspapers in Austria, Germany, and Switzerland, and found that different terminology was used to describe men and women after death. The men were more likely to be described as expert and knowledgeable in their fields and the women as more skilled in interpersonal relations (Kirchler, 1992).

Of all the methods discussed in this book, content analysis scores the highest marks in terms of ease of replication. It is easy for one person to repeat another's study as the materials are available and unchanged by the previous study. For example, a group of researchers kept track of the amount of radio air time devoted to country music and compared it with suicide rates for 49 U.S. cities. They found that the greater the air time of country music, the greater the white suicide rate (Stack & Gundlach, 1992). A second group of researchers analyzed the data and failed to find the hypothesized relationship (Maguire & Snipes, 1994). According to the initial researchers, the disagreement centered on the way in which the suicide rate was estimated. The measurement of air time was less ambiguous.

Content analysis allows for the simultaneous application of quantitative and qualitative techniques. The structural aspects of advertising or news reports can be counted. At the same time the content can be classified qualitatively according to the values or attitudes expressed. All types of material can be studied using content analysis.

Although many researchers use this technique with material already printed, it is also possible to generate new material for a content analysis. An Israeli psychologist performed a content analysis on written reports of dreams collected from Jewish and Arab fifth-to-seventh graders living in various parts of Israel and the West Bank (Bilu, 1989). Each dream was analyzed for the degree to which Jews appeared in Arab dreams and vice versa. There was also an analysis of instances of friendliness and aggression between the dream characters. In this case, the researcher did "react" with the participants in the sense of requesting them to write down their dreams.

On the debit side, content analysis can be a tedious and exacting activity. Imagine sitting at a library table with 10 years of magazines stacked in front of you. Each article must be classified along several dimensions. The first few issues are interesting. By the time the twelfth issue is done, you wonder why you embarked on the study. Content analysis requires patience and attention to detail. Yet there is an excitement that comes from seeing trends emerge as you proceed through a mass of printed material.

Finding Categories

The best way to select categories for classification is first to skim over the materials to identify the major themes. These can be listed as they are found. When the categories begin to repeat themselves (i.e., the material all seems to be covered by the previous categories), you can stop for the moment. Categories that overlap or duplicate one another can be combined. The resulting categories can then be tried on new materials to see how well they fit.

Example

Content analysis of responses to open-ended interview question: "What is the single most important reason why you shop in this store?"

Reason	Classification
"Prices are low"	Prices
"Near my home"	Location
"Friendly service"	Employees
"Prices cheap"	Prices
"Convenient"	Location
"Good value"	Prices
"Accompanied friend"	Other
"Store on my way to work"	Location

The list of categories must be comprehensive, covering all the items to be analyzed. When coding specific elements, it is important to record non-instances too. If you are going to count the number of women with gray hair shown on TV, you must also count all the women shown on the screen as a basis for comparison, and probably the men, as well. It is legitimate to use an "other" heading for unusual items that belong nowhere else and aren't sufficiently numerous to warrant a separate heading.

Establishing categories is not always easy. Classifying emotional themes in television serials will have a subjective component. Cartoons may be difficult to classify with respect to type of humor. Some cartoons may show a combination of categories (e.g., both aggressive and sexual, or absurd and sick). You may need to develop a system that allows sorting into more than one category. In general, structural items such as amount of space, time, and location tend to be more reliable than content themes, which are more subjective.

In the study mentioned earlier of TV commercials aimed at children, viewers were able to identify global themes when reviewing ads that told a story, as in the following examples:

A boy is too timid to ask a rider for a close look at his show horse. But having been encouraged by animate characters (Snap, Crackel, and Pop), the boy reflects that "if Rice Krispies can talk . . . so can I. Hey, Mister, can I see your horse?" He is rewarded with a ride.

Olive Oyl cries, "Popeye, space creatures are stealing Sweet Pea. Where's the spinach?" Popeye replies, "Can the spinach, I want my Instant Quaker Oatmeal." Fortified, he defeats the creatures.

A girl who is practicing hurdles takes a hard fall, and doubts she'll be ready for tomorrow's trials. Tony the Tiger says, "We'll try again after a complete breakfast including my vitamin-packed Frosted Flakes. They bring out the Tiger in you." The girl wins the race.

The pattern of initial doubt followed by success was termed "enablement." Six other themes were found in other ads: achievement, conflict, dependence, mood alteration, trickery, and violence. Each theme or category was operationally defined. For example, "trickery" was indicated when an ad showed one party attempting to dupe another out of the product, or when costumes, camouflage, misrepresentations, or manipulative communications were involved. "Mood alteration" was the category used when consumption or reference to the product resulted in the actor's experiencing a pleasurable or intense physical or psychological reaction such as smoke from the ears, levitating, or stars in the eye.

When the scoring units are selected and operationally-defined, a coding sheet is generated for the coders or judges who will classify the content and structure of the material into specific categories. The coding system will then require pilot testing. Table 11–1 shows categories used in a content analysis of the themes in letters published by advice columnists Ann Landers and Abigail Van Buren (Dear Abby).

At least two specific coding systems have been established for verbal materials. The Gottschalk analysis of verbal behavior is designed to uncover emotional themes (Gottschalk, 1995). The CHILDRES project at Carnegie-Mellon University provides a system for analyzing talk and has been used extensively in establishing a database illustrating children's language development. The coding system can be used for a number of different languages (MacWhinney, 1995; Sokolov & Snow, 1994). These techniques require time and training. The advantage is that the coding details have been worked out and comparisons can be made across content analyses at different times and different places.

Content analysis is being changed radically by developments in computer technology, particularly the use of scanners for both text and non-text materials. Computer analysis is ideally suited for analyzing material already available in electronic form, such as e-mail messages posted to mailing lists or newsgroups on the Internet. Printed matter can be computerized using a scanner.

Many aspects of scoring systems are easily transferred to computers, such as coding specific words into more general categories, for example, counting "wife,"

TABLE 11–1. Coding System for Advice Columns (Ann Landers and Dear Abby)

Newspaper _____   Name of coder _____

Date _____

Circle one: Ann   Abby

Circle one: Letter/communication #   1   2   3   4

Check main theme (1) per letter

TOPIC (describe if Other)

manners/etiquette/taste	_____	love, romance	_____
financial	_____	health	_____
dangerous behavior	_____	friendship	_____
filler/quote (columnist)	_____	booklet pitch	_____
inspiration/meaning of life	_____	other (describe)	_____

CONTENT TYPE

setting straight/revenge	_____	seeking advice	_____
opinion - for	_____	giving advice	_____
opinion - against	_____	factual info.	_____
opinion w/o advice	_____	complaint	_____
anecdote only	_____	braggadocio	_____
other (describe)	_____		

TARGET

children (inc. grown)	_____	spouse	_____
stepchildren (inc. grown)	_____	ex-spouse	_____
in-laws	_____	grandparents	_____
other relatives	_____	lover	_____
friends	_____	acquaintances	_____
strangers	_____	self	_____
readers (of column)	_____	other (describe)	_____

"son," and "grandpa" as "family members." Several computer programs exist for searching printed materials to find key words, phrases, or numbers. Search programs have been used by behavioral researchers since 1966 as a means of analyzing large amounts of written materials and eliminating coding errors (Stone & Kirsch, 1966). The availability of scanners allows computer analysis of nearly any printed materials. The programs become more complex when designed to function as artificial intelligence in categorizing ideas conveyed in speech. There are software programs for non-text items such as drawings, photographs, and video images. Weitzman and Miles (1995) review some of the software programs useful for content analyses. Another way to locate a program is to review the most recent literature on your topic, paying particular attention to finding content analyses (see Chapter 3). Searching an electronic database using keywords 'content analysis' and 'software' will provide many references.

In the future the use of hand tabulation of written material may be as infrequent as hand tabulation of statistical data. However, analogous to the situation in statistical analysis, there is value in a researcher's making an initial rough tabulation by hand of both content and structure items when beginning a content analysis in order to see that the scoring categories fit the material and that important items are not being overlooked. A hand-scored pilot study can serve as a check on the output of the computer analysis. Occasionally the computer printout shows results which appear strange or bizarre. The answer may be a coding error that has gone undetected. Hand analysis even on a small amount of data can help to catch such mistakes.

Sampling

Sampling techniques will vary depending upon the type of material and its location. When coding open-ended responses on a questionnaire, sampling is probably not relevant, as the entire set of responses would be coded. Where there is a lot of information available, such as back issues of a daily newspaper, selected subsets can be analyzed. The key issue in sampling is to select an unbiased assortment. Chapter 16 describes the sample types and their selection in more detail.

Sampling Print Media

Finding one biased textbook does not necessarily indicate a serious problem with school books in the community; nor is an analysis of a single magazine issue sufficient to reveal an editorial policy. A larger number of school textbooks or speeches must be analyzed. A single edition may be affected by extraneous factors, such as the time of year or some unusual event that may temporarily obscure long-standing policies. The greater the amount of material analyzed, assuming it is representative, the more valid the conclusions will be. Although the more-is-better rule applies in general, at some point the cost of increasing the amount of material will outweigh the benefits. If a monthly periodical is being examined over a 10-year period, there will be 120 issues available for study. For reasons of economy, the researcher may decide to reduce this number through sampling rather than use all of them. Probably a sample of six issues per year would be sufficient. However, the sample must be representative. The investigator cannot simply use those articles or speeches that support his or her beliefs or expectations.

The researcher must come up with a decision rule; for example, selecting every third issue of a magazine or every fifth article over a 2-year period. The important consideration is that the material selected be representative of the material as a whole, that the selection is free of bias.

Decisions must also be made about the unit of analysis. One can analyze sentences, paragraphs, pages, or entire articles. For example, in a study of magazine ads, should a single four-page ad be scored the same as four one-page ads? Is a large editorial cartoon on a topic equivalent to a small one? One approach is to score each item in two ways. First, count each article, advertisement, or cartoon as a separate unit regardless of size (e.g., the number of anti-politician cartoons on the editorial page regardless of their size). Second, tabulate them by the amount of space (column inches) they occupy.

Sampling Other Media

As with print media, unbiased decision rules must be made regarding the sample selected for analysis, and the same principles apply to other domains. Pre-scheduled time periods may work for current TV shows. The extent of the sample determines the degree of generalization possible. If only one TV channel is analyzed, conclusions can only be drawn about that single station. As noted above, the sampling must be systematic and unbiased.

Reliability

Scoring categories must be reliable. Two people doing a content analysis of the same article using a single list of categories should come up with similar results. Reliability is greatest when the scoring categories are clearly stated and do not overlap. This is accomplished by establishing clear decision rules or criteria for classifying the information. Reliability cannot be assumed even with something as seemingly obvious as gender in advertisements. Some ads deliberately obscure the sex of the models.

Computer scoring is very reliable in many situations. When programmed to note every occurrence of a word or phrase in the a body of printed material, the computer does it accurately and does not get bored or lose interest over time. When the scoring is done by hand, the first task in checking reliability is to train two or more people (coders) to use the scoring system. It is important that the training be leisurely and relaxed. The coders must be free to ask questions and express their doubts when they are uncertain. Even a good scoring system may seem unreliable if the coders are not properly trained. Training begins with a detailed explanation of the scoring system and categories, followed by practice in scoring material under the watchful eyes of the investigator. The material used should be similar to that in the actual research project. When the coder is uncertain how to classify something, it can be discussed immediately with the investigator. It may be that the categories are ambiguous and should be changed. At other times, the problem will be the coder's inexperience in using the system. If the coders still have problems after a few practice trials, then the classification system should probably be revised. It is wasteful to begin a lengthy content analysis with categories that are not reliable.

Limitations

The results of a content analysis are purely descriptive. They reveal the content and structure but not *why* they are that way; nor does the analysis reveal the impact of a communication upon the audience. This requires further investigation through observation, interviews, or experiments.

The researcher using content analysis is restricted to the materials available. Some topics are more likely than others to be covered in the media. Someone who is interested in media stereotypes of accountants or welders, for example, would have to search a long time and would probably find little that was applicable.

Content analysis deals with communication materials, not necessarily with outside reality. An increase in media coverage of robberies and burglaries may reflect less of an actual crime wave than an editorial decision to highlight crime during a particular month. The investigator must be careful not to assume that trends in written or pictorial materials automatically reflect changes in the outside world.

Summary

Content analysis is a technique for systematically describing written, spoken, or visual communication. The analysis can emphasize either the content of the material or its structure. The basis of content analysis is quantification.

The researcher uses material that is already available; there is no need for interaction with an actual subject. The method is well suited for cross-national comparisons and for examining trends over time. The material chosen for analysis must be selected in an unbiased way, and reliable categories must be used in the scoring.

The results of a content analysis are descriptive rather than explanatory. Analysis is limited to available recorded materials and is subject to any biases in these materials.

References

Barnett, A. (1990). Air safety: End of the golden age? *Chance, 3,* 8–12.

Bilu, Y. (1989). The other as a nightmare: The Israeli-Arab encounter as reflected in children's dreams in Israel and the West Bank. *Political Psychology, 10,* 365–389.

Cohen, A. (1990). Tehomot shel sina (Abysmal hatred). *Hetz, 1*(4), 3–12.

Gottschalk, L. A. (1995). *Content analysis of verbal behavior: New findings and clinical applications.* Hillsdale, NJ: Lawrence Erlbaum Associates.

Kirchler, E. (1992). Adorable women, expert men: Changing gender images of women and men in management. *European Journal of Social Psychology, 22,* 363–373.

MacWhinney, B. (1995). *The CHILDES project: Tools for analyzing talk* (2nd ed.). Hillsdale, NJ: Lawrence Erlbaum Associates.

Maguire, E. R., & Snipes, J. B. (1994). Reassessing the link between country music and suicide. *Social Forces, 72,* 1239–1243.

Moore, M., & Kramer, D. (1993). Value reflection in Israeli children's drawings during the Gulf War. *Archivio di Psicologia, Neurologia e Psichiatria, 54,* 3–12.

Rajecki, D. W., McTavish, D. G., Rasmussen, J. L., Schreuders, M., Byers, D. C., & Jessup, K. S. (1994). Violence, conflict, trickery, and other story themes in TV ads for food for children. *Journal of Applied Social Psychology, 24,* 1685–1700.

Sokolov, J. L., & Snow, C. E. (1994). *Handbook of research in language development using CHILDES.* Hillsdale, NJ: Lawrence Erlbaum Associates.

Stack, S., & Gundlach, J. H. (1992). The effect of country music on suicide. *Social Forces, 71,* 211–218.

Stone, P. J., & Kirsch, J. (1966). *The general inquirer: A computer approach to content analysis.* Cambridge, MA: M.I.T. Press.

Svensen, S., & White, K. (1995). A content analysis of horoscopes. *Genetic, Social, & General Psychology Monographs, 121,* 5–38.

Weitzman, E. A., & Miles, M. B. (1995). *Computer programs for qualitative data analysis: A software sourcebook.* Thousand Oaks, CA: Sage Publications.

Further Reading

Krippendorff, K. (1980). *Content analysis: An introduction to its methodology.* Beverly Hills, CA: Sage Publications.

Weber, R. P. (1990). *Basic content analysis* (2nd ed.). Newbury Park, CA: Sage Publications.

12 Personal Documents and Archival Measures

Personal Documents

Many important research questions concern behavior that is personal and private. Although it is possible to interview people on these matters, private documents provide an additional source of information. Among the types of personal documents used in behavioral research are diaries and journals kept by individuals on their own or written by individuals at the researcher's request, and letters.

There are important ethical considerations connected with the use of personal documents, especially in terms of protecting the confidentiality of the participants. Any research use of diaries and other personal documents containing private thoughts and actions must be done with extreme care and regard for the protection and welfare of the writer and others mentioned in the text.

Research Diaries

To unravel the mysteries surrounding migraine headaches, neurologist Oliver Sacks (1992) routinely asked his patients to keep detailed records of their migraine attacks. This allowed the patients to become co-investigators, assisting Sacks in his research, and at the same time providing a level of detachment for them as they described their subjective states. The diaries were particularly useful in understanding the circumstances of a migraine attack—where and when it took place, what the person was doing and feeling at the time, its severity or degree, the specific physical and mental symptoms, the duration of the attack, and the person's condition after the attack had passed. This information would be difficult to obtain from other sources.

A research diary generally is limited to a specific activity of concern to the investigator. For example, research diaries are used in nutritional research to measure food intake. Although it would be possible for a researcher to observe people eating at mealtime, being observed might influence how people behaved (fewer second portions?). Systematic observation would be time-consuming and omit snacks consumed between meals. An efficient alternative is a food diary in which people record what was eaten and the circumstances. In a study of the effects of social factors on food consumption, researchers paid a group of people to keep track of everything they ate over a one-week period, noting where it was eaten and the number of people present (see Figure 12–1). They found that people in groups ate more and their meals lasted longer than was the case when people were alone. As a check on the accuracy of the recording, each person's diary entries were checked by two other people who were physically present at the time. At the end of each week the researcher contacted participants by phone to clear up any problems concerning the diary entries (DeCastro, 1994).

Research diaries are most effective when entries are recorded during or immediately after the behavior occurs. The longer the interval between the behavior and the recording, the greater the likelihood of recall errors and distortions. The research diary allows the inclusion of subjective information (how the person felt at the time) and environmental variables (where the behavior took place and how many people were present), factors often omitted when recall procedures are used. In regard to food consumption, studies show that there is fairly good agreement between diary records and data from actual observation (DeCastro, 1994).

In constructing a research diary, a key issue is how long a period should be covered—one week, two weeks, a month? The answer depends, among other things, on the amount of cooperation that can be expected from the participants. People's motivation for continuous recording of behavior decreases rapidly over time. Research on food intake might require people to record for seven consecutive days in order to include both week and weekend days. Keeping a diary of mood changes may require a longer period, perhaps a month.

<u>Instructions:</u> Please fill out a separate form for each snack and meal. Record your feelings at the start, and fill out the remaining information. A snack is a small portion of food/drink that is eaten between meals. A meal is a sufficient amount of food/drink to satisfy the appetite and is eaten at a planned or scheduled time (additional directions are provided).

Full-Hungry	Sated-Thirsty	Depressed-Elated	Calm-Anxious
1 2 3 4 5 6 7	1 2 3 4 5 6 7	1 2 3 4 5 6 7	1 2 3 4 5 6 7

Day: Sa Su Mo Tu We Th Fr   Time: Begin _____ End _____ *am pm*

Meal _____ Snack _____   # of people: Male _____ Female _____

Pre-meal physical activity level:

    Very Light 1 2 3 4 5 6 7 *Very Strenuous*

Type of Food/Drink with Brand Names	Amount	Location
(continued)		

FIG. 12–1. Example of a food diary (adapted from DeCastro, 1994).

Activity Log

A research diary tends to be limited to the specific activities of concern to the researcher. An alternative approach is to study how much time people devote to different activities throughout the day, for example, watching television, reading, eating, etc. The choice depends on the goals of the research. If the researcher's sole interest is in food consumption, a research diary would be sufficient. However, if the aim is to compare time spent eating with time spent on other activities, an activity log would be needed.

As with research diaries, the investigator must decide how long a period should be covered in an activity log. It should be long enough to sample important times but should not be so long as to lose the cooperation of the participants. Another decision concerns the time intervals on the activity log. Depending upon the nature of the topic, some activity logs use 1-hour intervals, asking the person what they did between 8 A.M. and 9 A.M., between 9 A.M. and 10 A.M., and so on. Finding appropriate time units is very important. Information will be lost if the intervals are too long, but if the intervals are short, requiring frequent responses, the amount of paperwork increases and cooperation may decline. When the activity has a clearly defined beginning and end, logs can be kept in minutes (e.g., telephone calls: 9:18 to 9:21 A.M.,

Personal documents. Because studying so often took place at odd hours in odd locations, researchers asked students to keep diaries showing how much and where they studied.

9:36 to 9:45 A.M.). With activities that are loosely defined or highly variable, records can specify the primary activity that occurred during the period.

There is no advantage to specifying time units in advance for behaviors that are infrequent or unpredictable. People can make a note at the time of occurrence. In a study of tip-of-the-tongue memory (the feeling of being almost, but not quite able to recall a word or name) researchers asked a group of participants to record whenever this occurred over a several-week period. Participants only needed a piece of paper and pen or pencil. They didn't need separate pages with days and hours specified (Heine, 1994).

Some researchers equip participants with beepers that signal on a schedule set by the investigator. At the tone, the person logs in the requested information, for example, where they are and what they are doing.

Personal Diaries and Journals

The data sources mentioned thus far are prepared at the researcher's request. Researchers can also use existing personal documents. Some people have published their own journals. In other cases someone else, perhaps a relative, friend, or historian, has located an interesting diary and obtained permission for publication. Using the diary of a British writer, Franz (1995) analyzed the words and themes entered in 1914–15 when the writer was in her early twenties, and those of a decade later, 1924–25. In this way she was able to compare and contrast the writer's interests and outlooks at two life stages. Another researcher, interested in expressions of grief and bereavement, studied diaries of 56 people who experienced the loss of someone close to them. As the diaries spanned the nineteenth and twentieth centuries, the analysis provided insight into changes over time (Rosenblatt, 1983).

Diaries do not guarantee direct access to the unvarnished truth. People can and sometimes do lie in their diaries, inserting their wishes and dreams rather than what actually happened. The cartoonist Nicole Hollander in her *Sylvia* strip has a character who uses her diary to record her fantasies of giving advice to important people. There are also possibilities of distortion when diaries are edited for publication. An original unexpurgated (uncut) version of a diary may differ considerably from the published version available to the public. A dramatic example is the much-beloved *Diary of Anne Frank*. A comparison of the version published in 1947 with the original revealed that her father, who did the editing, removed many passages about his daughter's developing sexuality and conflicts with her parents. Other published diaries reveal different distortions, sometimes making a person appear in a more favorable light, but occasionally adding unfavorable experiences that never happened. There is the case of a frustrated naturalist, Bruce Frederick Cummings, who described his own death two years before it occurred (Steinitz, 1994).

Following recent court decisions that allow diaries to be subpoenaed in legal proceedings, many public figures have stopped keeping diaries or are very careful about what is included—further diminishing the diary as an accurate record of events. Columnist William Safire (1994) described diaries of public officials as "always self-serving and often too sloppy to be evidence" (p. A6). This does not mean that diaries are useless or invalid sources of information. It means that they are subjective accounts rather than objective records of what occurred; reconstructions of events rather than accurate transcripts. Where feasible, other sources of information should be examined to see if they support the diary account.

Letters

Occasionally a researcher gains access to letters or documents not intended to be made public. Letters of resignation and written complaints fall into this category. A restaurant manager may have a file of complaints. The personnel director of a company may have exit interviews with departing employees. Such records may be valuable sources of information about personnel procedures or health and safety practices. Researchers who gain access to private documents like these should be particularly careful of the privacy of the writer and any people mentioned in the letters.

Collections of letters written by famous individuals have found their way into print—for example, Freud's letters to Wilhelm Fliess (Freud, 1957) and van Gogh's letters to his brother Theo (van Gogh, Gogh-Bonger, & Gogh, 1955). Originally written as private correspondence, they have become public documents available for journalistic, historical, and psychological studies.

Combining the use of personal documents and simulation, Black (1993) systematically compared the content of genuine suicide notes with simulated notes produced by non-suicidal individuals.

Limitations

The successful use of research diaries and activity logs requires participants who are highly motivated and competent to maintain detailed records. Although personal documents can be analyzed in the same way as other written materials, using content analysis as described in the preceding chapter, interpretation requires caution. Material from diaries and letters may be unrepresentative. What does it mean that 18 out of 20 letters received by the City Parks Department are complaints? Statistical analysis of such letters is a poor guide to public attitudes. Bias can be assumed even when most of the letters and documents are favorable. Most of the people who write spontaneously on a topic feel strongly pro or con. When using material from personal documents, care must be taken to ensure that the statements are not taken out of context or selected in such a way as to ignore contrary information.

Life Histories

Accounts of people's life experiences provide a valuable source of behavioral information.

Autobiography

There are published autobiographies (people's accounts of their own lives) relevant to almost any conceivable topic, for example, autobiographies of mental patients, sports figures, physicians, prisoners of war, and criminals. Politicians frequently write autobiographies, as do film stars, singers, musicians, and artists. Occasionally a sufficient number of autobiographies on a topic is available to permit systematic analysis. Numerous scientists and explorers have written accounts of how they made their discoveries. Hundreds of published autobiographies of prison inmates are available. These accounts cover all time periods and many nations, permitting comparison of prisons across centuries and national boundaries. Prison autobiographies are particularly valuable as it is difficult for researchers to gain access to jails and prisons.

A history professor described his gradual loss of sight through disease, his life as a blind person, and subsequent return to sight through surgery (Hine, 1993). His observations and insights would be very difficult to obtain through any method other than autobiography. One can observe blind people without knowing what they are thinking and interview them without knowing the right questions to ask. Reading first-person narratives adds insight and is easy and enjoyable. Most can be finished in a single evening.

Biography

A biography is one person's life as seen by another person. Its value as a research document depends on the skill, diligence, and accuracy of the writer. The analysis of biographies of artists and inventors is a common approach in creativity research. An English researcher examined biographies of noted English and French poets, some going back 300 years, looking for signs of mental illness (Martindale, 1990). Another researcher studying the same issue combined the analysis of biographies with available medical records for major British and Irish poets (Jamison, 1993).

In theory, a biography written by another person should be more objective than an autobiography where the writer presumably has more investment in maintaining a favorable or at least marketable image of themselves. However, biographies written about the same individual can differ significantly from one another, even when the authors have access to the same material. Biography involves considerable interpretation on the part of the writer.

General Comments

A reference librarian can be helpful in locating published personal documents. An entire profession exists whose avowed goal is to help you gain access to information. Some electronic databases have specific listings in biography and autobiography. Another possibility is to send out a request for information on the Internet. A recent request for titles of autobiographies written by women who were hospitalized with severe depression produced several replies the following day.

Although material in personal documents and autobiographies can be quantified by means of a content analysis, much is lost in the process. Retaining them in narrative form provides *qualitative* data—information not reducible to quantity or amount. It is often difficult to demonstrate the reliability and generalizability of such accounts. Despite this drawback, qualitative information complements quantitative data in increasing our understanding of behavior and social processes.

Limitations

Published autobiographies are frequently biased. The material may have been edited to exclude embarrassing or sensitive sections. Authors often deliberately try to show themselves in a good light or try to support some specific cause. They may not be representative of others who have undergone similar experiences but have not written about them.

A behavioral researcher who uses biographical data needs to be aware that what A says about B's life may be as autobiographical about A as biographical about B. People exaggerate or omit important details in describing their own lives and probably do the same in describing the lives of others. Two different and independent types of information, such as a biography plus medical records in the case of illness, are probably better than two biographies, as biographers often borrow material from one another or use the same sources.

Archival Measures

Archives are public records and documents. They contain a wealth of information for the researcher. A century ago, the French sociologist Emile Durkheim (1897) examined records of suicides from all parts of Europe where such records were available. He found that suicide rates differed greatly among nations. Those nations that had the highest rates during one time period also tended to have the highest rates at other times. Durkheim's statistics were used to test various hypotheses. A common belief was that suicide increased with the temperature. Durkheim's data did not support this hypothesis; there was no straightforward relationship between temperature and suicide rate. What seemed most important was the cohesiveness of the society. When family ties, social relationships, and political ties were strong, the suicide rate was low. When the social fabric began to come apart, the rate rose.

Many statistics are readily available in government reports; other information requires a diligent search through newspaper files, crime statistics, biographical directories, and census records. Most of the other techniques discussed in this book require the researcher to go out and collect original data. For the archival researcher, the data are already available in almost limitless quantity. The process is sometimes termed *secondary research*, as the primary data already exist. The wealth of statistics from different regions and time periods carries the risk of providing more information than can be sorted into meaningful categories.

Uses

Government records are invaluable in a multimethod approach. What they lack in depth can be compensated for by their greater comprehensiveness and coverage over time. Unlike data collected for a research study, which tends to be a one-time activity, government statistics are collected repeatedly. Once an agency begins publishing statistics on some topic, it seems difficult to stop. This is advantageous to the researcher who wants to compare trends over time. However, the researcher must check to see that methods of data collection have not changed. Between 1979 and 1991, the basis for collecting British unemployment data was changed 30 times (MacDonald & Tipton, 1993). Imagine trying to do research comparing unemployment figures in England during this period. Storage issues also affect the reliability of archival data. Some governmental agencies routinely discard statistical records after a fixed time period.

Public records can be used as a check against interview and case study material. Anthropologists matched baptismal records with the stated ages of residents of Vilcabamba, Ecuador, where many residents claimed to live more than a century. Earlier reports stated that residents lived to age 130 and that a large proportion was over 65. However, inspection of the actual records showed no one older than 96 and an expected proportion of senior citizens. "It's clear that a few individuals were specifically lying about their age, but most of them believed what they were saying," the researcher declared. "There is apparently a natural inclination of the elderly in Vilcabamba to exaggerate their ages for reasons of status or celebrity . . . and they have been getting encouragement from both tourists and the scientific community to do that." Available records provided a check on the residents' self-reports (Forman & Mazess, 1978, p. A2)

Using baseball and basketball statistics collected since the 1920s, some researchers claimed to have documented the occurrence of the "home choke"—that professional sports teams play badly in decisive games under pressure from home audiences (Baumeister, 1995). Other researchers questioned the conclusions and argued for a home field advantage, noting that more recent games did not fit the home choke pattern (Schlenker, Phillips, Bonieski, & Schlenker, 1995). Despite the seemingly objective nature of the statistics, the debate continues because the numbers are not consistent across sports and over time.

Finding Data

Most reference libraries have statistical data from public records, including census statistics. There are also yearbooks, sourcebooks, and factbooks with public statistics on a wide range of topics. For information on the United States, the *American Statistical Index* lists the publications of more than 400 government agencies, including sources of consumer price index reports, education and employment statistics, and other data. The *Statistical Reference Index* provides a topical index to information gathered by state governments, universities, and private associations. These two indexes are available online and in bound volumes.

Many other official archives are available in electronic form. Researchers can access census data, economic statistics, voting records, and some survey results on the Internet. Survey research centers are putting their results on CD-ROM and online, making them available worldwide (with a fee for access). Archives of visual data are also coming online. More than illustrations to accompany written text, these photographic collections provide opportunity for study and research. There seems little doubt that the future of archival research will be found in electronic databases.

In seeking information, the researcher is not limited to the most obvious reports, such as crime statistics, voter registration lists, and census reports. Numerous private firms keep detailed records in specialized areas. In studying the community response to a crime wave, it would be interesting to examine the sales of deadbolt locks and burglar alarms. Since no central records for this exist, it would be the researcher's task to visit locksmiths in the community and compare sales for the same month over several years.

Collections in libraries and museums are a rich source of archival data. In one study, researchers examined more than 12,000 photographs and reproductions of works of art spanning fifty centuries across cultures around the world to find over a thousand cases depicting an unambiguous hand preference (e.g., tool or weapon use). From the earliest cases in 3,000 B.C. to the present era, 86 to 97 percent of the cases depicted a preference for the right hand (Coren & Porac, 1977).

Underreporting and Bias

No matter how carefully they have been collected and assembled, archival records are likely to contain some errors. The important question is whether the errors rule out the use of the records in a particular study. Records may be very useful for certain groups in society but not for others. For example, census figures are more accurate for the middle-class sections of the community than for the poor. Census figures reveal very little about illegal aliens, who are heavily concentrated in specific areas of the country. Many older people sink into poverty and disappear from public records.

Other statistics, such as those for victimless crimes, are so erroneous that they are virtually useless. Published statistics on suicide tend to be low due to underreporting. Many families conceal a self-inflicted death by attributing it to an accident. Fatalities involving a single automobile may in fact be suicides, although they are rarely classified as such. Whether or not death from drug overdose is classified as suicide is often a matter of chance.

Records for rates of robbery and rape also are underestimates. One method of correction is to estimate the extent of error in official statistics by getting an independent measure of victimization. For example, with regard to robbery rates, researchers ask a representative sample of people in a district whether or not they have been robbed during the past year. If 15 out of 100 residents report a robbery while police statistics show a rate of only 5 per 100, there is an assumed underreporting factor of 66 percent. If this error rate is found in other victim surveys, the police crime statistics in similar districts can be corrected by 66 percent to yield a more accurate picture of the number of robberies.

Another approach is to seek out those cities and agencies with the most detailed and accurate social statistics. Public health researchers in the United States have often been frustrated in keeping track of people with schizophrenia. When these individuals move, contact with public agencies in the original location is lost. To get around this problem, researchers on schizophrenia make use of records in Denmark, where social statistics are more accurate and comprehensive than those in the United States. Records of birth, death, family relationships, and hospital admissions going back hundreds of years can be found in district offices. While information obtained in Denmark can be generalized only with caution to the situation of schizophrenics in the United States, it can contribute to a multimethod research strategy. The Denmark data have different limitations than studies of mental patients in the United States, which tend to cover a large geographic area over a short time period.

Some bias can be estimated by supplementing social statistics on large populations with detailed case studies and interviews with smaller samples.

Limitations

A major concern in using archival data is the problem of the selective deposit of information. Many statistics, such as crime and illness rates, tend to be underreported. Other figures, such as unemployment and cost-of-living statistics, are occasionally manipulated for political purposes. Researchers tend to be justifiably suspicious of statistics compiled by individuals and agencies with little interest or stake in accuracy.

Classification systems and the quality of record keeping vary from one agency or city to the next. A felony in one state may be a misdemeanor in another. Methods used in gathering and classifying information change over time. Classification systems may not suit the researcher's purposes.

Summary

Personal documents provide a subjective view of events. They are especially useful for understanding private behavior. Asking people to keep research diaries or activity logs provides material for content analysis and requires motivated participants. Life histories should be analyzed with recognition of potential bias. Documents not intended for publication are also subject to bias and should be analyzed with respect for the privacy of the people involved. Personal documents and autobiographies provide valuable information on how the world appears from the inside looking out, which complements other behavioral methods that provide the view from the outside looking in.

Archives refer to public records including government documents and statistical reports, library and museum collections, and agency records. Archival material is very useful when combined with data collected by other methods. Archives are subject to the selective deposit of information reflecting changes in classification and policies or other sources of bias. Data may be underreported or manipulated for personal or political purposes.

References

Baumeister, R. F. (1995). Disputing the effects of championship pressures and home audiences. *Journal of Personality & Social Psychology, 68*, 644–648.

Black, S. T. (1993). Comparing genuine and simulated suicide notes: A new perspective. *Journal of Consulting & Clinical Psychology, 61*, 699–702.

Coren, S., & Porac, C. (1977). Fifty centuries of right-handedness: The historical record. *Science, 198*(4317), 631–632.

DeCastro, J. M. (1994). Methodology, correlational analysis, and interpretation of diet diary records of the food and fluid intake of free-living humans. *Appetite, 23*, 179–192.

Durkheim, E. (1897). *Le suicide: Etude de sociologie.* Paris: F. Alcan.

Forman, S., & Mazess, R. B. (1978, March 10). They either lie or forget. *Daily Democrat,* p. A2.

Franz, C. E. (1995). A quantitative case study of longitudinal changes in identity, intimacy, and generativity. *Journal of Personality, 63*, 27–46.

Freud, S., & Fliess, W. (1957). *The origins of psychoanalysis; letters, drafts and notes to Welhelm Fliess, 1887-1902.* Garden City, NY: Doubleday.

Heine, M. K. (1994). *Naturalistic and experimentally induced tip-of-the-tongue in three adult age groups.* Unpublished Ph.D. dissertation, University of California, Davis.

Hine, R. V. (1993). *Second sight.* Berkeley: University of California Press.

Jamison, K. R. (1993). *Touched with fire: Manic-depressive illness and the artistic temperament.* New York: Free Press

Macdonald, K., & Tipton, C. (1993). Using documents. In N. Gilbert (Ed.), *Researching social life* (pp. 187–200). London: Sage Publications.

Martindale, C. (1990). *The clockwork muse: The predictability of artistic change.* New York: Basic Books.

Rosenblatt, P. C. (1983). *Bitter, bitter tears: Nineteenth-century diarists and twentieth-century grief theories.* Minneapolis: University of Minnesota Press.

Sacks, O. W. (1992). *Migraine* (Rev. ed.). Berkeley: University of California Press.

Safire, W. (1994, August 18). Carte blanche to pry into our intimate thoughts. *Davis Enterprise,* p. A6.

Schlenker, B. R., Phillips, S. T., Boniecki, K. A., & Schlenker, D. R. (1995). Where is the home choke? *Journal of Personality & Social Psychology, 68*, 649–652.

Steinitz, R. (1994, July-August). Kiss and lie: Diaries vs. the truth. *Utne Reader,* 138–139.

van Gogh, V., Gogh-Bonger, J. v., & Gogh, V. W. v. (1955). *Verzamelde brieven van Vincent van Gogh* [Collected letters of Vincent van Gogh]. Amsterdam: Wereld Bibliotheek.

Further Reading

Allport, G. W. (1942). *The use of personal documents in psychological science.* New York: Social Science Research Council.

Denzin, N. K. (1989). *Interpretive biography.* Newbury Park, CA: Sage Publications.

Gottschalk, L., Kluckhohn, C., & Angell, R. C. (1945). *The use of personal documents in history, anthropology, and sociology.* New York: Social Science Research Council.

Hill, M. R. (1993). *Archival strategies and techniques.* Newbury Park, CA: Sage Publications.

James, J. B., & Paul, E. L. (1993). The value of archival data for new perspectives on personality. In D. C. Funder, R. D. Parke, C. Tomlinson-Keasey, & K. Widaman (Eds.), *Studying lives through time: Personality and development* (pp. 45–63). Washington, DC: American Psychological Association.

O'Brien, J. W., & Wasserman, S. R. (1989). *Statistics sources: A subject guide to data on industrial, business, social, educational, financial, and other topics for the United States and internationally* (12th ed.). Detroit, MI: Gale Research.

Runyan, W. M. (1982). *Life histories and psychobiography: Explorations in theory and method.* New York: Oxford University Press.

Stewart, D. W., & Kamins, M. A. (1993). *Secondary research: Information sources and methods* (2nd ed.). Newbury Park, CA: Sage Publications.

Tomlinson-Keasey, C. (1993). Opportunities and challenges posed by archival data sets. In D. C. Funder, R. D. Parke, C. Tomlinson-Keasey, & K. Widaman (Eds.), *Studying lives through time: Personality and development* (pp. 65–92). Washington, DC: American Psychological Association.

Wasserman, P., & Paskar, J. (Eds.) (1977). *Statistics sources* (3rd ed.). Detroit, MI: Gale Research.

Webb, E. J., Campbell, D. T., Schwartz, R. D., Sechrest, L., & Grove, J. B. (1981). *Nonreactive measures in the social sciences* (2nd ed.). Boston: Houghton Mifflin.

13   Case Study

In the field of cultural psychiatry, *koro* is a condition of panic regarding the possibility of genital shrinkage, coupled with fear of impending death. The condition has been reported primarily in the southern coastal provinces of China, occasionally as epidemics affecting hundreds or thousands of people. In 1984–1985 there was a massive koro epidemic involving more than 2,000 people in Guangdong, China. Teams of researchers from the Guangdong Psychiatric Research Institute and the University of Hawaii interviewed 232 koro victims (Tseng et al., 1988). Among the 232 cases, 84 percent involved males and 16 percent involved females. Most were between ages 10 and 25 years, the majority being adolescents. Because they embraced the folk belief that the shrinkage of the genitals was caused by the female fox spirit and could be fatal, most were already anxious when they heard the news about the spread of koro. Before their own attacks, about three-quarters had actually seen others having panic attacks and had witnessed other people attempting to assist a victim. Their own episodes usually began during the night. After the onset of chills, the males experienced a sensation that their penises were shrinking. Thinking this to be a fatal sign, they became panic-stricken and pulled at their penises while simultaneously shouting for help. They experienced anxiety (100%), tremors (69%), palpitations (65%), shouted in fear (68%), and were preoccupied with thoughts of impending death (62%). The female victims usually complained that their nipples were retracting or their sexual organs were shrinking.

Upon witnessing the episode, family members and neighbors reacted decisively in the belief that the victims were in need of rescue. They would physically pull at the sexual organs fearing that the genitalia might retreat into the abdomen and cause death. The victims were fed red pepper jam, black pepper, or ginger juice.

In the majority of cases, the attack was brief and ended within 20 to 60 minutes. Only a minority (22%) had a second attack, and very few had more than three attacks. After the panic subsided, most of the victims recovered completely. No one died of genital retraction, but there were several injuries due to mistreatment by others trying to be helpful.

Advantages of a Case Study

Unusual events like this call for innovative techniques. When there is no opportunity for a controlled experiment or before-and-after observations, the researcher may still want to undertake a careful investigation after the fact. A *case study* is an in-depth investigation of a single instance. It can involve a unit as small as an individual or as large as an entire community or region. It provides the opportunity to apply a multimethod approach to a unique event or setting. Unlike other methods that carve up a whole situation into smaller parts, the case study tends to maintain the integrity of the whole with its myriad of interrelationships. It represents a *holistic* approach to research, and rests on the assumption that understanding is increased by considering the entire entity rather than breaking it into its constituent parts.

The case study has a long and honorable history in clinical practice. What is lacking in breadth and generalizability may be compensated for by greater depth. When a physician comes across unusual symptoms, it is important to examine the patient's background and experience in great detail. Have other family members shown anything like this? Has the patient been exposed to toxic substances? Any recent foreign travel? If there appears to be a connection between the symptoms and some specific factor, a report may be published in a medical journal even though it is based on a single set of observations. The author hopes that others have come across patients with similar symptoms and can supply confirming or negative instances. When several case reports link the symptoms to a specific cause, then it is time to undertake a survey or experimental study. The first case report can begin a chain of events that produces an important discovery. Publication of the case study of the koro epidemic in Guangdong was followed by reports in the medical literature of individual cases of koro in other parts of the world.

Another advantage of the case study is its ability to catch the reader's interest. Reports of surveys or experiments often appear dull and dense (thick with references, tables, and graphs), making them difficult and slow to read. In contrast, many of the best-known case studies in the behavioral sciences can be read as easily and with as much enjoyment as a good novel or short story. There is a building up of suspense making the reader eager to turn the page to find out what comes next. Vivid details about particular cases can aid recall. Judgments about what motivates or causes behavior often are influenced more by vivid details of a single case than by statistical evidence that emerges from a review of the literature (Hamill, Wilson, & Nisbett, 1980). Although a single case is not sufficient for supporting or rejecting a hypothesis, it can lend support or shed doubt on the predictive power of the underlying theory. Many of the principles of children's intellectual development have been illustrated by case studies.

Choosing a Topic

There are no rules for selecting a topic worthy of detailed investigation. Most researchers choose things that are unusual and newsworthy, such as natural disasters, serious illness, riots, fads, and fashions. This has created the false impression that a case study can be used only with unusual events. There is no theoretical reason why the method cannot be applied to ordinary people doing ordinary things. The practical objection, of course, is that it is likely to make dull reading and no one will publish it. However, studies that may seem ordinary at the beginning can be of considerable scientific value. Shatz (1994) produced a highly-readable account (*A Toddler's Life*) of her grandson, Ricky. She uses the case study to illustrate general principles of child development from ages 2 to 4.

To supplement the study of a single event, case studies of other individuals or communities can be collected. The desire for multiple case studies from different disasters has encouraged international collaboration. Disaster researchers at Georgia Institute of Technology have an ongoing collaboration with their counterparts at Kyoto University in Japan (Abe, 1982). Researchers in Norway and Sweden have been studying railway engineers involved in accidents causing fatalities (Leymann, 1989). The small number of individuals and the unique circumstances connected with each accident have some of the qualities of a case study. The accumulation of individual accounts and the availability of information about the employees prior to the accident and of their fellow employees not involved in accidents also give the studies some aspect of a quasi-experiment or experiment-in-nature.

A case study has a temporal dimension—it shows the changes that occur over time. It also covers a wide net of informants and situations. This will probably require more time and effort on the part of a researcher than a comparison of two groups tested once (e.g., comparing the questionnaire responses of 20 individuals who had been in a natural disaster with responses from a control group, especially if testing can be done in a group session). The two approaches, the case study and the group comparison, produce different types of information, but ideally will be complementary. For example, following the case study of the koro epidemic reported at the beginning of this chapter, the research team made a follow-up study using a questionnaire and compared responses of a group who suffered koro with those of a group that had not, all from the same region. The koro victims were less critical in their thinking and more likely to accept koro-related folk beliefs (Tseng et al., 1992).

The case study is widely used in anthropology to study cultures, in sociology to study communities, and in clinical psychology to study individuals. Educational researchers employ the technique to study innovations, such as the response of students and teachers to a new curriculum or teaching method. It is far more economical to introduce a new approach in a single school, study it carefully in order to identify problems and remove the bugs, rather than to start with a large and expensive test trial.

Unlike before-and-after measurement, which examines changes on an objective test at two points in time, the case study focuses on the processes of change with attention to the role that individuals play in promoting or hindering a new program. For example, a case study may reveal that an innovation failed because it was imposed arbitrarily on key individuals who refused to support it, not because of its form or content. The richness and breadth of the material in a case study can help to explain the findings obtained from other methods.

Case studies provide illustrative examples within larger investigations using multiple methods. A case study can humanize a quantitative study and increase reader interest by connecting statistical findings to real-life examples. The koro study was not only about victims in the abstract, but about Mr. Gwee, an unmarried 28-year-old office worker who suffered a koro attack while preparing for an examination. One evening he heard sounds of a gong informing the populace of a panic in a nearby neighborhood. He suddenly became anxious and experienced his own koro attack. The researchers followed his life for several years afterward. He later married and advanced in his career.

The researcher's responsibilities do not end with collecting information. There remains the task of synthesis and analysis—putting together the information from various sources into a coherent whole. The case study generally (but not always) ends with some kind of synthesis and analysis. For each conclusion there needs to be evidence presented in the body of the report. There should also be feedback to the participants.

Unusual Individuals

What would you do if a dog walked into your classroom, sat down, and proceeded to talk? Would you look for more talking dogs to round out the study (Fox, 1992)? No, a researcher would probably do what colleagues have done for over a century, carefully document the single extraordinary case using a variety of different methods and approaches to chart the mental powers of the talking dog. Can it be taught to speak other languages, solve mathematical problems, and find its way home in the dark?

Case studies are commonly used with individuals who display unusual intellectual abilities. People who have been extraordinarily creative provide fascinating subjects for case studies. A recent book that explores the nature of leadership has chapters on Eleanor Roosevelt, Robert Oppenheimer, Pope John XXIII, and Margaret Thatcher, among others (Gardner & Laskin, 1995).

There is a large body of case study research of savants. They are more or less ordinary people who can perform extraordinary mental achievements, although sometimes they have severe deficits in some areas of mental functioning. Salo Finkelstein, a calculating genius from Poland, was tested extensively by researchers in Europe and the United States in the 1930s. He demonstrated his amazing ability to manipulate numbers on stage on several continents. Upon request, he could supply Pi to 300 decimal places and the logarithm of any number from 1 to 100 to seven decimal places. Finkelstein was hired by a broadcasting company to tally the returns from the 1932 American presidential elections because, it was believed, he was faster than any calculating machine at the time (Bousfield & Barry, 1933). Finkelstein's feat of memorizing Pi to 300 decimal places pales before that of Rajan in Minnesota who had memorized nearly 35,000 digits of Pi, among other numerical achievements (Fox, 1992). Jebediah Buxton, an English laborer with little education and low intelligence, worked more slowly than most other calculating geniuses. Once he mentally squared a 39-digit number although it took him 2.5 months to do it. He worked as a laborer and the highlight of his otherwise obscure life was a visit from Fellows of the Royal Society who asked him to solve a number of complex mathematical questions. He could calculate while working or talking and could solve two mathematical problems at one time without confusion (Barlow, 1969).

An Englishman named Christopher is a savant of a different type. Six weeks after birth he was diagnosed as brain damaged. Although suffering from major deficiencies with regard to eye-hand coordination, finding his way around, and understanding the viewpoints of others, he can read, write, and communicate in at least fifteen languages (Smith & Tsimpli, 1995).

Following up an unusual case is very useful in social science research. When a stereotype exists, for example, that only men are capable of becoming great chefs or great chess players, it is an open invitation for researchers to seek contrary instances of women who have succeeded in these fields. A case study would document their development, career, and answer the question of why so little is known about them or why their successes have disappeared from public view. A single case study may lead to investigating the effects of prejudice and discrimination against women. There is a saying that if you can teach a chicken to play the violin, you don't need a string quartet to prove it. When you can document the existence of top-ranked women chess players, it is sufficient to disprove the belief that no woman can become a chess expert. Such documentation stimulates questions about gender roles and about the nature of chess, including the fascinating origins of the game and why the pieces move as they do. The rules of chess are unusual in that the queen is the most powerful and most mobile piece on the board, capable of moving long distances in any direction, while the king is a weak piece, inhibited in movement, largely restricted to a home base and requiring constant protection from other pieces. All these details and more could be covered in a case study of women chess players.

Obtaining Cooperation

You will gain or lose people's cooperation in a case study by your manner of approach and interview style. An anthropologist interviewing natives in the Canadian Arctic had a difficult time explaining his purposes. The natives could not comprehend why he wanted to know the intimate details of their lives. He wasn't getting any cooperation until he admitted that his employer told him to get the information. *That* they could understand. Compliance with a supervisor's orders required no further explanation. The anthropologist was perceived as another person doing his job. In your own case study, you will find that people open up because they like you, trust you, and want to help you. This is particularly true if the study continues over a long period and involves personal revelations. Of all the research methods discussed so far, the case study places the most emphasis upon the researcher's style, approach, and personality.

With poor or needy individuals, money is helpful in obtaining cooperation. It conveys the researcher's seriousness of intent and the value placed on the information. Even with an affluent respondent, a token payment can be helpful. There is widespread belief in Western society that something obtained for nothing is not appreciated. However, there are situations in which money cannot be used. For example, one could not offer $100 to the mayor or city planner to discuss zoning policies. Offering payment would be insulting, unethical, and probably illegal.

Avoid overselling your project in order to gain people's cooperation. Listen to their objections to your study before you begin. Encourage them to express any doubts they might have, such as fears for their privacy, the possibility of bad publicity for the community, and so on. It may be easier to work out ways to deal with these objections at the outset than in the midst of gathering data.

Make sure that you contact the key individuals involved with the issue you are studying. At the close of an interview, ask for the names of others who should be contacted. There is nothing more embarrassing, after you have finished your case study and left the area, than finding out that you neglected to interview important sources. Box 13–1 summarizes the skills needed by a case study researcher.

Cross-verification

A description from a single observer should be regarded as tentative. When three or four people independently provide similar accounts, it seems more substantial. Cross-checking the accounts of independent observers is one means of assessing

---

BOX 13–1. Case Study Skills

(Adapted from Yin, 1994, p. 56)
The researcher should possess the following attributes.

1. Be able to ask good questions.
2. Be a good listener.
3. Be adaptive and flexible, recognizing unexpected situations as opportunities to gain more knowledge.
4. Have a firm grasp of the issues being studied, for example, planning, politics, disease, etc.
5. Be unbiased by preconceived notions.

reliability in a case study. For example, a tornado victim may tell the researchers how he tried to help other people after the twister struck. Other accounts may indicate that the first individual was dazed and groggy and had to be led to safety. Do not conclude that the first respondent is an unreliable liar. Distortion becomes a topic of investigation. How consistent are people's accounts of their own actions during and after a calamity? We are led directly to a study of how people put unwelcome thoughts out of their minds.

A researcher should not challenge the respondent even when an account seems biased or incorrect. You are not the district attorney conducting a cross-examination. The goal is to obtain the respondent's point of view. Verification comes afterward. You must convey the impression of being a good listener. The respondents' knowledge that you have access to neighbors, newspaper reports, and public records will keep them from straying too far from the truth. Deliberate collusion among townspeople in concocting a false story is a possibility, but it does not occur often.

Differences between two accounts may reflect the way each person saw the situation. The person who spent several days in an evacuation camp after a tornado may have a different view of events than the person who stayed in town removing debris. Each of the views is accurate but is based on a limited range of experience. Inconsistencies in people's narratives can provide valuable leads. The researcher is a bit like the psychoanalyst who pays special attention to distortions and omissions. Asking for further elaboration is a better way of internally checking a story than challenging people as to their truthfulness or objectivity. Cross-verification is also possible through a multimethod approach. Perhaps better than all other techniques, the case study lends itself to the use of multiple sources and techniques for gathering information.

The validity of a case study is enhanced by using multiple approaches and then integrating the information through a process of triangulation or converging operations as described in Chapter 1. Interviews are usually an intrinsic part of a case study. Other useful techniques are observation, trace measures, and the analysis of public records.

Observation

Case studies may benefit from the systematic application of observational procedures. The case study of a child may include observations of behavior on the playground, in the classroom, or in other settings. For conducting a case study of an organization, participant observation (see Chapter 4) will be useful. Although there can be problems in being objective, some researchers study organizations to which they belong.

Trace Measures and Physical Artifacts

A case study of a tornado would necessarily include descriptions of damage and debris. Analysis of graffiti would be useful in a case study of teenage gangs. Case studies of some mental patients have included examples of their artwork. The cat paintings of Louis Wain, a famous British artist, showed his progression into severe mental disorder. The early cats were happy and socially active while the last ones exploded into color and energy, losing their feline features (Parkin, 1983).

Public and Private Records

When a case report involves a newsworthy event, other records may be available. The researchers who studied the koro epidemic found hospital records that documented earlier occurrences of the condition. In other case studies, the most relevant records are census statistics, school district records, crime reports, or the multitude of other available public documents. For supplementing interview or observational material, consider the archival sources described in Chapter 12.

Diaries are often included as part of a case study. The researcher may be able to obtain residents' diaries covering the period before a natural disaster. See Chapter 12 on the use of personal documents in research. These can be very useful in shedding light on the situation before the researcher arrived at the scene.

Limitations

Generalization from a case study is necessarily limited. Often an event is selected because it is atypical. No matter how many people were interviewed in Guangdong, China, and no matter how much time was spent in the area by the research team, this was only a single koro epidemic. It is appropriate to draw conclusions from the data (e.g., the panic was brief in the vast majority of cases), but the findings cannot be generalized to other koro outbreaks without further study.

Because so much depends on the researcher's personality and approach, a case study is difficult to repeat. The situation of two researchers conducting *independent* case studies of the same event virtually never occurs. For some topics, generalizability (external validity) can be increased by multiple case studies. The earlier example of railway engineer accidents is a multiple case study (Leymann, 1989).

In case studies that take place after the fact, the researcher must depend upon people's recollections of events. After a crisis, memories are likely to be selective and distorted. With dramatic events, behavioral effects may continue for years, and it will be difficult to determine when the study should end.

Summary

A case study is an in-depth investigation of a single instance. This method emphasizes the individuality and uniqueness of the participants and the setting. Reliability is obtained through cross-verification of people's accounts. Multiple methods, including observation, the analysis of physical traces, and public and private records are useful in supplementing interview data.

Generalization from a case study is necessarily limited. The event studied is likely to be atypical. People's recollections of past events are likely to be selective and distorted.

References

Abe, K. (1982). *Introduction to disaster psychology*. Tokyo: Science Publishing.

Barlow, F. (1969). *Mental prodigies*. New York: Greenwood Press.

Bousfield, W. A., & Barry, H. (1933). The visual imagery of a lightening calculator. *American Journal of Psychology, 45*, 353–358.

Fox, P. W. (1992). Fragments of understanding: The psychological study of retarded savants. *Contemporary Psychology, 37*, 221–222.

Gardner, H., & Laskin, E. (1995). *Leading minds: An anatomy of leadership*. New York: Basic Books.

Hamill, R., Wilson, T. D., & Nisbett, R. E. (1980). Insensitivity to sample bias: Generalizing from atypical cases. *Journal of Personality and Social Psychology, 39*, 578–579.

Leymann, H. (1989). *Psychological effects of fatal accidents on the track—the reaction of the railway engineer* (abstract of current research, Division of Social and Organizational Psychology). Solna, Sweden: National Institute of Occupational Health.

Parkin, M. (1983). *Louis Wain's Edwardian Cats*. London: Thames & Hudson.

Shatz, M. (1994). *A toddler's life: Becoming a person*. New York: Oxford University Press.

Smith, N. V., & Tsimpli, I. (1995). *The mind of a savant: Language learning and modularity*. Cambridge, MA: Blackwell Publishers.

Tseng, W-S., Mo, K-M., Jing, H., Li, L-S., Ou, L-W., Chen, G-Q., & Jiang, D-W. (1992). Koro epidemics in Guangdong, China: A questionnaire survey. *Journal of Nervous & Mental Disease, 180*, 117–123.

Tseng, W-S., Mo, K-M., Li, L-S., Chen, G-Q., Ou, L-W. & Zheng, H-B. (1988). A sociocultural study of koro epidemics in Guangdong, China. *American Journal of Psychiatry, 145*, 1538–1543.

Yin, R. K. (1994). *Case study research: Design and methods* (2nd ed.). Thousand Oaks, CA: Sage Publications.

Further Reading

Riley, M. W. (1963). *Sociological research: A case approach*. New York: Harcourt, Brace, & World.

Stake, R. E. (1995). *The art of case study research*. Thousand Oaks, CA: Sage Publications.

Wallace, D. B., & Gruber, H. E. (1989). *Creative people at work: Twelve cognitive case studies*. New York: Oxford University Press.

Withers, C. (James West, pseud.) (1945). *Plainville, U.S.A.* New York: Columbia University Press.

Yin, R. K. (1994). *Case study research: Design and methods* (2nd ed.). Thousand Oaks, CA: Sage Publications.

14   Using the Internet

The Internet is a new and exciting communication system. We include it in this book on research methods because it has become a major tool for obtaining and dispensing information. The Internet provides access to individuals and to databases. Access to the Internet requires a computer. Other aspects of computer use in research, such as running experiments or statistical analysis, are covered in the next chapter. Technically, the Internet is an extensive international network of computers that can interact with one another. It is a decentralized system available to anyone who can get access to it. Most colleges and universities have Internet connections as do governmental agencies. Access is also available through commercial services such as CompuServe and America Online. The actual connection is made either through an electronic network at an institution or by using a modem to send and receive information on a private telephone line.

The use of the Internet in behavioral research has expanded tremendously during the past few years. It has potential application for almost every research method discussed in this book. This chapter describes some of the ways that the Internet is currently being used in behavioral research and something about its potential, with the realization that a printed textbook cannot capture a fast-changing and expanding technology. The author of a recent book on the Internet acknowledged his inability to keep pace with fast-breaking developments, commenting that "A book that tried to keep up to the minute with the Internet would never get written" (Shirky, 1994, p. 167).

We will avoid getting into the technical aspects of the Internet or specific commands. These are best learned through first-hand experience using the software available to you. Once you get online (linked into the Internet) and start experimenting with the system, it is easy to find your way. The Internet is user-friendly, and one step leads to another. The system was originally designed to withstand a nuclear war, so it is very rugged and you can't break anything. Don't panic if you make a mistake. By reading the screen carefully, you may find an "error message" with instructions as to how to set things right (Shirky, 1994).

There are a number of subsystems operating on the Internet. You can think of them as alternative communication routes. The most frequently used ones are discussed in the following sections.

e-mail

Electronic mail (e-mail) is a way of sending messages to another person's computer using an electronic address. Here is an example of an e-mail address (that of the first author):

basommer@ucdavis.edu

The first segment identifies the individual; @ identifies the particular computer system to which the message is sent. The address can be entered in either lower or upper case letters, or a combination of the two.

Some instructors use e-mail for class projects. Each student is given a list of e-mail addresses of other class or team members, plus the instructor's address. When questions arise, such as the wording of items on a questionnaire or how to score unusual responses, messages can be rapidly exchanged. Even if someone is not in the office or at home at the time, the message will remain on the computer until it is retrieved. There is no fear of disturbing a conference or waking up other people's roommates. An e-mail message can be responded to whenever the recipient gets around to it. It can be stored on the machine, forwarded to others, and printed out (hard copy) for future reference. Some of the privacy and etiquette issues connected with e-mail remain to be resolved; e-mail is neither a fully public nor completely private form of communication. As a consequence, it probably is not a good idea to assume confidentiality or to forward another person's message without their approval.

Besides its use in class projects, e-mail facilitates contact with researchers at other locations. There is not a central directory for listing of e-mail addresses. The easiest strategy is to contact the institution with which the person is affiliated. The institution may have a list or directory of individual e-mail addresses. One Internet manual suggests calling the person on the telephone to request their e-mail address. Even if you don't reach the person directly, the individual answering the call may be able to provide an e-mail address.

There are several other ways of finding e-mail addresses that we will describe here, although you may need to read the rest of the chapter before they make sense to you. If you can access the World Wide Web (to be discussed shortly), there is a web site for college e-mail addresses (see Box 14–2). The list includes colleges and universities worldwide, but not all are included. The American Psychological Association (APA) home page on the Web provides access to a list of academic departments and research institutions which may (or may not) release e-mail addresses for specific individuals. If you cannot find a specific institution listed, contact a college nearby for the address of the one you want. For example, if you wanted someone at the University of Tampere in Finland (which is not listed), you could try the cognitive program at the University of Helsinki or the psychology program at Stockholm University, both of which are listed, and see if someone there has the address you want. Our point here is that there are lots of ways to use the network to get information. The Hanover College home page maintains a list of psychology departments on the Internet, including separate lists for Canada, Britain, and Ireland.

Mailing Lists

Mailing lists also use e-mail connections. A *mailing list* consists of a group of subscribers to a central address. Subscribers exchange information on a specific topic. There are mailing lists for nearly all behavioral science topics, including research methods. Messages are sent to a central address and then distributed to subscribers. Some lists are open exchanges in that and all communications are automatically distributed. Others have a moderator who screens messages for appropriateness before sending them to subscribers. You can become part of a mailing list by sending a request to subscribe. Once you are on the list, messages are sent directly to your e-mail address.

There are two important addresses: one for subscribing and the other for communicating with the other people on the list. The *list server* (sometimes called a *list processor*) does the bookkeeping. The list server is your contact address for subscribing, unsubscribing, and finding out who else is on the list. The second address is that of the *list* itself. Here is an example of the first step—getting on the list:

On the address line: listserv@⟨server address⟩
In the message space: subscribe ⟨list⟩ ⟨your name⟩

For the St. Johns University Virtual Psychology List, we sent the following e-mail message:

On the address line: LISTSERV@SJUVM.STJOHNS.EDU
In the message space: SUBSCRIBE VIRTPSY BARBARA SOMMER

You don't need to add your own e-mail address because it is automatically included as the return address on your message. You will get a very prompt response via e-mail.

To *unsubscribe*, send the following:

On the address line: listserv@⟨server address⟩
In the message space: unsubscribe ⟨list⟩ ⟨your name⟩

Once you are on the list, you use the *list* address (different from that of the list server) to communicate with other subscribers. The *list* address that you will use for sending messages to others on the list begins with the list name (rather than LISTSERV or LISTPROC). For sending messages use the following format:

On the address line: ⟨list name and address⟩
On the subject line: ⟨what your message is about⟩
In the message space: ⟨your message to people on the list⟩

The St. Johns University Virtual Psychology list name and address is VIRTPSY@SJUVM.STJOHNS.EDU, and that is the address used for all communications among subscribers to that particular mailing list.

Joining a list is like meeting new people at a party with whom you have something in common. The first step is introductions. It is courteous to introduce yourself by posting a note to the list noting your specific interests in the topic, e-mail address, and affiliation (for example, department or college). You may receive reminders of proper "netiquette," such as keeping communications brief, avoiding hostile remarks, and giving proper credit to others on the list if you borrow their ideas. You may also be asked to read a list of answers to frequently asked questions in order to avoid needless duplication.

Mailing lists are very useful for exchanging information. One can ask for assistance in solving research problems, find out how other researchers deal with similar situations, enlist aid in finding suitable tests for specific purposes, and locate special categories of respondents. One person might send out a query on the creativity mailing list to find out if anyone knows of a test that can be used with teenagers. Another person might ask if the test is available in translation. There is often much to be learned from reading the exchange of questions and answers.

Newsgroups

Newsgroups are public discussion groups that are also organized around specific topics. Newsgroups are part of a system called *Netnews* or *Usenet*. Newsgroup messages are posted in an accessible location rather than sent out to individual subscribers. It is up to you to find and read them. It's like a posting on a bulletin board. You can see what is posted, select the communications that interest you, and either read them on the screen or print them out for later reference. You can respond to the posted messages and post your own. An instructor may set up a newsgroup for a class in order to facilitate the exchange of information and views. Newsgroups are accessed by programs called *newsreaders*, such as *Tin* and *NewsWatcher*.

Be advised that there are thousands of newsgroups on almost every subject imaginable. Lists of newsgroups are sent to local sites, such as the mainframe computer of a university. There are lists of lists available; one example is the Psychology and Support Groups Newsgroup Pointer (see Box 14–2 for address). Using such a list, you can see at a glance whether there are any newsgroups on topics of particular interest to you.

Many newsgroups maintain a list of frequently-asked questions (FAQ List). If you are interested in a particular group, find out if there is a FAQ List available. It may answer many of your questions.

We recognize that if you are not familiar with the Internet, the many new terms may be daunting. We have provided an alphabetized list of key terms and abbreviations along with their definitions in Box 14–1.

BOX 14–1. Glossary for the Internet

Archie—a software program for searching publicly-accessible files on the Internet. Archie can find the name and address of publicly accessible files when you enter a specified keyword.

Electronic abstracts—many behavioral science journals have abstracts available through online services such as PsycINFO or ERIC.

Electronic journals—similar to printed journals, except that they are available electronically (online) and are more timely.

File Transfer Program (FTP)—allows the user to transfer large or complex files from one computer to another on the Internet.

Gopher—allows user to search and retrieve information from a wide range of locations.

Home page—Web pages set up to allow access to related materials. From a college home page, one could obtain admissions information, lists of departments or majors, a history of the institution, names of noted graduates, a campus map, and other relevant information.

Internet—an extensive network of computers linked so that they can interact with one another.

Internet Relay Chat (IRC)—a multi-user, multi-channel network that allows Internet users to converse in real time.

List processor—see *List server*

List server—manages and distributes communications among members of a mailing list, also called a *list processor*.

Mailing list—an organized group for a discussion on a specific topic. Once you subscribe to a list (join), you receive all the materials sent to list members via the list-server.

Modem—A device that allows computer signals to be sent over a telephone line. A modem can be internal (built into the computer) or external.

Moderator or *Host*—a central e-mail address serving a group of users, such as subscribers to a mailing list, where messages are screened before they are distributed.

Newsgroups—open forums or bulletin boards for discussion of specific topics.

NetNews or *Usenet*—a collection of newsgroups enabling local users to communicate with each other and with other users, nationally and internationally.

Overload—the likely result of spending too much time on–line.

Usenet—see NetNews.

Veronica—literally Very Easy Rodent-Oriented Network Interface to Computing with Archie; facilitates subject or keyword searches on Gopher.

World Wide Web—also known as WWW or the Web; a system of linked information sources using text, graphics, and sound.

World Wide Web

The *World Wide Web* (also known as WWW or the Web) is a very popular communication system for several reasons. One is that it is not limited to what can be typed on a keyboard. Images and sound can be transmitted. Another impressive feature is its interconnectedness. One moves easily from one document or place to another. That is why it is called a web. It is truly an international creation with multi-colored images, sound and animation, and possibilities for obtaining further information by clicking on particular words or icons.

Specific software (called a *browser* program) is required for navigating the Web (examples are *Netscape* and *Mosaic*). Navigation can be slow if you are using a modem on your telephone line. It works much faster on institutional networks which have their own computer lines. You use the browser software to locate the particular system that you want to use (in this case, the WWW). Each system on the Internet has a URL (Universal Resource Locator) which is an address. The URL for the Web is http:// followed by the specific address you want to access.

Home Pages

The Web works through a system of home pages. These are constructed by individuals or organizations. The home page usually serves as an entry to additional information on the topic. Many of the major national and international social science organizations have home pages. For example, the home page of the American Psychological Association (APA PsychNet) contains extensive information about developments in the field of psychology, including a guide to library resources, locating information on standardized tests, lists of behavioral science archives and software, and guidelines on using PsycINFO (including a sheet containing the most frequently asked questions).

True to its name, the Web is very useful for making connections between researchers in different locations and different fields. As an example, one of us has been doing research on migraine headaches. Reviewing published journal articles on migraines revealed a possible relationship between migraine headaches and motion sickness. This was a new issue for us. A Web search under motion sickness turned up a military laboratory studying pilot training for high-speed jet aircraft where motion sickness could have serious consequences. The home page of the military laboratory contained names of contact people. A series of inquiries (the first ones went nowhere) turned up a person who provided very useful information about unpublished studies done in military installations. As these studies were not part of the published literature, the Web gave access to new information not otherwise available.

Besides providing a wealth of detail, the home pages often connect with other home pages within the same or related fields. The APA home page is linked to the home page of the American Psychological Society (APS). APS has links to the Australian, British, Canadian, and German psychological associations, and to the Council of Canadian Departments of Psychology. It is also linked to the Hanover College home page, which in turn connects with other behavioral science organizations. This gives you an idea of the multifaceted networks on the Web. Box 14–2 lists some useful home page addresses.

In addition to viewing home pages of related organizations, it is possible to do searches on the Web using key words. The browsing software (e.g., Netscape or Mosaic) will have a search capacity. For example, entering a key word, such as "creativity" or "depression" produces an enormous amount of information, including titles of relevant books and articles, conference proceedings, organizations interested in the topic, research institutions, etc. Each of these leads can be followed by going to its Web address. In addition to the general search capability of the browser program, there are several search programs with their own home pages. Two examples are Webcrawler and YAHOO. Their addresses are listed in Box 14–2.

BOX 14–2. Some Useful Web Addresses

Note: Developments on the Internet are taking place so rapidly that we cannot guarantee that all of these addresses are current. They worked the last time that we tried them. Linkages exist among the various addresses and lists. If you don't succeed in finding a specific source through one entrance, try another, or do a search. Don't be intimidated.

Two search programs (there are others)
   Webcrawler
      http://webcrawler.com/
   YAHOO
      http://www.yahoo.com/
American Psychological Association (APA)
   http://www.APA.org/
American Psychological Society (APS)
   http://psych.hanover.edu/APS/
Clearinghouse for Subject-Oriented Internet Resource Guide (electronic journals, discussion groups, conferences, and key people in many fields)
   http://www.clearinghouse.net/
Office of Research Integrity, U.S. Public Health Service (contains material on research ethics)
   http://phs.os.dhhs.gov/phs/ori/ori_home.html
Scholarly journals distributed via the World Wide Web
   http://info.lib.uh.edu/wj/webjour.html
PsychWeb (psychology-related information for students and teachers)
   http://www.gasou.edu/psychweb/psychweb.htm
EFF's Guide to the Internet (formerly The Big Dummy's Guide to the Internet)
   http://www.eff.org/pub/Net_info/EFF_Net_Guide/
Glossary of Internet Terms
   http://www.matisse.net/files/glossary.html
Psychology & Support Groups Newsgroup Pointer
   http://www.coil.com/~grohol/news.htm

Researchers can use the Web to learn more about new standardized tests and software packages. For example, two researchers at LaTrobe University in Australia developed a software program for doing content analysis of written material. Information about the software program is available on the home pages of the university. Researchers interested in content analysis see for themselves the output of the program and what it can do for their own research. Some standardized tests useful in research can be viewed on distributors' home pages.

Today the situation is a little like garage sales in a few front yards requiring separate trips to check each seller's wares, but in time one can expect the sellers to assemble on a single Web site, offering a virtual bazaar of electronic support materials for behavioral research. The Web makes available a tremendous amount of material of uneven and unknown quality. One cannot assume that the material is accurate, comprehensive, or current. You can use it to get ideas and identify potential sources of information, but this is not the same as a literature review. The quality of the material depends upon who has collected it; very little information is peer-reviewed. There is some fascinating material available along with some odd stuff.

Electronic Newsletters, Journals, and Abstracts

Newsletters on specialty topics and some behavioral science journals are available by subscription on the Web. The APA and APS home pages have links to tables of contents and some summaries to journals in psychology and related areas.

Other publications are directly available online, for example, the *Electronic Journal of Sociology*, *Psycloquy*, and the *Journal of Artificial Intelligence Research*. For a comprehensive list, see Scholarly Journals distributed via the World Wide Web (address listed in Box 14–2).

Non-Web Information Sources

There are other information sources on the Internet that do not require Web access. Gopher and FTP are also URLs (Universal Resource Locators). It is not necessary to have Web browser software to access them, although it can be used. Use of these URLs can be frustrating. As on the Web, many leads go nowhere. Connections may not work, lines are often busy, and your downloading (transfer) attempts may fail. It takes a while to learn how to use them efficiently.

Gopher allows you to explore, search, and retrieve information from various locations. It does not have the graphic capabilities of the WWW. Gopher uses a series of menus and is quite user-friendly. In most cases you simply connect with your institutional computer and type in "gopher." You'll see a menu and one option will read something like "Other Gopher and Information Servers." These will then take you most anywhere. Try the various options, and use the term *Veronica* to do a keyword search. You will see Veronica (Very Easy Rodent-Oriented Network Interface to Computing with Archie) somewhere on a menu, or try typing it in.

Gopher is useful for tracking down people at various institutions. For example, you can access most college sites and get a listing of faculty, staff, and sometimes students, often with e-mail addresses. Some of the electronic journals described above can be accessed via gopher. It also provides an uneven range of information covering specific topics, book reviews, and personal messages, and it has lots of dead ends.

Some of the material you locate can be downloaded to your computer within the program, for example, e-mail communications, newsgroup notices, and gopher findings. Other information, such as public records and public domain software, must be transferred using a File Transfer Protocol (FTP). *Archie* is a search program you can use for locating such information. We find Archie and FTP to be uneven in their ease of use. Another option is WAIS (Wide Area Information Service) for searching over 500 indexed databases. If you are after information not available through other means, find out the specifics on using these programs from your local computing service.

Using the Internet to Conduct Research

On the last occasion we checked, there were five experiments being run through the Hanover College home page: two on visual perception, one on auditory perception, and two in social perception. We took part in one of the social perception studies, which involved making judgments about the attractiveness of different body types. There were 27 judgments to be made, each involving a pair of human figures. After we completed the series, a message appeared on the screen thanking us for our participation and informing us that the results of the experiment would be posted on the Hanover College home page at some future time. One problem with the experiment was the time required for the stimulus figures to appear on the screen. The procedure took over five times as long as it would have if the figures had been presented in a paper-and-pencil format. On the positive side, the experimenters were able to test volunteers in distant locations with a minimum of effort and cost. As with any research involving a self-selected group of volunteers, characteristics of participants may confound the findings. Sampling problems may be reduced in the future as more people are linked to the Internet and sampling procedures can be used in selecting respondents.

The Internet can be used to recruit research subjects in general, as was done on the Hanover College home page, or to locate people with specific characteristics. It would be especially useful for finding people with particular characteristics or interests.

As access to the Internet becomes more widespread, the potential for its direct use in research increases. Individuals across many settings can be given questionnaires and the text of their answers captured and filed. Tests involving visual material can be placed on Web pages where they can be accessed and responded to by people in distant locations. An example of an experiment suitable for the Internet is shown in Figure 14–1.

The potential for cross-cultural research is enormous. Imagine a research collaboration between your class and one in France, involving surveys in the two nations with shared results. The Internet can be used to locate a suitable class for the collaboration (e.g., a research methods class at a French university), to gain the cooperation of the instructor and the class, to agree on the questions asked in the survey and the instructions to respondents, to check the translation, to develop scoring criteria for the answers and how to handle problem responses (i.e., people who did not appear to understand the instructions), to exchange the collected data, for conducting the statistical analysis using similar software programs, and for exchanging successive drafts of the report for editing.

Researchers who wanted to conduct experiments simultaneously in two nations could make all the advance arrangements on the Internet, including the instructions for the experimental session. This would be much faster and easier than at-

Judging the Length of Lines

On each of the figures below, indicate which of the line segments is the longer, the Left or the Right, by clicking on the appropriate box. If they are equal, click on Equal. There are 15 stimulus figures, and the experiment will take approximately 10 minutes.

Which of the two sections below is longer, the Left, the Right, or are the two lines Equal?

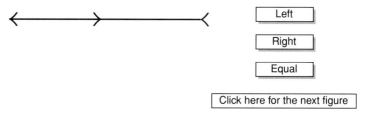

| Left |
| Right |
| Equal |

| Click here for the next figure |

(End of series)

If you are willing, we would like you to answer a few background questions. The information will help us to interpret the results. Please click on the appropriate boxes.

Gender: | Female | | Male |

Age: | Under 18 | | 18 – 23 | | 24 – 30 | | 31 – 60 | | over 60 |

Thank you for your participation in this study. The results will be posted on this home page when enough data have been collected. If you would like additional information about the experiment, click on the box below.

| More information, please. |

(leads to e-mail message form addressed to researcher)

FIG. 14–1. Perception experiment appropriate for the Web.

tempting to obtain agreement through a succession of letters and working drafts going back and forth for everybody's approval, and much cheaper and more efficient than telephone, conference calls, or faxes. Cross-national research used to take months or years to arrange and carry out. Now it can be done electronically within a single semester.

As more individuals are linked to the Internet, electronic panels can be formed. In survey research, a *panel* is a group of respondents selected for their particular characteristics, who agree in advance to take part in future surveys. Commercial survey firms pay panel members for their participation, but this may not be necessary in student projects or where the respondents have a personal interest in the topic. Since the same people are interviewed on repeated occasions, the panel method is particularly useful for comparing opinions over a period of time.

It is also possible to conduct real-time conversations through *Internet Relay Chat* (IRC). These "chat rooms" introduce the possibility of conducting interview studies or focus groups. At present the technology is still in a developmental stage and sampling issues would have to be resolved, but the prospects are exciting.

The use of the Internet itself can be an object of study, for example, examining characteristics of users, message content in newsgroups, and frequency of contact. Communications can be printed out and stored for later analysis. The material can be scored electronically using one of the programs developed for content analysis. Some mailing lists, newsgroups, and home pages keep records of the number of messages sent and received.

Overview

The Internet is a wonderful information and communication tool with an almost unlimited potential in behavioral research. It can be used to contact members of your class working on a group project, to contact researchers in different locations, or to administer questionnaires, experiments, and standardized tests. The multimedia potential of the Web makes it suitable for auditory and visual stimuli. The Internet can be used to locate and obtain data files and to link researchers to mailing lists and newsgroups, plus providing an almost unlimited amount of information on the World Wide Web. There are risks involved, particularly in regard to the quality of the information, overload, and short-cuts. Except for a few electronic behavioral science journals, the information available on the Internet is not peer-reviewed, and the quality is variable. Some of the material may be solid, but there is no guarantee.

A major risk in using the Internet for obtaining background information is overload. It is an open-ended system, with each item leading to others with no end in sight. One can sit for hours browsing different sites. This can be very distracting and counter-productive when an assignment is due the next day.

Because of its speed and flexibility, the Internet seems like a wonderful short-cut to obtain information needed for a term paper. A search can turn up pages of text, plus access to other sites providing additional materials. If you are writing a term paper on a topic, it is tempting to think that a Web exploration can replace an actual library search. Unfortunately this is not the case. First, the quality of what is available is variable, and there is no assurance that it is current, comprehensive (covering all the important aspects of the topic), or accurate. Some topics work better than others on the Web. We initiated a search using "autism" as a key word and came up with book titles, names of institutions doing research on autism, lists of organizations distributing information, various home pages, and some biographical accounts. All this would be good background information in doing a report, but it would not be sufficient material for actually writing the report. Our search under the heading of "imagery" produced material primarily of interest to geographers and others concerned with satellite viewing of the earth. Material on the psychological aspects of imagery could be more easily retrieved from one of the psychological data bases, such as PsycINFO. A search under "migraine" turned up a newsgroup with periodic postings of information, lists of support groups, treatment centers, and migraine associations, titles of recent books, and an 11-page summary of answers to frequently asked questions about migraines (FAQ List). There was considerable material on unusual treatments for migraines using herbs, acupuncture, and diet. Some of the information differed from that provided in the technical literature.

Surf the net, cruise the Web, fly through hyperspace, but don't try to write a term report or conduct a literature review based exclusively on what you find there. Even when an abstract is available electronically, it is only a guide to whether or not the article is relevant to your interests. An abstract is too brief to be taken as an accurate guide to the research results. If you are going to cite an article, for example, as supporting or not supporting a given finding, you should consult the actual article and not simply the abstract. To do this you will have to tear yourself away from the computer screen, leave the colorful images and infinite possibilities of the Web, and return to the campus library to consult the actual materials. If your library is online, you can quickly find out whether the book or journal is part of the library's collection and obtain the call numbers (some systems will tell you whether or not the material has been checked out).

Summary

The Internet provides opportunities for communication among researchers, access to information, and potential for collecting new data. To use the Internet, you must be able to log on to a computer (a server) connected with the network.

Direct communication between individuals is accomplished through *e-mail*. *Mailing lists* provide for the exchange of information among subscribers to the list. *Newsgroups* allow the posting of messages on publicly-accessible bulletin boards. The *World Wide Web* (WWW or the Web) has graphic and sound capabilities and consists of home pages with a wide-range of information. Many academic and professional organizations have home pages that provide links to other information sources. The Web can be searched using subject headings and keywords.

Other resources are *Gopher* and *Archie*. Information on their use is readily available from technology support services at colleges or from the suggestions for further reading at the end of this chapter.

In addition to the exchange of information, researchers are using the Internet to distribute questionnaires and conduct experiments. A major problem is possible bias in sample selection. Communications on the Internet may themselves become objects of study by means of a content analysis.

As with any information source, it is important to distinguish between accurate, useful information and that which is irrelevant, inaccurate, or simply distracting.

References

Shirky, C. (1994). *The Internet by e-mail*. Emeryville, CA: Ziff-Davis Press.

Further Reading

Braun, E. E. (1994). *The Internet directory*. New York: Fawcett Columbine.
Gilster, P. (1994). *Finding it on the Internet: The essential guide to archie, Veronica, Gopher, WAIS, WWW (including Mosaic), and other search and browsing tools*. New York: Wiley.
Gilster, P. (1994). *The Internet navigator* (2nd ed.). New York: Wiley.
Hahn, H., & Stout, R. (1994). *The Internet complete reference*. Berkeley, CA: Osborne McGraw-Hill.
Li, X., & Crane, N. (1993). *Electronic style: A guide to citing electronic information*. Westport, CT: Meckler.

15 Equipment

Equipment refers to the hardware and materials used in research. There are a number of equipment uses: presenting stimuli, recording responses, analyzing data (including statistical analyses), presenting results, and showing the settings and procedures.

Presenting Stimuli

Many laboratory experiments in psychology require equipment for presenting stimulus materials in the form of photographs, slides, audio recordings, and videos. There is an increasing use of computers in presenting and accurately timing stimulus presentation. Computer use is extensive in research on perception and attention. Variables such as background/foreground contrast, size, and context (surrounding area) can be systematically manipulated in order to measure the effect on the speed and ease with which something is heard or seen. Virtually all of the classic perception studies are amenable to computer presentations.

The computer is ideal for research on language and speech perception. The sound components can be altered in order to explore the point where recognition of the word no longer occurs (e.g., to find the point where an accent renders the word incomprehensible to a particular listener). Visual and auditory stimuli can be combined. Lip movement and sounds can be matched and mismatched in talking heads. Time to recognition of a particular word or sound is easily tracked by using a voice-activated timing system. The speed at which information is delivered to the viewer can be controlled.

Computer use involves two components: the machine (hardware) and a software package. *Hardware* refers to the physical parts, the actual machine. *Software* consists of programs or packages that direct the computer to perform specific tasks. Software tells the machine what to do.

There are three general levels of software for running experiments. In the first category are pre-designed packages for specific procedures. These are the least flexible, but the easiest to run. The second set is basic design software that allows some modification but does not require knowledge of computer programming. The third level requires you to design your own software and requires knowledge of computer programming. This takes a considerable amount of time, but you get exactly what you want.

A major consideration in selecting and designing software for either recording observations or running experiments is the timing—measuring length of presentation or response times. The built-in timer on a computer will probably not be sufficiently accurate. Timing software can be purchased for specific programming languages. If you decide to use an existing software package, be sure to look at its timing capabilities. Don't rush out and buy software that may be available at your institution.

The use of computers in running experiments is a rapidly developing field. An excellent way to get current information is to:

1) Talk with an instructor or researcher who has a computer-based research laboratory.

2) Do a literature search using the keywords "instrumentation software." Search your topic of interest adding "computer" as a keyword.

3) Skim recent issues of *Behavior Research Methods, Instruments, & Computers*. This scientific journal is full of articles about computers in behavioral science research.

Many studies in social or clinical psychology or education do not require the use of a computer for presenting stimuli. A slide or overhead projector may be sufficient, or perhaps a piece of apparatus that can be purchased from an equipment company. Some equipment may be resting unused in a storage closet at your institution or can be time-shared with another investigator. Scrounging for apparatus and software is good training for a researcher. If you decide to continue in behavioral research as a career, you are likely to be searching for apparatus, supplies, and funds throughout your professional life.

Recording Responses and Collecting Data

In addition to presenting stimuli, various types of equipment can be used for recording responses in both the laboratory and field. The increasing availability of computers has led to real-time experiments—that is, recording human–computer interaction as it is happening. Subjects' responses can be accurately timed and recorded directly by the computer without requiring the researcher to perform an additional data entry step. This automation minimizes error. Then the information can be electronically saved to a file for later analysis.

A laptop computer can be very useful in collecting observational data, particularly when its use will not influence ongoing behavior. Behavioral sequences can be systematically recorded by entering pre-established symbols for actions and events, and recording the frequency and duration of particular behaviors. As noted above, the entire process can be automated by using appropriate software.

Audio cassette recorders are valuable in obtaining samples of speech and language use in various settings. Conversational interactions and patterns can be captured for analysis. Recordings of meetings permit the analyses of timing of state-

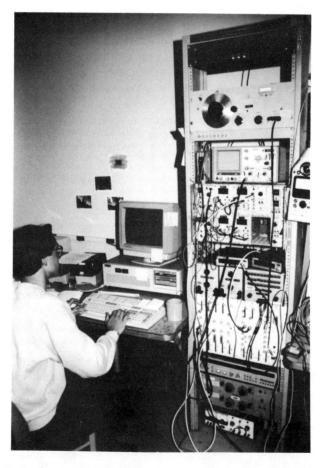

Equipment designed to measure neural activity from the auditory nerve. Not every experiment requires apparatus so elaborate.

ments and silences at a meeting. Much of the research on male-female conversational interactions has been based on data collected by cassette recording. Transcribing the material and printing it out allows coders to categorize responses without knowledge of the gender or other characteristics of the speaker.

A videocamera is particularly useful for recording complex interactions that are difficult to observe and analyze at the time they occur. Behavior can be recorded at one time and analyzed later. Material can be played many times so that details and complex interactions can be accurately noted. The technology is well suited for analyzing sequential behaviors, such as how one person approaches another or how people wait in line. Video images capture subtle changes in direction of gaze, facial expression, body position and posture, as they occur in response to external events. A videocassette recorder can be used to record television programs for later analysis.

Videotaped interviews require planning and a warm-up period. Don't go into a setting cold and expect to interview people there. Check out the location in advance, particularly the lighting and sound environments. Is there too much background noise from a ventilating system or street traffic? Such considerations should be checked out prior to the formal taping session. No matter how well you know the person and the place, the presence of a camera can change the quality of interaction and a warm-up period will be needed. Arrange beforehand to have some friendly and interesting questions or comments to offer before the filming or in the early stages. The important thing is to get the respondent's attention off the camera and on to the interaction with you. A shoulder- or hand-held camera is both awkward and intimidating during an interview. It is preferable to keep the camera off to the side while talking to another person.

An advantage of these recording techniques is that the categorizing or coding of behavior can be done later at a more leisurely pace than is possible in the field, and the scoring can be checked for reliability. Systematic sampling techniques can be applied, for example, randomly selecting five- or ten-minute segments from a 3-hour sequence.

A limitation of primary data obtained by photography or recording is that the presence of a camcorder or recorder may bias ongoing behavior. It is difficult to be unobtrusive carrying a camera or operating a casette recorder. A Canadian research team studying eating was aware that videotape would provide more precise records of what people ate at meals, but they still avoided videotaping because of the likelihood that it would distort behavior (Clendenen, Herman, & Polivy, 1994).

One possibility is to ask people to take pictures or do recording themselves. That reduces the sense of intrusiveness, although the potential for bias remains. Researchers interested in studying children's view of nature distributed inexpensive recyclable cameras to elementary school children and asked them to photograph the outdoors. The photographs were analyzed for objective features, such as the number of natural elements in the picture compared to people or buildings (Johnson & Monear, 1994). In another study, researchers asked school children in Germany and the United States to take pictures illustrating what "war" and "peace" meant to them. Each student was loaned a Polaroid camera with built-in flash and loaded with film. When a student returned the printed photographs, a structured interview was conducted on the meaning of each picture in relation to war and peace (Dinklage & Ziller, 1989).

Analyzing Recorded Data

There is computer software available for content analysis of text and some images, but material from audio- and videotapes needs to be transcribed. It is more common in behavioral research to code videotape data than to transcribe it literally, which would be very arduous and time consuming (i.e., describing every word and movement). See Chapters 8 and 11 for discussions of coding procedures. Videotapes made in the field also will require coding.

One potential disadvantage of videotape recording is the tremendous amount of information collected. Taking pictures of everything going on can be wasteful and time consuming for data analysis. A better approach is to have some idea in advance of what you want to record. Viewing angle is very important, especially if there is to be a systematic analysis of the data that requires consistency in what is being recorded from one time to the next.

Another limitation of both audio- and videotape material is transcription. Unless you have a special tape player with a foot-*reverse* pedal (and very few tape players have this), the transcriber will have to reverse and re-run the tape manually whenever a word or phrase is unclear. As most conversations are full of half-spoken and half-heard phrases, accurately transcribing the audio portion will involve as many as 8 hours per hour on tape. Unless there was an observer with the recording machine who kept written notes of who was speaking, the transcriber will have difficulty identifying people's voices, particularly when only brief statements or interjections are made. This problem is reduced in the case of videotape, but the process of transcription is equally cumbersome.

Statistical Tabulations and Analyses

Calculators and computers greatly reduce the time required for quantitative analyses.

Calculators

Many makes and models of hand calculators are available. Some are as expensive as a microcomputer and can do almost as much. Others are inexpensive models that can perform simple arithmetic operations but not much else. In between are many low- and moderate-priced calculators that will perform most of the major operations needed for statistical tests. The complexity of a keyboard doesn't necessarily reflect its potential utility. In choosing a calculator, look for the term *sta-*

tistics in the description, rather than business or engineering applications. For most behavioral research, there is no need to transform gallons into liters or compute compound interest. Logarithms can more efficiently be looked up in statistical textbooks, on those rare occasions when they are needed in behavioral research, than retrieved on a calculator. We have not found programmable calculators to be especially useful to beginning researchers. At the point when students are ready to write programs, they would be better served by a computer that will open many more avenues for analysis than are available with a calculator.

Some features increase the usefulness of a calculator for behavioral research. These features are identified by symbols or terms found on particular keys or just above. When a symbol is written above rather than on a key, a separate function button (F) must be pressed first. Symbols vary among different makes or models even when the operations they perform are similar.

Box 15–1 lists useful keys that reflect our experiences with the computational needs of beginning researchers. For those whose work becomes highly specialized, certain keys such as mean ($\bar{X}$ or M) or percentage (%) may increase efficiency, even though these operations can be performed using other keys with little extra effort. The keyboard symbols may vary slightly according to make or model.

Computers

Nearly all universities and colleges, and many other institutions and organizations, such as school districts and corporations, provide access to personal computers

---

BOX 15–1. Essential and Useful Features in Calculators

STO or M	Memory storage. Used for placing items into memory to make them available in subsequent calculation. Several memories are better than one. Essential.
RCL	Memory recall—recalls items placed into memory. Essential.
x^2	Squares each number. Essential.
$\sqrt{x}$	Square root key. Essential.
SS, Σx^2, $\Sigma+$	Sum of squares. Key used for squaring numbers individually and then summing them. Very useful.
σ, s, SD, S.DEV	Standard deviation. Very useful.
r, corr	Correlation coefficient or Pearson *r*. Very useful.
t or t_{ind}	*t* ratio for independent scores. Very useful.
t_{dep}	*t* ratio for dependent (correlated) scores. Occasionally useful.
χ^2	Chi-square. Occasionally useful.
F	*F* ratio—used in analysis of variance. Occasionally useful.
Var or s^2	Variance or square of the standard deviation. Occasionally useful.
RAN	Random number generator. Useful in selecting samples.

(PCs) for both data analysis and word processing. These include standard desktop versions and small portable laptop models. An advantage of using the computers available at school or your workplace is that there is generally a knowledgeable staff person available to assist with computer problems.

If you are considering the purchase of a PC, read some of the inexpensive paperback books that offer useful hints before you spend your money (see "Further Reading" at the end of this chapter). Talk with friends about their computers.

A PC has a system unit (system box or central processing unit), which does the computing, a monitor (screen), a hard drive or hard disk (place for storing information), a keyboard (for entering information), and a printer. Each of these components varies in price depending on whether you go for the basic version or the upscale one (i.e., a color monitor, an extended keyboard, and a laser printer).

Software for Data Analysis

The computers available to you may be equipped with software, or they may be on a network where software is shared. If you buy a new computer, the purchase price will probably include a software bundle—programs for word processing and some data management. A spreadsheet is probably included. A spreadsheet is the grid on which you enter your raw data. Database management and spreadsheet programs might help you organize information, but they will be of limited value in statistical analysis.

In selecting a software package for data analysis, look for the key term, *statistical analysis*, in the title or description. There are many good programs. The more sophisticated software packages are SPSS, SYSTAT, SAS, StatView, JMP, Minitab, and BMDP. The cost of these packages ranges from $500 to $3,000. Two moderately priced packages (under $500) are NCSS (Number Crunching Statistical System) and WinStat. There is a good chance that your school or organization already owns one of them and may have a site license, meaning that people affiliated can use the program (but not install it on their own machines).

Before purchasing a software package, find out the level of your system software and the amount of memory on your machine. There are student versions that use less memory and are available at a much lower cost. These tend to be limited in the number of variables and cases that can be processed, but generally will meet the needs of the beginning researcher. Examples that do not exceed $100 (and some are considerably less) are NCSS Student, StataQuest, Statistics with Stata, SPSS, StatView Student, MYSTAT, and Student Edition of Minitab. If your library has the Computer Articles database, you can use these software titles as the subject or keyword and get up-to-date information (see Chapter 3 on library searches). The Computer Articles database covers 200 computer-related magazines and journals. You read abstracts of the latest reviews and sometimes download the actual text of the article, getting the price and other pertinent information.

Each program is slightly different. You will find that once you have learned to use one software package, you will be able to learn another. Most software comes with a tutorial, a learning module to familiarize the user with the program. Although it might seem tedious, it is extremely worthwhile to go through the tutorial before attempting to use the program. You will be saved considerable time and aggravation later by getting an overview of the software's uses, functions, and commands. At the same time, learn the precise meaning of all the terms used. Some of these will be ones that you encountered in Chapter 6 (Experimentation), in particular, *variable* and *value*, and in Chapters 18 and 19 on statistics.

Finding Help

Many colleges and universities offer courses for students and staff on the use of computers and on managing data files. Extension courses are also common. Although you may not find that all the information is pertinent to your interests, such classes often provide valuable time- and money-saving tips.

Chances are that your institution or organization will have trained computer specialists on the staff. They are hired to help you. There are also a number of paperback books available in the computer section of bookstores. Talking to friends and associates who have been in a similar situation may be the easiest way to get assistance.

Data Presentation Using Computer Software

Behavioral scientists often present data in tables. With a good software package, it is possible to construct them in a presentable style. Most programs also have a graphics capability, allowing presentation in visual form. This may be useful in showing relationships that have a particularly interesting or clear pattern. Properly labeling everything requires considerable attention to detail. You may have to make some changes to conform to a required style. Chapter 20 and the example in Appendix C show the APA (American Psychological Association) style requirements.

With a few adjustments it is possible to make tables, charts, or both from the same data set. The software manual will explain the construction of graphs and tables. Don't overwhelm yourself or anyone else who reads the paper with duplicate tables plus graphs for every single comparison.

Illustrating Settings and Findings

Photography is invaluable for showing experimental rooms, apparatus, and simulations. The space station environment described in Chapter 7, involving Ken talking to an upside-down Derek, is presented more clearly in a photograph than in words. Visual images can have great impact in their portrayal of events or situations. Showing the type of graffiti found on city walls is more dramatic than a simple verbal description and presents the wall-writing in its natural context, illustrating the dozens of initials and statements, some deliberately intended to cover up others.

Photographic documentation is essential in a case study of a physical setting with its unique conditions. Photography can document what the town looked like after a tornado or flood. Photographs also can document ordinary aspects of life and elements likely to be overlooked because they are so commonplace. Participant observations of a small rural auto repair shop were greatly enriched by photographs showing the organization of space inside the shop, the exterior yard, and the junked cars waiting to be cannibalized for future projects (Harper, 1987). Sequences of photographs showed how the shop owner organized the repair process, depicting things as he saw them, offering the mechanic's perspective. The book contains over a hundred photographs coordinated with descriptions and interview data.

The decision on whether to use print or slide film depends on your purposes. Converting from one format to the other is expensive and there is a loss in sharpness. Prints have the advantage of not requiring a projector. They are more portable. However, if you want to show scenes to an audience, you will probably need slides. Slides and movie films can be transferred to videotape for presenting research results to an audience.

Audiotapes are not as useful as slides and video for presenting the results of behavioral studies. Unless an audio recording is professionally made and edited, there are likely to be fuzzy and unintelligible spots that are confusing and frustrating to the audience. Editing requires expensive equipment, trained personnel, and much time and effort. Some audiences become restless and bored hearing an audiotape without seeing anything on the screen.

Helpful Hints

The following suggestions are offered as guides to the purchase and use of cameras and recorders.

Still Camera

A sophisticated, expensive camera is unnecessary. A single-lens reflex camera that will cost around $200 will probably be sufficient. Many cameras of this variety focus automatically, a very helpful feature in candid photography in public locations where there is insufficient time to change the focus on each exposure. Cameras that do everything except click the shutter are called "point-and-shoot." They automatically adjust for film speed, the light value, and distance to the subject. The disadvantage is that you have less control over the picture because the camera makes many of the key decisions. After you have become proficient in using a point-and-shoot camera, you can decide if you need a more sophisticated model that gives you more control over the picture. Behavioral researchers who use photography as part of their professional work own several cameras. A good combination is a small point-and-shoot camera that is easily taken on trips and into the field, and a larger, more complex camera for serious documentation.

When using a camera in field work, you must plan for adverse conditions. Picture taking is generally forbidden in bars, gambling establishments, prisons, and hospitals. Adverse environmental conditions include rain, power failure, and illumination too dim for most natural light photography. There are three solutions to the low-light problem. The first is the use of an inexpensive strobe attachment, whose chief disadvantages are distortions in color and light reflection as well as intrusiveness. It is difficult to remain in the background when you are using a strobe. Another possibility is to use high speed films and "push processing." The speed of the film is written as the ASA number on the side of the film. The higher the number, the more useful the film will be under low-light conditions. If necessary the film speed can be "pushed" even higher through special processing. You should discuss this with a photo lab before you take pictures, to learn the maximum "pushing" that can be handled locally. The third method for handling weak illumination is to use time exposures. This requires a tripod along with a shutter release. Good pictures are possible in a dimly lit area if exposure time is sufficiently long. The chief disadvantage is that any movement will blur a portion of the picture.

Wind, rain, and snow create problems for a field photographer, but they are all solvable with the right equipment and advice. Cameras made for underwater photography can be used in the rain. Cheap protection can be obtained by wrapping the camera in a transparent plastic bag. This will produce some distortion, perhaps not unpleasant from an aesthetic standpoint. There are also methods for making sound recordings under adverse weather conditions. Advice can be obtained from local radio personnel or audiovisual specialists.

There are ethical and legal considerations in photographing people as part of a research study. Because laws vary from place to place, it is worthwhile to check with a local photographer before undertaking a research study involving camera work. The APA Code of Ethics calls for obtaining permission from research participants prior to filming or recording them. This is not a requirement in naturalistic observation in public locations where the photographs will not be used in a manner that could cause personal identification, discomfort, or harm (APA, 1992)

Check out the location in advance before taking the pictures. Think through what you want to capture on film. One session may not be enough. Often a close inspection of the developed photos shows elements previously missed, and it is likely that you will need to return for additional photos.

Audiocassette Recorder

An inexpensive tape recorder can do most of the things an expensive one can do. You don't need tremendous fidelity for most purposes. The omnidirectional (all-directional) microphone that comes with most tape recorders is satisfactory for recording the normal range of voice frequencies. A voice-activated model will save tape in recording group discussion but will lose information about pauses and silences. *Consumer Reports* is a good source of information about audio equipment.

If you want to play tapes to an audience, you will probably need a good player with at least two speakers. A good amplification system makes the difference between a clear presentation and a confused, bored, and irritated audience.

There are very few situations in which we would recommend the use of hidden microphones. There are serious ethical problems in using them.

An audio specialist can help you select the right equipment for a special recording situation. Some microphones, for example, completely block out background noise; others record background and foreground equally. Know what is available and choose accordingly.

Video Camera

Cameras may be hand-held, wall-mounted or used with tripods for stationary recording. Videocameras differ in special features and some are much easier to use in the field than others. Special lenses are available, including wide-angle lenses useful for indoor recording, telephoto lenses for long-distance pictures, and macro lenses for close-up work. Some machines have built-in microphones and headsets for continuously monitoring audio quality. Other models allow for remote operation both in recording and playback. Some cameras allow for the insertion of titles, date, and elapsed time, and combine both recording and playback systems.

Videocassette Recorder (VCR)

The various types of VCRs are not necessarily compatible with one another or with home television sets. Professional models cost more than consumer models and produce a higher quality picture. Tapes for professional models are usually more expensive than those for consumer models. The choice of machine for research depends on the quality level needed and compatibility between recorder and playback machine.

Some machines allow the possibility of playing tapes in slow motion. This may be a useful feature in interaction analysis. A "search mode" enables the researcher to locate needed items on a tape visually. For any type of content analysis, a "Pause" or "Freeze Frame" control will allow for the extended analysis of single frames. In some machines the frozen frame may be too fuzzy or unstable for serious analysis. For on-air recording, a counter will be helpful for making notes of significant features for later analysis. Video printers are available for making hard copy from video images. Slides and movie films can be transferred to videotape for presenting research results to an audience.

Summary

Equipment refers to hardware and related materials used in research. Photographs, slides, audio recordings, and video can be used for presenting stimuli to research participants. Computer software is available for both stimulus presentation and recording participant responses. Laptop computers are useful for recording field observations.

Collecting data by audio or video recording requires considerable planning. An advantage is that the obtained material is available for repeated viewing (or listening) and coding. However, the use of recorders may bias behavior. Another disadvantage is that reducing the recorded information to a manageable quantifiable level takes considerable time and effort.

Calculators and computers can reduce the time required for statistical description and analyses. Select a calculator that has some memory capacity and keys for calculating square roots and for squaring numbers. Having the capacity to accumulate the sums of the squares is very useful.

Computer analyses involve hardware and software. Hardware refers to the machine and its parts; software tells the computer what to do. Select a software package with statistical capabilities. Chances are that you are involved with an organization that has available software. Student packages can be purchased at low cost.

A camera is very useful in illustrating the research setting, as well as enriching the description of research findings. Still cameras are inexpensive and easy to use, as are audiocassette recorders. Video cameras and VCRs vary considerably with regard to capabilities and cost.

References

American Psychological Association. (1992). *Ethical principles of psychologists and code of conduct.* [brochure]. Washington, DC: Author.

Clendenen, V. I., Herman, C. P., & Polivy, J. (1994). Social facilitation of eating among friends and strangers. *Appetite, 23,* 1–13.

Dinklage, R. L., & Ziller, R. C. (1989). Explicating cognitive conflict through photo-communication; the meaning of war and peace in Germany and the United States. *Journal of Conflict Resolution, 32,* 1–19.

Harper, D. (1987). *Working knowledge.* Chicago: University of Chicago Press.

Johnson, G. R., & Monear, J. (1994). A child's view of the urban forest. *Journal of Arboriculture, 20,* 336–340.

Further Reading

Bear, J., Pozerycki, D. M., & Bear, J. (1992). *Computer wimp no more: The intelligent beginner's guide to computers.* Berkeley, CA: Ten Speed Press.

Becker, H. S. (1981). *Exploring society photographically.* Evanston, IL: Mary and Leigh Block Gallery.

Ziller, R. C. (1990). *Photographing the self.* Newbury Park, CA: Sage Publications.

16   Standardized Tests and Inventories

Not surprisingly, many students are anxious before taking exams. To investigate this phenomenon, a researcher administered a standardized test for state anxiety (which is connected with a mood or situation) to a research methods class early in the semester. The test used, the State-Trait Anxiety Inventory (Spielberger, Goruch, & Lushene, 1970), consisted of 20 statements, such as "I feel calm" or "I feel upset" to be rated by the student in terms of how well the term applied: not at all, somewhat, moderately so, and very much so. This inventory yields an overall state (situational) anxiety score.

A few weeks later, on the day of the first exam, the inventory was given again. A comparison score from the two administrations showed a significant increase in state anxiety on the day of the exam. However, there was no relationship between the amount a student's anxiety had increased and his or her actual exam performance. That is, students whose anxiety levels soared did neither better nor worse on the average than students whose anxiety levels changed little. Also, there was no relationship between anxiety on the day of the exam and how well the student performed on the exam.

What Is a Test?

A *test* or *inventory* in the behavioral sciences is a systematic procedure for comparing people's performance, feelings, attitudes, or values. Those tests that are most useful in research have been *standardized*. This means that the test has been published and is available, and that its questions and methods of administration

226

are so fixed that the scores of people tested at different times and places can be compared. A standardized test usually has *norms*, which are statistical summaries of the performance of specified groups who have been given the test. The method for administering the test (how the test is to be given) and norms are included in the manual that accompanies the test. The manual for the State-Trait Anxiety Inventory, described at the beginning of the chapter, contains norms obtained from several hundred college students, providing a base of comparison for new data.

Test Reliability and Validity

Test reliability refers to the stability of measurement over time. When a person's data entry skills are measured on two occasions, the scores should be similar unless something significant has happened in the interval between the tests. Reliability is often measured by a *reliability coefficient*—a coefficient of correlation between two administrations (see Chapter 18 for a discussion of correlation). Reliability information is generally included in the test manual along with validation information.

The *validity* of a test is the extent to which it measures what it is supposed to measure. Validity is judged by three types of evidence—construct, content, and criterion. *Construct validity* refers to the association of the test scores with specific theoretical constructs. Does the inventory connect with something beyond itself? Does the measure rest on a logical base? A valid personality test should be based upon or related to a major theory of personality.

Content validity refers to the degree to which the test items reflect the domain that the test claims to cover. A test intended to measure achievement motivation should not contain items dealing with mechanical ability. The item "I feel down in the dumps" would have high content validity on a depression inventory but not on an intelligence test. Grade point average (GPA) has high content validity on an inventory covering academic achievement but low content validity if included as a measure of adjustment. In recent years American courts have looked at content validity in deciding whether or not a test is discriminatory. If a particular test is used for selecting police officers, then there must be evidence that the individual questions are relevant to police work. The latter decision could be based on the judgment of experienced police officers.

The third aspect, *criterion validity*, shows that the test score is related to other measures of the characteristic. A common method for determining criterion validity of a new test is to compare scores on the new test with those of earlier tests that measure the same characteristics. There are two subtypes of criterion validity: *concurrent validity*, the relationship between the test score and related tests or measures, and *predictive validity*, the ability of the test score to predict future behavior. Predictive validity has considerable practical significance in personnel selection and the identification of people at risk for certain problems who might benefit from additional assistance or counseling. To summarize, the elements of validity are:

Construct   The relationship of the test to theory
Content   The relevance of the items to the behavior measured
Criterion   The relationship of the test to other measures
    Concurrent   Correlation with existing tests or measures
    Predictive   Ability to predict future behavior

Using Tests and Inventories

Technically speaking, standardized tests are less a method of research than tools, like apparatus. They are used most frequently in research in education and psychology, less often in anthropology, sociology, and political science. The researcher's use of tests is likely to be different from their use in career planning, counseling, or personnel selection. Some of the most commonly used standardized tests are IQ tests, personality tests, occupational inventories, and school achievement tests (Box 16–1). There are also specialized instruments such as self-esteem measures, sex-role inventories, environmental rating scales, and other topical tests used in specific areas of research.

Some tests are designed for group administration, while others are constructed for individual administration. Most group-administered tests can be given by a relatively untrained person and scored by computer. The interpretation of the results (the meaning of scores on the various parts of the test) must be done by a knowledgeable person. Other tests are designed to be individually administered, scored, and interpreted by a trained examiner.

Personally constructed instruments, such as a questionnaire used for a single project or an examination given by a college instructor, do not qualify as standardized tests, but with sufficient development, revision, and the compilation of norms, these instruments could become standardized tests. The advantages of using a standardized test are that someone else has done the work of developing the test and there are likely to be comparison data available. You need not develop your own measure of hypnotizability or employee morale; there are tests already available. Booklets and answer sheets are printed and norms allow comparison of new scores with those of others who have taken the test. Some tests are accompanied by test keys that allow you to score the answers yourself; others must be mailed to a testing service, where they are scored and analyzed for a fee.

Many standardized tests are culture-specific. An intelligence test developed in one nation may not be useful or valid in another. There may be serious problems with some of the questions or tasks required. This does not mean that international norms for standardized tests are impossible to achieve. It does mean that further examination and administration is necessary before a test can be assumed valid in another country. For example, when researchers in Italy translate psychological tests developed in Germany, they must standardize the tests on an Italian sample before they assume validity for use in Italy. Researchers comparing intellectual abilities in different cultures may try to select tests that do not depend so heavily on language, such as Raven's Progressive Matrices which uses manipulation of geometric designs to measure intellectual abilities. Although Raven's Matrices are

BOX 16–1. Common Types of Standardized Tests in Educational and Psychological Research

Test type	Purpose	Examples*
School achievement	To determine a person's academic level	Wide Range Achievement Test, California Achievement Test
Intelligence (group administration)	To measure how a person's intellectual performance compares with that of others in the same age group	Kaufman Adolescent and Adult Intelligence Scale, Raven's Standard Progressive Matrices
Intelligence (individual administration)	To obtain a detailed picture of an individual's intellectual abilities, primarily for clinical use	Wechsler Adult Intelligence Scale, Stanford-Binet Intelligence Scale
Personality	To measure various dimensions of normal personality, such as introversion, independence, practicality, etc.	California Psychological Inventory, 16PF, Myers-Briggs Type Indicator
Mood	To assess emotional state	Profile of Mood States, MAACL-R (mood checklist)
Clinical	To identify patterns of behavioral dysfunction	MMPI, Beck Depression Inventory
Occupational interests	To determine interest in specific vocations or in general career categories	Stone Interest Inventory, Kuder Occupational Interest Survey
Specialized abilities	To measure abilities in such areas as music, art, languages, etc.	Standardized Tests of Musical Intelligence, Modern Language Aptitude Test, General Clerical Test

* Only a few tests in each category are listed here. Many others can be found in the catalogs of test distributors. Tests are constantly being revised. Check catalogs for the latest version.

not completely free of the effects of living in a specific culture, they are probably more culture-fair than tests that depend on language.

Some tests have multiple forms for use with different groups and nationalities. As an example, the Sixteen Personality Factor Questionnaire (16PF) has norms for use with different age groups, including a preschool version, an early school version, a children's form, a secondary school form, and a version for those 16 years and older. There are German and Spanish language editions, and test forms in Braille and on videotape using sign language.

Standardized tests are not suitable for all research questions. Very few of the research problems discussed in previous chapters can be addressed by a standardized test. No commercial questionnaire will tell you what college students think about the cafeteria food; the same is true of student attitudes toward peer counseling or financial aid. Even those standardized tests on which the most work has been done, such as measures of intelligence and school achievement, have many limitations and may not be usable for the particular groups you want to test.

Locating Suitable Tests

Your first task is to find out whether appropriate tests are already available. There are several sources. First, you can look at previous research on the topic. Have studies similar to yours employed standardized tests? If not, the answer may be that none is available.

A very comprehensive index is *Tests in Print (TIP)*, providing a bibliography of all known commercially available English tests in print (Murphy, Conoley, & Impara, 1994). *TIP IV* has thousands of test entries and serves as an index for the *12th Mental Measurements Yearbook* (Conoley & Impara, 1996). The *Mental Measurements Yearbook* provides test reviews and reference information for over 400 available tests. Earlier editions are still useful. These resources are also available on CD-ROM.

Another source is Sweetland and Keyser's *Tests: A comprehensive reference for assessments in psychology, education, and business* (1990). The third edition contains information on 3200 assessment instruments. There is a subject index and a brief description of each test. That volume is accompanied by several volumes titled *Test Critiques* that provide excellent descriptions of many tests. Both of these major sources provide price information and the names and addresses of test suppliers.

The Educational Testing Service (ETS) publishes lists of inventories by subject matter area. The six volumes cover cognitive, aptitude, intelligence, affective, personality, vocational, attitude, and achievement tests (ETS, 1986–92). On the Internet, ERIC's Clearinghouse on Assessment and Evaluation has a test locator for the ETS collection. A search by topic produces descriptions and references (but not the tests themselves). Chapter 3 describes ERIC and other electronic databases, and Chapter 14 serves as an introduction to the Internet.

There is also a *Directory of Unpublished Experimental Mental Measures* that provides information about non-commercial experimental test instruments for research in psychology, education, sociology, and related fields (Goldman & Mitchell, 1995). Most of these do not qualify as standardized tests, but some are on the way to standardization. Earlier volumes might also be of help if you cannot locate the most recent one.

Sometimes separate versions of tests are available for children or adolescents.

There may be versions in different languages. Some tests have both short forms for brief administration and longer forms for more detailed assessment. A few tests offer training videos for test administration. Some tests are available as computer software. Questions are shown on a video screen and the respondent selects an answer. The respondent's score on various parts of the test, plus an overall test score are automatically calculated. The program may use pictures, sound, or both. For example, in test of vocabulary, a voice asks the respondent to indicate which of three pictures is associated with a particular word. A test of auditory perception (the ability of a person to hear varying levels and types of sound) uses a Macintosh computer with a stereo sound output. In the future, most psychological tests will probably be available as software.

Ask knowledgeable individuals whether they know of tests or inventories appropriate for your purposes. Try an Internet search using terms listed under Test Types in Box 16–1. You will probably locate home pages of test publishers. Faculty members in departments of education and psychology, personnel managers, school guidance counselors, and others who use standardized tests in their work may have catalogs from test suppliers. It is not easy for a beginner to sort through numerous catalogs and find the right test. Discussing your needs with a qualified test specialist is helpful.

Obtaining the Tests

Some tests are available only to members of professional societies, such as the American Psychological Association. Access to these tests is restricted to prevent their unauthorized use. Information on availability is contained in most test catalogs. If the test you are considering has restricted distribution, you must either be personally qualified or find someone who is. The personnel department of your company or the counseling bureau of your school probably has a qualified test professional. This person may have a copy of the test on file or can obtain a sample copy for you to examine. For a small charge, most test suppliers will send sample kits containing a single copy of the test booklet, a test manual containing norms, and scoring sheets. The sample kit should be closely scrutinized before any decision is made about ordering multiple copies. For most standardized tests, permission must be obtained from the holder of the copyright (usually the publisher) to make copies of or modify the test in any way. Test publishers, who are commercial firms, are likely to charge a fee for reproducing tests.

We offer a word of caution about changing standardized tests. Once you begin tinkering with a test by removing some items or changing the wording or instructions, you lose the benefits of standardization. The norms for the test will no longer be valid. A compromise solution, when you find a test that seems good but does not do everything you want, is to leave the test intact but add additional items. This allows you to use the earlier norms and at the same time to introduce new questions tailored to your specific purposes. You can score the results in two ways, first in terms of the original version of the test, and second, to include the new items.

Constructing a Test

If you cannot locate the test you need in catalogs from test suppliers or published work on the topic, a remaining option is to develop a test of your own. This will be time consuming so the decision should not be made lightly. Making up a standardized test, with score sheet and norms, requires far more time and effort than composing a questionnaire or list of interview questions.

The sequence of steps involved in compiling a standardized test is shown in Box 16–2. The first task is to define the performance or behavior to be measured. This is a more difficult task than it sounds. Let us use bicycle riding as an example of a common ability for which few or no standardized tests are available. If you wanted to compare the bicycle riding skills of individuals or groups, you would probably have to make up your own test. Defining the skill will raise some important questions. Should you include items pertaining to mountain bikes and trail riding? What about skills for long distance touring or racing? Or riding a unicycle? These are certainly "skills," but they may not be particularly relevant if your concern is with safety in local bicycling. One approach to defining the topics to be included in a test is to consult previous research. What aspects

---

BOX 16–2. Steps in Constructing a Standardized Test

1. Define the performance to be measured
   a. Check previous research
   b. Consider your own experience
   c. Consult with recognized authorities
   d. Convert accumulated materials into behavioral measures
2. Compile potentially useful items
   a. Eliminate duplications and inconsistencies
   b. Construct draft instrument
3. Pilot test the items
4. Make necessary revisions and do subsequent pilot testing and revision
   a. Decide on length and format
   b. Collect responses from a new sample
   c. Do an item analysis
   d. Select final item set
5. Compose final version
6. Check reliability by administering test to same individuals on two occasions. Check split-half reliability. Make necessary revisions
7. Check validity by comparing scores with known abilities or performance
8. Establish norms
   a. Administer tests to different groups
   b. Compile scores according to relevant categories (e.g., age, education, experience, etc.)
9. Publish or disseminate test

---

of performance have been deemed important or relevant by other investigators? Another possibility is to consult with recognized authorities and cycling organizations. What sort of skills do safety officials and leaders of cycling clubs feel are important for bicyclists? Major cycling organizations have material on the Internet. General statements must be made specific and defined in terms of observable operations.

The behavioral items collected from all sources must be examined to remove obvious duplications and inconsistencies. See that important issues are covered and that the instrument is not too long. The revised list of items can be tried out on an exploratory basis with a small number of respondents. The goal at this point is to get the bugs out of the procedure. Several successive revisions of the preliminary version of the test will be required. Then the almost-final version of the test must be further refined through an *item analysis*. Detailed methods for undertaking an item analysis can be found in Murphy and Davidshofer (1994). An item analysis shows the degree to which the various items "hang together." Items that produce responses unrelated to those of the other questions are probably measuring a different type of ability and can be removed from the instrument.

Establishing the reliability of the revised instrument is done by administering the test to the same individuals on two separate occasions. If the test is reliable, those individuals who score high on the test the first time should also score high on the second administration. Many standardized tests will also have alternate versions. Constructing alternate versions requires additional effort, but it will increase the practical and research usefulness of the instrument.

One approach to validity is to administer the test to people known to be high or low in the skill being measured. Presumably a group of experienced cyclists should perform better on a test of bicycle skills than a group of inexperienced cyclists. Another approach to validation could test individuals who have been involved in bicycle accidents. We could predict that when matched for age, cycling experience, amount of riding per week, and other relevant background factors, individuals who have been involved in a bicycle accident should perform worse on a test of bicycle skills than individuals who have not been involved in an accident. These are only a few of the ways in which a standardized test can be validated.

The next step is to compile norms from various groups. A test of bicycle skills should probably include norms for different age groups. The norms would be compiled by administering the test to samples of respondents at different age levels and tabulating the results. This will allow scores of people to be compared with those of their own age groups.

If all of the preceding steps have been done, and the test appears promising in predicting bicycle skills, the next step will be to publish the results and make them available to researchers and cycling organizations. Encouraging researchers to try out the test will assist in developing norms for other geographic areas and types of samples. Some test publishers actively solicit researchers to aid in the development and revision of tests, for example, to produce a version in another language or to modify the adult version for use with children or adolescents.

Projective Tests

Projective tests deliberately use stimuli that are vague or incomplete. It is assumed that the respondents fill in the blanks or gaps by *projecting* their personal concerns and experiences. In sentence completion tests, the respondent adds an ending to an incomplete beginning, for example, "When I think of home I think of. . . ." or "Old people worry about. . . ." Two widely-used projective tests are the Rorschach Inkblot and the Thematic Apperception Test (TAT). The Rorschach is the successor to the Stern Cloud Pictures Test in which the respondent was shown pictures of clouds and asked what the clouds resembled. Rorschach, a Swiss psychiatrist, replaced the clouds with ten inkblots. The TAT consists of a set of pictures of blurred people in ambiguous situations. The respondent is asked to tell a story about what is going on in the picture. On the assumption that young children will identify more readily with animals than with humans, a children's version of the TAT uses drawings of animals.

Because the responses to projective tests are open-ended, their interpretation requires considerable training on the part of the clinician or researcher. Often the style of responding (e.g., hesitation or embarrassment) is more important than the content of the response. Some objective scoring techniques have been developed and computer software is available. Multiple-choice versions of the inkblot test suitable for group administration are available and have been used in cross-cultural studies as the stimulus figures do not involve language.

Limitations

Standardized tests are not available for many topics that an investigator wants to study. When tests are available, the norms may not be appropriate for groups other than those on which the test was standardized. Many standardized tests have been criticized as being culturally biased. Standardized tests are primarily useful for people similar to those on whom the norms were collected. The apparent precision of test scores is often misleading. The important issue is how well the test measures what it is supposed to measure.

Personality tests tend to stigmatize people who diverge from conventional social norms. Some of the questions on personality tests are intrusive. You must be sensitive to the way the question appears to respondents and outside agencies. It is difficult to defend some of the questions about personal habits and sexual preferences included on some major personality tests.

Low reliability is a serious shortcoming of projective tests. Two psychologists examining the same record are likely to develop different interpretations.

Summary

Standardized tests, which are available from test supply firms, have norms that can be used in interpreting results. *Reliability* refers to the stability of measurements over time. Three aspects of test validity are *construct*, the relationship of test to theory, *content*, the relevance of the items to the behavior measured, and *criterion*, the relationship of the test to other measures. Standardized tests tend to be culture-specific. The most common types measure school achievement, intelligence, personality, clinical symptoms, occupational interests and skill, and specialized abilities in areas such as music, art, and languages. Many standardized tests are not appropriate for groups other than those on whom the norms were established.

Information about tests and their availability can be found in *Tests in Print* (*TIP IV*) and the *Mental Measurements Yearbook*, available in print or CD-ROM at most reference libraries. Another source is *Tests* (Sweetland & Keyser, 1990). The Internet is also a resource for finding references to tests and inventories.

Many tests can be administered and scored by computer. There may be separate versions in different languages and for use with special groups of respondents. Constructing a new standardized test is a difficult and time-consuming task because of the need to establish reliability and validity, and to collect norms from different segments of the population. Problems of reliability and the extensive time required for training and analysis limits the use of projective tests in research.

References

Conoley, J. C., & Impara, J. C. (1996). *The 12th mental measurements yearbook*. Lincoln: Buros Institute of Mental Measurements, The University of Nebraska-Lincoln.

Educational Testing Service. (1986–1992). *The ETS Test Collection catalog* (Numbers 1–6). Phoenix, AZ: Oryx Press.

Goldman, B. A., & Mitchell, D. F. (1995). *Directory of unpublished experimental mental measures* (Vol. 6). Washington, DC: American Psychological Association.

Murphy, K. R., & Davidshofer, C. O. (1994). *Psychological testing: Principles and applications* (3rd ed.). Englewood Cliffs, NJ: Prentice Hall.

Murphy, L. L., Conoley, J. C., & Impara, J. C. (1994). *Tests in print IV: An index to tests, test reviews, and the literature on specific tests*. Lincoln: Buros Institute of Mental Measurements, The University of Nebraska-Lincoln.

Spielberger, C. D., Gorsuch, R. L., & Lushene, R. E. (1970). *STAI manual for the state-trait anxiety inventory*. Palo Alto, CA: Consulting Psychologists Press.

Sweetland, R. C., & Keyser, D. J. (1990). *Test: A comprehensive reference for assessments in psychology, education, and business* (3rd ed.). Austin, TX: Pro-Ed.

Further Reading

Beere, C. A. (1990). *Sex and gender issues: A handbook of tests and measures*. New York: Greenwood Press.

Crocker, L. M. (1986). *Introduction to classical and modern test theory*. New York: Holt, Rinehart and Winston.

Cronbach, L. J. (1990). *Essentials of psychological testing* (5th ed.). New York: Harper & Row.

Hammill, D. D., Brown, L., & Bryant, B. R. (1992). *A consumer's guide to tests in print* (2nd ed.). Austin, TX: Pro-Ed.

Murphy, K. R., & Davidshofer, C. O. (1994). *Psychological testing: Principles and applications* (3rd ed.). Englewood Cliffs, NJ: Prentice Hall.

Robinson, J. P., Phillip R. Shaver, Lawrence S. Wrightsman (Ed.). (1991). *Measures of personality and social psychological attitudes*. San Diego: Academic Press.

Walsh, W. B., & Tyler, L. E. (1989). *Tests and measurements* (4th ed.). Englewood Cliffs, NJ: Prentice Hall.

17 Sampling

Americans' sex lives are conservative and not particularly active, according to a much-publicized survey (Laumann, 1994). Reading about the survey, several questions immediately come to mind. How many people were surveyed? How were they selected? Who were they? What were they like—how old, where were they from, what were their educational levels? These questions concern *sampling*, the selection of a subset of cases from some population of interest. It is very rare for an investigator to be able to study all the people or cases in a given category. Some selection is necessary and must be done in an unbiased way if it is to yield valid information.

The entire group of people or cases of direct interest to the investigation is called the *population*. The smaller group selected for study is called the *sample*. The sample is used to make generalizations about the population from which it was drawn. The degree to which the sample differs from the population is termed *error*. There are two general sources of error: sampling error and sample bias.

Sampling error refers to chance variations among samples selected from a single population. Imagine a person who draws successive samples of 50 marbles each from a large bowl containing 1000 marbles, half black and half white. After each selection is noted, the marble is returned to the bowl. Some samples would contain a majority of black marbles and others a majority of white marbles. Ideally, if there were enough trials, the characteristics of all the samples would *average* 25 white marbles and 25 black marbles. However, any single sample of 50 marbles is likely to deviate from this average. The difference between the samples and the actual population characteristics (50% black and 50% white) is the *sampling error*. It can never be totally eliminated, but it can be estimated statistically.

If one third of Canadian adults favor the Conservative party, then 33.3 percent of a representative sample of Canadian adults should favor the Conservative party (or 333 out of a sample of 1,000). Deviation from 33.3 percent in the sample percentage represents sampling error. A common method of reducing the influence of sampling error (chance variation) is to draw a large sample. As the sample size approaches the population size, it becomes a more accurate representation.

Sample bias refers to error introduced by a sampling procedure that favors certain characteristics over others. In selecting the marbles from the jar, it is possible that the black marbles, by absorbing heat, are slightly warmer than the white marbles. The blindfolded subject may unconsciously select the warmer black marbles. This source of error could be reduced by having the blindfolded subject wear gloves. In the example of Canadian adults, interviewing only in Quebec would introduce sample bias. Sample bias occurs when the sample fails to represent the population because of some factor in addition to chance. Increasing the sample size is *not* effective in reducing sample bias. The source of the bias must be identified and then reduced or eliminated. To summarize, sampling error (error due to chance) cannot be completely eliminated, but can be minimized and estimated. Sample bias can be eliminated by using careful design and sampling procedures.

Types of Samples

There are two general ways of constructing samples: probability (representative) sampling and nonprobability sampling, with variations within each type.

Probability Sampling

Probability samples are those in which the probability for the inclusion of any given individual is known. Two variants of probability sampling are *random samples* and *stratified samples*. These sampling techniques produce the most representative samples—samples that are most like the population from which they are drawn.

Random Sample

In random sampling, every individual in the entire population being studied has an equal likelihood of being selected. For random sampling, the researcher must have access to each member of the population, that is, know how many individuals there are and how to reach them.

Visiting a college campus and interviewing every fourth person on the sidewalk will *not* yield a random sample of the student body because each student will not have an equal chance of being selected. The chances of being selected will be affected by the location, time of day, personal inclination, and so on.

Drawing names out of a hat containing the names of all students in the class is one way of randomly selecting a sample of students in the particular class. Another procedure is to assign a randomly-generated number (numbers that follow no particular pattern) to each case in the population and use those numbers to select the sample, for example, taking the case with the highest number, then the next highest, and so on until the desired sample size is reached. Or one could start with the lowest number. Some calculators have a special key, identified as RAN, for generating random numbers. Another way of making a random selection is to use a table of random numbers, such as Table A–5 in Appendix A. The researcher can start anywhere in the table and proceed in any direction.

Example

Researchers wanted a sample of twenty students from a middle school population of 148. They obtained a list of all 148 students. Using the table of random numbers in Appendix A–5, beginning at the top of the second column (an arbitrary choice), they assigned a number to each of the 148 names as follows:

Student name	Random numbers from Table A–5
Amos, F.	17
Baker, J.	46
Cassandro, P.	09
Daheb, M.	72
Foushee, A.	09
. . .	
Vigil, K.	42
Weber, L.	35
Yoshimura, M.	88

For their sample, they selected the twenty students with the lowest numbers. Duplicate numbers occur by chance and should be included. If some of these students cannot participate, additions to the sample can be made from among those with the next lowest numbers.

Stratified Sample

A stratified sample is a variation of the random sample. Instead of selecting each case randomly, criteria are set up to ensure representation of particular groups within the sample proportionate to their numbers in the population. For example, if the population in question is made up of 55 percent males and 45 percent females, then a stratified sample is set to have 55 percent males and 45 percent females. Similar criteria may be set for age, occupation, religion, and other variables of interest. Within categories, individuals are chosen randomly. Public opinion polls rely on stratified samples. They select a relatively small number of families to represent various levels of age, income, region, ethnicity, and other variables. The use of a stratified sample requires an accurate knowledge of the characteristics of the population. The school researchers in the earlier example might want their student sample to be stratified with regard to gender and grade. They would need to know the breakdown of these variables for the entire school in order to obtain their samples.

Nonprobability Sampling

Samples in which the likelihood of selection is not actually known are called non-probability samples. There are three general types: *quota samples*, *purposive samples*, and *convenience samples*. Nonprobability samples are generally not an accurate representation of the population. There are circumstances where a non-representative sample is satisfactory or even desirable for particular research purposes. More typically, a non-representative sample is a result of researchers being unable to obtain representative samples.

Quota Sample

Quota sampling describes the situation where the investigator deliberately sets sample proportions that are different from those existing in the population. These proportions are specified according to the goals of the investigation. For example, researchers at a middle school may have a particular interest in the attitudes of incoming (grade 6) and outgoing (grade 8) students and therefore select a sample with 50 percent from grade 6 and 50 percent from grade 8, even though that distribution does not mirror the actual composition of the student body.

Using a quota sample is a way to insure representation of particular members of the population. The individuals selected within each quota should be chosen randomly in order to avoid bias; but the entire sample itself is not truly representative of the population.

Purposive Sample

A *purposive sample* targets the individuals thought to be most central to the research question. For example, a study of city policy may require interviews with particular individuals in key leadership positions. A random sampling of all city officials would be time consuming and may miss some of the most important people.

For an experiment studying the effect of two types of video terminal monitors on employee productivity, it makes sense to select the employees who will be using the system most often to be the experimental and control subjects. The trade-off is more detailed information on immediate users, but limited generality to all potential users.

A special type of purposive sample is the *snowball sample* where the researcher asks respondents for other persons to contact. This technique is useful when studying particular groups where membership may not be obvious or where access to members may be difficult, for example, drug users, prostitutes, or gang members. A research team used snowball sampling to study marijuana use in two Midwestern U.S. cities (Hirsch, Conforti, & Graney, 1991). Acknowledging that this approach would not yield representative samples, the investigators chose snowball sampling as a means of penetrating a relatively closed population of individual engaged in an illegal activity.

Convenience Sample

Convenience sampling is taking what you can get. Interviewing people on a particular day in a shopping mall, observing students at lunchtime on campus, or studying the bears at a temporary campsite in Yellowstone, all use convenience samples. A volunteer sample, comprised of people who are willing to participate in a research project, is a convenience sample, and the characteristics and behavior of volunteers may be quite different from those of non-volunteers.

Generalization from Probability and Nonprobability Samples

Probability samples are more representative and therefore allow greater generalization to the population from which they are drawn. Returning to the distinction between sampling error and sample bias, a properly drawn probability sample will be free of sample bias, and sampling error can be dealt with statistically. Probability samples do not permit generalization *beyond* the population sampled. The findings from a study of one school cannot be generalized to another. Bear behavior in Yellowstone may differ considerably from that observed in Yosemite.

Nonprobability samples may be easier to obtain, but provide limited and possibly misleading information about the population. There is always the possibility of sample bias in addition to sampling error. In a quota sample, random selection within each quota permits generalization to that particular group, but the findings cannot be generalized to the population as a whole (because it was not randomly sampled as a whole). In the middle school example of a quota sample (selecting from grades 6 and 8), the researcher can generalize to 6th and 8th graders based on the samples that were randomly selected, but cannot generalize the overall findings to the school as a whole.

Purposive samples are select and often small, and a particular respondent's point of view cannot be assumed to represent the views of other group members. The advantage is in obtaining an insider's unique perspective.

Convenience samples can be made more representative by taking steps to approach random selection and reduce bias, such as making observations at different times of day and on different days of the week. Setting decision rules ahead of time is a good procedure, for example, interviewing every fifth person entering the mall, or for a taste test, selecting the fourth tomato from the lower left-hand corner in the display at each of four grocery stores. The point is to try to approximate randomness in the technical sense (to provide as equal an opportunity for selection as is possible) and to devise ways of reducing or eliminating sources of error by setting unbiased decision rules ahead of time.

How Large a Sample?

Other things being equal, large samples provide more reliable and representative data than small samples. A sample of 50 marbles randomly selected from the 1,000-marble bowl is likely to show less deviation from the true characteristics of the marble population in the bowl than will a smaller sample of 10 marbles. If half of the marbles are black and the other half white, it would be unusual to select 40 black and 10 white marbles but one wouldn't be surprised to draw a sample of 10 marbles that contained 8 black and 2 white marbles.

In deciding on sample size, one needs to consider both statistical logic and practicality. The reduction in sampling error that results from a large sample may not be worth the extra time and effort required to obtain the additional data. Some public opinion polling firms find that they can make accurate predictions of voting trends based on interviews with a representative sample of 2500 individuals. To increase the sample to 5000 or 10,000 would reduce sampling error but would not be worth the extra time, effort, and expense. In public opinion surveys, time is very important. The extra two days that might be required to double the sample would make the results less useful to the client.

Sample size should be specified in advance in order to avoid the accusation that data collection was halted as soon as the results supported the hypothesis. The following factors should be considered in making a decision on sample size:

1. *Size of population.* Large populations call for larger samples. For a survey of library *readers*, a sample of 100 individuals would probably be sufficient. For a survey of library *employees*, this would be far too many. There may not even be 100 employees.

2. *Available resources and time constraints.* Pilot testing will reveal the cost in terms of time and effort for data collection. The *maximum* size of the sample can be determined from constraints such as the time required for each interview or to run each subject in an experiment, the availability of equipment, or the researcher's time commitments.

3. *Strength of the effect.* Smaller samples are sufficient for stronger or more straightforward effects. When the independent variable has a strong and clear effect on the dependent variable, a smaller sample can be used. For example, only a few subjects would be needed to demonstrate the effect of five ounces of alcohol on reaction time. A much larger number of subjects would be necessary to determine the effect of one ounce of alcohol, as the small amount produces inconsistent and often contradictory results. Similarly, if all the voters on an issue have made up their minds, the election outcome can be predicted from a smaller sample than if many voters are undecided.

4. *Number of analyses to be performed.* Multiple comparisons require larger samples. If the researcher wishes to compare groups within the sample by dividing it according to social class, age, ethnicity, and gender, the sample must be large enough to include a sufficient number of individuals in each of the smaller categories.

5. *Refusal and spoilage rates.* Sample size should be increased to allow for unusable data. Keep in mind the number of people who will be unable to follow instructions on a questionnaire, do not return the survey forms, drop out of an experiment, or terminate the interview prematurely. A questionnaire given to and collected from a group of office employees at their place of work is likely to have a high return rate, perhaps in excess of 80 percent, while the same questionnaire mailed to an unselected group of individuals with a request to return by mail may have a return rate of less than 10 percent.

Gaining Access

Most of the studies undertaken in a research methods class will involve people and places on campus. Access isn't much of a problem when observing other students eating in the cafeteria or sitting in the library, interviewing roommates, or distributing questionnaires to other classes. Once you leave the campus, access can be a problem. Before you consider how to sample within a group outside the campus, you first have to get access to the group. This is in addition to approval from an Institutional Review Board. It takes further time and effort to locate a *gatekeeper*, a person who can give you access to a needed population. Gatekeepers may be people in official positions. For example, if you want to survey nursing home patients, you will need formal approval from the director, and perhaps a governing board or outside agency. A household survey may require approval from city officials or the police. Personal contact is helpful in obtaining assistance from a gatekeeper. A good way to find the gatekeeper is to use local networks, finding a friend, family member, or local official who can make the first contact. For example, in order to find out how colleges selected athletes, a researcher wanted to interview a large number of coaches. He began by contacting the coaching staff on his own campus, who put him in touch with coaches at other institutions. A similar sequence could be used in a study of police, architects, or nursery school workers. Start by enlisting the assistance of local practitioners, acquaintances, or friends of friends, who can then help you approach their colleagues in other locations.

Measuring Non-respondent Bias

The question that frequently arises in survey research is whether the people who respond are representative of the total population, or whether there is some bias in who responded and who did not. There are several methods used by survey researchers to answer these questions. The easiest approach is to compare the characteristics of the respondents with known characteristics of the population. A second method is to compare answers of early and late respondents. A survey of community attitudes may produce a 25 percent return rate for the first mailing of the questionnaires. A follow-up letter enclosing an additional copy of the questions may add another 12 percent. The latter group represents people who did not respond to the first survey (i.e., non-respondents on the first pass). Differences between the characteristics of the two groups indicate respondent bias—that the early responders are different from the later responders and also may differ from those who did not respond at all. If the respondents in the second mailing are similar to those from the first mailing, the possibility of a response bias appears less likely.

A third method is to directly contact non-respondents. In a mail survey, telephone interviews can be attempted with people who did not return their questionnaires. A goal of the interview is to find out if those people who did not return their questionnaire are similar to those who did.

A similar issue arises in generalizing research findings based on volunteer samples. Sampling bias can be checked by contacting people from the population who did not volunteer and comparing their characteristics with those of the people who did volunteer. For example, researchers who recruit subjects for experiments from introductory psychology classes can compare the characteristics of the volunteers with those of students in the same classes who did not volunteer—either by interviewing non-volunteers or using course or college records.

Describing the Method of Sampling

The survey report should include a description of the sampling along with the other procedural information. Here is an account of the methods used in a telephone survey of consumer attitudes toward food preservatives:

> A questionnaire developed for a survey of 370 consumers from the Statistical Metropolitan Survey Area of Seattle-Everett, Washington, was adapted for use in this survey. Structured interviews were conducted in the same district by telephone. Phone numbers were selected at random from the telephone directory; 220 households were contacted and 170 usable replies were obtained. Only persons responsible for the major food purchases for the household unit being studied were interviewed. Each interview took 5 to 7 minutes, and all were conducted by the same interviewer.

Limitations

A sample that is perfectly representative is difficult to obtain. For example, census records are probably out-of-date, not everyone is listed in the telephone directory, and door-to-door surveys find many people unavailable or refusing to be interviewed. The resulting sample may be subject to sample bias, and therefore, confidence in the generalizability (external validity) of the findings is reduced.

Summary

The entire group of people in a category is called a population. The smaller group selected for study is called a sample. Probability samples are more accurate representatives of the population. In a random sample, each member of the population has an equal chance of being selected. A stratified sample is selected so that its characteristics are proportionate to those present in the total population.

There are three types of nonprobability samples: quota, purposive, and convenience. In a quota sample, the selection categories are specified according to the needs of the investigation. A purposive sample targets key individuals for study. A convenience sample uses what's available.

The degree to which the sample differs from the population is termed error. Two major sources of error are sampling error and sample bias. Sampling error refers to chance variations among samples selected from the same population. It affects both probability and nonprobability samples and is reduced by increasing sample size. Sample bias refers to error introduced by a sampling procedure that favors certain characteristics over others. Sample bias can be eliminated by using probability samples. Sampling procedures that approach randomness and unbiased decision rules can reduce sample bias in quota, purposive, and convenience samples.

The generalizability of a probability sample is limited to the population from which it is drawn. Generalizations based on nonprobability samples are more limited.

Other things being equal, large samples provide more reliable and representative data than small samples. The decision on sample size is influenced by the size of the population, available resources and time constraints, strength of the effect, number of comparisons to be made, and expected refusal and spoilage rates.

Without access there can be no sampling. Gaining access requires permission from gatekeepers who may need to consult with other authorities.

Non-respondent bias refers to differences between those who participate and those who do not. Techniques used to assess the possibility of respondent bias in surveys are comparison of respondent characteristics with known population characteristics, comparison of early and late respondents, and comparison of respondents with a sample of non-respondents contacted by other means. Similar techniques can be used for experiments or simulations in order to compare volunteers with non-volunteers.

References

Hirsch, M. L., Conforti, R. W., & Graney, C. J. (1991). The use of marijuana for pleasure. In J. W. Neuliep (Ed.), *Replication research in the social sciences* (pp. 485–498). Newbury Park, CA: Sage Publications.

Laumann, E. O. (1994). *The social organization of sexuality: Sexual practices in the United States.* Chicago: University of Chicago Press.

Further Reading

Backstrom, C., & Hursh-Cesar, G. (1981). *Survey research*. New York: Wiley (see Chapter 2).

Fink, A. (1995). *How to sample in surveys*. Thousand Oaks, CA: Sage Publications.

Henry, G. T. (1990). *Practical sampling*. Newbury Park, CA: Sage Publications.

Kraemer, H. C., & Thieman, S. (1987). *How many subjects?* Beverly Hills, CA: Sage Publications.

Sudman, S. (1983). Applied sampling. In P. H. Rossi, J. D. Wright, & A. B. Anderson (Eds.), *Handbook of survey research* (pp. 145–194). New York: Academic Press.

18   Descriptive Statistics

You've made your survey or run your experiment or collected systematic observations; now what? Chances are you have a stack of scored materials that you need to make sense of. These are your *raw data*. Obviously you have to reduce the stack to manageable proportions. That is the job of descriptive statistics—to summarize quantitative data (numbers) in an understandable and meaningful way. A *statistic* is defined as a quantitative characteristic of a sample, thus descriptive statistics are numerical descriptions of samples.

The first step in summarizing your research findings is to look at the type of measures you have for each of your outcomes (dependent variables). A review of the Levels of Measurement section in Chapter 10 may be useful. Chances are that some of your data will be *categorical* (nominal) and other results will be *continuous* (measured along a continuous dimension). The type of descriptive statistics used depends on whether the outcome measure is categorical or continuous.

Categorical refers to variables that have levels that are mutually exclusive.

Examples of Categorical Variables

Outcome variable	*Values assigned to each case*
Smoking status	Smoker, Nonsmoker
Hair color	Brunette, Blond, Redhead

| Political affiliation | Republican, Democrat, Independent |
| Gender | Female, Male |

The levels are discrete; each individual case is assigned to one or another category. The measurement for each individual case in the sample occurs at a *nominal* level of measurement (see Chapter 10). No true quantity is indicated. Sometimes nominal levels are labels with numbers, for example, male = 1 and female = 2, or smoker = 1 and non-smoker = 0. Note that these numbers do not refer to quantity or amount. There are not intermediate values. Counts, such as the number of cases in a category, represent frequencies. They do not represent values or levels of a variable.

Continuous variables are those whose levels can take on any value within the lowest and uppermost limit of the variable.

Examples of Continuous Variables

Outcome variable	Value assigned to each case				
Exam score (20 possible)	0–20				
Age	0 (birth)–100+ yrs. (for humans)				
Degree of agreement	5	4	3	2	1
	agree very much	agree	neither agree nor disagree	disagree	disagree very much

With some variables, the measurement can be either categorical or continuous, depending on how it is measured by the researcher. For example, hair color could be measured categorically (blond, brunette, or redhead) or on a continuous scale or dimension ranging from dark to light. Human age can be measured continuously as years, months, days, or classified categorically, for example, child, adolescent, adult, and senior.

You can change the level of measurement from continuous to categorical (nominal), but not the reverse. If you only have nominal data, meaningful numbers cannot be assigned. For example, checking blond, brunette, or redhead does not provide enough detail for putting each individual on a scale from dark to light hair color. You will know whether the respondent is blond, but you won't know how blond he or she might be. The range of values is not continuous; the intermediate values are not known.

Descriptive Statistics for Categorical Measures

The first step in summarizing categorical results is to tabulate them in *contingency tables*. A contingency table shows the levels of the independent or predictor variables at the top and levels of the dependent variable at the side. The cells contain *frequencies of occurrence* (counts) of the possible combinations of levels. For example, assume that you observed 210 bicyclists at an intersection, noted their gender, and kept track of whether or not they came to a full stop at a stop sign.

RESPONSE TO STOP SIGN	GENDER	
	Male	Female
Stop	66 (72.5%)	126 (60%)
No Stop	25 (27.5%)	84 (40%)
Total	91 (100%)	130 (100%)

Including percentages enables the viewer to tell at a glance that proportionately more males than females stopped and that a majority of both genders stopped.

Descriptive Statistics for Continuous Measures

When the outcome is a value taken from a continuous measure, such as a score on a test or an attitude scale, the first step is to order the entire set of scores from highest to lowest. The following example of a creativity test illustrates the construction of descriptive statistics for continuous data. The test question is "How many uses can you think of for a top hat?" Possible answers include a scoop, a target, a container, a musical instrument, something to throw snowballs at, a paperweight, a vase, or something to keep sugar or fish in, and a mouse might use it for a boat on the water. The test-taker receives a point for every new category of use; answers that a top hat could be used as a vase, a sugar bowl, and fishbowl earn only one point, as these are all single uses of the top hat (i.e., as a container). Table 18–1 shows the raw data from 16 subjects.

Because more than one person earned the same score, a summary is made using a frequency distribution with the scores (number of uses) listed in descending order (see Table 18–2). The score (X) is listed in one column, and a second column shows the frequency of occurrence (f).

The data are still not sufficiently summarized to qualify as descriptive statistics. It can be packed down further. Two aspects must be described, *central tendency* and *variability*.

Before we go on, one comment is necessary regarding the categorical-continuous distinction. One could argue that the number of uses for a top hat isn't really a continuous variable because there can't be 1.5 or 5.63 uses. However, most behavioral researchers treat variables with ordinal and interval levels of measurement as continuous, even though the intermediate values are not obvious.

TABLE 18–1. Number of Uses for a Top
Hat Given by 16 Students

Subject #	Number of uses
1	8
2	5
3	5
4	11
5	6
6	7
7	6
8	4
9	9
10	4
11	5
12	7
13	6
14	6
15	8
16	7

Measures of Central Tendency

Central tendency refers to a number (statistic) that best characterizes the group as a whole. The *average* is a synonym for central tendency. It expresses the outcome at a glance. There are three types of averages: mean, median, and mode.

TABLE 18–2. Frequency Distribution Showing the Number
of Uses for a Top Hat Given by 16 Students

Number of uses (X)	Frequency of occurrence (f)
11	1
10	0
9	1
8	2
7	3
6	4
5	3
4	2

Mean (M)

The mean is the arithmetic average. It is the sum of all scores divided by the number of cases. The statistical formula is

$$\text{Formula: } M = \frac{\sum X}{N}$$

where M = mean
$\sum$ = sum of
X = raw score
N = number of cases

Example

The mean of the creativity scores is calculated for the test scores as follows:

$$\text{Sum of all scores } \sum X = 104$$
$$\text{Number of test scores } (N) = 16$$
$$\text{Mean } (M) = \frac{104}{16} = 6.5$$

When data are in a frequency distribution, remember to take into account how often each score occurs (see Table 18–3 for Top Hat example). The procedure for calculating the mean from a frequency distribution is as follows:

Multiply each score (X) by its frequency (f), number of times specified value has occurred.
Add those together.

TABLE 18–3. Calculation of the Mean from a Frequency Distribution

X	f	fX
11	1	11
10	0	0
9	1	9
8	2	16
7	3	21
6	4	24
5	3	15
4	2	8

$N = 16 \quad \sum (fX) = 104$

$$M \text{ (Mean)} = \frac{\sum (fX)}{N} = \frac{104}{16} = 6.5$$

Divide by the total number of cases.

$$\text{Formula: } M = \frac{\sum (fX)}{N}$$

The mean is the most frequently used measure of central tendency. It is considered the most reliable of the three measures.

Median (Mdn)

The median is the midpoint of a distribution. When all the scores are arranged from highest to lowest, half of the scores will fall above the median and half will fall below.

To calculate the median, arrange all the scores from highest to lowest. The median is the middle score. If there is an even number of scores, calculate the midpoint by averaging the two scores closest to the middle (add them and divide by two). Table 18–4 shows the calculation of the median for the top hat

TABLE 18–4. Calculation of the Median Number of Uses for a Top Hat

Rank all scores from highest to lowest and find the middle score	Find the score (X) of the middle case in the frequency distribution

Creativity score (X)		X	f	
11		11	1	
9		10	0	
8	N = 16	9	1	
8	8 scores (50%	8	2	8th and 9th
7	of all scores)			(middle cases
7	above	7	3	fall here.
7		6	4	← Median = 6
6		5	3	
		4	2	
Median = 6		N = 16		
6				
6		One-half of 16 is 8. Find the 8th and 9th		
6	8 scores (50%	cases in the frequency distribution,		
5	of all scores)	counting either from the top or bottom.		
5	below	The median is the score lying between		
5		them.		
4				
4				

problem. Calculating the median from a frequency distribution (the right-hand column on Table 18–4) is useful when there are too many scores to list individually.

The median is a better indicator of central tendency than the mean when there are a few extremely high or extremely low scores. It is less influenced by extremes than is the mean. In the top hat example, the median is 6 and the mean is 6.5, elevated by the extreme case of the person who generated 11 uses.

Mode

The *mode* is the single score that occurs most often in a distribution. Of the three measures of central tendency, it is the easiest to compute but often the least informative, as it provides only a rough estimate of central tendency. Table 18–2 indicates that four people gave six uses for a top hat—more than gave any other single number of uses. The *mode* of this distribution is therefore 6. It is not unusual for a distribution to have more than one mode. When there are two modes, the distribution is called *bimodal.*

Measures of Variability

Variability refers to the spread or dispersion among a set of scores.

Range

The most simple measure of dispersion (variability) is the *range,* the difference between the highest and lowest score. To compute the range, simply subtract the lowest score from the highest. On the Top Hat problem, the highest score was 11 and the lowest was 4; the range is $11 - 4 = 7$.

Standard Deviation (SD)

A second and more statistically useful indicator of variability or dispersion is the *standard deviation.* The standard deviation is a more complicated statistic than the range and is more useful for statistical purposes. It is more useful because unlike the range, which simply indicates the difference from highest to lowest score, the standard deviation takes into account the degree to which the scores cluster around the mean. Note that the standard deviation is used with the mean, but not with the median or mode.

The standard deviation takes into account the distance of each score from the mean of the distribution. The larger the standard deviation, the greater the spread of scores around the mean. A small standard deviation indicates that most scores are grouped closely around the mean. Figure 18–1 shows two sets of scores that have identical means, medians, and ranges, but different standard deviations.

```
x    x     x           x              x     x           x
0  1  2  3  4  5  6  7  8  9  10  11  12  13  14  15  16  17  18  19  20
                    Set A scores (X_A)
```

$\Sigma X_A = 65$

(sum of scores)

```
                          x
                          x
x                    x  x  x                                   x
0  1  2  3  4  5  6  7  8  9  10  11  12  13  14  15  16  17  18  19  20
                    Set B scores (X_B)
```

$\Sigma X_B = 65$

(sum of scores)

Descriptive Statistics for Set A
N_A = 7 (number of cases)
M_A = 9.3 (Mean)
SD_A = 7.63 (Standard Deviation)

Descriptive Statistics for Set B
N_B = 7 (number of cases)
M_B = 9.3 (Mean)
SD_B = 5.82 (Standard Deviation)

FIG. 18–1. Example illustrating two sets of scores (7 each) with same central tendency and range but different patterns of variability.

A formula for computing the standard deviation is:

$$SD = \sqrt{\frac{\sum X^2 - \frac{\left(\sum X\right)^2}{N}}{N}}$$

where SD = standard deviation

$\sum X^2$ = each score squared and then summed

$\left(\sum X\right)^2$ = all scores summed and then squared

N = number of cases

Do not be surprised if you find other formulas for calculating the standard deviation. They vary among statistics texts. Sometimes the formula will show *N*-1 in the denominator instead of *N*. Using *N* provides the standard deviation of the sample. *N-1* gives an estimate of the population standard deviation. Most calculators provide keys for calculating either one. Table 18–5 shows the calculation of the sample standard deviation for the results of the Top Hat study. In calculating a standard deviation, it is not necessary to list the scores from highest to lowest. They can be written in any order.

An individual's score can be expressed in standard deviation units (called a *standard score* or *z-score*) which allows a quick assessment of how far that individual is above or below the mean. Another index is the *variance* or square of the standard deviation (SD^2 or s^2).

This may be the time to stop momentarily. The next part of the chapter will deal with graphs. However, before going on, you may wish to review some of the earlier parts of this chapter.

TABLE 18–5. Calculation of the Standard Deviation for the Top Hat Study

Number of uses for a top hat X	X^2	
11	121	
9	81	$\text{S.D.} = \sqrt{\dfrac{\sum X^2 - \dfrac{\left(\sum X\right)^2}{N}}{N}}$
8	64	
8	64	
7	49	
7	49	$= \sqrt{\dfrac{728 - \dfrac{10{,}816}{16}}{16}}$
7	49	
6	36	
6	36	
6	36	$= \sqrt{\dfrac{728 - 676}{16}}$
6	36	
5	25	$= \sqrt{\dfrac{52}{16}}$
5	25	
5	25	$= \sqrt{3.25}$
4	16	
4	16	$\text{S.D.} = 1.80$

$\sum X = 104 \quad \sum X^2 = 728 \quad N = 16$

$\left(\sum X\right)^2 = (104)^2 = 10{,}816$

Figures

Up to this point, data have been presented in statistical tables. It is also possible to present the same information in figures, sometimes called charts or graphs. You need to decide whether the information is presented more clearly in text (written description), in a table, or as a figure. Sometimes a combination of techniques works best, with some written description and other results displayed in a graph. Chapter 20 provides more detailed information about the use of tables and figures in the results section of a research report.

Types of Figures

Many different types of graphs or charts are available in computer software, sometimes under slightly differing names. For example, a bar graph in one program may be called a bar chart in another. The type of graph you select depends upon what you wish to communicate. A well-drawn graph can make it easier to see and understand information. There are many tempting variations in computer software with the capacity for multiple labels, shading, and three-dimensional presentation. Beware of overdoing it and creating "chart junk"—excessive clutter that leads to information overload. Rule number one is to keep the figure clear and simple.

Bar graphs

Figure 18–2 is a bar graph. Other terms are *column charts* or *histograms* (a particular type of bar graph). Generally, the levels of the independent or predictor variable are shown along the horizontal axis. The values of the dependent variable (outcome) are shown on the vertical axis.

Line Graphs

For a line graph, the data points are plotted and then connected with lines (see Figure 18–3). It is a good way to illustrate an overall trend or pattern. The values of the independent variable (preferably continuous) are plotted along the horizontal axis, and the dependent variable along the vertical axis.

Pie Charts

Pie or round graphs are good for showing the relationships of parts to the whole. Don't try to depict more than five segments because the graph becomes cluttered and difficult to read. Arrange the segments in order, from largest to smallest, us-

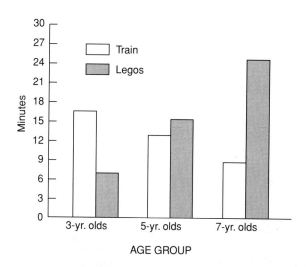

FIG. 18–2. Median length of time spent playing with two types of toys, by age group (40 children per group).

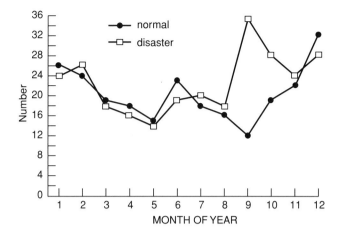

FIG. 18–3. Mean number of tranquilizer prescriptions per month during disaster year and the previous year.

ing patterns to distinguish them with the darker shading for the smaller segments. Figure 18–4 illustrates students ratings of cafeteria food.

Guidelines for Figures

1. Take time to plan the figure in advance. Be prepared to try different arrangements. You probably won't get it right on the first try.

2. Present only essential facts; don't clutter the figure with unnecessary information or decoration.

3. Make it easy to read; use clean lines.

4. On the horizontal axis, numbers run from left to right, beginning with the low numbers.

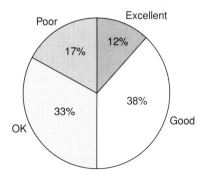

FIG. 18–4. Student ratings of cafeteria food ($N = 254$).

5. On the vertical axis, low numbers are placed at the bottom.

6. The entire graph and everything on it should be clearly labeled. Define all symbols used. Provide a caption beneath, describing the contents.

7. When comparing different-sized groups, use percentages or proportions instead of frequencies (counts).

8. The overall impression conveyed by a graph is affected by the ratio of the vertical to the horizontal axis. Some writers suggest keeping the vertical axis about three-quarters as long as the horizontal axis.

Summary

The original scores on a measure constitute the raw data. The type of descriptive statistics used depends upon whether the outcome measure is categorical or continuous. Categorical variables are those whose levels or values are discrete (nominal). Continuous variables have values that can be represented along a sliding scale or continuous dimension.

For categorical outcomes, the first step is to arrange the data in a contingency table. The counts or frequencies of occurrence within each category can be described by percentages or proportions.

For continuous variables, the data set is described in terms of both its central tendency and its variability (spread or dispersion of scores). The measures of central tendency are the the *mean* (arithmetic average), *median* (middle score, when scores are arranged in order), and *mode* (the most frequently-occurring score). Variability of scores is described by the *range* or *standard deviation*. The standard deviation indicates the degree to which the scores cluster around the mean. The *variance* is the square of the standard deviation.

Figures present data in visual form. The best figure to use is the one that depicts the particular data set in the most clear way.

Further Reading

Bruning, J. L., & Kintz, B. L. (1987). *Computational handbook of statistics* (3rd ed.). Glenview, IL: Scott, Foresman.

Cleveland, W. S. (1993). *Visualizing data*. Summit, NJ: Hobart Press.

Kosslyn, S. M. (1994). *Elements of graph design*. New York: W.H. Freeman.

Phillips, J. L., Jr. (1996). *How to think about statistics* (5th ed.). New York: W. H. Freeman.

Tufte, E. R. (1990). *Envisioning information*. Cheshire, CT: Graphics Press.

Utts, J. M. (1996). *Seeing through statistics*. Belmont, CA: Duxbury Press.

Zeisel, H. (1985). *Say it with figures* (6th ed.). New York: Harper & Row.

Sample Problems

1. A college coach was interested in comparing the quality of players from urban and rural high schools. She rated each player's ability as Excellent, Good, and Fair. From the urban schools, there were 10 Excellent players, 17 Good, and 9 Fair. From the rural schools there were 5 Excellent players, 7 Good, and 15 Fair.

    a. Put the data on a contingency table.

    b. Show the appropriate descriptive statistics on a table.

    c. Illustrate the descriptive statistics on a bar graph.

2. Here are scores from 10 sixth-grade boys who participated in a study of running speed. Compute the following descriptive statistics: mean, median, range, and standard deviation.

Name	Time (in seconds)
John	52
Willis	62
Ricardo	47
Henry	59
Tran	50
Josh	72
Kevin	50
P.K.	71
Raphael	48
Morris	50

Answers to Problems

1. a. Contingency table

HIGH SCHOOL

	Urban	Rural
Excellent	10	5
Good	17	7
Fair	9	15
Total	36	27

COACH'S RATING

b. Descriptive statistics

Percentage of players from urban and rural schools rated as Excellent, Good, and Fair by college coach.

COACH'S RATING

HIGH SCHOOL	Excellent	Good	Fair	Total
Urban (n = 36)	27.78	47.22	25.00	100.00
Rural (n = 27)	18.52	25.93	55.56	100.01

c. Bar graph

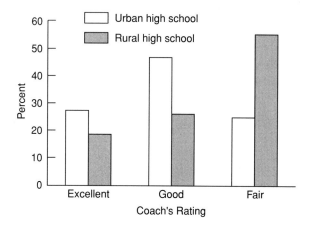

2. Descriptive statistics
   Mean = 56.1
   Median = 51 (midpoint between 50 and 52)
   Range = 72 − 47 = 25
   Standard Deviation = 8.916*

* Some calculators use a slightly different formula, employing $N − 1$ rather than N in the denominator. In that case, the standard deviation is 9.398.

19 Inferential Statistics

"Smoke Gets in Your Eyes" is a very romantic song but not a very pleasant experience for many people. A graduate student wanted to find out whether people stood farther away from smokers than from nonsmokers (Anthony, 1977). She recruited student volunteers from psychology classes. When they arrived at the designated room, each volunteer was introduced to the research associate (a person working with Ms. Anthony) and asked to "choose the distance most comfortable for conversation between you and this person, assuming you had just met." Once the student had created a comfortable conversational distance, a tape measure was used to calculate it in centimeters. During approximately half of the 76 sessions, the research associate was smoking a cigarette. During the other sessions, the associate did not smoke.

Anthony found that students stood a mean distance of 62.5 cm from the nonsmoking associate. When the associate was smoking, the distance was 80.3 cm.

From these average distances, it appeared that the cigarette had an effect on conversational distance. However, there may have been a large overlap in the scores, and perhaps only one or two extreme scores were responsible for these differences. For example, a single student who remained 4 m away from a smoking person might have been responsible for the entire difference. A procedure is needed for deciding when a difference is reliable and when it is due to chance fluctuations, perhaps the result of a few extreme scores in one group. One solution is to repeat the study and see if similar differences are found. Another approach is to test the reliability of differences between groups using an *inferential* test. *Inferential statistics* permit generalization from samples to populations.

First, Some Background

Chapter 16 on sampling described the process of generalizing from a *sample* to a *population*, making inferences from a part to the whole. There were two problems that arose in doing this. One was *sampling error,* chance fluctuation that is inevitable when taking small samples from large populations. The second problem was *sample bias*, which comes from faulty sample selection resulting in a subset that does not accurately represent the population. Statistical techniques are used to take care of the problem of *sampling error*, the chance fluctuation one must expect. Statistical manipulation *cannot* solve problems of inadequate or biased sampling. That is a research design problem. Statistics cannot salvage an inadequately designed or poorly conducted piece of research. To repeat, statistics are used to deal with sampling error, to estimate the role of chance in the findings.

Note to the reader: If you have not taken a course in statistics, this chapter will seem more difficult than others because of the many new terms and formulas. It is probably best to read this chapter for understanding the first time through, rather than to attempt to grasp all the details of each statistical test. Do not be concerned if you cannot understand immediately how these tests can be applied. This will come in time as you work with actual data.

Testing the Null Hypothesis

The idea that any differences in an experiment are due to chance fluctuations and that the independent variable has no effect on the dependent variable is called the *null hypothesis* (H_0). In a technical statistical sense, the null hypothesis is the assertion that the samples being measured are all drawn from the same population with regard to the outcomes under study.

This is a conservative way of phrasing the research question; the null hypothesis predicts that there will be no reliable difference between groups. In the preceding example, the null hypothesis is that the two samples tested (those approaching the smoker or the nonsmoker) do not differ in average conversational distance.

Following a statistical test, the null hypothesis is either accepted (no difference) or rejected (there is a reliable difference). When the null hypothesis is accepted, the researcher concludes that the independent variable had no effect on the outcome. If the null hypothesis is *rejected* (the difference was *not* due to chance), then the conclusion is that there was an effect. Acceptance or rejection of the null hypothesis can be done quickly and easily when you know the techniques. Formulas and tables necessary for interpreting the results have been worked out by statisticians.

Alternative Hypothesis

The alternative hypothesis is your working or research hypothesis. It is called the *alternative hypothesis* because it is an alternative to the null hypothesis. The alternative hypothesis is stated in positive terms—that there will be a difference between groups or that the independent variable will have a significant effect on the dependent variable.

Testing the null hypothesis may seem odd because you are usually more interested in confirming the alternative hypothesis. This is probably what you were interested in initially. Nevertheless, statistical practice requires that the fate of the alternative hypothesis actually rests on acceptance or rejection of the null hypothesis.

Probability Levels

In using inferential statistics, it is the null hypothesis that is tested. Whether or not your own hypothesis can be accepted depends on whether you are able to reject the null hypothesis that no reliable difference exists. Rejecting the null hypothesis is a gamble. The *probability level* of a statistic indicates the odds. If the probability of the difference occurring by chance alone is less than 5 in 100, then most researchers are willing to gamble that the outcome is *not* one of these five cases, and will therefore reject the null hypothesis and accept the research hypothesis that a genuine difference exists.

A common practice in the social sciences is to use the .05 probability level for testing the null hypothesis. This is also called the *.05 level of significance* and is abbreviated as $p < .05$ (the direction of these symbols is important, $<$ is less than, and $>$ is greater than). When the odds of a difference being due to chance are less than 5 in 100 ($p < .05$), the null hypothesis will be rejected. When the likelihood of a difference being due to chance is more than 5 in 100, then the null hypothesis—that the difference is probably due to chance—can be accepted. Some researchers prefer the .01 level of significance ($p < .01$), rejecting the null hypothesis only if the odds of a difference being due to random fluctuation are less than 1 in 100. The .01 probability level reduces the likelihood of mistaking a chance difference for a genuine difference.

Do not confuse statistical significance with practical importance. To say that a difference is "statistically significant" means only that it is not due to chance. With very large samples, even a tiny difference can be statistically significant even though it probably will not have much practical relevance.

Statistical Tests for Continuous Data

The two most common tests for continuous data are the *t* test and analysis of variance. Both of them look at differences between means. The *t test* is used for comparing two groups. *Analysis of variance* (ANOVA) is used for comparing differences among two or more groups. Both of these tests take into account the amount of overlap in the distribution of scores in order to make a judgment about the significance of the *difference between means*.

A Precondition

Before either test can be employed, there is an important condition that must be met. The distribution of scores in the population from which scores were drawn

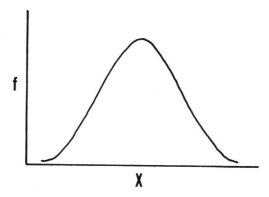

FIG. 19–1. Normal curve.

should approximately follow the normal curve. A perfect normal curve is the symmetrical bell-shaped curve shown in Figure 19–1. Characteristics measured in nature among large populations often produce this kind of frequency curve. If we measure the length of tigers' tails, the age at which children lose their milk teeth, or the production of fruit during the growing season, we would get a heavy concentration of scores in the middle with scores diminishing in frequency to the two ends of the curve. In a perfectly normal distribution, the mean, median, and mode are identical.

Most distributions of behavioral data do not perfectly match a bell-shaped curve but rather approximate it, as in Figure 19–2. This is acceptable for using a test for continuous data.

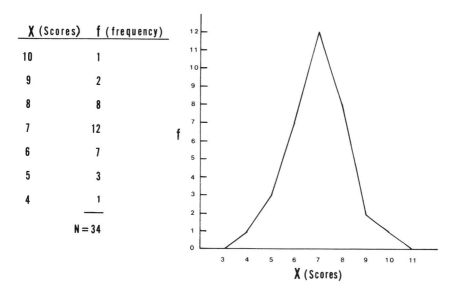

FIG. 19–2. Normally distributed data and frequency polygon.

Sometimes a distribution of scores deviates markedly from a normal curve. This happens when there are many extreme scores at the upper or lower ends of the distribution, as in Figure 19–3. Such distributions are said to be *skewed*. It is necessary to know whether data approximate a normal curve or instead are skewed in order to select the best statistical technique for describing them and testing any differences between groups. When the data are continuous and the frequency distribution is close to normal (it will rarely be a perfectly normal curve), then a *t* test or ANOVA can be used. If your results are skewed, but you think the characteristic being measured is probably normally distributed in the population, then you can still use a *t* test or ANOVA. If you think the population data do not approximate a normal curve, then sort your continuous data into two or three categories, and use the Chi-square test described later in this chapter.

There are many computer software packages that can be used for statistical calculation (see Chapter 15). Appendix C offers helpful tips for data entry and analysis by computer. The next sections (and Appendix B) provide formulas for hand calculation and also offer advice in interpreting computer-generated results.

Comparing Two Groups—the t Test

The *t* test assesses the significance of the difference between the *means* of two groups of scores. The numerical result of this test is called a *t ratio*, an inferential statistic. There are two formulas for a *t* test. One is used when the two groups are independent, that is, two different subject samples are being compared. The other is used when the two groups being compared have been matched on some characteristic, or the same people have been tested before and after an experimental treatment. The resulting scores are called *paired*, *matched*, or *correlated measures*.

Doing a *t* test requires obtaining three different numbers: the *t* ratio, degrees of freedom (*df*), and the *p* value (probability) associated with the *t* ratio. Degrees of

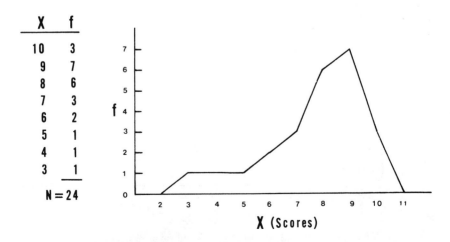

FIG. 19–3. Skewed data and frequency polygon.

freedom (*df*) are related to the sample size and number of levels of the independent variable. The probability (*p*) value is used in deciding whether to accept or reject the null hypothesis.

t *ratio for Independent Groups*

A *t* ratio evaluates the difference between two means against the amount of variability within each group of subjects. Conceptually,

$$t = \frac{\text{Difference between means}}{\text{Measure of variability in both groups (pooled within-group variance)}}$$

The formula for calculating a *t* test for independent groups and an example of its use are shown in Box 19–1.

BOX 19–1. Calculation of a *t* Test for Two Independent Groups

Two groups of employees are given a test. One group contains five people, the other six. Do the employees in Group 1 score significantly higher than the employees in Group 2, or is the difference between them the result of random fluctuation?

Scores on Test

Group 1 (X)	Group 2 (Y)
4	4
5	9
5	2
3	3
3	3
	4

The formula for a *t* test for independent groups is

$$t = \frac{M_X - M_Y}{\sqrt{\left[\frac{\left(\sum X^2 - \frac{\left(\sum X\right)^2}{N_X}\right) + \left(\sum Y^2 - \frac{\left(\sum Y\right)^2}{N_y}\right)}{N_X + N_Y - 2}\right] \cdot \left[\frac{1}{N_X} + \frac{1}{N_Y}\right]}}$$

M_x = mean for Group 1
M_y = mean for Group 2
X = score in Group 1
Y = score in Group 2
N_x = number of scores in Group 1
N_y = number of scores in Group 2

Computation

Step 1. Add up scores in Group 1: $\sum X = 20$.

Step 2. Square total for all scores in Group 1: $\left(\sum X\right)^2 = (20)(20) = 400$.

Step 3. Square *each score* in Group 1. Add together $\sum X^2 = 84$.

Step 4. Find number of scores in Group 1: $N_x = 5$.

Step 5. Compute mean for Group 1: $M_x = \sum X \div N_x = 4.0$.

(Steps 6–10 repeat above for Group 2)

Step 6. $\sum Y = 25$.

Step 7. $\left(\sum Y\right)^2 = 625$.

Step 8. $\sum Y^2 = 135$.

Step 9. $N_y = 6$.

Step 10. $M_y = 4.17$.

Step 11. Enter these figures in the formula for the t test for independent groups.

$$t = \frac{4.0 - 4.17}{\sqrt{\left[\dfrac{\left(84 - \dfrac{400}{5}\right) + \left(135 - \dfrac{625}{6}\right)}{5 + 6 - 2}\right] \cdot \left[\dfrac{1}{5} + \dfrac{1}{6}\right]}}$$

$$= \frac{-.17}{\sqrt{\left(\dfrac{4 + 30.83}{9}\right)(.20 + .17)}} = \frac{-.17}{\sqrt{(3.87)(.37)}}$$

$$= \frac{-.17}{\sqrt{1.43}} = \frac{-.17}{1.20} = -.14$$

Step 12. Compute degrees of freedom: $df = (N_x - 1) + (N_y - 1) = 4 + 5 = 9$. Check Table A–1 in Appendix A. For 9 degrees of freedom, Table A–1 shows that a t ratio of 2.26 or greater is required for significance at the .05 level. As $t = .14$ (the minus sign can be ignored), this difference is *not* significant.

Interpreting the t Ratio

Once you have calculated the t ratio, the next step is to find out the probability (p value) associated with it. The sign ($+$ or $-$) of the t ratio tells you the direction of the difference between the means, but this is not important in interpreting the statistical significance of the t ratio, so it can be ignored momentarily.

A small probability (p value of .05 or less) allows you to reject the null hypothesis and conclude that there is a reliable difference between the means. However, the p value also indicates the likelihood that you are making a mistake in rejecting the null hypothesis. For example, if the probability associated with your statistic is .05, you have a 1 in 20 (5 out of 100) chance of being wrong in assuming that you found a true difference (if the null hypothesis were in fact true). This is called a *Type 1 error* (rejecting the null hypothesis when it is true). Although it might seem better to be conservative and require a smaller probability (e.g., a .01 level) before rejecting the null hypothesis, there is a trade-off. You may be more confident about rejecting the null hypothesis, but there is a second error, which involves missing a true effect. A more thorough discussion is beyond the scope of this book. For now, simply specify in your research report the level of significance that your statistic reached, either *not significant* or whether it has a probability less than .01 or less than .05.

Hand Calculation

Box 19–1 provides all of the steps for hand calculation. First the formula is followed for calculating the *t* ratio. Then the degrees of freedom (*df*) is computed. Finally, the probability of your *t* ratio is estimated by using the table of Critical Values (Table A–1 in Appendix A). If the *t* ratio that you computed is *less* than the value listed in the .05 column at the appropriate *df*, then you must *accept the null hypothesis*. If your *t* ratio equals or is greater than the Critical Value listed in the .01 column, then you reject the null hypothesis at the .01 level of significance. If it only exceeds the Critical Value at the .05 level, then you can reject the null hypothesis at the .05 level but not at the .01 level of significance.

Understanding the Computer Printout

If you are using a computer program, the printout will give you the *t* ratio, the degrees of freedom (*df*) and the exact probability of the *t* ratio. The interpretation is the same as the final stage described in the preceding section on hand calculation. You don't need to consult the table of Critical Values in Appendix A because the computer has given you the exact probability of your *t* ratio.

When the raw data illustrated in Box 19–1 are entered into a computer program for analysis, the obtained *t* ratio of -0.14 has 9 degrees of freedom (*df*) and a probability (*p* value) of 0.89. The probability is greater than .05, so the null hypothesis must be accepted—leading to the conclusion of no reliable difference between the group means.

t *Ratio for Paired Scores*

When two sets of scores are matched in some way, such as the same individuals tested before and after an experimental treatment, or pairs of scores obtained from siblings or twins, the *t* test for paired scores is used. The formula and an example of the calculations are shown in Appendix B–1. If you use a computer program to calculate the *t* ratio, be sure to indicate that you are contrasting means from matched or paired groups rather than from independent groups.

Degrees of freedom (*df*) for a *t* test with paired or matched scores are the number of pairs of scores less one. For example, if 16 subjects are tested and then retested, then $df = 15$.

Analysis of Variance (ANOVA)

When you want to compare more than two means, use Analysis of Variance (ANOVA). The principles of interpreting differences are similar to those for the *t* test. Like the *t* test, ANOVA is used to judge the reliability of differences between means. Its advantage is that it can be used for more than two means at a time, or it can be used instead of *t* for two means. The inferential statistic produced by ANOVA is called an *F* ratio.

One-way ANOVA

A one-way or single-factor ANOVA is a statistical analysis of one independent variable, comparing two or more levels. Here is an example with three means. An aviation researcher is interested in the effect of sleep deprivation on information processing by air traffic controllers. The independent variable is sleep deprivation measured at three levels: none, slight, and moderate deprivation. The dependent variable is the number of mistakes made on a radar detection task. Four subjects are randomly assigned to each group (sleep deprivation condition), giving a total of 12 individuals in the study. The raw data are presented in Table 19–1.

The question to be answered by the statistical analysis is whether or not the means of these three groups differ significantly from one another (i.e., more than would be expected by chance). We are concerned with the differences *between* groups, but we gauge the chance variation by looking at the variability of scores *within* each group. *F* is a ratio of the average between-group (numerator) to the average within-group variability (denominator). In this example, ANOVA calculates a measure of the differences between the groups with respect to the number of mistakes and evaluates that against the distribution or spread of mistakes within each group. The between group differences must be substantially greater than those within groups in order for the differences between means to reach statistical significance. Looking at the means on Table 19–1, it appears that sleep deprivation leads to more errors, but the differences between groups are not large and could reasonably be attributed to chance. The ANOVA will allow us to decide the odds of that being the case.

TABLE 19–1. Sleep Deprivation Data

Group 1		Group 2		Group 3	
No deprivation	Number of mistakes	Slight deprivation	Number of mistakes	Moderate deprivation	Number of mistakes
Subject 1	1	Subject 5	3	Subject 9	2
Subject 2	2	Subject 6	2	Subject 10	3
Subject 3	0	Subject 7	3	Subject 11	4
Subject 4	2	Subject 8	4	Subject 12	4
Means	1.25		3.0		3.25

Hand Calculation

The formulas and an example of the calculation are found in Appendix B–3. The statistic to be tested is the F ratio. As with the t ratio, you need to use a table of Critical Values (Table A–6 in Appendix A) in order to decide whether or not to reject the null hypothesis. Follow the instructions in Appendix B–3 for calculating df (degrees of freedom) and using Table A–6 in Appendix A. The F ratio must equal or exceed the value shown on the table to justify the conclusion of a difference among the means.

Understanding the Computer Printout

When the data from the sleep deprivation study are processed by computer, the output will include a table like the one shown in Box 19–2. The exact probability for F is given, so you do not need to consult the table of Critical Values to make your decision. Box 19–2 provides a more detailed description of the components of the ANOVA table. In the sleep deprivation study, the obtained F had a p value of .025, which allowed the aviation researcher to reject the null hypothesis (because the probability is less than .05) and conclude that sleep deprivation did increase the number of mistakes.

Locating the Differences

Additional tests called *mean comparisons* or *contrasts* can be made to find exactly where the significant difference lies. In our example, the difference between groups 1 and 2 and between 1 and 3 was significant, while the difference between groups 2 and 3 was not. For computer analysis, the contrast/comparison tests are usually included with the ANOVA software. Formulas for hand calculation can be found in advanced statistical textbooks.

Advanced ANOVA designs

There are many variations of the ANOVA design, each requiring a different set of calculations. The interpretation of the F ratio is fundamentally the same across the various designs.

ANOVA for Groups of Unequal Size

In natural experiments or observational studies, it is common to have unequal numbers of subjects in different treatment conditions. Alternative calculations must be used to take into account the unequal numbers. Computer programs for calculating ANOVA easily accommodate unequal sample sizes, or you can find the appropriate formula in an advanced statistics textbook.

BOX 19–2. Interpreting an ANOVA Table

Example from the sleep deprivation study

ANALYSIS OF VARIANCE

SOURCE	SUM-OF-SQUARES	DF	MEAN-SQUARE	F- RATIO	P
GROUP	9.500	2	4.750	5.700	0.025
ERROR	7.500	9	0.833		

SOURCE	= sources of variability in the study.
GROUP	= the independent variable.
ERROR	= fluctuation due to chance or individual differences.
SUM-OF-SQUARES (*SS*)	= a measure of variability, the sum of squared deviations from the mean.
GROUP *SS*	= amount of variability among the group means. It is the between-group variability, the treatment effect.
ERROR *SS*	= within-group variability. It is a pooled measure showing the dispersion of the members of each group from their group mean (each of the three sleep deprivation conditions contributes to it).
DF	= degrees of freedom
MEAN-SQUARE	= SUM-OF-SQUARES divided by DF (degrees of freedom).
F	= the arithmetic result of dividing the GROUP MS by the ERROR MS (the ratio of between-group variability to within-group variability).
P	= the probability associated with F.

Slight differences in notation are to be expected across computer programs and statistics textbooks.

Factorial Design

ANOVA can be used for studies involving more than one independent variable or factor. When multiple levels of more than one factor are used, the design is termed *factorial*, for example, two-factor or two-way ANOVA, three-factor or three-way ANOVA. Sometimes you will see an ANOVA described as a 3 × 2. That would be an analysis of 3 levels of one independent variable (e.g., age) and 2 levels of a second independent variable (e.g., gender).

The research design for the sleep deprivation study could be modified by introducing three levels of job experience as an additional factor: less than 1 year experience, 1 to 5 years experience, and more than 5 years experience. Such a design would allow for assessment of the effects of sleep deprivation, assessment of the effects of job experience, and an assessment of a possible *interaction* between the two. For example, sleep deprivation may be less important for experienced than for beginning air controllers. An *interaction* is when the outcome produced by changes in one variable differs depending upon the levels of a second variable. The potential for judging interactions makes the factorial design a very useful one. In these cases, separate F ratios are generated for each factor and for the interaction.

Repeated Measures Design

When the same subjects are studied at different times or under different conditions, the design is called *repeated measures*. In the air controller example, it would have been possible to study the same subjects under the different conditions of sleep deprivation.

The design is very powerful or sensitive as it permits the measuring of individual differences in detecting the effect of the different levels of the independent variable. *Individual differences* are the result of each person's unique set of characteristics. If different groups of subjects are compared, some of the difference in their average performance will be the result of different treatment and some will be due to differences in their unique characteristics. So the between-group comparison has two sources of variation, treatment (different levels of the independent variable) plus individual differences. Within the group, differences are *only* due to the unique characteristics of each person, because the group has received the same experimental treatment. With a repeated measures design, the variability due to individual differences is measured and taken into account—the subjects or participants are the same in the different treatment conditions.

As with unequal subjects, a repeated measures design requires a different formula. If you use a computer, be sure to request the analysis for *repeated measures*.

Analysis of Covariance (ANCOVA)

This technique takes into account scores on some other variable believed to affect the action of the independent variable. For example, a coach evaluating the effects of practice on long-jump performance might want to take athlete's height into account. Height, measured in inches or centimeters, could be added as a co-variate. As with the designs described above, a special formula is needed.

In the air controller example, instead of introducing amount of experience as a second factor (independent variable with three levels), we could take it into account statistically by using years of experience for each subject as a co-variate and including it in an ANCOVA calculation. Analysis of covariance would tell us the effects of sleep deprivation, after making an adjustment for years of experience.

Multivariate Designs (MANOVA)

In ANOVA, only one dependent variable is used per analysis. There are also *multivariate* procedures in which the relationship between two or more dependent variables enters into the statistical calculation. These are complex and generally done by computer. While relatively easy to generate because the computer does the work, their interpretation requires a well-grounded understanding of statistical concepts and inference.

There are other variations of the ANOVA technique that are beyond the scope of an introductory course in research methods. Many colleges and universities teach advanced statistics courses devoted entirely to Analysis of Variance. Additional information on ANOVA can be found in the books listed at the conclusion of this chapter.

A Statistical Test for Categorical Data: Chi-square

When your data are not in a continuous distribution, but instead are grouped into categories, a very useful statistical test is Chi-square. The symbol is χ^2. *Chi* is a Greek letter pronounced *ki*, as in *kite*. χ^2 is used to test whether the pattern of the actual results (counts in categories) differs reliably from what would be expected by chance. There are computer programs for Chi-square, but it is an easy statistic to compute using a calculator.

Hand Calculation

Start with the *Observed frequencies (O)*, the raw data (frequencies, *not* percentages) arranged in the appropriate cells of a contingency table. Then compute the *Expected frequencies (E)* by following the steps listed in Box 19–3. The Expected frequencies (E) represent the null hypothesis—what you would expect by chance.

After the E frequencies are calculated, the Chi-square statistic is computed. The formula for the Chi-square and a computational example using the bicycle observations are shown in Box 19–4.

Understanding the Computer Printout

The printout will give you the Chi-square statistic, the degrees of freedom (*df*) and the exact probability of χ^2. The decision is made on the same basis as with the *t* and *F* ratios. If the probability is less than .05, then reject the null hypothesis and conclude that the observed pattern differs more than expected by chance.

When the raw data illustrated in Box 19–4 are entered into a computer program for analysis, the obtained χ^2 of 4.313 has 1 degree of freedom (*df*) and a proba-

BOX 19–3. Calculation of Expected Frequencies (E)

Description of the study: A class in research methods was interested in whether men or women bicyclists were less likely to come to a full stop at a stop sign at a major intersection near the college campus. They made 20-minute observations during weekday afternoons over a 2-week period. Each cyclist was classified as having stopped or not stopped at the sign. The statistical question is whether the pattern of stopping differs by gender. Or (null hypothesis) if the observed difference between groups (men and women) is no greater than expected by chance.

Step 1. Arrange the observed counts in a *contingency table* with the predictor or independent variable at the top (levels in columns) and the other variable at the side (levels in rows).

For the bicycle study, this is a table with two columns and two rows (2 × 2 table). Each cell shows the number of individuals meeting the conditions described in the two margins (e.g., 66 males stopped at the sign). These are the observed frequencies (O). As a convention, the individual cells of the table are lettered.

	GENDER	
	Men	Women
STOP Yes	A 66	B 25
No	C 126	D 84

Note: This arrangement is called a contingency table because cell membership is *contingent* upon the variable levels shown on the margins. In this example, being in cell A indicates that the person is male and has stopped at the sign.

Step 2. Calculate the totals for each row ($A + B$ and $C + D$) and for each column ($A + C$ and $B + D$).

	GENDER		Row totals
	Men	Women	
STOP Yes	A 66	B 25	91
No	C 126	D 84	210
Column totals	192	109	

Step 3. Compute the Expected frequencies (E). This is done by multiplying each cell's column total by its row total and dividing by the grand total ($N = 301$). Enter each on the contingency table.

Cell A   192 × 91 ÷ 301 = 58.05
Cell B   109 × 91 ÷ 301 = 32.95
Cell C   192 × 210 ÷ 301 = 133.95
Cell D   109 × 210 ÷ 301 = 76.05

GENDER

	Men	Women	Totals
STOP Yes	A 66 [58.05]	B 25 [32.95]	91
No	C 126 [133.95]	D 84 [76.05]	210
Totals	192	109	

The E values for the column cells should add up to the marginal total for the column, and the E values in the row cells should equal the total for the row. If they do not, check your calculations.

Rationale: The Expected frequencies (*E*) are those that would occur due to chance alone. The characteristics of the sample as a whole, expressed in the marginal totals, are used to calculate the expected values for each cell in the contingency table. In this example, out of the entire sample of people, 192 stopped. To put it another way, 192/301 of the entire sample stopped at the sign. Furthermore, 91 of the people in the sample were male. Based on the characteristics of the sample (marginal totals), if no other factors were influencing behavior, we would expect 192/301 of the 91 males to stop at the sign. This gives the expected value of 58.05. The arithmetic shown above is an easier way to do the computations.

bility (*p* value) of 0.038. The probability is less than .05, so the null hypothesis can be rejected.

Limitations of Chi-square

The Chi-square statistic becomes unreliable when the *expected* frequencies (*E*) are very small (i.e., less than 5). It should never be used when an expected frequency is 0. Note that this applies only to *E* rather than to the observed frequencies (*O*), which can be any size, including zero.

A contingency table can contain any number of levels (rows or columns), but the Chi-square statistic becomes difficult to interpret when the number of levels gets beyond 3 or 4 per variable.

Examples of contingency table layouts

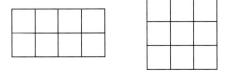

Note to the reader: This is good a place to stop and review this material.

BOX 19–4. Calculation of Chi-square

Formula for Chi-square:

$$\chi^2 = \sum \frac{(O - E)^2}{E}$$

The frequencies shown in Box 19–3 are used in this example.

Step 1. For each cell, subtract the expected value (E) from the observed value (O), square this figure, and divide by E. Sum the resulting numbers.

$$\text{Cell } A \quad \frac{(66 - 58.05)^2}{58.05} = \frac{(7.95)^2}{58.05} = 1.09$$

$$\text{Cell } B \quad \frac{(25 - 32.95)^2}{32.95} = \frac{(7.95)^2}{32.95} = 1.92$$

$$\text{Cell } C \quad \frac{(126 - 133.95)^2}{133.95} = \frac{(7.95)^2}{133.95} = .47$$

$$\text{Cell } D \quad \frac{(84 - 76.05)^2}{76.05} = \frac{(7.95)^2}{76.05} = .83$$

$$\chi^2 = 1.09 + 1.92 + .47 + .83 = 4.31$$

Step 2. Compute the degrees of freedom for the contingency table. Formula for degrees of freedom for the Chi-square:

$$df = (\text{number of rows} - 1)(\text{number of columns} - 1)$$
$$df = (2 - 1)(2 - 1) = 1$$

Step 3. To find the significance of the obtained Chi-square statistic, consult Table A–2 in Appendix A. Find the appropriate degrees of freedom ($df = 1$) in the left-hand column and then move to the right to the probability level (.05 or .01) columns. Table A–2 shows that with one degree of freedom, a Chi-square of 3.84 (the critical value) or greater is required to reject the null hypothesis at the .05 level.

Step 4. The obtained Chi-square value for the bicycle observations is 4.31 which is larger than 3.84. Therefore, we can conclude that there was a reliable gender difference in ignoring the stop sign at this intersection. *Note:* If you feel that a .01 level of signif- icance is more appropriate for judging whether or not there is a gender difference, you would have to *accept* the null hypothesis and conclude that the difference was due to chance (i.e., not a true difference). The decision about probability level should be made before calculating the statistic.

Step 5. The direction of the difference can be seen by transforming the contingency table frequencies to percentages.

Did not come to a full stop:

  126/192 of the men = 65%
  84/109 of the women = 77%

Correlation

The statistical tests mentioned thus far have dealt with differences between groups either by testing differences between means (*t* test and ANOVA), or by comparing observed with expected frequencies of occurrence (Chi-square). Another issue of concern to the researcher is *correlation*. Correlation refers to an association between scores on two variables for the same individuals or cases.

Correlations are often used to make predictions from one variable to another. For example, we could ask the question, "Is there a relationships between education and income?" One way to answer this question is to collect data on people's income in middle age and compare it with their formal education. For a visual picture, each case can be put on a *scatterplot*, also called a *scattergram* or *scatter chart*. The horizontal axis represents the levels or values of one variable (X), and the vertical axis shows the levels or values of the second variable (Y). Each dot represents an individual case. Figure 19–4 shows income and education data from a group of 20 individuals.

The pattern of dots in Figure 19–4 reveals a fairly clear trend for income to rise with years in college. This is called a *positive relationship* or *positive correlation*; an increase in one variable is accompanied by an increase in the other.

It is also possible for two variables to be *negatively correlated*; that is, as one variable increases, the other variable decreases. This is also called an *inverse relationship*. An example of a negative correlation would be that between children's hostile behavior and rating of liking by peers. In general, the more hostile children would be less liked, and the less hostile children would be more liked.

Although a scatterplot provides a visual picture of the association between two variables, a more precise indication of the degree of relationship is generally used

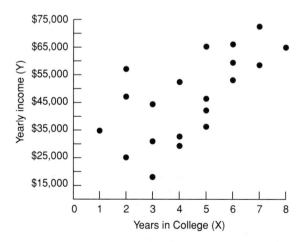

FIG. 19–4. Scattergram showing the relationship between amount of formal education and income level (*N* = 20).

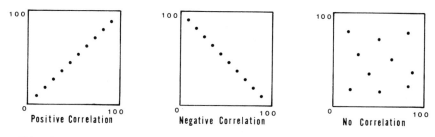

FIG. 19–5. Scattegrams produced by positive, negative, and absence of correlation.

in reporting research findings. That statistic is called a *correlation coefficient,* a number that can range from +1.0 through −1.0. A correlation coefficient of +1.0 indicates a perfect positive relationship, like that shown in the first scatterplot in Figure 19–5.

A perfect negative relationship, such as that shown in the second scatterplot, produces a correlation coefficient of −1.0. The higher the correlation coefficient, either in a positive or a negative direction, the stronger the association (positive or negative) between two variables.

The absence of any relationship, such as in the third scatterplot, produces a correlation coefficient of 0. This is the null hypothesis—that there is *no relationship* between two sets of scores.

The correlation coefficient for the scatterplot in Figure 19–5 is .646 (the + is understood by the absence of a minus sign), showing a positive relationship between education and income. Another example of a positive correlation is .872 between IQ test scores when people are tested twice, demonstrating good test-retest reliability. In contrast, a correlation coefficient of .024 between intelligence and musical ability is extremely low and has no predictive value.

Correlation does not imply causation. The fact that two variables are correlated does not mean that one causes the other. In the example of college education and income, it is tempting to assume that going to college produced the higher income later in life. However, it may be that people who attended college came from wealthier families in the first place. Or some factor *other* than the two variables being measured may be the cause of the relationship, such as qualities of perseverance or ambition.

Pearson Product-Moment Coefficient (r)

When both sets of scores to be correlated are continuous, a Pearson product-moment coefficient (*r*) is a widely-used statistic. Here is an example of data appropriate for correlational analysis:

A teacher predicted that pupils who do well in arithmetic are also good spellers (a positive correlation). The highest possible arithmetic score was 10, and the highest possible spelling score was 20.

Test Score

Student	Arithmetic	Spelling
Jeanine	8	13
Howard	6	8
Ky-Van	5	7
Blossom	10	14
Hugh	7	12
Bradford	9	15
Clayton	6	3
Lorraine	3	3

Hand Calculation

The formula and computational example for r are shown in Appendix B–3.

Understanding the Computer Printout

The usual computer printout for a correlation produces a correlation matrix. Here is an example using the Arithmetic and Spelling scores.

PEARSON CORRELATION MATRIX

	ARITH	SPELL
ARITH	1.000	
SPELL	0.881	1.000

MATRIX OF PROBABILITIES

	ARITH	SPELL
ARITH	0.000	
SPELL	0.004	0.000

NUMBER OF OBSERVATIONS: 8

In the top matrix the correlation (r) is shown in the cell at the intersection of the two variables. The other correlations are 1.000 because each variable correlates perfectly with itself.

The second matrix lists the probability of each r. In this example, the probability (p value) of $r = .881$ is .004, a great deal less than .01. Thus, we can reject the null hypothesis and conclude that there is a significant positive correlation between performance on the arithmetic test and performance on the spelling test for these 8 pupils.

Spearman Rank-order Coefficient (r_S)

The Spearman Rank-order Coefficient (r_S) is an alternative formula for computing correlation. One reason for using (r_S) instead of the Pearson r is because Pearson r can be distorted by extreme scores. Another use for the Spearman r_S is with ordinal or ranked data (see Chapter 10). Although the numbers in a ranked series increase in value, the distance between each rank may not be equal. Computation of Spearman r_S requires that the data be ranked. Thus, any scores must be transformed to a rank order before the coefficient is calculated.

Like Pearson r, Spearman r_S is a coefficient ranging from $+1.0$ to -1.0 and is interpreted the same way. Some textbooks use the Greek letter *rho* (ρ) to represent the Spearman coefficient.

Computing Ranks

Putting scores in rank order simply requires giving the highest score a rank of 1, the next highest is 2, and so on. With tied scores, compute an average rank by adding together the ranks that would be occupied by these individuals and divid-

---

BOX 19-5. Ranking Procedure for Tied Cases

General rule for ranking ties: Assigned rank is calculated by summing the ranks occupied by the tied cases and assigning each case the average rank. The next case in the ranking is given the next rank that has *not been included* in the averaging for the ties.

The following list represents yearly income for 9 people. The data are being transformed from measurement in dollar amounts to rank order.

Income	Rank
$130,000	1
$80,000	2
$50,000	3.5
$50,000	3.5
$40,000	5
$20,000	7
$20,000	7
$20,000	7
$15,000	9

Example #1: The two individuals earning $50,000 occupied the third and fourth positions. Their ranks are computed by summing $3 + 4 = 7$ and dividing by 2 (number of individuals tied for that rank) = the tied rank score of 3.5. When you assign tied ranks to two individuals, you use up two ranks in the series. The two individuals earning $50,000 both received ranks of 3.5, using ranks #3 and #4, therefore the next person in the series receives a rank of 5.

Example #2: The three individuals earning $20,000 are tied for the sixth, seventh, and eighth places, respectively. To compute their tied rank scores, add all three ranks together and divide by the number of individuals ($6 + 7 + 8 = 21 \div 3 = 7$). Each of the three individuals earning $20,000 receives a tied rank score of 7 (a combination of ranks 6, 7, and 8). The next individual receives a rank of 9.

ing by the number of individuals obtaining the score. Box 19–5 shows how to deal with tied ranks.

Hand Calculation

Here is an example of using a Spearman r_S to compare a coach's ranking of runners and their subsequent performance at a track meet. The coefficient will reveal the level of accuracy of the coach's assessment.

Runner	Coach's ranking before the race	Order of finish in the race
Nguyen	1	4
Smolenski	2	6
Jones	3.5	7
Rodrigues	3.5	1
Heinz	5	2
Tomatsu	6	5
Harris	7	3

The formula and computation of Spearman Rank-order Coefficient (r_S) are shown in Appendix B–4. For the above data, $r_S = -.241$. Looking at the Table A-3 in Appendix A will reveal that p value is less than .05 ($r_S = .241$ does not equal or exceed the critical value of .714). The null hypothesis must be accepted—that the coach's predictions bore no relationship to actual performance in the race.

Hand calculation of the r_S coefficient is feasible only when there is a small number of cases. It would be very time consuming to rank more than 30 scores.

Understanding the Computer Printout

The computer printout will look very similar to that described for Pearson r. The important thing to remember is asking the computer to compute the correct coefficient (Pearson or Spearman).

Correlating a Continuous Variable with a Ranked Variable

If one of the variables is continuous and the other is ranked, simply transform the continuous scores into ranks (from highest to lowest) and use the Spearman r_S formula (and pay attention to the initial ordering when you are interpreting whether or not the correlation is positive or negative).

Other Measures of Correlation

There are many other correlation coefficients not described here. You can find information about them in statistics textbooks and in manuals for statistical software packages. For this chapter, we felt it was important for you to learn these two important tests. As you go further into research, you can obtain information about alternative correlational tests as needed.

Presenting the Results of Statistical Tests

Box 19–6 shows the format to be used in presenting the results of your statistical analysis. Chapter 20 (Writing and Reviewing a Research Report) provides examples of how the findings are described.

Limitations of This Chapter

This chapter is intended as an introduction to a few basic techniques. Of necessity, many other useful statistical tests have been omitted. The student who would like to know more about statistical analysis should consult a statistics textbook in the area. There are books available for the beginner as well as for advanced learners.

At this point, we will repeat something said at the beginning of this chapter: Do not be concerned if you have not understood everything about inferential statistics. The origin of many statistical tests goes far beyond what is needed to use them in practice. Once you start working with actual data, the meaning of the tests, as well as their limitations, will become more clear.

BOX 19–6. Presenting the Results of Statistical Tests According to the Publication Manual of the American Psychological Association

The number within the parentheses is df (degree of freedom), $<$ means *less* than, and $>$ means *greater* than. If the results reach the required level of statistical significance, you will reject the null hypothesis.

$t(74) = 3.36, p < .01$
$F(2,9) = 5.7, p = .025$
$\chi^2 (1, N = 310) = 4.31, p < .01$
$r(6) = .973, p = \ < .01$
$r_S(5) = .793, p = \ < .05$

If p is *greater* than .05 (you will accept the null hypothesis), you can either specify the probability or simply indicate *ns* (not significant).

$r_S(5) = -.243, ns$
$t(9) = -0.14, p = .89$

BOX 19-7. Common Statistical Notations

$<$	Less than.
$>$	Greater than.
N	Number of scores.
df	degrees of freedom.
p	Probability that the results of a statistical test are due to chance.
ns	Not significant.
M	Mean (arithmetic average).
X	An individual score.
M_X	Mean of the preceding set of scores (X scores).
Y	An individual score (used for a second set of scores).
N_Y	Number of scores in the preceding set (Y scores).
Σ	Sum (Greek letter, SIGMA).
ΣX	Sum of all the individual X scores.
ΣX^2	Sum of squared X scores. Each score is individually squared and then all the squared scores are added together.
$(\Sigma X)^2$	Sum squared. First, the individual scores are added together, giving a single sum; then, this sum is squared.
SD	Standard deviation, a descriptive statistic that indicates variability or dispersion, often noted as σ (Greek letter, sigma).
SS	Sum of Squares, refers to sum of squared deviations from the mean.
MS	Mean square; SS divided by df.
t	t ratio, an inferential statistic used for contrasting two means.
ANOVA	Analysis of Variance
F	F ratio, an inferential statistics used for contrasting two or more means. Calculated by ANOVA.
χ^2	Chi-square, an inferential statistic used for analyzing categorical scores.
r	Pearson product-moment coefficient; a measure of correlation for continuous data.
r_S	Spearman rank-order coefficient; a measure of correlation for ranked data.

Summary

Inferential statistics are used to take sampling error (chance variation) into account in interpreting research results. They cannot eliminate problems introduced by inadequate or biased sampling or other research design flaws. The null hypothesis

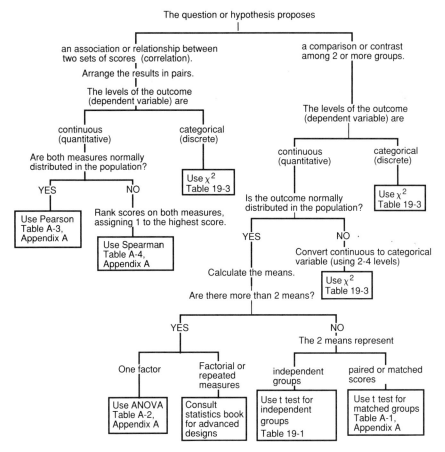

FIG. 19–6. Decision tree for selecting the appropriate statistical test (among those described).

is the assumption that any connection between the independent or predictor variables and dependent variables is due to chance. Inferential statistics are used to test the null hypothesis. Rejecting the null hypothesis leads to acceptance of the alternative or working hypothesis, that the independent variable does make a difference. The usual probability levels used for rejecting the null hypothesis are the .05 or .01 levels of statistical significance.

Both the *t* test and ANOVA (Analysis of Variance) are used for testing the significance of differences between *means*. Groups or samples of individuals are contrasted or compared. ANOVA is used to contrast two or more means. A *t* test does the same thing but is restricted to two means. There are two formulas for a *t* test; one for independent groups and the other for paired scores. ANOVA also has different formulas for independent groups (with a different formula when sample sizes are unequal) and repeated measures. Variations on ANOVA are Analysis of Covariance (ANCOVA) and multivariate analysis (MANOVA).

When the measures are categorical (it is not possible to calculate a mean), or with a skewed distribution, use Chi-square (χ^2). The Chi-square statistic tells whether or not the observed pattern differs significantly from what would be expected by chance.

Correlation answers a different type of question. It indicates the *degree* of a relationship between two variables for the same set of cases. A correlation may be either positive or negative. If both variables are continuous, use the formula for Pearson *r*. If the data are skewed or if one or both of the variables is ranked (or-dinal data), use the formula for Spearman r_S (after ranking the continuous data).

Box 19–7 lists all of the statistical notations and definitions used in these chapters. Figure 19–6 can be used as a guide in selecting an appropriate statistical test for your data.

Reference

Anthony, K. (1977). On cigarette smoking—Where do you stand? *GASP Educational Foundation News,* *11*, p. 3.

Further Reading

Bruning, J. L., & Kintz, B. L. (1987). *Computational handbook of statistics* (3rd ed.). Glenview, IL: Scott-Foresman.

Gravetter, F. J., & Wallnau, L. B. (1995). *Essentials of statistics for the behavioral sciences* (2nd ed.). St. Paul, MN: West.

Keppel, G. (1991). *Design and analysis: A researcher's handbook* (3rd ed.). Englewood Cliffs, NJ: Prentice Hall.

Mohr, L. B. (1990). *Understanding significance testing.* Beverly Hills, CA: Sage Publications.

Siegel, S., & Castellan, J. J. (1988). *Nonparametric statistics for the behavioral sciences* (2nd ed.). New York: McGraw-Hill.

Utts, J. M. (1996). *Seeing through statistics*: Belmont, CA: Duxbury Press.

Sample Problems

1. Describe in words the meaning of each of the following statistical expressions.

$$t = 2.53$$

$$N = 20$$

$$\sigma = 1.9$$

$$df = 18$$

$$p < .05$$

$$r = .41 \ (p < .01)$$

$$r_S = .30 \ (p < .05)$$

$$r = .15 \ (p > .10)$$

$$t(18) = 2.53, p = .05$$

2. A college instructor wants to see if there is a difference in the final grade between students who participate frequently in class and those who never say a word. In a class of 26 students, the instructor identified 6 participants and 7 nonparticipants. Below is a list of the final grades of these students (A = 4 pts., F = 0 pts.). Apply a t test for independent measures to see if there is a significant difference between the final grades of high and low participants. Be sure to use the correct table in Appendix A for evaluating your result.

Final Grade (A = 4, B = 3, C = 2, D = 1, F = 0)

Frequent participators $n = 6$	Non-participators $n = 7$
4	4
4	3
3	3
3	2
3	2
1	1
	1

3. Use a t test for *dependent measures* to see if subjects in an attitude change experiment became more favorable to space exploration after seeing a NASA film.

Attitude scale score

Name	Before film	After film
Matt G.	62	64
Eva B.	71	75
Hamadi R.	68	67
Gretchen H.	51	52
Okimo M.	58	61
Maria G.	84	85

4. Is there a correlation between age and speed on a running test? Compute the Pearson product-moment coefficient using the formula in Table B-3, Appendix B. Then compute a Spearman rank-order coefficient using the formula in Table B-4, Appendix B. After you have done this, check the appropriate significance tables in Appendix A to find out whether these coefficients are statistically significant.

Age (years)	Running speed (in seconds)
12	20
13	18
13	19
14	14
15	17
16	16
16	13
16	15

Answers to Problems

2. $t(11) = 1.16$, *ns* (difference was not significant).

3. $t(5) = -2.33$, *ns* (difference was not significant).

4. Spearman $r_S(n = 8) = -.744, p < .05$ (significant at the .05 level). Pearson $r(6) = -.785, p < .05$ (significant at the .05 level).

20 Writing and Reviewing a Research Report

Set aside a special time for writing and editing your report. Don't expect to complete the analysis of your data and hand in the final report a few days later. Several drafts will probably be required. It is important to get feedback from other people. Early drafts should be labeled as preliminary and dated.

There are two general classes of scientific reports. One is an article for a scientific journal and the other is a technical report written for a specific client or audience. The journal format is easier to use for hypothesis-testing studies. Opinion or attitude surveys and evaluation studies are more easily written in technical report form. The rules for the form of a scientific article are quite precise. Technical reports can be much more varied in style and order of presentation. The deci-

sion regarding the form of data presentation will depend on the type of dissemination you want. If you desire to write articles for other researchers, you will have
to learn journal style.

Article for a Scientific Journal

Many scientific periodicals require that contributors follow a specific style. This
is usually mentioned in the inside front cover of the journal under the heading "Instructions to contributors." When you write for a specific journal, be sure to check
these instructions before beginning the report.

As the American Psychological Association (APA) is used by many behavioral
and social science journals, we will cover it in detail. Once you have mastered one
style, it is relatively easy to transform your article into another style. The APA
publication manual can be ordered from the APA Order Department, P.O. Box
2710, Hyattsville, MD 20784.

The layout or format of a manuscript prepared in APA style includes the following sections: Title page, Abstract, Introduction, Method, Results, Discussion,
and References. Each section is described in more detail below, but first it is helpful to have an overview of the manuscript: The *Abstract* is a very concise summary of the paper. The *Introduction* tells the reader about the topic—what the issue is, what is known about it, and your specific focus. The *Method* section
describes what you did. The *Results* section tells what you found. The *Discussion*
describes what your findings mean in the light of the information you presented
in the introduction. It is the interpretive segment of the paper and loops back to
answer the issues raised in the introduction. The *Reference* section contains a list
of articles and other sources mentioned in the report.

There is very little guesswork in writing an APA style paper. The rules for coverage are clearcut, although sometimes the boundaries are fuzzy between what belongs where within each section. The topic and what is known or theorized are
presented in the introduction. The method and results sections are direct and factual. Interpretation belongs in the discussion. The manuscript is typed double-
spaced with 1-inch margins, using a 12-point font. You should consult the APA
Publication Manual for detailed information. Be sure to examine the manuscript
example illustrated in Appendix D.

Title Page

The first page of the manuscript contains the title of the paper, authors' names,
their institutional affiliations (university, private firm, government agency, etc.),
and the running head. The title summarizes the main topic or key variables studied and should be about 10 to 12 words in length. Avoid unnecessary words in the
title, such as "An Experimental Study of . . ." or "A Research Investigation

into. . . ." They take up space and don't add content. Examples of suitable short titles would be "Achievement Motivation in Brazilian Children" or "The Effects of Amphetamine on Reaction Time." The running head is an abbreviation of the title and should not exceed 50 typewritten characters counting letters, punctuation, and spaces. Running heads for the titles mentioned above would be "Achievement Motivation" and "Amphetamine Effects." An example of a title page for a submitted article is found in Appendix D.

Abstract

The abstract is a very brief summary of the article. Because this is all of the report that most people are likely to read, it must be accurate, self-contained, and concise. It should be about 100 to 120 words in length. Someone reading an abstract should be able to see at a glance what was studied, what was done, and the outcome.

It is often difficult to compress the information, and there is no point in attempting to write the abstract before you write the paper. For guidance, read the abstracts found when searching the PsycINFO database (Chapter 3).

The abstract is printed on a separate page in the manuscript. It follows the title page and precedes the introduction. See the example in Appendix D.

Introduction

The introduction contains a statement of the problem, its theoretical and practical significance, and its place in a larger body of knowledge. Begin the introduction with a paragraph clearly indicating the topic under study.

Following the opening paragraph, present what is known on the topic. This is your review of the literature. In this section you are telling the reader what other researchers have found regarding your specific topic. Stick to the essentials, that is, previous findings that are directly pertinent to your study. See Appendix D for examples of citation style within the body of the article.

In the last paragraph of the introduction, define the key variables and describe the purpose or rationale of what you did in your study. This segment includes the specific questions or hypotheses.

Method

Describe what you did and how you did it. The interested reader should be able to repeat the study from the account provided. The details are described in subsections under appropriate headings. Most methods sections have several sub-sections, depending upon the type of study.

Participants

The participants are the respondents or subjects of study—who was observed, who answered the interviewer's questions, or who filled out the survey. Give the number of individuals and describe the relevant characteristics, such as gender and age. For example, "Thirty-one men and twenty-three women students in an Introductory Psychology class at a large midwestern university filled out the questionnaire." Also describe how the sample was selected and the degree to which they represent the population of interest. For a content analysis of magazines or videos, a participants section would be unnecessary.

Apparatus/Materials

Instrumentation or materials used are described in this section, including observation sheets, checklists, or standardized tests. The actual title can be altered to better fit the topic (e.g., substituting a more appropriate term for apparatus).

Examples:

Materials
Personality was assessed by the 44-item Big Five Inventory which consists of five factors that measure. . . .
Apparatus
A pre-programmed computer was used to measure reaction time within 1/1,000 of a second.
Questionnaire
The four questions used to determine the respondent's attitudes toward the environment were. . . .
Materials
All of the episodes of General Hospital during the first two weeks of November 1995 were videotaped and used for the analysis.

Setting

Observational studies often require a description of the setting in which the information was collected, for example, a description of the site or event where the study took place. This information might be combined with that describing the research subjects.

Procedure

Describe how the data were obtained. In addition to the actual data collection, this section would include information about training for interviewers or experimenters, a description of the physical setting in which the data were collected, instructions to the participants, and mention of any special problems that were addressed. Describe any pilot tests or reliability checks made on procedures, checklists, or equipment. For a content analysis, describe the development and use of the coding categories.

Results

This is the place for factual information about what was found. Opinions and interpretations are reserved for the discussion. Begin the section with the findings most relevant to the hypothesis or problem. Then present any secondary or related findings. The order of presenting results should follow the order of the hypotheses or questions raised in the introduction. Don't skip from hypothesis 1 to 3 and then back to 2. Let the reader see how each hypothesis fared before going on to the next.

Do not overwhelm the reader with raw data. Be sure to present summary (descriptive) statistics such as number of individuals in each group, percentages, or measures of central tendency (mean or median) and variability (range or standard deviation). Then use the inferential statistics as justification for statement of difference or statistically reliable findings. Do not include formulas.

APA style uses standard symbols for presenting descriptive statistics and specific formats for inferential ones. See Box 20–1 for examples. Most word processing programs have a "Symbol" font which will allows you to print the appropriate statistical symbol. Draw by hand those that you cannot find.

There are no fixed rules concerning the amount of numerical and statistical information to present. The best solution is to examine the results sections in recent issues of the journal you have selected.

For reporting decimal places, the general principle is to present summary statistical numbers carried to two decimal places beyond the raw data.

Tables and Figures

If they are needed, most tables and figures will be presented in the results section. *Tables* refer to tabular information, such as lists of terms or columns of numbers or percentages. *Figures* are charts, graphs, drawings, photographs, or any other type of pictorial information.

Tables and figures are useful for presenting information that cannot be easily summarized in a sentence, particularly where there are multiple comparisons and several sets of numbers to show. Save them for your most important data as they are more expensive to produce than text.

Each table and figure must have a numbered descriptive title, for example, "Figure 1. Creativity Scores by Respondent Age." The sample report in Appendix D contains an example of a table. Figures (and tables) do not speak for themselves. Many readers automatically skip them. In the appropriate section of the text, you must refer the reader to each table or figure.

BOX 20–1. Presenting Results APA style (see also Boxes 19–6 and 19–7).

Do *not* begin a sentence with a number; spell it out, for example, "Thirty-two children were observed. . . ." It is okay to use numerals within the sentence. "The researchers observed 32 children. . . ."

Boxes 19–6 and 19–7 at the end of Chapter 19 list the symbols and formats. In written text, use the percent symbol(%) only when it is preceded by a numeral. Use the word "percentage" when a number is not given, for example, ". . . for 18% of the rats" or "The percentage of rats. . . ." *Exception:* In table headings and figure legends, use the symbol % to conserve space.

When presenting many numbers, be sure their order is clear by clarifying the order, for example, "Means for Trials 1 through 4 were 2.43, 2.59, 2.68, and 2.87, respectively" *or* "In order, means for Trials 1 through 4 were 2.43, 2.59, 2.68, and 2.87."

Do *not* provide inferential statistics when the difference is not statistically reliable (you still need the descriptive statistics). Simply state that the difference was not significant. For example, "There was no significant difference between the lower division mean of 1.71 and the upper division mean of 2.81."

Use the following formats as examples for describing statistically significant outcomes:

"As predicted, the first-grade girls reported a significantly greater liking for school ($M = 4.63$) than did the first-grade boys ($M = 1.38$), $t(22) = 2.62, p < .01$."

"The means for the long, medium, and short retention intervals were 1.38, 4.62, and 5.11, respectively. An analysis of variance indicated a significant retention interval effect, $F(1,34) = 123.07, p < .01$."

"There was a negative relationship between the age of the driver and the number of traffic citations, $r(43) = -.32, p < .05$."

The number in parentheses after the inferential statistic is *df* (degrees of freedom).

For categorical data organized on a contingency table for analysis, do *not* present the contingency table in the written report. Instead, use percentages, in either the text or a table. For example, "For the men, 37% smoked at least one cigarette during the evening, while 62% of the women at the party smoked at least one cigarette, $\chi^2(1, N = 85) = 5.19, p < .05$." The first number within the parentheses is *df* (degrees of freedom).

When you have the exact probability (from a computer printout), you may use that for your *p* value by substituting = for <, for example, $\chi^2(2, N = 110) = 7.38, p = .025$. (The example applies to other inferential statistics, such as *t*, *F* and *r*.)

Examples

The 9-year-olds were more active than the 11-year-olds under the practice condition (see Figure 1).

Table 1 shows that Group 1 scored significantly higher than the other two groups on the reactivity test, $F(2,119) = 4.99, p < .01$.

Figures and tables are numbered with arabic numerals (1, 2, 3) in order of appearance. In the manuscript, they follow the reference list. Answer the following questions as you construct each table or figure:

Is the table or figure necessary?

Does every column have a brief explanatory column heading?

Do the percentage columns add up to 100?

Are the above criteria met for rows?

Is the table or graph simple, clean, and free of extraneous detail?

Is it easy to understand—is its purpose readily apparent?

Are the vertical and horizontal axes of graphs labeled correctly?

Is the table or figure numbered and given a clear title?

Is the table or figure referred to in the text?

For details on submitting figures for publication, consult the APA publication manual (American Psychological Association, 1994).

Discussion

This is your opportunity to interpret the findings, discuss their significance, and suggest directions for future research. Open the discussion section with a clear statement about the answers to the questions raised in the introduction and describe support or nonsupport for your hypotheses. There is no need to repeat everything that was said in the results. Instead, describe how your findings fit existing theories and other research in the field (that was reviewed in the introduction). What general conclusions can you draw? Based on what you have learned, what issues should be investigated next? What are the flaws and limitations in your study? If you were to repeat the study, what would you change?

In other words the discussion fits your particular piece of research into the context that you established in the introduction. It completes the work at hand, which is to add new information or knowledge, and points ahead to future research.

References

All citations mentioned in the manuscript must be listed in the reference section, and everything listed must be cited in the text. The list does *not* include relevant work not specifically mentioned. A long list of references is no mark of scholarship if the articles have come from secondary sources (accounts about other people's work) and you have not read the original articles. Reference lists should be triple checked. It is frustrating to try to locate an article from Volume 12 that was listed as Volume 21, or to finally discover that a book author's name is Chemminski rather than Hemminski. You can use the Internet to access library databases in order to check the accuracy of your references (see Chapter 14).

The specific form for the references will be determined by the periodical or audience for whom you are writing. The APA publication manual requires the following form.

Article reference:

Smith, R. S., & Jones, D. A. (1991). Children's response to colored glasses. <u>Journal of Child Development, 30,</u> 14–26.

Book reference:

Brown, O. (1989). <u>Organizational behavior</u>. New York: Smith Publications.

Chapter in an edited book:

Elms, A. C. (1994). Keeping deception honest: Justifying conditions for social scientific research stratagems. In E. Erwin, S. Gendin, & L. Kleiman (Eds.), <u>Ethical issues in scientific research: An anthology</u> (pp. 121–140). New York & London: Garland Publishing.

As described in Chapter 3, there are computer software packages that manage references and format them in various styles. These programs also allow you to directly download the results of your library search by computer, so that you do not need to retype the references.

Helpful Hints

Avoid plagiarism by placing quotation marks around any material that is quoted verbatim. To *plagiarize* is to pass off someone else's work as one's own. It is unethical and often illegal. All direct quotations must include a reference citation with the page number of the quoted material. The following example illustrates APA style:

> According to Luster and McAdoo (1995), "Academic success in school may not be the only way in which the school context contributes to individual differences in self-esteem" (p. 454).

If the quotation is extensive, permission to quote is likely to be required by the holder of the copyright. The exact length allowed without specific permission varies. The APA allows quotations of up to 500 words from their journals without explicit permission, but you still must indicate the source of the material being quoted. Using drawings, figures, graphs, or tables from published work is also likely to require permission. With material that is *paraphrased* (expressed in your own words rather than the author's), omit quotation marks, but be sure to provide a citation indicating the source.

Avoid footnotes wherever possible. Footnotes break the continuity of a passage, and many readers will ignore them. Long footnotes that contain detailed explanations are rarely appropriate. The information should be included in the body of the report or omitted.

Appendix D shows the format for citations within the manuscript. If you have more than one citation for the same sentence, put them in alphabetical order.

The style of journal articles tends to be impersonal and the use of first person pronouns such as "I" and "we" is discouraged. Refer to yourself as "the researcher" or "the investigator." Words such as "data" and "criteria" are plural; the singular forms are "datum" and "criterion," respectively. A common error is incorrect placement of the apostrophe. Note the differences between the simple plural (subjects), the singular possessive (subject's), and the plural possessive (subjects').

Use an active rather than passive voice when possible (e.g., "Observers recorded the number of occurrences" rather than "The number of occurrences was recorded by observers.") Use nonsexist language—either make gender pronouns plural, "they" rather than "he/she" or use "he or she". Avoid jargon (unnecessary technical terms).

Double check all the tables for misprints. Double check the names of people cited in the literature review and triple check the reference list at the end of the report.

Be sure to show a draft of your report to other people before the final version is written. Discussing it with people not directly involved with the issues may provide fresh ideas.

Technical Reports

Often a study is written for a specific client, such as an organization, firm, or public agency that sponsored the research. The format, style, and layout of the report probably will differ from the style of a journal article. Some clients want everything included; others want only brief accounts of the major findings. Don't hesitate to check the form, style, and length used by others who have written similar reports. Consider this part of the literature review. You won't need to follow the style used by others exactly, but it is important to know how they have presented their work. Two widely used style manuals are the *Chicago Manual of Style* (University of Chicago Press, 1993) and the U.S. Government *Style Manual* (United States Government Printing Office, 1986). An example of a technical report can be found in Appendix E.

The length of the report depends largely on the wishes of the sponsor and the projected audience. The decision involves a compromise between presenting sufficient information so that the findings and basis for the recommendations are clear but not giving so much detail that people will be discouraged from reading the document. You can assume that your audience consists of busy people. Therefore, clarity, brevity, and ease of understanding are essential.

Large organizations such as government agencies or corporations that commission numerous printed documents may require a specific format and style for all technical reports. The report may use a standard cover displaying the corporate symbol and statement of endorsement by an executive officer. Advance approval may be necessary before a report is officially released. Prior to writing a technical report for a sponsor, check in advance about approval policies.

Current technology makes it easy to place illustrations on the cover. If the cover is dull, people may be reluctant to open the report and read the contents. Unless the sponsor of the research prohibits it, we like to use photographs on the cover of technical reports, either taken as part of the research or posed afterward. Some experimentation with the copy machine is necessary to get the correct light values for reproducing photographs. Photographs and drawings can enliven the text also. A study of housing needs of the elderly might include pictures of senior citizens and various housing options. Do not overlook the dramatic potential of visual materials.

Submit an advance draft of a report for approval to the sponsor and key participants before the final version is completed. This allows you to catch mistakes as well as ambiguous or controversial statements. Words can mean different things to different people. Even seemingly non-controversial terms can cause problems in some circumstances. We once described a preschool as a "child care center." The draft created an immediate uproar, as preschool operators associate "child care" with the absence of a formal program. "Nursery school" was similarly rejected.

No matter how careful you are with the wording of a technical report, there is no substitute for an early reading of a draft by someone from the intended audience. Mark the cover at the top "Draft Report, For Comments Only" and attach a letter indicating the specific date by which the comments should be returned.

Executive Summary

Unlike a journal article, which begins with a brief abstract, a technical report should begin with an executive summary. This is a much longer section than an abstract. It should be able to stand alone, covering all the necessary information—the problem, method, results, and conclusions. As with a journal abstract, the executive summary is written *after* the report (even though it is presented first).

Appendix

A technical report is likely to conclude with an appendix section. This is the place for all supplementary materials not included in the main body of the report. Appendices are arranged in sequence with letters (e.g., Appendix A, Appendix B, etc.). The appendix contains material that is *not essential* for understanding the report. It will be used most often by readers with a special interest in the topic who want detailed information. Typical items considered for inclusion in the appendix are

1. Score sheets, questionnaires, or observation sheets used in the study. An exception would be instruments that are commonly used and widely available. These can be omitted.

2. Detailed tables and charts primarily for reference purposes. Tables and figures necessary for the reader's understanding should be placed within the text.

3. Lists of technical terms. For a general audience, technical terms should be defined as they occur in the text.

4. Other relevant documents not essential to the reader's comprehension of the report. These might include the sign-up sheet for recruiting subjects, interviewer instructions, instructions for coding interview data, the follow-up letter to respondents who did not reply, etc.

Writing a Critique

The preceding section of this chapter concerned the written form of a research paper. Another writing task in science involves the preparation of a *critique* or critical review of a single paper or series of papers on a specific topic. Despite its semantic resemblance to negative criticism, the tone of a critique may be positive, neutral, or unfavorable. The critique is central to the *peer review* of scientific work. This is the process by which submitted articles are evaluated by those knowledgeable in the field (i.e., scientific peers). Most journals in the behavioral sciences require that an article pass through peer review before it is published. This can be a long and tedious process in which numerous requests for revisions are made before the article is accepted. Some editors remove all identifying information about the authors from a paper before it is sent out for review. This is called a *blind review* system. An unpublished manuscript submitted for a journal review is considered privileged information, that is, it cannot be quoted or cited without the written permission of the author. Reviewers may be asked to destroy the manuscript when they have completed the review.

Box 20–2 shows the evaluation forms used by two behavioral science journals. The first journal requests its reviewers to rate the paper along specific dimensions before coming up with a recommendation, while the second one requests a recommendation followed by written comments.

Sometimes a critique of a published article is part of a class assignment. When making your critique, keep in mind that most journals put severe space limitations on authors. A master's or doctoral thesis is likely to run 50 to 200 pages, but a journal article describing the identical study may be only a fraction as long. The information is presented in a highly compressed form. Box 20–3 lists questions for you to ask as you read through an article. In addition to guiding your critique or review, these questions can be used to review and evaluate your own reports.

Need for Empathy

Doing research yourself provides a good perspective for evaluating the work of others on the same topic. This is the basis of peer review, in that experienced researchers are likely to be familiar with previous work. They also are aware of the difficulties in studying certain issues. Personality researchers know the problems in securing honest responses to personal questions. Experimentalists realize that

BOX 20–2. Examples of Two Evaluation Forms for Journal Reviews

Title of Paper and Author:
Reviewer Number:
Please fill out the following, in addition to your typed comments.

1. Style. Is the writing clear and the statements of theory or results unambiguous? (circle one) yes   no
   If *no*, please give guidance for rewriting.
2. Literature review. Does the paper mention the necessary references? (circle one) yes   no
   If *no*, please list the omitted ones in your comments.
3. Methods. Have the authors used the best methods available? (circle one) yes   no
   If *no*, please comment.
4. Interpretation. Have the authors given the appropriate interpretation to their data? (circle one) yes   no
   If *no*, please comment.
5. Significance. Is this paper a significant contribution to its field? (circle one) yes   no
   If *no*, state reasons.
6. Recommendations: (check one)
   Accept as is
   Accept subject to specified revision
   Revise and resubmit
   Reject

Manuscript Review Form

Manuscript Number: Reviewer Number:
Manuscript Title:
   Please review this manuscript within the next 30 days,
providing us with your objective evaluation of its publishability.
Recommendation: (check one)
___ Publish as is
___ Publish with noted revisions
___ Not publishable in present form
___ Better suited for another journal (specify name)
___ Not publishable
General Comments for Editor/Author:

some subjects won't show up for their scheduled appointments or will incorrectly perform their assigned tasks, leaving blank spaces in the data. Psychophysiologists know how time consuming and expensive it is to simultaneously record physiological and psychological processes. They understand why a study of drug effects might use only 12 subjects. In most social psychological experiments, this number would be too small for valid generalizations.

BOX 20–3. Checklist for Reviewing a Research Report

I. Introduction and background.
   A. Is the problem clearly stated?
      1. What questions are posed by the researchers?
      2. Are the hypotheses or goals of the study clearly stated?
   B. Is the important background literature (earlier work in the field) included?
II. Research methodology
   A. Are the methods appropriate to the goals of the study?
      1. Do they fit the question?
      2. Was the choice of methods dictated by the goals of the study (the problems), or simply a matter of expedience (the course of least resistance)?
   B. Is the sample appropriate, given the nature of the study (i.e., is it representative of the population of interest)?
      1. Were the participants selected in such a way as to avoid bias?
      2. Is it a special group whose characteristics may influence the outcome in particular ways?
      3. Does the sample make sense for the hypotheses being tested?
   C. What outcome is being measured?
      1. How is it measured?; for example, a paper-and-pencil test, an open-ended questionnaire, a time measure, counts of some activity, statistics from a government report, etc.
      2. Are questionnaires, surveys, or tally sheets described in sufficient detail for the reader to judge their adequacy?
      3. Are laboratory instruments adequately described?
      4. In observational studies, is the selection and training of observers described?
      5. Is evidence of reliability presented (i.e., reliability of instruments, interobserver reliability, test-retest information, etc.)?
   D. Does the procedure do what it is supposed to do?
      1. Is the logic of the procedure correct?
      2. Were all sources of bias (subject, experimenter, responder, interviewer, setting, etc.) eliminated or controlled?
III. Description of findings
   A. What answers were obtained to the questions posed?
      1. Are the findings clearly presented with adequate descriptive statistics (e.g., number of cases, mean, median, standard deviation, or range)?
      2. Are the statistical tests (inferential statistics) appropriate to the data?
   B. Are the findings correctly interpreted?
      1. Are the conclusions based on the results?
      2. Is the level of generalization appropriate?
         a. Is it justified by the sample?
         b. Is it justified by the research design?
      3. Are procedural weaknesses noted? Are the limitations of the study discussed?

Not every study needs to be ground-breaking or earth shaking. Much of science is comprised of small studies, each adding to the store of knowledge. There will be occasional major breakthroughs in a field, but don't expect every paper to do so. A minor study may be valuable in pointing toward a new or different direction, even though it may not have traveled far along the way. A review should enlarge the reader's understanding of the good and bad features of a study. Some critiques are unbalanced in that they provide no guidance to the author as to how the paper could be improved. When you review a paper, ask yourself what new information you are providing that will be of assistance to the author. In addition to the specific comments you've made about the clarity of the abstract, the appropriateness of the method and so on, indicate how the study and write-up could be improved. Be sure to described the good points as well as the deficiencies.

Summary

Journal articles are written in a specific style. In APA style the sections are abstract, introduction, method, results, discussion, and references. Technical reports are more variable in format and often begin with an executive summary and end with the appendix. In writing papers, it is necessary to avoid plagiarism and provide credit to others whose work is used. Peer review refers to a critique by someone knowledgeable in the field. In preparing a critique it is important to provide positive suggestions for improvement as well as criticism of weak points.

References

American Psychological Association. (1994). *Publication manual of the American Psychological Association* (4th ed.). Washington, DC: Author.

United States Government Printing Office Staff. (1986). *Style manual* (Rev. ed.). Washington, DC: U.S. Government Printing Office.

University of Chicago Press. (1993). *The Chicago manual of style* (14th ed.). Chicago: Author.

Further Reading

Day, R. A. (1994). *How to write & publish a scientific paper* (4th ed.). Phoenix, AZ: Oryx Press.

Dorsten, L. E. (1996). *Interpreting research in the social and behavioral sciences.* Los Angeles: Pyrczak Publishing.

Houp, K. W., Pearsall, T. E., Tebeaux, E., & Redish, J. (1995). *Reporting technical information* (8th ed.). Boston: Allyn & Bacon.

Loke, W. H. (1990). *A guide to journals in psychology and education.* Metuchen, NJ: Scarecrow Press.

Pfeiffer, W. S. (1994). *Technical writing: A practical approach* (2nd ed.). New York: Merrill.

Pyrczak, F., & Bruce, R. R. (1992). *Writing empirical research reports: A basic guide for students of the social and behavioral sciences.* Los Angeles: Pyrczak Publishing.

Rosnow, R. L., & Rosnow, M. (1995). *Writing papers in psychology: A student guide* (3rd ed.). Pacific Grove, CA: Brooks/Cole.

Zeisel, H. (1985). *Say it with figures* (Rev ed.). New York: Harper & Row.

21 After the Report

Jason Tyburczy, an undergraduate psychology major, studied human–animal interaction in a veterinary hospital waiting room. It was an interesting setting where humans, dogs, cats, birds, and occasional rodents and snakes coexisted in very close quarters. Tyburczy observed pet owners and interviewed them about their level of satisfaction with the visiting area. Having completed the study, he was faced with the question of what to do with the findings. He mailed a copy of the report to the hospital director. No response came back. This lack of spontaneous feedback is fairly typical among recipients of survey results.

Tyburczy next considered various publication outlets. He went to the university library and consulted a reference librarian. He described the study and his ideas about who might be interested in the results. The librarian suggested a number of periodicals. Tyburczy looked at copies to find out which were the most suitable. After some deliberation, the choice narrowed to either a national or a state veterinary journal. The chances of publication seemed better in the state journal, so this was the outlet selected.

The report was rewritten in a style appropriate for the periodical and submitted. A few months later, a favorable review was received along with a request for revision. The revised paper was eventually accepted by the journal and appeared in print 7 months later. A copy of the published article was sent to the hospital director and this time a formal letter of thanks was received. Apparently the published article was more impressive than the typed draft report. A year later, the director requested a copy of the findings for use in renovating the waiting area. Several additional requests for reprints and further information about the study were also received.

Completion of a study is not the end of a chapter. In terms of feedback and application of the findings, it is a beginning. There are a number of steps that can be taken after the report is written. These steps include feedback to the participants, conducting further research on the topic, and submitting the write-up as an article for a technical journal or some other type of periodical.

Feedback to Participants

A researcher has an ethical responsibility to provide feedback to those who participated in the research. This is in addition to the debriefing session immediately following the research procedure. When people have invested time and effort or allowed their privacy to be invaded, the least they are owed is information about how the study came out. If you have surveyed the opinions of a group, they should be given a written or oral account of the results. Feedback is also necessary in observational research. If you have done behavioral mapping in a park, for example, the park manager will be interested in the findings. When students conducted observational studies in our campus library, they sent a written report to the campus librarian. When a class has participated in a group experiment, feedback can be given as an in-class presentation, or the class invited to a poster session where the results are described.

Further Research

A good study will probably raise more questions than it answers. What begins as a small investigation can easily mushroom into a large research program requiring a major commitment of time and effort. Procedures developed in study may be extended to new classes of problems or people. Or the original sample can be retested using different procedures.

Beginning researchers tend to think in terms of single studies. Experienced researchers think in terms of larger programs in which several related studies are linked together. A research program is economical in time and effort since later studies build on procedures developed in previous work. A follow-up study is also the opportunity to correct the mistakes made earlier. There is a saying among researchers that a first study is *always* flawed. Beginning researchers may not realize this if they read only published articles in which everything seems correct. Many published papers are not first studies but third or fourth attempts to wrestle with a difficult and complex problem. The final version looks methodologically correct because the studies were repeated several times, and the manuscript underwent numerous revisions prior to publication.

Publishing the Findings

Very few studies conducted as part of an introductory class will be publishable by themselves. Typically, a first-time project will require additional studies using improved methods before it is publishable. At the point when the research provides new or interesting valid information, various types of outlets are available. We will start out discussing publication in research journals.

Research Journals

The review of papers submitted to scientific journals is a time-consuming process. A typical sequence of events is shown in Figure 21–1. For a paper submitted to a behavioral science journal, it is likely that editorial review will take 3 to 9 months, not including needed revisions. If a paper is accepted, there is likely to be a 12-month delay before it is finally published. This may seem a long wait but it is typical. Experienced researchers deal with the numerous delays by conducting several studies that overlap in time. While one study is being reviewed, the researcher is working on others which are in various stages of completion. There are also less time-consuming types of dissemination, such as presenting the results at a professional meeting.

Choosing a Journal

Discuss possible publication outlets with those experienced in the specialty area. Also see where related articles have been published. Then visit a university library

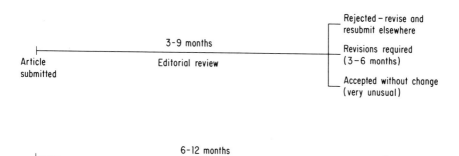

FIG. 21–1. Timetable for publication in a behavioral science journal.

and look over the most likely prospects. In some fields there is a wide choice among publication outlets. There are more than a dozen English language journals that carry papers on social psychological topics. The same is true of journals in animal behavior. However, in some specialty areas, such as program evaluation or environmental education, the choice among potential outlets is more limited. Check the table of contents and the editorial policy statement of a journal before considering a submission. Journal titles can be misleading, as in the case of *Psychological Bulletin,* which carries lengthy reviews, while the *Psychological Review* publishes mainly theoretical articles, and *Contemporary Psychology* publishes book reviews only on request from the editors. Often a beginning researcher is wise to choose a less prestigious journal with a lower rejection rate than a top journal that rejects 9 out of 10 papers.

Paralleling the distinction between basic and applied research made in Chapter 1, some journals specialize in basic research while others emphasize applied studies. Because they publish different types of articles, they reach different audiences. Before choosing a journal, check where it stands on the basic-applied continuum. Otherwise you risk having an article rejected by a basic science journal as "too applied" or rejected by an applied journal because it is "too theoretical." You can make this judgment by looking at the articles published. Another strategy is to examine a bibliography on your topic, or your own reference list, and see which journals are represented. If a journal has published several papers on a topic, the editors are likely to be receptive to further studies that extend the earlier work.

Submit an article to only one journal at a time. Many journals require a statement to accompany each submission stating that the article is not being submitted anywhere else.

Some journals have submission fees; others charge authors of accepted papers according to article length. For some journals, these charges may be waived for students and others without support funds, and other journals charge no fees. This information is available in the instructions to authors section of the journal, which is often found on an inside cover.

Drafts

It is standard practice to circulate preliminary versions of papers to colleagues for their comments. Their input will be invaluable in preparing the final draft for submission. Date the cover page of a preliminary draft and write at the top "Draft copy—for comments only" or "Draft copy—not to be cited." This will indicate to the recipient that the contents are subject to revision before the final draft is submitted.

Dealing with Rejection

The rejection rate among major behavioral science journals is high. For some journals it can reach 80 to 90 percent of all submitted papers. Others have a more favorable ratio. When a paper has been rejected, it can be revised on the basis of reviewer comments and sent to a second journal for consideration. It is inappropriate to submit an article to more than a single journal at a time. Develop backup plans for a second or third journal in case the first choice rejects the paper.

Preprints

When an article has been accepted for publication, it is indicated on the cover page of the final version by the notation "In press, Journal of. . . ." It is legitimate to send copies of an accepted final version (this is called a *preprint*) to interested colleagues who would otherwise wait many months to see it published. Recipients of an "in press" article will be able to cite the article in their own writings. An article formally accepted for publication has virtually the same status and legitimacy as a published article. Note that an article "in press" has been formally accepted for publication, while one "in preparation" is still in the process of review or revision.

Page Proofs

A journal editor may make minor editorial changes on an article accepted for publication. Any changes will be indicated on the page proofs sent to the senior author. This will be the last opportunity to correct typographical or other errors. This is *not* the time to add new material to an article that has already been accepted. Editors discourage this practice and the journal may charge a stiff fee for each line of page proof altered by the author.

Reprints

A *reprint* is an individual copy of a particular article. Although some journals require authors to buy reprints as a condition of publication, purchasing reprints usually is an optional matter. Some journals supply a small number of free reprints to authors. Others charge for all reprints. They may also allow authors to photocopy their own articles and distribute photocopies (the journal usually holds the copyright to the article). Check the policies of the journal in regard to authors' rights to photocopy their own papers. Ordering reprints is generally done on a separate form that accompanies the page proofs.

Other Publication Outlets

Many research projects, although methodologically sound with clear positive results, will not be suitable for research journals. Sometimes the findings are too local or specific. As an example, a study of cheating among students in a college, or of bicycle accidents in a community, will probably be considered of local interest but not publishable in a research periodical. Fortunately, there are numerous alternatives to journal publication that can be used to communicate with an interested audience. These outlets include newspapers, newsletters, and trade magazines. One student who systematically observed campus bicyclists published his findings in *Bicycling* magazine. The student whose salad bar observations were mentioned in Chapter 4 published them in a restaurant magazine. Another student who studied older people in a city park published her findings on the op-ed page of the local newspaper.

Publication can also be a means of direct feedback to the participants, as in the case of a student who surveyed members of a food co-op and then summarized her findings in an article published in the co-op newsletter.

There are many alternative to publishing in journals, especially when the findings have local significance. There is a wide range of periodicals available. However, the article must be tailored to the particular publication to which it is submitted.

Application

The goal of a study may not be further research but application, such as using the information to change policies and practices in an organization. When application is the researcher's goal, a scientific article by itself may be insufficient for changing long-established attitudes and procedures. Consider writing an article for a periodical directed specifically to practitioners. Most occupations, professions, and specialities have periodicals concerned with applied issues. Your reference librarian can help locate appropriate outlets for applied studies. Such outlets will require a more lively writing style and format than is customary for a scientific journal. However, even in an applied article, busy administrators may not see the potential usefulness of the findings. A common response among administrators to research findings is that they are interesting but not directly relevant. There are always reasons why things should be left unchanged. The researcher may have to convince busy administrators of the value and relevance of the findings through personal discussion.

Application is also an opportunity to learn the limitations and shortcomings of a study. The researcher becomes aware of questions that should have been included on the survey but were omitted, or questions that yielded ambiguous answers. This may demonstrate the need for further studies on the topic to pinpoint problems and develop solutions.

It is difficult to predict what parts of a study will be most useful in applied settings. In several of our surveys for nonprofit organizations, it has been the demographic information that yielded the most interesting information from the client's perspective. Surprisingly, many organizations and agencies do not have an accurate idea of who they serve. As an example, a class project involved interviews with customers shopping for donated clothing at a thrift store. The management believed that most of the customers had large families. The survey showed the opposite to be true. A possible explanation is that large families have more opportunities than small families for hand-me-downs. This information on family size, thought to be of only incidental interest by the research team, helped the store to define its customer population and improve its outreach program.

Box 21–1 shows the correspondence between the instructor who supervised the class project at the thrift store and the regional chief executive officer (CEO). The first letter illustrates the form of a cover letter for a research report in an applied study, and the replies give detailed feedback on the utility of the findings to the client.

Research can be a valuable tool in the change process, but by itself will probably not be sufficient to alter long-established attitudes and practices. The action

---

BOX 21–1. Correspondence About a Research Report

Dear (CEO):

I am pleased to enclose the report on the survey undertaken by the students last quarter. As you will see, the survey shows . . . (description of major findings presented for emphasis).

We hope you find the report informative and helpful. This was a very good learning experience for the students. Sandy, Janee, and Elizabeth felt that they received excellent cooperation from the store and the customers, and appreciate the opportunity to put their research training to practical use. We look forward to your comments on the recommendations. Sincerely,

(Professor)

Dear (Professor):

I reviewed the study your students made at our store with my staff and we were quite surprised with many of their findings. Without the survey report, we would still be unaware of many factors that are considered to be of prime importance in our operations. First of all, let me inform you that we received many compliments from our customers on the method of conducting the survey. There was not a single negative reaction by any of our customers. (Detailed reaction to survey results—six paragraphs!)

For the first five months of the year, our sales have been $63,325 over the same period last year. I feel sure that at least part of the increase resulted from the information we gained through your team survey. Please accept our sincere appreciation for the efforts and extend our thanks to Sandy, Janee, and Elizabeth for their outstanding work in undertaking the survey. Sincerely,

(CEO)

Dear (Professor):

I really appreciate your assistance to the store. The customer survey was very helpful and the manager is considering all of your recommendations. The revenues from the store have helped place over a hundred disabled people in our community for the last five years. Your students' research will allow us to be more effective and productive. Thank you very much.

(President of the Board of Directors)

research approach described in Chapter 1 called for a combination of research and technical assistance in which the clients (potential users of the information) are intimately involved in all stages of gathering, analyzing, and disseminating the information. When people have been personally engaged in a study, they are more likely to understand the methods used in gathering the information and the implications of the findings. However, there is no sure and easy road to applying behavioral science findings. Changing organizations is as difficult (perhaps more so) as changing individuals. Several specialty areas such as organizational development and program evaluation have developed around the issue of organizational change.

News Releases

In addition to reaching other researchers through a scientific article, practitioners through a trade publication, and a client through a technical report, a researcher may also want to bring the findings to the attention of a wider audience, such as readers of local newspapers or the audience of local TV stations. This requires a different format and style than is appropriate for a journal article or technical report. Place the maximum emphasis on the findings and their implications for action, and eliminate any jargon. Even a modest study by a student researcher may rate a column in the local press if the issue is newsworthy. Such articles should not be a dull presentation of the results, boring the reader with endless statistics. A lively writing style can help maintain reader interest in the study without unduly distorting the findings.

There are dangers in premature media exposure. Not only can this disrupt a study in progress, but it also raises serious ethical questions if the findings contain errors. Science depends heavily upon *peer review*, which is the time-consuming process by which researchers critically evaluate one another's work before it is published. Scientists will be severely criticized by colleagues if they hold press conferences before their findings are reviewed by other researchers.

Professional Meetings

Many professional organizations make it a policy to encourage student presentations and establish special sessions at their meetings for such papers. There are also student organizations that hold conferences to discuss research. This is excellent practice for subsequent presentations at professional meetings. It can also provide useful feedback and is a positive addition to your application if you apply to graduate school. Information on regional, national, and international conferences is available on the Internet along with abstracts of recent presentation. Look for the name of the sponsoring organization.

Three common formats used at professional meetings are panel discussions, individual presentations, and poster sessions. A panel discussion brings together a number of people around a theme or topic. The panel moderator often is the organizer of the session. The ground rules for the presentation are established in advance. In addition to the topic, panelists are told the order of presentation, how long to speak, and the length of the question-and-answer period. In an individual presentation, themes may vary considerably, although such presentations are often grouped in a topical area, such as social psychology or vocational education. Again, the ground rules will be stated in advance.

Tips for Talks

When speaking at professional meetings, keep the following points in mind. Communication intended to be spoken requires a different style than does written communication. Assuming that you have already done a written report, you should prepare a separate outline for a talk. It is boring to hear someone read a manuscript word for word.

Memorize your introduction and conclusion. By having the introduction memorized, you can start out loud and clear, thereby getting the attention of the audience, and sounding like you know what you are talking about. If you lose them during the talk, stating "in summary" or "in conclusion" will bring them back for your closing remarks.

Address the audience (not the blackboard, your notes, or the slide screen). Be careful not to let your voice drop below an audible level at the end of your sentences. If you must turn away, pause in your talk.

Check the clock. A major goal of presenting a talk to a live audience is to obtain feedback, therefore leave time for questions. A few well-made points will be more productive than trying to cram all of your study into a 15-minute session. If you run out of time, don't speed up. Cut to the conclusion and end gracefully.

Use visual aids wherever possible. Showing an audience what the experimental room or observational sheet looked like will have more impact than a verbal description. Things that people can see are likely to be remembered better than things merely described. Also, preparing visual aids helps you organize your talk. The ease of making transparencies for overhead projectors in copy machines has made this a very common method for presenting data at professional meetings. One can make transparencies of tables, charts, or illustrations directly from printed materials. However, don't get carried away and bombard your audience with complex tables of numbers. Select only the most important information for visual presentation and make sure in advance that it can be seen and understood by the audience in the time available. Know how to operate the audiovisual system prior to the session. Turn off the projector when there is no need for it. This saves energy and reduces noise and distraction. Be prepared to go forward in the event of technological failure.

Practice your talk on friends or colleagues beforehand. This will enable you to keep within the time limit and smooth out the rough spots. Practice for content (meaning) and for physical presentation. Being able to practice in the actual room and try out your recordings, overheads, or slides is even better. If this is impossible, arrive early to familiarize yourself with the room and check out the audiovisual equipment.

Frequent problems at talks include the following: previous session runs over and your talk starts late, faulty or incomplete introduction, microphone improperly adjusted or not working (e.g., emits high-pitched whistle), distracting noises outside of the room, difficulty in locating proper switches for dimming lights, a slide in wrong order or upside down, other slides under- or overexposed making them too dark or too light, and talk exceeds time limit. Keep these in mind during your rehearsal, and their occurrence will come as less of a shock.

Poster Sessions

Poster sessions are visual displays with the authors present for informal discussion. Individuals or groups of researchers prepare a poster board prior to the meeting. They are assigned a fixed amount of space, for example, 3 × 4 feet. All the materials, including charts and illustrations are produced ahead of time. These are assembled and displayed for a few hours in a large room containing dozens of poster boards with researchers standing beside them. Interested viewers stroll up and down the aisles stopping to look at the boards and commenting or asking questions. Many researchers like the poster session format because it involves interaction with people who are specifically interested in the topic. A poster session is listed in the conference program and is a positive feature on a graduate school application.

It is important to create an interesting display with very large, bold, easy-to-read type. Use illustrations to attract attention and show the research conditions and findings (see Figure 21–2). Copy machines can enlarge letter-size type and illustrations. Cut and paste as needed. You can also have small prints or slides enlarged for use on a poster. It is a good idea to have copies of a summary sheet to provide on request, or you can have a sign-up sheet and send interested people copies of the original paper. See Figure 21–2 for poster format.

Summary

A single study points the way to other studies, leading to a research program involving several linked investigations. Potential authors need to exercise care in choosing from among available journals and have back-up plans in case the first journal rejects the paper. A manuscript is likely to go through several revisions (drafts) before it is finally accepted for publication.

A study may also have implications for practice. Practitioners can be reached through articles in occupational or trade periodicals. Action research stimulates change by involving the potential users of the information in the research process.

Select a Font size such as **this bold 24-point font that is readable from 9 feet away.**

Use a larger Font such as 36-point bold for

TITLES & Section Headings

Where possible, illustrate your points graphically with photos, images, sketches, charts, tables. <u>Example</u>: (should be enlarged for a poster)

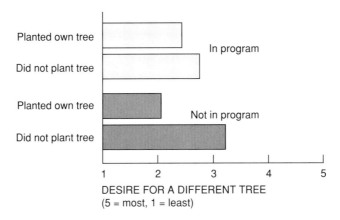

Your text might look like this:

TITLE OF PAPER
Author, Affiliation
Section Headings
* Outline format for text
* No need for full sentences
* Use and label graphics

FIG. 21–2. Suggestions for poster presentations.

News releases and talks at meetings provide additional ways of getting your information to an audience. Three types of conference presentations are panel discussions, individual presentations, and poster sessions. Keep your presentations lively and to the point using audiovisual aids when feasible. Practice your presentation ahead of time.

Further Reading

American Psychological Association. (1994). *Publication manual of the American Psychological Association* (4th ed.). Washington, DC: Author.

Anholt, R. R. H. (1994). *Dazzle 'em with style: The art of oral scientific presentation.* New York: W.H. Freeman.

Day, R. A. (1994). *How to write & publish a scientific paper* (4th ed.). Phoenix, AZ: Oryx Press.

Loke, W. H. (1990). *A guide to journals in psychology and education.* Metuchen, NJ: Scarecrow Press.

22 Concluding Notes

This book began with an introduction to the multimethod approach. This was followed by a discussion of reviewing the literature and research ethics. We then moved to specific methods. First came observational methods, including behavioral and cognitive mapping; experimental design; interviews and questionnaires; followed by the content analysis and the case study. We also described the data sources provided by personal documents and archives, and research uses of standardized tests, equipment, calculators, and computers. Having many techniques at your disposal is like being a skilled worker with a kit full of tools. In all likelihood, several tools rather than one will be needed on a specific job. Training and experience will aid you in their selection and use.

The statistical tests described in Chapters 18 and 19 are likely to seem abstract and difficult until you try to use them with your own data. When the data have a personal significance because you have collected them yourself, the application of statistical tests will be more satisfying and meaningful than when you are using arbitrary numbers from a textbook example. Knowing the origins of statistical tests is not necessary in order to use them. Descriptive statistics are tools for reducing a mass of numbers to a few informative figures such as percentages, means, and standard deviations. Inferential statistics are ways of analyzing data that allow you to choose among alternative explanations. The chapters on reports and follow-up activities attempted to place the research process within the larger context of science and practice.

Before closing, we would like to offer a few additional suggestions to the beginning researcher. Some of these apply to specific techniques, others to behavioral research in general.

Helpful Hints

Always check reliability. No matter how simple and straightforward the behavior being observed, it is still necessary to check observer reliability. Remember the adaptation of Murphy's law—if something can be misinterpreted, it will be. The number of people in a room should be easy to record reliably. Not so—people come and go and move about. Even a count of billboards, road signs, or some other tangible items is likely to produce discrepancies between observers. Questions arise as to whether store signs along the road count as billboards, whether a sign divided into two parts is considered two signs or one, and so on. A scoring

315

system considered reliable in earlier studies may be interpreted differently by a new observer.

Replication is useful. Don't worry if halfway through your research, you discover that someone has done a similar study. Science depends on repeated observations. If you come up with the same results, you have done a good job. If your results differ, this indicates a problem that must be resolved either through a finer-grained analysis or additional research.

Don't include too much in a single study. For a beginning researcher, there is a great temptation to keep on adding experimental conditions or test questions in the hope of positive results. There is the feeling of foreboding that the study will end inconclusively. Attempting to "cover yourself" by adding more conditions may create additional problems. Every new variable increases the likelihood of finding relationships due to chance. If you compare enough things enough times, relationships will be found. Do not deceive yourself that such findings are meaningful. With unpredicted findings in a multivariable study, it is necessary to repeat the study at least one more time before there is any assurance that the obtained difference is not a random fluctuation.

Be careful about data collected by others. A tired interviewer may not be strongly motivated to do a good job. Occasionally interviewers have interviewed themselves and written the replies as if they came from other people. One pollster admitted that the if you hire somebody with any intelligence, after the tenth interview they are going to sit down and make up the other twenty-five. This view may seem cynical, but it illustrates the need to check that field interviewers and observers are actually doing their job.

Specify in advance the characteristics for including subjects in the study as clearly and explicitly as possible (e.g., a good command of English, good eyesight and hearing with corrective devices, over age 18 and under 60, and so on). If possible, list the ways to identify non-serious answers in advance. One possibility is to discard replies that show a fixed or illogical pattern. There is reason to question the seriousness of someone who checks "strongly agree" to every statement, including those for and against an issue. Some researchers automatically discard any questionnaire that shows a stereotyped pattern of responses. Another way of determining non-serious answers is to ask the same questions several times in slightly different form. The person who strongly agrees with one form of the statement but disagrees with another is not a reliable respondent. It is useful to consult with colleagues, other researchers, or fellow students before discarding data. Occasionally, a response that looks unusual will make sense if you know the respondent's particular situation. Obtaining a second opinion will help answer the criticism that replies were rejected because they did not fit the hypothesis.

Double check information. Always check what you are told by those in authority. Seemingly factual statements such as "The park closes at 6:30 P.M." or "All the dormitory residents occupy double rooms" may be incorrect. It is surprising how often administrators are out of touch with what is going on in their own departments. The custodian is likely to know more about people's working habits than the company president. Don't be offensively distrustful of what people say or challenge their statements. Quietly check the facts and figures to see if they are accurate, complete, and current. Numerous horror stories could be recited of people who based their research projects on what authorities told them. A researcher studying litter in city parking garages was told that the garages were swept every morning. Not so, she found, during several preliminary visits. The floors were cleaned once every 2 days at most. Had she not inspected the garages, her estimates of litter would have been grossly inflated.

Double check any maps or floor plans that are being used in an observational study. A faulty floor plan can invalidate otherwise good observations. In one study, observers recorded classroom participation in several lecture halls. It was later found that one observer had included an extra row of chairs and another had not indicated clearly the front of the room and occasionally reversed front and back locations. Neither of these errors was detected until after the study was completed. All their data had to be discarded.

Don't overanalyze data. Only so much can be learned from a single study. Once the totals and averages have been computed, the major trends should be apparent. Overanalysis is a common error among beginning researchers, who are so eager to fully interpret the data that they tend to inflate the results. The amount of "noise" in behavioral research requires caution in interpreting trends that are not obvious. If 69 percent of the managers and 62 percent of the clerical employees are satisfied with working conditions, the similarity between the two groups seems more significant than the difference.

When the major findings have been extracted from the data, you should seriously consider (1) stopping because you have learned what you wanted, or (2) undertaking another study. Either of these options is likely to be more sensible than spending the next 6 months attempting to squeeze the last bit of information out of the data. People become attached to their data. This is normal; it is good to feel positive toward your findings. However, you should look upon each study as an attempt to answer certain questions. When this has been done, it is time to develop the implications of the findings and answer new questions that have arisen during the study. The danger of becoming bogged down in the data is particularly serious if your results have been analyzed by computer, creating a tremendous stack of printouts. You should accept the fact that most of the comparisons are probably not worth understanding or analyzing. Including them in the report will overwhelm the reader and detract attention from the major findings.

Not every study need be earthshaking. Science is a cumulative enterprise. Breakthrough discoveries occasionally occur, but most scientific investigation consists of small studies that shed light on one particular aspect of a topic.

Don't be concerned about the possibility that your methods or findings will be stolen. It is not necessary to copyright your term paper or class project. Sharing your findings with colleagues and fellow students can yield valuable feedback and ideas.

Don't be overly caught up in novelty. Doing good research does not require demolishing all previous studies in the field. Behavioral science is based on a steady accumulation of solid studies that improves our understanding of human behavior. This includes small and large studies, minor and major adaptations of previous work, new studies, and replications.

Avoid jargon in talking with outsiders. Scientific terms are intended for communication within the scientific community. A technical vocabulary is essential for keeping terms distinct and meaningful. Nonetheless, the same terminology that is helpful in communicating with other scientists may be a source of confusion and resentment when used with outsiders. Behavioral research is increasingly a collaborative effort, requiring communication with technical people from related fields and with lay people.

Be a responsible critic. Don't seize upon the limitations of a study in order to dismiss the entire project. Every study has its flaws. A responsible critic is obliged not only to indicate the nature of any limitations but how they operate to distort the data. Most of the landmark studies in behavioral research, including the classic investigations of Sigmund Freud, Jean Piaget, and Margaret Mead, were severely flawed in their methodology. The person who blazes a trail into a forest should not be criticized for not building a four-lane highway.

Be especially tolerant of the work of beginning researchers. They are the future of science. Try to specify what is good as well as what is missing in their studies.

Appendix A Critical Values

TABLE A–1. Critical Values for t Test[a]

Degrees of freedom (df)	Probability level[b]	
	.05	.01
5	2.57	4.03
6	2.45	3.71
7	2.36	3.50
8	2.31	3.36
9	2.26	3.25
10	2.23	3.17
11	2.20	3.11
12	2.18	3.06
13	2.16	3.01
14	2.14	2.98
15	2.13	2.95
16	2.12	2.92
17	2.11	2.90
18	2.10	2.88
19	2.09	2.86
20	2.09	2.84
25	2.06	2.79
30	2.04	2.75
40	2.02	2.70
50	2.01	2.68
100	1.98	2.63
∞	1.96	2.58

[a]Abridged from Fisher and Yates, *Statistical tables for biological, agricultural, and medical research* (London: Longmans Group, Ltd.), 6th ed., 1974. (Previously published by Oliver and Boyd, Edinburgh.) Used with permission of the authors and publishers.

[b]These are *two-tailed* probability levels. They are used when the investigator has made no specific prediction about the direction of the difference. A *one-tailed* test is used when the investigator has predicted the direction of the difference. The probability levels for a one-tailed test are half those of a two-tailed test. Since two-tailed tests are more conservative, it is good practice to use them routinely.

TABLE A–2. Critical Values for Chi-square Test[a]

Degrees of freedom (df)	Probability level	
	.05	.01
1	3.84	6.64
2	5.99	9.21
3	7.81	11.34
4	9.49	13.28
5	11.07	15.09
6	12.59	16.81
7	14.07	18.48
8	15.51	20.09
9	16.92	21.67
10	18.31	23.21
11	19.68	24.73
12	21.03	26.22
13	22.36	27.69
14	23.68	29.14
15	25.00	30.58
20	31.41	37.57
30	43.77	50.89

[a]See footnotes for Table A–1.

TABLE A–3. Critical Values for Pearson Product-
moment Correlation Coefficient $(r)^a$

Degrees of freedom[b] (df)	Probability level	
	.05	.01
5	.754	.874
6	.707	.834
7	.666	.798
8	.632	.765
9	.602	.735
10	.576	.708
11	.553	.684
12	.532	.661
13	.514	.641
14	.497	.623
15	.482	.606
16	.468	.590
17	.456	.575
18	.444	.561
19	.433	.549
20	.423	.537
25	.381	.487
30	.349	.449
40	.304	.393
50	.273	.354
60	.250	.325
80	.217	.283
100	.195	.254
200	.138	.181
300	.113	.148
400	.098	.128

[a]See footnotes for Table A–1.

[b]df = number of pairs − 2.

TABLE A–4. Critical Values for Spearman Rank-order Coefficient (r_s)[a]

Number of pairs N	Probability level[b]	
	.05	.01
5	.900	1.000
6	.829	.943
7	.714	.893
8	.643	.833
9	.600	.783
10	.564	.746
12	.506	.712
14	.456	.645
16	.425	.601
18	.399	.564
20	.377	.534
22	.359	.508
24	.343	.485
26	.329	.465
28	.317	.448
30	.306	.432

[a]Reprinted with permission from E. G. Olds, Distributions of sums of squares of rank differences for small numbers of individuals. *Annals of Mathematical Statistics*, 1938, 133–148.

[b]Unlike the earlier tables, which contain two-tailed probability levels, the levels for *rho* are one- tailed levels. They assume that the researcher has predicted the direction of the relationship as positive or negative. If no prediction has been made, the researcher can use the more conservative .01 probability levels.

TABLE A–5. Abridged Table of Random Numbers

73	17	86	15	27	10	42	72
64	46	07	88	76	45	61	55
19	09	22	09	35	99	76	34
08	72	60	22	84	17	81	39
90	09	97	61	90	37	23	52
34	43	09	17	30	20	59	61
02	48	34	21	18	03	99	61
45	90	33	88	89	70	04	80
03	61	05	61	77	70	17	47
05	56	83	78	26	48	35	06
15	86	60	14	49	10	51	17
38	07	45	88	06	06	29	92
60	22	86	92	52	31	00	47
81	94	25	53	73	89	42	62
87	97	01	09	03	40	86	12
17	35	11	60	12	23	83	26
71	27	96	45	07	60	71	82
66	38	80	72	74	42	21	53
94	84	69	37	69	35	59	32
03	26	07	66	93	88	48	54

TABLE A–6. Critical Values of F*

Degrees of freedom in denominator	Degrees of freedom in numerator													
	1	2	3	4	5	6	7	8	9	10	20	50	100	∞
1	161 **4052**	200 **5000**	216 **5402**	225 **5625**	230 **5764**	234 **5859**	237 **5928**	239 **5980**	241 **6022**	242 **6056**	248 **6208**	252 **6302**	253 **6334**	254 **6366**
2	18.51 **98.50**	19.00 **99.00**	19.16 **99.17**	19.25 **99.25**	19.30 **99.30**	19.33 **99.33**	19.36 **99.34**	19.37 **99.36**	19.38 **99.38**	19.39 **99.40**	19.44 **99.45**	19.47 **99.48**	19.49 **99.49**	19.50 **99.50**
3	10.13 **34.12**	9.55 **30.81**	9.28 **29.46**	9.12 **28.71**	9.01 **28.24**	8.94 **27.91**	8.88 **27.67**	8.84 **27.49**	8.81 **27.34**	8.78 **27.23**	8.66 **26.69**	8.58 **26.30**	8.56 **26.23**	8.53 **26.12**
4	7.71 **21.20**	6.94 **18.00**	6.59 **16.69**	6.39 **15.98**	6.26 **15.52**	6.16 **15.21**	6.09 **14.98**	6.04 **14.80**	6.00 **14.66**	5.96 **14.54**	5.80 **14.02**	5.70 **13.69**	5.66 **13.57**	5.63 **13.46**
5	6.61 **16.26**	5.79 **13.27**	5.41 **12.06**	5.19 **11.39**	5.05 **10.97**	4.95 **10.67**	4.88 **10.45**	4.82 **10.27**	4.78 **10.15**	4.74 **10.05**	4.56 **9.55**	4.44 **9.24**	4.40 **9.13**	4.36 **9.02**
6	5.99 **13.74**	5.14 **10.92**	4.76 **9.78**	4.53 **9.15**	4.39 **8.75**	4.28 **8.47**	4.21 **8.26**	4.15 **8.10**	4.10 **7.98**	4.06 **7.87**	3.87 **7.39**	3.75 **7.09**	3.71 **6.99**	3.67 **6.88**
7	5.59 **12.25**	4.74 **9.55**	4.35 **8.45**	4.12 **7.85**	3.97 **7.46**	3.87 **7.19**	3.79 **7.00**	3.73 **6.84**	3.68 **6.71**	3.63 **6.62**	3.44 **6.15**	3.32 **5.85**	3.28 **5.75**	3.23 **5.65**
8	5.32 **11.26**	4.46 **8.65**	4.07 **7.59**	3.84 **7.01**	3.69 **6.63**	3.58 **6.37**	3.50 **6.19**	3.44 **6.03**	3.39 **5.91**	3.34 **5.82**	3.15 **5.36**	3.03 **5.06**	2.98 **4.96**	2.93 **4.86**
9	5.12 **10.56**	4.26 **8.02**	3.86 **6.99**	3.63 **6.42**	3.48 **6.06**	3.37 **5.80**	3.29 **5.62**	3.23 **5.47**	3.18 **5.35**	3.13 **5.26**	2.93 **4.80**	2.80 **4.51**	2.76 **4.41**	2.71 **4.31**
10	4.96 **10.04**	4.10 **7.56**	3.71 **6.55**	3.48 **5.99**	3.33 **5.64**	3.22 **5.39**	3.14 **5.21**	3.07 **5.06**	3.02 **4.95**	2.97 **4.85**	2.77 **4.41**	2.64 **4.12**	2.59 **4.01**	2.54 **3.91**
11	4.84 **9.56**	3.98 **7.20**	3.59 **6.22**	3.36 **5.67**	3.20 **5.32**	3.09 **5.07**	3.01 **4.88**	2.95 **4.74**	2.90 **4.63**	2.86 **4.54**	2.65 **4.10**	2.50 **3.80**	2.45 **3.70**	2.40 **3.60**
12	4.75 **9.33**	3.88 **6.93**	3.49 **5.95**	3.26 **5.41**	3.11 **5.06**	3.00 **4.82**	2.92 **4.65**	2.85 **4.50**	2.80 **4.39**	2.76 **4.30**	2.54 **3.86**	2.40 **3.56**	2.35 **3.46**	2.30 **3.36**

df														
13	2.21 / **3.16**	2.26 / **3.27**	2.32 / **3.37**	2.46 / **3.67**	2.67 / **4.10**	2.72 / **4.19**	2.77 / **4.30**	2.84 / **4.44**	2.92 / **4.62**	3.02 / **4.86**	3.18 / **5.20**	3.41 / **5.74**	3.80 / **6.70**	4.67 / **9.07**
14	2.13 / **3.00**	2.19 / **3.11**	2.24 / **3.21**	2.39 / **3.51**	2.60 / **3.94**	2.65 / **4.03**	2.70 / **4.14**	2.77 / **4.28**	2.85 / **4.46**	2.96 / **4.69**	3.11 / **5.03**	3.34 / **5.56**	3.74 / **6.51**	4.60 / **8.86**
15	2.07 / **2.87**	2.12 / **2.97**	2.18 / **3.07**	2.33 / **3.36**	2.55 / **3.80**	2.59 / **3.98**	2.64 / **4.00**	2.70 / **4.14**	2.79 / **4.32**	2.90 / **4.56**	3.06 / **4.89**	3.29 / **5.42**	3.68 / **6.36**	4.54 / **8.68**
16	2.01 / **2.75**	2.07 / **2.86**	2.13 / **2.96**	2.28 / **3.25**	2.49 / **3.69**	2.54 / **3.78**	2.59 / **3.89**	2.66 / **4.03**	2.74 / **4.20**	2.85 / **4.44**	3.01 / **4.77**	3.24 / **5.29**	3.63 / **6.23**	4.49 / **8.53**
17	1.96 / **2.65**	2.02 / **2.76**	2.08 / **2.86**	2.23 / **3.16**	2.45 / **3.59**	2.50 / **3.68**	2.55 / **3.79**	2.62 / **3.93**	2.70 / **4.10**	2.81 / **4.34**	2.96 / **4.67**	3.20 / **5.18**	3.59 / **6.11**	4.45 / **8.40**
18	1.92 / **2.57**	1.98 / **2.68**	2.04 / **2.78**	2.19 / **3.07**	2.41 / **3.51**	2.46 / **3.60**	2.51 / **3.71**	2.58 / **3.85**	2.66 / **4.01**	2.77 / **4.25**	2.93 / **4.58**	3.16 / **5.09**	3.55 / **6.02**	4.41 / **8.28**
19	1.88 / **2.49**	1.94 / **2.60**	2.00 / **2.70**	2.15 / **3.00**	2.38 / **3.43**	2.43 / **3.52**	2.48 / **3.63**	2.55 / **3.77**	2.63 / **3.94**	2.74 / **4.17**	2.90 / **4.50**	3.13 / **5.01**	3.52 / **5.93**	4.38 / **8.18**
20	1.84 / **2.42**	1.90 / **2.53**	1.96 / **2.63**	2.12 / **2.94**	2.35 / **3.37**	2.40 / **3.45**	2.45 / **3.56**	2.52 / **3.71**	2.60 / **3.87**	2.71 / **4.10**	2.87 / **4.43**	3.10 / **4.94**	3.49 / **5.85**	4.35 / **8.10**
25	1.71 / **2.17**	1.77 / **2.29**	1.84 / **2.40**	2.00 / **2.70**	2.24 / **3.13**	2.28 / **3.21**	2.34 / **3.32**	2.41 / **3.46**	2.49 / **3.63**	2.60 / **3.86**	2.76 / **4.18**	2.99 / **4.68**	3.38 / **5.57**	4.24 / **7.77**
30	1.62 / **2.01**	1.69 / **2.13**	1.76 / **2.24**	1.93 / **2.55**	2.16 / **2.98**	2.21 / **3.06**	2.27 / **3.17**	2.34 / **3.30**	2.42 / **3.47**	2.53 / **3.70**	2.69 / **4.02**	2.92 / **4.51**	3.32 / **5.39**	4.17 / **7.56**
40	1.51 / **1.81**	1.59 / **1.94**	1.66 / **2.05**	1.84 / **2.37**	2.07 / **2.80**	2.12 / **2.88**	2.18 / **2.99**	2.25 / **3.12**	2.34 / **3.29**	2.45 / **3.51**	2.61 / **3.83**	2.84 / **4.31**	3.23 / **5.18**	4.08 / **7.31**
50	1.44 / **1.68**	1.52 / **1.82**	1.60 / **1.94**	1.78 / **2.26**	2.02 / **2.70**	2.07 / **2.78**	2.13 / **2.88**	2.20 / **3.02**	2.29 / **3.18**	2.40 / **3.41**	2.56 / **3.72**	2.79 / **4.20**	3.18 / **5.06**	4.03 / **7.17**
100	1.28 / **1.43**	1.39 / **1.59**	1.48 / **1.73**	1.68 / **2.06**	1.92 / **2.51**	1.97 / **2.59**	2.03 / **2.69**	2.10 / **2.82**	2.19 / **2.99**	2.30 / **3.20**	2.46 / **3.51**	2.70 / **3.98**	3.09 / **4.82**	3.94 / **6.90**
200	1.19 / **1.28**	1.32 / **1.48**	1.42 / **1.62**	1.62 / **1.97**	1.87 / **2.41**	1.92 / **2.50**	1.98 / **2.60**	2.05 / **2.73**	2.14 / **2.90**	2.26 / **3.11**	2.41 / **3.41**	2.65 / **3.88**	3.04 / **4.71**	3.89 / **6.76**
∞	1.00 / **1.00**	1.24 / **1.36**	1.35 / **1.52**	1.57 / **1.87**	1.83 / **2.32**	1.88 / **2.41**	1.94 / **2.51**	2.01 / **2.64**	2.10 / **2.80**	2.21 / **3.02**	2.37 / **3.32**	2.60 / **3.78**	3.00 / **4.61**	3.84 / **6.64**

Appendix B   Statistical Tests

TABLE B–1. Calculation of a t Test for Matched Scores

A group of workers is given a hand steadiness test before and after taking a drug. Does the drug have a significant effect on their performance?

Score on Hand Steadiness Test

Employee name	Before	After	d	d^2
Bill	72	70	+2	4
John	81	78	+3	9
Mary	75	74	+1	1
Sue	77	78	−1	1
Al	84	80	+4	16
Sam	72	72	0	0

Step 1. Compute the difference (d) between each person's scores before and after taking the drug. Subtract each *after* score from each *before* score. Pay close attention to the sign (plus or minus) of each difference (d).

2. Square each difference (d^2).

3. Compute $\sum d = 9$

   Note: Pay close attention to plus and minus signs.

4. Compute $\left(\sum d\right)^2 = 81$.

5. Compute $\sum d^2 = 31$.

   Note: All numbers here are positive since they have been squared.

6. $N = 6$.

7. Enter figures into formula. The formula for a t test for matched scores is:

$$t = \frac{\dfrac{\sum d}{N}}{\sqrt{\dfrac{\sum d^2 - \dfrac{\left(\sum d\right)^2}{N}}{N(N-1)}}}$$

d = difference between the matched scores
N = number of *pairs* of scores

Computation

$$t = \frac{\dfrac{\sum d}{N}}{\sqrt{\dfrac{\sum d^2 - \dfrac{(\sum d)^2}{N}}{N(N-1)}}} = \frac{\dfrac{9}{6}}{\sqrt{\dfrac{31 - \dfrac{81}{6}}{6(6-1)}}}$$

$$= \frac{1.5}{\sqrt{\dfrac{31 - 13.5}{30}}} = \frac{1.5}{\sqrt{.58}} = \frac{1.5}{.76} = 1.97$$

8. Compute degrees of freedom. For related scores, $df = N - 1 = 6 - 1 = 5$.

9. Check Table A–1 in Appendix A. The critical value for t to be significant at the .05 level for 5 degrees of freedom is 2.57 or greater. Since this t ratio is only 1.97, it is *not* significant.

TABLE B–2. Calculation of a One-way Analysis of Variance (ANOVA)

Step 1. Arrange the scores by groups.

Group 1		Group 2		Group 3	
No deprivation	*Number of mistakes*	*Slight deprivation*	*Number of mistakes*	*Moderate deprivation*	*Number of mistakes*
Subject 1	1	Subject 5	3	Subject 9	2
Subject 2	2	Subject 6	2	Subject 10	3
Subject 3	0	Subject 7	3	Subject 11	4
Subject 4	2	Subject 8	4	Subject 12	4

The results of each set of steps are entered on an ANOVA table:

ANOVA Table

Source	SS	df	MS	F
Total	SS_{tot}			
Treatment	SS_{bet}			
(deprivation groups)				
Error	SS_{within}			

A. Calculation of the total sum of squares (SS_{tot}).
NOTE: If you are using a calculator with a X^2 key, you can do steps 2 and 3 at the same time.

Step 2. Add the scores in *each* group. This is the *sum* for each group.

	Group 1	Group 2	Group 3
	1	3	2
	2	2	3
	0	3	4
Sum	$\underline{2}$	$\underline{4}$	$\underline{4}$
	5	12	13

Step 3. Square each individual score and add these squared values together.
$$1^2 + 2^2 + 0^2 + 2^2 + 3^2 + 2^2 + 3^2 + 4^2 + 2^2 + 3^2 + 4^2 + 4^2$$
$$= 1 + 4 + 0 + 4 + 9 + 4 + 9 + 16 + 4 + 9 + 16 + 16$$
$$= 92 \text{ This is } \sum X^2$$

Step 4. Add all the group sums (in step 2) together to get the sum for all scores, the grand total.
$$5 + 12 + 13 = \sum X_{tot} = 30$$

Step 5. Square the grand total (step 4).
$$\left(\sum X_{tot}\right)^2 = (30)^2 = 900$$

Step 6. Divide the result of step 5 by N, the total number of cases.
$$N = 4 + 4 + 4 = 12$$
$$\frac{\left(\sum X_{tot}\right)^2}{N} = \frac{900}{12} = 75$$
This is called the *correction factor*.

Step 7. Subtract the *correction factor* (step 6) from the result of step 3, the sum of the squared values.
$$\sum X^2 - (\text{correction factor}) = 92 - 75 = 17.0$$
This is the *total sum of squares* (SS_{tot}).
Enter it in the ANOVA table (see model table in Section H).

B. Calculation of the between group sum of squares (SS_{bet}).

Step 8. For *each* group, square the sum (step 2) and divide by the number of scores in the group.
$$\frac{5^2}{4} + \frac{12^2}{4} + \frac{13^2}{4} = 84.5$$

Step 9. Subtract the correction factor (step 6) from the value in step 8.
$$84.5 - 75 = 9.5$$
This is the between groups sum of squares (SS_{bet}).
Enter this value in the ANOVA table.

C. Calculation of the within group sum of squares (SS_{within}).

Step 10. Subtract the between group sum of squares (step 9) from the total sum of squares (step 7)
$$17 - 9.5 = 7.5$$
This gives the within group sum of squares (SS_{within}). Enter in the ANOVA table.

D. Calculate degree of freedom (df) and enter on the ANOVA table.

Step 11. For SS_{tot} df_{tot} = (total number of cases) − 1
                    $df_{tot} = 12 - 1 = 11$

     For SS_{bet} df_{bet} = (number of groups) − 1
                    $df_{bet} = 3 - 1 = 2$

     For SS_{within} $df_{within} = df_{tot} - df_{bet}$
                    $df_{within} = 11 - 2 = 9$

E. Calculate mean squares (MS) for the *between* and *within* group measures.

Step 12. The mean squares (MS) are computed as SS/*df*. (Note: MS_{tot} is not needed.)

$$MS_{bet} = \frac{SS_{bet}}{df_{bet}} = \frac{9.5}{2} = 4.75$$

$$MS_{within} = \frac{SS_{within}}{df_{within}} = \frac{7.5}{9} = .83$$

Enter these in the ANOVA table.

F. Calculate the *F* ratio.

Step 13. $F = \dfrac{MS_{bet}}{MS_{within}} = \dfrac{4.75}{.83} = 5.72$

Enter the value on the ANOVA table.

G. Statistical significance.

Step 14. See Table A–6 in Appendix A to find the probability associated with the *F* ratio. There were 2 degrees of freedom (*df*) in the numerator of the *F* ratio, and 9 *df* in the denominator. Using Table A–6, first go across the columns until you reach 2 *df* for the numerator, then proceed down this column until you reach 9 *df* for the denominator. This shows that for the differences among the means to be significant at the .05 level, the obtained *F* ratio must equal or exceed 4.26, and to be significant at the .01 level, must equal or exceed 8.02.

Because the obtained statistic, 5.72, exceeds the critical value at the .05 level, we can reject the null hypothesis at the .05 level, and conclude that sleep deprivation has a negative impact on task performance. See the notation, $p < .05$, on the ANOVA table.

H. Model ANOVA Table.

Source	SS		df	MS	F
Total	SS_{tot}	17.0	11		
Treatment (deprivation groups)	SS_{bet}	9.5	2	4.75	5.72 $p < .05$
Error	SS_{within}	7.5	9	0.83	

TABLE B–3. Computation of the Pearson Product-Moment Coefficient (*r*)

Example: A teacher predicted that pupils who do well in arithmetic are also good spellers (a positive correlation). The highest possible arithmetic score was 10, and the highest possible spelling score was 20.

Step 1. Sum X scores: $\sum X = 54$.

Step 2. Square $\sum X$: $\left(\sum X\right)^2 = 2916$.

Step 3. Square each X score.

Step 4. Sum the squared X scores: $\sum X^2 = 400$.

Step 5. Repeat steps 1–3 for the Y scores.

Step 6. Multiply each X score its corresponding Y score (XY column).

Step 7. Sum XY products: $\sum XY = 573$.

Student	Arithmetic score (X)	Spelling score (Y)			
	X	Y	X^2	Y^2	XY
Jeanine	8	13	64	169	104
Howard	6	8	36	64	48
Ky-Van	5	7	25	49	35
Blossom	10	14	100	196	140
Hugh	7	12	49	144	84
Bradford	9	15	81	225	135
Clayton	6	3	36	9	18
Lorraine	3	3	9	9	9

$$\sum X = 54 \quad \sum Y = 75 \quad \sum X^2 = 400 \quad \sum Y^2 = 865 \quad \sum XY = 573 \quad \left(\sum X\right)^2 = 2916.$$

Step 8. Count the number of pairs: $N = 8$.

Step 9. Insert these figures into the formula for r:

$$r = \frac{N\sum XY - \left(\sum X\right)\left(\sum Y\right)}{\sqrt{[N\sum X^2 - \left(\sum X\right)^2][N\sum Y^2 - \left(\sum Y\right)^2}}$$

$$r = \frac{8(573) - (54)(75)}{\sqrt{[8(400) - 2916][8(865) - 5625]}}$$

$$= \frac{4584 - 4050}{\sqrt{(3200 - 2916)(6920) - 5625}} = \frac{534}{\sqrt{(284)(1295)}}$$

$$= \frac{534}{\sqrt{367,780}} = \frac{534}{606.45} = .881$$

Step 10. Compute the degrees of freedom: $df = N - 2$, where N is the number of pairs: $df = 8 - 2 = 6$.

Step 11. Interpreting the significance of r. Consult Table A–3 in Appendix A. Find $df = 6$ in the first column; then move to the right, to the column indicating the .05 level of confidence. The table indicates that when $df = 6$, a coefficient must be at least .707 to be statistically significant at the .05 level. This value of .707 holds for *both* positive and negative coefficients. The sign of the coefficient is unimportant in testing whether or not it is statistically significant. The sign *is* important in determining the direction of the relationship.

Step 12. The obtained coefficient in this example is .881 permitting rejection of the null hypothesis. The sign of the coefficient (+) indicates that there is a positive association between spelling and arithmetic. We are able to conclude that students who do well in arithmetic are good spellers, and students who spell poorly also do poorly in arithmetic.

TABLE B–4. Computation of the Spearman Rank-order Coefficient (r_s)

Example: Do the coach's rankings predict performance in the track meet?

Step 1. Check to see that all ranking (including ties) has been done correctly (see Chapter 18 for dealing with tied scores).

Step 2. Compute the difference (d) between the coach's rankings and the actual performance for each individual.

Step 3. Square each difference and sum them: $\Sigma d^2 = 69.50$.

Runner	Coach's ranking before the race	Order of finish in the race	d	d^2
Nguyen	1	4	−3.0	9.00
Smolenski	2	6	−4.0	16.00
Jones	3.5	7	−3.5	12.25
Rodrigues	3.5	1	2.5	6.25
Heinz	5	2	3.0	9.00
Tomatsu	6	5	1.0	1.00
Harris	7	3	4.0	16.00
			$\Sigma d^2 =$	69.50

Step 4. Count the number of pairs: $N = 7$.

Step 5. Enter these figures in the formula:

$$r_S = 1 - \frac{6\Sigma d^2}{N(N^2 - 1)}$$

$$r_S = 1 - \frac{6(69.50)}{7(49 - 1)} = 1 - \frac{417}{336} = 1 - 1.241 = -.241$$

Step 6. Evaluating r_S. Table A–4 in Appendix A shows the significance levels for r_S. Ignore the sign ($+$ or $-$) when using the table of critical values. Look in the left-hand column under N. Note that this column uses the number of pairs (N) rather than degrees of freedom. The table shows that with an N of 7, r_S of .714 or greater is required for significance at the .05 level. Because the obtained coefficient in this example was .241, we accept the null hypothesis and conclude that there was no reliable relationship between the coach's ranking and the runner's performance in the race.

Appendix C   Using Computer Software for Data Analysis

The various software packages for statistical analyses were listed in Chapter 15. Although each one will have its own unique characteristics, the general procedures for data entry and analysis will be similar. The following guidelines will be appropriate for most software, but you will have to familiarize yourself with each program's particular characteristics. Most packages include a tutorial, that is, a learning module to familiarize the user with the program. While it might seem tedious, it is extremely worthwhile to go through it at the beginning. You will be saved considerable time and aggravation later by getting an overview of the program's uses, functions, and commands, and be sure to learn the precise meaning of all the terms used.

After you have read about the program and gone through the tutorial, run a test program before you enter your actual data. Make up a list of five or six single-digit numbers, and calculate the sum, mean, and standard deviation (if you have a calculator). Then enter the numbers into the computer, request the statistics just described, and see if you get the correct results. In this way you will have more confidence in the results from your larger data set. Also, it is extremely frustrating to enter long columns of numbers only to discover that you have done it wrong and must re-enter the entire set.

Remember that the computer is a very single-minded concrete thinker that works methodically, step by step. It just does it very fast. If you work step by step and not so fast, you will be successful in using the system. All variables are of equal importance to the computer. It makes distinctions only on the basis of your commands. A trial run with a small set of numbers will save you great amounts of time and effort in avoiding problems that will be more difficult to trace in your actual data.

List Comparisons, Contrasts, and Correlations

Before you begin entering your research results, make a list of the questions or hypotheses that led to the data collection in the first place. These will serve as a guide for data entry and analysis. Specify the comparisons you wish to make. For example, will you be comparing the means of two groups (*t* test or ANOVA), or analyzing a contingency table (Chi-square)? Or perhaps you want to see if two variables are associated with each other (correlation). Having these in mind will help you in knowing what information needs to be entered and what information you will want to request.

Statistical work on the computer has two aspects: data entry and data analysis. The most time will be spent on entering the data and checking it for accuracy. All the numerical information you wish to use must be correctly entered into the computer and properly saved for subsequent use. The second step is for you to request the specific analyses—statistical summaries and tests. These may include both descriptive statistics and inferential statistics (see Chapters 18 and 19).

Data Entry

The program will have an editor which is a numbered spreadsheet, the grid on which you enter your data. Generally you will enter the variable name at the top of a column and then list the obtained values below. Figure C–1 shows the data entry for Problem #3 at the end of Chapter 19.

The first variable is likely to be the subject or observation number. You must make up a name for each variable, usually limited to eight letters (five in some programs) without spaces or symbols. This is the *variable label*. For subject or observation number you might use SUBJ, NUMBER, or ID. Even if the program assigns a case number (as in Figure C-2), you should enter your own because if you reorder your subjects or cases, the computer will simply renumber them in consecutive order, thereby losing the original order.

SUBJ	NAME	BEFORE	AFTER
1	Matt	62	64
2	Eva	71	75
3	Hamadi	68	67
4	Gretchen	51	52
5	Okimo	58	61
6	Maria	84	85

FIG. C–1. Example of data entry, using problem #3 at the end of Ch. 19.

	SUBJ	GROUP	GRADE
1	1	Participator	4
2	2	Participator	4
3	3	Participator	3
4	4	Participator	3
5	5	Participator	3
6	6	Participator	1
7	7	Nonparticipator	4
8	8	Nonparticipator	3
9	9	Nonparticipator	3
10	10	Nonparticipator	2
11	11	Nonparticipator	2
12	12	Nonparticipator	1
13	13	Nonparticipator	1

FIG. C–2. Example of data entry, using problem #2 at the end of Chapter 19.

The *value* indicates the level of the variable. In Figure C–1, the BEFORE and AFTER measures were quantitative. The variable GENDER would have two values, Male and Female. If you use a number for your value level, for example, 1 = Male, and 2 = Female, be sure to make a codebook in which you keep all pertinent information, so that you will have it at a later date, or so that someone else can figure out how you coded the information.

If you are comparing different groups of respondents, you will need to indicate the group to which each score belongs. Figure C–2 shows the data entry for Problem #2, at the end of Chapter 19.

Missing Data

The next task is to learn how missing data are handled. The software package will tell you what to use for missing information. Usually the space is left blank or a point (.) is inserted. Do *not* use zero. The computer will simply read 0 as the value for the variable and include it in all calculations.

Backup Copies

We cannot stress enough the importance of making a backup copy of your data entries on a diskette that you keep yourself. Unimaginable things can happen to data you have entered into computer memory. Expect it to be lost, either from your own or some external cause. Extremely hot weather can lead to extensive use of air conditioning, which in turn can lead to power fluctuations in an entire city that may affect your individual computer. If you share computer use, there is little control over the activities of others. Panic and paranoia are easily avoided by having a personal copy of your data set.

Data List

After the raw data have been entered, print out your entire data file. This is called a *data list*. Use this to check and double check your entries. Keep it. If all else fails (i.e., your file disappears and your backup diskette melts) at least you will have a typed copy. It is tempting to rush ahead to the final analysis, but save paper and first make sure all your entries are correct. It is best to read your raw data aloud to another person who checks the entries on the data list. After you make changes, be sure to recopy the corrected file onto your backup diskette.

Data Analysis

Once your data entries are checked and corrected, the analysis is amazingly fast. Following the instructions of your particular software package, you simply request the statistics you want and answer the computer's queries about which variables you wish to use. Here the discussion in Chapter 6 on experimentation will be helpful. You will need to specify which variable represents the outcome, or dependent variable, and which variable or variables comprise the independent or predictive ones. Sometimes these will be referred to as the grouping variable or groups, as when comparing two groups on some outcome.

Be sure to request both descriptive and inferential statistics. You need the descriptive information (e.g., percentages, sample size, means, ranges, and standard deviations) in order to fully understand the meaning of the inferential statistics.

Look at the results and see if they make sense. If the scores range from 40 to 100, the mean cannot be 22.57. Check to see that the number of cases (N) corresponds with your knowledge of the number in your sample. Make sure that you didn't inadvertently correlate one of your key variables with the subject numbers. If you have been paying attention to your data during the study, there should be no big surprises in the data analysis.

Label your output. Write notes on the printout indicating the date and type of analysis made. You may need to add some identifying information by hand. Otherwise, you may look at the printout a few weeks later and not have any idea which analysis it represents. Once you gain an understanding of the process, you are likely to start making a number of subset analyses (e.g., selecting only males and then comparing the under-30 group with the 30-and-above group). Keeping a record of your computer runs with the dates is useful. Box C–1 lists the necessary steps for data entry and analysis.

Avoid Blind Analysis

The computer has greatly extended the range of statistical techniques available to researchers. It can perform operations in a matter of seconds or minutes that would take hours or days to analyze with a calculator. The positive effect of this has been to increase the number and types of possible analyses, but the freedom of choice brings the risk of asking the computer to perform analyses that the researcher does not understand. It probably won't help to take a complicated printout of data to a statistical consultant in the hope that he or she can make sense of it. The consultant may be familiar with the statistical test but not the nature or limitations of the data being analyzed.

BOX C–1. Steps in Data Entry and Data Analysis

Data Entry

1. Read over the material accompanying the statistical package you will be using.
2. Go through the tutorial.
3. Run a small data set as a test, including an entry with a missing value.
4. Resolve any problems by either going to the software manual, the tutorial, or asking a knowledgeable person.
5. Make a list of the questions and hypotheses that led to data collection.
6. Enter your raw data.
7. Make a backup copy of your data on a separate diskette.
8. Print out a data list, adding labels and date.
9. Thoroughly check the data list for errors, circling corrections in red.
10. Correct errors and make a new backup copy.

Data Analysis

1. Consult your list (#5 above). Decide the specific statistics you need. (Actually this decision should be made much earlier, during the study design phase.)

   a. Descriptive statistics: Do you need percentages, or means and standard deviations (including the Ns)?

   b. Inferential statistics: Does the study call for a Chi-square test, a t test, or ANOVA? Is there a basis for doing a correlation? If so, should you request a Pearson or Spearman coefficient? (When the time comes, review Chapter 19.)
2. Request the desired statistical analyses.
3. Examine the output to see if it makes sense.
4. Label the output, adding date, variable and value labels, and other information or notes that you may wish to have at a later time.

As a general rule, a researcher should not travel too far beyond the bounds of personal understanding in doing a statistical analysis. The problem was less serious with hand calculation where one could gain familiarity with a technique in the course of doing the computations. Today, a computer does everything so quickly that there is little time for understanding to develop. You should read about a statistical method before asking the computer to perform it. This doesn't mean that you have to understand the derivation of all the formulas in order to apply a statistical test. What is needed is a general understanding of the nature of the test and the assumptions behind it, what it can and cannot do, and the meaning of key concepts and terms. This understanding can be gained from reading some of the statistical textbooks listed in the further readings section at the conclusion of Chapter 19.

Appendix D   Example of a Manuscript Prepared According to the Publication Manual of the American Psychological Association

Running head: MUSIC AND WALKING

Music and Walking Speed*

Jean Davidson and Mary Li

West Australia College

*This paper is a fictitious account, presented solely as a model
of APA style.

Abstract

Walking speed was timed for male and female pedestrians on a
public sidewalk with fast, slow, or no music playing in the
background ($\underline{n}$ = 20 per condition). Pedestrians in the fast music
condition walked more rapidly than those in the other two
conditions. Slow music did not reduce walking speed, relative to
the no music condition. Walking speed did not differ by gender in
any of the three conditions. The findings support elements of
Mayfield's organismic theory of activation effects.

Music and Walking Speed

Does ambient stimulation increase arousal? Late-night drivers often turn up radio volume in hopes of staying awake on the road. Increasing stimulation is a common response to feelings of boredom. Mayfield (1947) proposed a theory of organismic activation to explain the effects of background stimuli on arousal. According to the theory, increased arousal or activation is an adaptive response to increases in background stimuli, unless such stimuli are competing directly with the activity taking place. Considerable research has been done to test the theory in the laboratory and field situations. Garcia's (1988) review of the literature on the effects of increasing stimulation showed that research results generally support the theory.

In related research Araujo (1965) found that slow music did not increase activity levels of subjects performing mechanical tasks, and in fact had a slowing effect. In addition she reported that loud music led to a reduction in speed of solving logical and mathematical problems. Other studies have looked at the effects of social stimuli. During meals, the presence of other people at a table tends to increase eating speed, but if the other individuals deliberately eat in a slow manner, the activation effect disappears (Guenther & Stratton, 1985).

To sort out these somewhat contradictory findings, research is needed that compares the effects of differing levels of background stimuli on arousal within a single modality. Organismic theory predicts that any stimulus that is not competitive with ongoing activity will increase arousal. Araujo's inhibition theory predicts that increased levels (levels above ongoing activity) will increase arousal only as long as they do not interfere with ongoing activity, and that stimulation lower than the current level will decrease activity.

In the present study, activation is measured by walking speed and the background stimulus condition is music level. Unlike earlier studies comparing a music with a no music condition (Becker, 1991; Remick, 1982) the present study uses three levels of the experimental variable: fast music, slow music, and no music. The effects are tested under naturalistic conditions using the procedure developed by Kinefelter (1986) for measuring walking speed on public sidewalks. Organismic theory predicts that both the fast and slow music conditions should increase walking speed, relative to the no music condition. On the other hand Araujo's inhibition theory suggests that walking speed would be increased only in the fast music condition, and that the slow music might actually reduce walking speed relative to the no music condition.

Method

Setting

The study took place in a public park in Perth, a city of 1 million population, situated in Western Australia. The park is located in a busy downtown area with considerable foot traffic on the public sidewalks bordering the park on three sides. The specific location was the north sidewalk, the same location used by Li (1995) in her study examining the effects of group size on walking speed. The distance included in the present experiment is 120 meters. Earlier research by Kinefelter (1986) showed that the average time taken by a lone pedestrian to walk this section of sidewalk was 92 seconds, with a range from 72 to 104 seconds. The particular length of sidewalk was selected because of its public location, ease of observation from a nearby building, and the proximity of a grassy area where music could be played unobtrusively.

Participants

The participants in the experiment were 60 single adults, judged to be between 18 and 50 years of age, seen walking alone on the designated stretch of public sidewalk. Groups or parents with children were excluded from the study. Following a predetermined sampling plan, an equal number of male and female pedestrians was timed on the sidewalk.

Materials

The music selections used in the study were obtained from a list developed by Harrison and Moore (1983). These researchers had asked respondents to rate approximately 100 different musical selections as to preference (like-dislike) and activity level (fast-slow). The ratings were made on a 7-point scale with a neutral middle point. For the present study, two selections whose average ratings on the fast-slow scale that were at least 1 point above the neutral point, and two musical selections with an average rating at least 1 point below neutral. All four music selections were in the middle range of preference. The music was played on a Sony tape recorder located 2.7 meters from the sidewalk and played at moderate volume, measuring 72 decibels on a hand-held Smith Audiometer, Model C2. The volume is consistent

with that used by other people in the park with tape players or
radios.

Design and Procedure

The tape player was placed about mid-block, alongside the co-
investigator, a young woman sitting on a blanket facing away from
the sidewalk. The conditions (2 fast music selections, 2 slow
music selections, and no music) were presented in random order,
with the pattern and times noted by the co-investigator. Using a
prepared list of the music selection order, she noted the gender
and identifying attire of each passerby. Sessions were conducted
on Tuesday, Wednesday, and Thursday, from 1:30-4:30 p.m. The
weather was warm and sunny on all three days.

Walking speed of pedestrians, coming from either the east or
west, was timed by observers stationed on the roof of a 3-story
building across the street. They were unaware (blind) as to the
presence or absence of music, or the type of music played. Once it
was agreed by the two observers that the pedestrian met the
conditions of the study (alone and between the ages of 18 and 50),
the pedestrian was timed as to how long he or she took to cover
the designated section of sidewalk. While one observer timed each
individual, the other observer wrote down identifying information
(gender and attire) to be matched with the on-site record of which
type of music was being played. Interobserver reliability was
established by a correlation of .94 ($p < .001$) between the times
recorded independently by the two observers in a trial sample.

A total of 63 participants were observed in the study, but
three had to be excluded from the sample. In one case the person

stopped midway along the sidewalk, turned around, and walked back in the original direction. The other two excluded cases were individuals walking in opposite directions who stopped in the middle of the sidewalk for an extended conversation. The sampling period of the study was increased to included additional cases to make up for the three who were excluded. The final sample size was 60, equally divided over the three experimental conditions with of an equal number of men and women in each condition (n = 10).

Results

Table 1 shows the walking speed results of women and men in each of the three music conditions. As there were no significant differences by gender in any of the three conditions, the times were combined for further analysis.

When the results were combined across gender, Table 2 shows that music type had a significant effect on walking speed [F (2/57)= 3.97, p < .05].

To find out which specific differences were significant, t-tests were done for the possible comparisons (no music vs. slow music, no music vs. fast music, and slow music vs. fast music). The fast music produced faster walking times than either slow music [t(38) = 2.61, p < .01], or no music [t(38) = 2.31, p < .05]. The difference between mean pedestrian speed for slow music and no music was not significant.

Figure 1 shows the number of pedestrians in the fast and slow music conditions who walked either faster or slower than the mean speed for the no music group.

Discussion

The findings support a modified version of Mayfield's organismic activation theory. Only the more active background stimuli (fast music) significantly increased walking speed of pedestrians. Neither a speeding up nor slowing down of activity was associated with the slow music, relative to no music.

There was no confirmation of Araujo's inhibitory effect although the mean difference was in that direction. Other studies have found inhibition effects when the music interferes with the task or distracts from the activity, as in the case of loud music which can reduce problem solving efficiency (Araujo, 1965; "Loud Music Kills," 1989) or when the music is extremely liked or disliked (Teen Tips, 1994). The present study did not test possible interference effects as there is no indication that music would interfere with an activity as fundamental as walking. The music selections used in the present study were all in the middle preference range. Preference might be a confounding variable in that liked music might engage the attention of the passerby leading to a slower walking speed. In contrast, disliked music might serve as an aversive stimulus and quicken departure from the scene. Further research is needed to determine how preference interacts with music type (fast vs. slow) as an influence on activation level.

References

Araujo, L. (1965). Effect of music on problem solving. Journal of Western Musicology, 13, 213-217.

Becker, H. M. (1991). Effect of music on counting speed. Journal of Industrial Productivity, 136, 1014-1016.

Garcia, N. Q. (1988). Environmental stimulation in practice. Journal of Reviews, 9, 14-22.

Guenther, I., & Stratton, J. (1985). Social facilitation of eating speed. Psychology, 6, 27-32.

Harrison, A. H., & Moore, M. M. (1993, April 26). What do people really like? American Music, 36, 16-18.

Kinefelter, P. V. (1986). Ergonomic Measurement. Los Angeles: California University Press.

Li, M. S. (1995, May). The effect of groups size on walking speed. Paper presented at the annual meeting of the Society for Aerobics and Health, Corvallis, OR.

Loud Music Kills.(1989, June 30). The Portland Herald, p. B3.

Mayfield, R. U. S. (1947). Organismic theory: The role of environmental stimulation. Dixon, CA: Earthwatch Press.

Teen Tips. (1994). Studying to music: Do's and Don'ts. [brochure]. Radio City, NY: Author.

Remick, J. (1982). The differential effects of country music and the blues. In H. Weber & K. M. Lasswell (Eds.), Music and the American Experience, (2nd ed., pp. 88-97). Fargo, ND: Prairie Press.

Table 1

Walking Speed by Music Type, for Women and Men

Music type	Women			Men		
	$\underline{M}$	$\underline{SD}$	$\underline{n}$	$\underline{M}$	$\underline{SD}$	$\underline{n}$
No music	98.18	11.95	10	98.52	15.67	10
Slow	98.82	16.75	10	101.91	14.52	10
Fast	90.45	11.39	10	87.14	14.06	10

Table 2

Walking Speed by Music Type

Music type	$\underline{M}$	$\underline{SD}$	$\underline{n}$	
No music	98.35	13.56	20	
Slow	100.36	15.34	20	
Fast	88.79	12.57	20	

Figure Caption

Figure 1. Number of people by music type who walked faster or slower than the No Music mean (98.35 seconds).

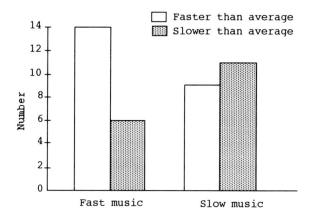

Appendix E Example of Style Used for a Technical Report

The following technical report was prepared for a university department of rhetoric and communication. The report describes a survey conducted among students enrolled in the major. The full 42-page document consisted of a cover page, table of contents, a two-page executive summary, an acknowledgement, 15 pages of single-spaced text and tables, a page of references, and a 22-page appendix containing material too detailed for the body of the report. To increase reader interest, the cover and the text contained photographs of student discussion groups. As our purpose here is to illustrate the format and style of a technical report, detailed findings and discussion in the report have been abridged.

Student Opinion of the Major in Rhetoric and Communication

May 1995

```
report included a photograph
here on the title page
```

A report of a self-survey in the Department of Rhetoric and Communication. Prof. _____ was the Principle Investigator and the survey was supported by the campus Teaching Resources Center.

Table of Contents

Executive Summary

A survey was undertaken among undergraduate majors in Rhetoric and Communication (RCM). Questions on the five-page questionnaire came from surveys of graduating seniors, a previous major survey in the _____ Department, and from faculty, staff, and students in the RCM Department. Questionnaires were distributed and collected on the first day of class. Returned questionnaires were received from 235 students, representing 67% of the 350 majors. Answers were recorded on scantron cards with space left at the end of the questionnaire for written comments.

The two most significant reasons for becoming an RCM major, far outdistancing any of the other answers, were the interest and career relevance of the subject matter. Student-faculty contact in the major was very good, with almost two-thirds of the respondents having a conversation with an RCM faculty member in the office, and one-third having a conversation with a faculty member outside the office during the past year. Almost half had talked with a peer adviser. Enrollment in internships, organizations connected with the major, and in individual study courses was relatively low.

Regarding aspects of the department program, students gave highest ratings to the faculty, followed by courses, class size in lower division courses, and advising. Two items were rated as poor, information about the honors program and student voice in department policies. There was a consensus that the major allows students to graduate in four years if they want. Students also felt that they learned some important ideas or applications in their RCM classes, and would overwhelmingly recommend the major to others. Very few would change their major at this point even if it would not slow down their time to graduation. The majority believe that there is at least one RCM faculty member who knows them well enough to write a recommendation letter.

Catalog descriptions are felt to be accurate and waiting lists for over-subscribed courses are handled fairly. However, many students do not feel that they have the opportunity to meet other RCM majors. There is a division of opinion about the amount and type of computer instruction available from all campus sources. Approximately 30% are satisfied with campus instruction in using computers, 30% dissatisfied, and the remainder undecided. Students are split as to whether they would prefer more essay questions on examinations and are opposed to more term papers.

Students believe that RCM classes are typically more relevant to their career interests than other courses they have taken, and reject the idea that the courses are less demanding or not as interesting as other courses on campus. RCM classes are considered to be sufficiently sensitive to gender and diversity issues. Educational objectives of the major are perceived to be clear, with a sufficient variety of courses to meet students' educational needs. Respondents strongly rejected the idea that a statistics course should be required for the major.

Results from the survey have been discussed at a department colloquium, and copies of this report will be distributed to faculty, staff, and the peer advisers. The report will play a role in future department planning and in the ongoing review, which calls for information on many of the questions addressed in the survey.

Acknowledgment

(list of individuals who assisted in the survey and acknowledgment of their contributions)

Background

During the academic year 1994–95 the Department of Rhetoric and Communication consisted of 8 ladder faculty, 3 lecturers, 3 staff, 18 graduate students, and 350 undergraduate majors. To find out how the majors felt about all aspects of the program, a survey was undertaken. The procedure was similar to student evaluation of teaching except that it applied to the major program rather than to individual courses.

. . . . A major includes many things other than individual courses, such as student organizations connected with the major, internship and research opportunities, and exposure to new technologies, none of which are likely to be covered in teaching evaluations collected in specific courses.

. . . . There is currently a lack of information about student opinions regarding issues in the major. The survey procedure described here can fill this gap while providing information that will be useful in department planning and in administrative reviews.

Method

With the permission of the instructor, questionnaires were distributed by an undergraduate student on the first day of all classes meeting the spring quarter 1995. The questionnaires were filled out anonymously and collected in class. A total of 235 students completed the questionnaire, representing 67% of the 350 declared majors. We have no explanation for the third of declared majors missed in the survey, except that they may not have been enrolled in any RCM class this quarter. Because the questionnaires were distributed and collected in class, sources of bias in terms of motivation or interest should be minimized. The high percentage of majors completing the survey suggests that the responses can provide a valid picture of student views of the program.

The five-page questionnaire consisted of 72 multiple choice questions to be answered on accompanying scantron sheets. Space was left at the end of the questionnaire for comments, which were analyzed separately (See Appendix). Many of the items came from a 1990 survey given in the Department and a questionnaire administered to Baccalaureate recipients. Other items were contributed by

RCM faculty, staff, and the peer advisers who saw the questionnaire through several iterations. To increase interest in the survey, nine drawings of famous orators and people of letters were photocopied on the pages. Students were told that the person making the most correct identifications would receive a twenty-five dollar purchase order at the campus bookstore. The scantron sheets (Form F-158) were scored by the Teaching Resources Center who provided an ASCII file on a diskette.

The frequencies and means for each item are contained in the Appendix. The text of the report will highlight the more important findings and their implications.

Results

Respondent Characteristics. The sample consisted of 39% seniors, 40% juniors, 17% sophomores, and 3% frosh. The high percentage of upper division students is not uncommon in surveys of majors, as many students do not declare their majors until they have attained upper division standing. More than half the respondents (59%) had taken 5 or more upper division RCM courses. Of the specialty areas within the department, students were most interested in interpersonal communication and mass communication, with less interest in organizational communication and rhetoric.

[describes demographic characteristics of the sample]

Motivation for becoming an RCM major. The two most significant reasons for becoming an RCM major, far outdistancing any of the other items, were the interest and career relevance of the subject matter. These were far more important than the possibility of finishing quickly, friends in the major, or having a good experience in lower division courses. It seem clear that there is something in the subject matter that holds student interest and keeps them in the major.

Student experiences. Almost two thirds of the respondents had a real conversation (more than a signature) with an RCM faculty member in the office, and over a third had a conversation with a faculty member outside of the office. Almost half had talked with a peer adviser. However, involvement in internships, organization connected with the major, and enrollment in individual study courses was minimal. The relatively low percentage taking internships shows need for additional outreach.

Student evaluation of program quality. Students were asked to rate aspects of the program along five-point scale from very good (5) to very poor (1). Table 1 summarizes means for the student ratings. Faculty received the highest ratings, followed by courses, class size in lower division courses, peer advising, faculty advising, advice from all sources on major requirements, and staff advising. Two items had ratings in the poor category—information about the honors program, which had a modal response of "very poor," and student voice in department policies. Other items which were only slightly above average on the scale were op-

TABLE 1. Student Ratings of Program Quality

RCM faculty	4.11
RCM courses	4.08
Class size in lower division courses	4.00
Peer advising	3.82
Faculty advising	3.82
Advice (all sources) on major requirements	3.77
Staff advising	3.70
Textbook quality	3.62
Advice (all sources) on college requirements	3.62
Textbook prices	3.18
Class size in upper division courses	3.15
Availability of RCM classes	3.11
Advice on internships and individual study	3.11
Opportunities for skill in public speaking	3.08
Student voice in department policies	2.90
Information about honors program	2.23

portunities to gain public speaking skills, availability of courses in the major, class size in upper division courses, advice on internships and individual study classes, and textbook prices.

Agreement items. Students were asked to express their degree of agreement with various statements about the program along 5-point scales from strongly agree (5) to strongly disagree (1).

[evaluations of specific aspects of the program—several pages of text and tables follow]

Discussion

[implications of the results for planning in the major]

References

[list of articles cited in the report]

Appendix

A. Instructions used in administering questionnaires.
B. Questionnaire with percentage responses.
C. Questionnaire with response frequencies.
D. Comments written on the questionnaire.
E. Percentages from 1993 survey of RCM Baccalaureate recipients.
F. Poster announcing feedback session for RCM Department.

Glossary

Accidental Sample   Nonprobability sample comprised of those individuals available for study. Sometimes called a convenience sample.

Accretion   Buildup of a residue or product of an interaction; something added to the situation.

Action Research   Combines the testing of theory with application. Approach pioneered by Kurt Lewin.

Aggregate Data Analysis   Studying the characteristics of groups using census data or other social statistics.

Alternative Hypothesis   Working or research hypothesis, an alternative to the null hypothesis, stated in positive terms (i.e., that there will be an effect).

Analysis of Covariance (ANCOVA)   Takes into account scores on some other variable believed to affect the action of the independent variable.

Analysis of Variance (ANOVA)   Statistical technique for comparing differences between means. See Chapter 19 for computational procedures.

Anonymity   Researcher does not know the identity of the participants in the study.

ANOVA   See *Analysis of Variance.*

Applied Research   Uses systematic procedures to provide answers to pressing questions. Motivated primarily by the need to solve an immediate problem.

Archie   Program for searching publicly-accessible files on the Internet.

Archives   Public records and documents.

Attitude Scale   Type of questionnaire designed to produce scores indicating the overall degree of favorability of a person's attitude on a topic.

Autobiographies   People's accounts of their own lives.

Average   Generic term referring to various measures of central tendency—the mean, median, and mode.

Balance   In survey research, balance refers to the neutrality of questions and providing sufficient items so that those favoring one view are balanced by an equal number favoring the other view.

Bar Graph   A figure constructed of bars.

Basic Research   Investigation designed to answer general long-range questions. Motivated primarily by curiosity or testing theory.

Behavior Setting   Geographic location linked to customary patterns of behavior.

Behavioral Map   Chart of individuals' locations and movements, how they actually distribute themselves in a particular area or location. Maps can be place-centered or individual-centered.

Behavioral Range   Number of different settings that an individual enters during a given time period.

Bibliography   Listing of titles and citations on a topic.

Bimodal   Having two modes.

Biography   One person's life as seen by another person.

Blind review   All identifying information about the authors are removed from a paper before it is sent out for review.

Blind Testing   In sensory evaluation or drug research, blind testing indicates that the subject is not aware of the identity of the stimulus. If the experimenter is also unaware of the identity of the stimulus, this is called a *double blind procedure*.

Browser Program   Required for navigating the World Wide Web.

Case Study   In-depth investigation of a single instance. The unit can be as small as an individual or as large as an entire community.

Casual Observation   Observation without prearranged categories or scoring system. Eyeball inspection of what is happening.

Categorical   Refers to variables that have levels that are mutually exclusive.

Causal Relationships   Patterns of cause-and-effect.

Central Tendency   Number (statistic) that best summarizes the characteristics of a sample as a whole.

Chi-square (χ^2)   Statistical test used with categorical data to test whether an obtained distribution of scores differs reliably from what would be expected by chance.

Closed Questions   Respondents are asked to choose among fixed alternative answers; also known as multiple-choice questions.

Codebook   Listing of variable names and value labels used in a computer analysis or content analysis.

Coding   Transformation or reduction of raw data into a set of standard categories for statistical analysis. Frequently used in scoring responses to open-ended interview questions and in content analysis of mass media.

Cognitive Maps   Mental representations of places.

Column Chart   See *bar graph*.

Comparative Rating Scales   Respondent compares individual with others in the same category.

Concurrent Validity   Correlation of a test with present behavior, or with other existing tests or measures; one type of criterion validity.

Confidentiality   Participant or respondent identity is known to researcher but is not publicly revealed. Frequently achieved by removing identifying information from published reports.

Confounding   Confusion of the effects of variables, resulting in an inability to determine which variable is the cause of an observed effect.

Connotative Meaning   Subjective or personal meaning of something, as distinct from its physical characteristics.

Constants   Qualities that do not vary.

Construct Validity   Linkage of the test measurement to specific theoretical constructs, the relationship of test to theory.

Content   Subject matter; in content analysis, refers to specific topics or themes, in contrast with format that refers to form or structure.

Content Analysis   Technique for systematically describing the form and content of written or spoken material. Frequently used for quantitative study of mass media.

Content Validity   Degree to which test items assess the domain that a test claims to cover, the relevance of the items to the behavior measured.

Contingency Table   Table used to record the relationship between two or more variables. The observed frequencies are placed into the cells of the table.

Continuous Variable   Variable whose levels can take on any value within the lowest and uppermost limit of the variable, for example time or income.

Control Group   Subject group that resembles the experimental group in every respect except that it is not exposed to the independent variable. Used to control for the effects of extraneous variables on the dependent variable.

Convenience Sampling   Taking what you can get as your sample.

Converging Operations   A number of different research techniques are applied, each with somewhat different limitations and yielding somewhat different data.

Correlated Measures   Groups being compared have been matched on some characteristic, or the same people have been tested before and after an experimental treatment.

Correlation   Association between two sets of scores. Often expressed in terms of a *correlation coefficient*.

Correlation Coefficient   Indicates the degree of relationship between two sets of scores, a number that can range from $+1.0$ through -1.0.

Counterbalancing Reversing the order of presentation of variables.

Criterion Validity   Relationship of the test scores to other measures of the same characteristics.

Criterion Variable   See *dependent variable*.

Critique   Critical review of a single paper or series of papers on a specific topic.

Cross-sectional Study   Comparison of different groups at a single time.

Cumulative Scores   Accumulation of frequencies from the bottom to the top of a frequency distribution, formed by starting at the bottom of a frequency distribution and summing all the frequencies at and below each level.

Current Contents   Electronic and print database.

Data List   Printout of the computer file containing a complete data set.

Database   Listing of information.

Degrees of Freedom (*df*)   Number of values that are free to vary after certain restrictions have been placed on the data. Used to evaluate the results of various statistical tests; related to the sample size and number of levels of the independent variable.

Dependent Variable   Consequence or outcome of the manipulation, the variable that is affected by the independent variable; synonyms are *outcome, response*, or *criterion variable*.

Depth Interview   Form of unstructured interview in which the interviewer follows the respondent's answers with a request for more information at an increasing level of depth.

Descriptive Statistics   Techniques to organize and summarize data. Numerical values describing the characteristics of a sample.

Document Type   Index term in many electronic bases that allows searching the literature for specific types of articles, such as reviews, bibliographies, book reviews, etc.

Double Blind Procedure   Research design in which neither the experimenter nor subject is aware of the treatment condition to which the subject has been assigned.

Electronic Abstracts   Abstracts available through online services.

Electronic Journals   Journals available online.

Empirical Research   Involves the measurement of observable events.

Equivalent Forms   Two different, but comparable forms of a scale; used for assessing reliability or to avoid practice effects.

ERIC   Educational Resources Information Center of the U.S. Department of Education; also an electronic and print database.

Erosion   Deterioration or wear that provides an index of usage patterns; something is worn down or removed.

Error   Degree to which the sample differs from the population.

Ethnography   Type of qualitative research involving the description and study of specific peoples and places.

Expected Frequencies (E)   Represent the null hypothesis—what you would expect by chance.

Experimental Group   Subjects exposed to the levels of the independent variable; also called the *treatment group*.

Experimental Variable   Variable that is manipulated or systematically altered by the experimenter; synonyms are *independent variable*, or *predictor variable*.

External Validity   Generalizability of research findings.

Extraneous Variables   Variables, in addition to the independent variable, that might be affecting the dependent variable (outcome).

Face Validity   Appearance of being a valid measure of something; a measure that "looks right" to an outside observer. A form of *content validity*.

Factor   Independent variable or treatment. A study investigating the effects of age and education on attitude would be a two-factor study. If additional factors, such as gender were added, this would become a multifactorial study.

Factorial Design   ANOVA design involving more than one independent variable (factor).

Field Experiment   Experiment in which the independent variable is manipulated in a natural setting rather than in a laboratory.

File Transfer Program (FTP)   Used to transfer Internet files.

Focus Group   Group interview designed to explore what a specific set of people think and feel about a topic.

Format   Structure; pertains to the appearance, order, and wording of items in a questionnaire or interview; in contrast to content, which refers to meaning.

Frequency   Number of times a score or category level occurs.

Frequency Distribution   Arrangement of scores from highest to lowest, together with the frequency of each score.

Gatekeeper   Person who can provide access to a population.

General Laws   Principles that help explain behavior in a variety of situations.

Gopher   Program for searching and retrieving information on the Internet.

Graphic Rating Scale   Respondent places a mark along a continuous line.

Halo Effect   Tendency to make ratings of specific characteristics on the basis of an overall impression.

Hard Disk or Drive   Piece of computer hardware that can store a large amount of information, permitting complex data processing.

Hardware   Machine parts of a computer.

Histogram   Particular type of bar graph.

Home Page   Web pages set up to allow access to related materials.

Horizontal Axis   Straight line at the base of a graph.

Hypothesis   Testable statement logically derived from theory or observation; can be either confirmed (accepted) or disconfirmed (rejected).

In Press   Article that has been formally accepted for publication.

Independent Variable   Variable that is manipulated in order to measure its effect on some outcome; synonyms are *experimental variable*, or *predictor variable*.

Individual Differences   Each person's unique set of characteristics.

Individual-centered Map   Follows a particular individual or individuals across time and location.

Inferential Statistics   Statistical techniques used to make generalizations from samples to populations.

Informed Consent   Those who participate in research studies should understand what is involved and freely consent to participate.

Institutional Review Board (IRB)   Group of people with formal responsibility for reviewing submitted research proposals in terms of ethics and protection of the participants.

Instrumental Research   Undertaken as an academic, vocational, or professional requirement. Goal is to demonstrate competence in research.

Intensive Interview   See *depth interview.*

Interaction   Using ANOVA, the outcome produced by changes in one variable differs depending upon the levels of a second variable.

Internal Validity   Degree to which a procedure measures what it is supposed to measure.

Interval Scale   Level of measurement that provides information about size or direction, plus having equal intervals between scale points.

Inventory   See *test.*

Inverse relationship   See *negative correlation.*

Item Analysis   Shows the degree to which the various items in a scale or test "hang together."

Latent Content   Less obvious or more hidden information.

Legend   Title and brief description accompanying a table, figure, or graph.

Level   Amount or value of a variable; dimensions along which a single variable differs. Using hair color as a variable, the levels are blond, brunette, etc.

Level of Significance   See *probability level.*

Library of Congress Subject Heading Index   Listing of topics under which books are catalogued in libraries.

Life History   Biographical technique useful in qualitative research.

Likert Scale   Type of attitude scale containing statements that are clearly favorable or clearly unfavorable to which respondent indicates degree of agreement.

List Processor   See *List server.*

List Server   Manages a mailing list, also called a *list processor.*

Longitudinal Study   Study of an individual or group over a long time period.

Mailing List   Organized online discussion group.

Mainframe Computers   Computers capable of manipulating large data sets, generally available only at large institutions.

Manifest Content   Content that is obvious and conveyed in spoken or written information.

Matched Groups   Assigning subjects so that the experimental and control groups are as similar as possible. A means of controlling extraneous variables.

Matched Scores   See *correlated measures.*

Mean (M)   Arithmetic average; sum of scores divided by the number of cases.

Mean Comparisons   Comparisons or contrasts between individual means to locate where the significant difference lies.

Median (Mdn)   Midpoint of a distribution when all the scores are arranged from highest to lowest. Half the scores fall above the median and half fall below.

Mode   Single score that occurs most often in a distribution. If there are two modes, the distribution is called *bimodal.*

Modem   Allows computer signals to be sent over a telephone line.

Multivariate Design   Involves more than one dependent variable.

Natural Experiment   Study that uses a naturally occurring event or policy change as the independent variable; a *quasi-experiment.*

Negative Correlation   As one variable increases, the other variable decreases, also called an *inverse relationship.*

NetNews or *Usenet*   Collection of newsgroups.

Networking   Strategy of gaining information by using the references in recent articles to find other related articles or information.

Newsgroups   Online public discussion groups.

Nominal Measures   Characteristics assigned to categories. No underlying continuous dimension.

Nonprobability Samples   Likelihood of selection is not known to the researcher. Three general types are quota, purposive, and accidental samples.

Normal Curve   Symmetrical bell-shaped curve which often approximates the frequency of occurrence of events in nature.

Norms   Statistical summary of people's performance on tests or inventories.

Null Hypothesis (H_0)   Assumes that differences produced by the research manipulation are due to chance fluctuations and that the independent variable has no effect on the dependent variable.

Observed Frequencies (O), Raw data (frequencies, *not* percentages).

Online   Electronic communication via the Internet.

Online Catalog   Computerized reference index.

OPACs   Online Public Access Catalogs

Open-ended Questions   Respondents provide their own answers.

Operational Definition   Defining a variable by how it is measured. Intelligence can be operationally defined as a score on an IQ test.

Ordinal Scale   Characteristics can be ordered along an underlying dimension, but no information is provided about the distance between points, only provides information about increasing or decreasing size or direction.

Outcome   See *dependent variable*.

Paired Comparisons   Two items are presented and the person asked to compare them.

Paired Scores   See *correlated measures*.

Panel Study   Frequently used in public opinion research, in which the same sample of respondents is interviewed on repeated occasions.

Paraphrase   To express in your own words rather than those of the originator; interviewer's record of what the respondent meant.

Participant Observation   Observer becomes part of the event being studied and uses this position to make observations.

Peer Review   Process by which submitted articles are evaluated by those knowledgeable in the field.

Person-centered Map   Diagram showing a person or group's movements and activities over a specified period of time.

Pilot Study   Preliminary use of a procedure designed to identify problems and omissions before the actual study is conducted.

Place-centered Map   Diagram showing how individuals arrange themselves at a particular site.

Plagiarize   To pass off someone else's work as one's own.

Population   Entire group of people or cases of direct interest to the investigation.

Positive Correlation   An increase in one variable is accompanied by an increase in the other.

Poster Session   Visual display of papers at a conference with the authors present for informal discussion.

Predictive Validity   Ability of a measure to predict future behavior; a subtype of criterion validity.

Predictor Variable   See *independent variable*.

Preprint   Copy of an accepted final version of a journal article.

Primary Source   Original source of information.

Probability Level   When used in statistics, it indicates the likelihood that an obtained difference on a statistical test is due to chance alone.

Probability Sample   Sample that is drawn in such a way that the probability for the inclusion of any given individual can be estimated. Two general types of probability samples are *random samples* and *stratified samples*.

Probe   Question or comment during an interview designed to keep the person talking or obtain clarification.

Program Evaluation   Systematic procedures used to determine the effectiveness of a program.

Projective Test   Instrument used in clinical testing and research that relies on questions or stimuli that are deliberately vague or incomplete.

Psychological Abstracts   Print database.

Psychophysics   Connection between the physical qualities of objects and their sensory attributes; very important in sensory evaluation.

PsycINFO   Online version of *Psychological Abstracts*.

Purposive Sample   Type of nonprobability sample in which the individuals considered most relevant to the issue studied are selected for inclusion.

Quantification   Expressing information in numbers.

Quasi-experiment   Nonrandom assignment of subjects to conditions; the experimenter lacks direct control over the independent variable, also called a *natural* experiment.

Questionnaire   Series of written questions on a topic about which the respondent's opinions are sought.

Quota Sample   Nonprobability sample in which the investigator deliberately sets sample proportions that are different from those existing in the population.

Random Assignment   An individual is as likely to be put in one research group as in another; the decision depends on chance alone.

Random Sample   Type of probability sample in which every individual in the entire population being studied has an equal chance of being selected.

Range   Measure of dispersion or variability, computed by subtracting the lowest from the highest score.

Ratio Scale   Level of measurement that contains information on direction, possesses equal intervals, and an absolute zero point.

Raw Data   Firsthand scores or measures. The actual measurements or data collected before they have been reduced, coded, or analyzed.

Reactivity   Effect of the research upon the participants and the data collected.

Refereed Paper   One that has been through a peer review process.

Regression   Pertains to correlation; the relationships between sets of scores.

Reliability   Consistency in measurement; the repeatability or replicability of findings, stability of measurement over time.

Reliability Coefficient   Coefficient of correlation between two administrations of a test or other measures.

Repeated Measures Design   Research design involving the same subjects studied at different times or under different conditions.

Replication   To repeat an earlier study to see if its findings can be duplicated.

Reprint   Copy of a journal article, usually printed at same time as publication.

Response   See *dependent variable*.

Reviewing the Literature   Finding out about previous research on a topic.

Salience   Importance of an issue in people's minds.

Sample   Subset of a population.

Sample Bias   Error introduced by a sampling procedure that favors certain characteristics over others.

Sampling   Selection of a subset of cases from some population of interest.

Sampling Error   Chance variation among samples selected from a single population.

Scale   Series of ordered steps at fixed intervals used as a standard of measurement.

Scatterplot   Visual plot of a correlation, also called a *scattergram* or *scatter chart*.

Secondary Research   Archival research using existing primary data.

Secondary Source   Second-hand report of information.

Semantic Differential   Rating scale developed by Charles Osgood for measuring the meaning of concepts.

Semistructured Interview   All respondents are asked the same questions, but the order in which they are asked may differ.

Set   Tendency to respond in a particular way.

Simulation   Deliberate creation of an artificial reality. Depends less on literal resemblance than on functional resemblance.

Single-subject Research   Instead of testing many people at one time, a researcher tests one individual over an extended period.

Skewed Distribution   Distribution of scores that deviates markedly from a normal curve.

Snowball Sample   Type of purposive (nonprobability) sample in which the researcher asks respondents for other people who should be contacted.

Socially Desirable   Refers to a bias toward expected or socially-desirable statements or responses.

Software   Programs for computers.

Split-half Reliability   Dividing a scale or test into two halves which are then compared.

Standard Deviation   Measure of dispersion or variability; abbreviated s, *σ*, or *SD*.

Standard Score   Score expressed in standard deviation units, also called a *z-score*.

Standardized Interview   See *structured interview*.

Standardized Test   Refers to a test that has been published with normative data and is administered in a fixed way.

Statistic   Quantitative characteristic of a sample.

Step Scale   Rater selects one of a graded series of levels.

Stimuli   General term used to refer to the material to which participants are expected to respond.

Stratified Sample   Type of probability sampling in which the characteristics of the sample are selected to be proportionate to those present in the total population.

Structure   In content analysis, refers to form.

Structured Interview   Questions are formulated beforehand and asked in a set manner in a specified order; a *standardized interview*.

Subjects   Research participants or respondents.

Survey Research   Systematic gathering of information about people's beliefs, attitudes, values, and behavior.

Systematic Observation   Employs a scoring system and prearranged categories that are applied consistently.

Test   Systematic procedure for comparing people's performance, feelings, attitudes, or values.

Test Reliability   Stability of measurement over time.

Test-retest Reliability   Measure given to the same person on two occasions and the results are compared.

Theories   Logical constructions that explain natural phenomena.

Thesaurus   Dictionary of terms used as topic headings in an index such as Psychological Abstracts.

Time Sampling Procedure   Specific times are selected according to a sampling plan for recording observed activities.

Trace Measures   Physical remains of interaction after the individuals have departed. Two types of physical traces useful in behavioral research are accretion and erosion.

Transcription   Putting interview or questionnaire responses into clear form for data analysis.

Treatment Condition   Refers to the presence of the independent variable, as opposed to the control condition in which the independent variable is absent.

Treatment Group   Subjects exposed to the levels of the independent variable; also called the *experimental group.*

Treatments   Levels of the independent variable.

Triangulation   Use of more than one method, observer, and site to provide additional checks on a single observer's account.

True Experiment   Experimenter is able to assign subjects to treatment and control conditions either randomly or by some other unbiased method.

Type 1 Error   Rejecting the null hypothesis when it is true.

Unstructured Interview   Although the interviewer has a general topic in mind, there is no predetermined order or specified wording to the questions.

Usenet   See *NetNews.*

Value   Level or amount of a variable.

Value Label   Label or name assigned to the variable level that is being represented as a number in a computer analysis (e.g., female = 1).

Variability   Amount of spread or dispersion within a distribution of scores.

Variable   Any characteristic or quality that differs in degree or kind. Variables have values or levels and may either be continuous or categorical.

Variable Label   Label or name representing a variable in a computer analysis, usually restricted to five or eight letters.

Variance   Square of the standard deviation; abbreviations are s^2 or σ^2.

Verbatim   Recorded exactly as spoken.

Veronica   Literally Very Easy Rodent-Oriented Network Interface to Computing with Archie; facilitates subject or keyword searches on Gopher.

Vertical Axis   Perpendicular line showing the graph boundary. Often used to indicate frequency.

Within-subjects Design   See *repeated measures design.*

World Wide Web   Online system of linked information sources, also known as WWW or the Web.

Name Index

Subject Index